THE
EXECUTIVE
WAY

Calvin Morrill

THE EXECUTIVE WAY

Conflict Management in Corporations

THE UNIVERSITY OF CHICAGO PRESS

CHICAGO AND LONDON

Calvin Morrill is associate professor of sociology at the University of Arizona.

The University of Chicago Press, Chicago 60637
The University of Chicago Press, Ltd., London
© 1995 by The University of Chicago
All rights reserved. Published 1995
Printed in the United States of America
04 03 02 01 00 99 98 97 96 95   1 2 3 4 5
ISBN: 0-226-53873-7 (cloth)

Library of Congress Cataloging-in-Publication Data

Morrill, Calvin.
    The executive way : conflict management in corporations / Calvin Morrill.
        p.   cm.
    Includes bibliographical references and index.
    1. Conflict management.   2. Conflict management—Case studies.
3. Executives.   I. Title.
HD42.M67   1995
658.4—dc20   94-33344
                                                                    CIP

⊗ The paper used in this publication meets the minimum requirements of the American National Standard for Information Sciences—Permanence of Paper for Printed Library Materials, ANSI Z39.48–1984.

To Keith and Ruth Morrill

CONTENTS

FIGURES
AND TABLES

CASES

Preface and Acknowledgments

At the heart of this book is a seemingly paradoxical question: How can conflict management among corporate executives appear to be a process of reflective individualism and be socially determined? On the one hand, popular conceptions of corporate executives portray conflict management (and all decision making) among high-ranking managers as an affair of conscious choice and guile. We are constantly bombarded, for example, by mass mediated images of calculatingly shrewd business managers who are able, because of their superior reflection and skills, to "best" their colleagues and rival corporations. In other popular images, corporate executives and their corporations are portrayed as being locked into particular practices or "stuck" in intractable "ways of doing things." Many corporate executives are shrewd and quite resourceful as the empirically grounded chapters in this book make clear. Yet, as this book also makes clear, executives, and perhaps all disputants in familiar, local contexts, manifest such qualities within habitualized routines: aggrieved parties typically opt for conflict management scripts that are well known to them or at least feel well known to them. These routines—customs of conflict management—thus provide the foundations for normative orders at the executive levels.

But disputants do not slavishly obey socially determined scripts to the letter. Disputants deploy conflict management scripts in pragmatic ways, adapting as best they can to the normative constraints and opportunities of their local social contexts. At a social level there exist elective affinities between particular types of social contexts and the routine ways disputants interpret and pursue grievances, but within such routines, individual variation also exists. In social contexts in which stable constellations of conflict management practices predominate, routine conflict management could even be said to mirror and express nonconflict relations. Routine conflict thus reproduces its social context over time and, ironically, can obstruct fundamental social change as disputants come to vest salient aspects of their personal and social identities in how they pursue their grievances against one another.

The synthesis of scripted pragmatics in conflict management places this book at the interstice of several research questions, themes, and traditions. My introduction to this project squarely originated in structural-behavioral theories of social control and conflict management in the sociology and anthropology of disputing. Indeed, I entered this project with three simple questions about the moral order of corporate executives: What are the issues over which corporate executives have conflict among themselves? How do corporate executives manage conflict among themselves? What explains executive patterns of conflict management? Answering these questions required close-up looks at the behavior of social control and conflict management among corporate executives through prolonged fieldwork. My empirical materials emerged from nearly two years of ethnography among executives in thirteen corporations. I conducted informal and formal interviews of over two hundred executives and several dozen other personnel holding a variety of lower ranks and statuses in their corporations. Midway through the interviews, I gained observational access to several executive contexts which yielded data on executive daily routines, meetings, presentations, and social activities. I also collected numerous internal documents regarding corporate life and executive contexts, as well as published materials on each of the thirteen corporations in the study.

My immersion in this empirical context and my subsequent analyses of the data, however, demanded more than a fleeting glance at formal organization as just another research site in which to study conflict management. The properties of formal organization as a conceptual domain required that it be theoretically linked with conflict management in some meaningful fashion. The more I worked on the project, the more I became convinced that such a linkage could be achieved only by more systematic attention to the pragmatics of conflict management and the cultural side of organizations, particularly how executives make sense of their local social contexts, frame their grievances, and enact conflict management scripts with their colleagues. As such, this project is as much an excavation of a social setting little visited by sociological and anthropological fieldworkers—the corporate suites of

America—as it is an extension and recombination of theoretical leads from structural-behavioral theories of conflict management and interpretive theories of formal organization.

What Lies Ahead

Chapter 1 provides the intellectual context of the study, including brief reviews of previous ethnographies of corporate executives and work on organizational conflict. The chapter also outlines my theoretical approach, concluding with some expectations about the social contexts in which confrontational conflict management and third-party settlement are likely to occur. In chapter 2, the demographics of the executives in the study are discussed, including the proportions of women and minority members among organizational elites. The first part of the chapter provides thumbnail descriptions of the thirteen corporations in the study and then highlights some of the general similarities of executive demographics and experience. The second half of chapter 2 highlights the differences between three types of executive contexts in the study: mechanistic bureaucracies, atomistic organizations, and matrix systems.

Chapter 3 turns to the specific topic of executive conflict management. The first half of the chapter focuses on general tendencies across the executive contexts under study, again paying particular attention to variation in conflict management pursued by women and minorities. The objective of the second half of chapter 3 is to compare a variety of correlates with the aggregate patterns of executive conflict management collected in the thirteen organizations in the study. Using the aggregate analyses of chapters 2 and 3 as backdrops, chapters 4, 5, and 6 offer thick descriptions of the social contexts and conflict management patterns among executives in three organizations: Old Financial, Independent Accounting, and Playco. At the end of each of these chapters, grounded hypotheses about conflict management, managerial behavior, and context are offered as well. Chapter 7 concludes the book by examining some of the general implications of the findings at the individual and group levels, for organizational analysis, and for wider society. My personal experiences as a field-worker as well as the details of the methods and dilemmas in the field appear in appendix A. Appendix B contains several additional data tables which augment the aggregate analyses in chapters 2 and 3, and the qualitative analyses in chapters 4 through 6. Appendix C contains a glossary of indigenous terms used by Playco executives to describe various features of their context.

Background and Acknowledgments

I came to this project through an invitation by Donald Black, then the assistant director of the Center for Criminal Justice at Harvard Law School, to participate in a number of group discussions on social control in organizational life during winter 1983. The discussion group included Black, M. P. Baumgartner, and Mark Cooney. The original plan was to conduct research on conflict management in business organizations, with special reference to executives and other managers. Few studies of this kind existed at the time, and Black was convinced that there would be significant sociological payoff for anyone who could study conflict management close-up in the upper levels of large business corporations. Funding and time constraints prevented the group from meeting more than a few times or carrying out collaborative research, but Black, who became my dissertation adviser, suggested that I undertake the research as my doctoral dissertation. His suggestion certainly sparked my interest, but at the time I had no idea how inspired Black's suggestion was as I embarked on a multiyear ethnography of disputing among corporate executives.

Black was well aware of my family background through several enjoyable and illuminating one-on-one discussions we had on Friday afternoons in his office at the law school's Pound Hall. He knew that I had grown up in a middle-class family of entrepreneurs, who as leaders of their own small business organizations could be considered executives in their own right. He also knew that I had the chance through family ties to sporadically meet and become acquainted with corporate executives. But he did not know how closely the specific theme of organizational conflict management resonated with my family experiences. While growing up, the central topic in many serious conversations between my parents focused on conflict management and rules of all kinds—grievances my parents had against colleagues and vice versa and problems between people in their workplaces. From my vantage point, business appeared to be less an affair of pure economics than about interpersonal and intergroup conflict management. I became fascinated with how my parents and those they worked with handled trouble among themselves, and how people broke, bent, and flouted authority of all kinds. I began to note all the ways people pursued their grievances and engaged in the social control of others, including creating conflicts where there seemed to be none in order to achieve ulterior objectives or simply to shake things up. I also became interested in the strategies that the targets of social control used to resist those who pursued grievances against them. As a result, I became an informal participant- observer in business "cultures of conflict management" at an early age. The sociohistorical context of the 1960s galvanized my interests when the behavior which fascinated me in my family's business dealings—conflict and authority—exploded onto the scene as the issues of the day for wider society, for nearly every childhood friend I had, and for myself as I navigated my primary and secondary education.

The "slippage" between my personal but limited exposure to corporate executives and what I read about them during the 1980s further piqued my curiosity about executive life. President Ronald Reagan not only declared "morning in America" in 1981, but also that American economic and social salvation lay in the unbridled development of the capitalist enterprise. American financial institutions and the mass media reveled in his declaration as the country experienced an economic boom unrivaled since the immediate aftermath of World War II. Along the way, corporate executives emerged as popular heroes, although their direct effects on the productivity of their corporations and their current folk-hero status are questionable in light of the economic uncertainty of the early 1990s. With a few notable exceptions, the executives I had met while growing up did not seem at all like those I read about in the early and mid 1980s. The executives I met seemed less like mavericks than rule followers, more confined by their local contexts and at the whim of forces outside their control than independent decision makers. I recall thinking to myself that perhaps my direct experience with executives was somehow biased or that I had not picked up what made these men (and they were all men) different from the corporate managers about whom I read. As the paradox noted above suggests, I came to view these images of executives not as an either-or phenomenon, but as part and parcel of the same process of enacting routine conflict management and being a high-ranking corporate manager.

The personal and intellectual origins of this book are no more diverse than the people who have offered me their support during the ten years since I began the fieldwork for this project. First and foremost, I want to thank the hundreds of corporate executives and other personnel who took the time to talk with me, allowed me to listen to their conversations, and (almost) tirelessly answered what must of have seemed to them an endless stream of inane and obvious questions. Although some informants will view the contents of this book as unflattering, I have tried to represent executive life under trying circumstances in a relatively dignified yet sometimes wry manner—just the way informants themselves saw many of the events I describe and interpret.

I owe a particular debt of gratitude to Donald Black, Harrison White, and Alessandro Pizzorno, who shepherded my first pass at writing up a portion of my fieldwork in the form of a doctoral dissertation. As mentioned above, Black cultivated and refocused my interests in social control and conflict management by introducing me to his own structural-behavioral framework based on the cross-cultural literature on law, conflict management, disputing, and social control. Black has unflinchingly provided constructive criticism and support of my intellectual efforts over the past several years, and has read several of my papers in preparation of this manuscript, all of which helped me to hone my ideas. Even more important, Black continues to teach me by example the commitment required for serious, sustained intellectual life. White taught me that social life is not all that it seems on the surface (or as presented in most conventional social science) and challenged me to undertake field study in executive contexts. When I returned from the field, White challenged me again to dig deeper into my data to find more fundamental and unexpected sociological payoffs. Pizzorno taught me to subject my analytic inclinations to continual real-world criticism lest I be seduced by ideas completely removed from the phenomenology of everyday life. Finally, Steve Cornell first introduced me to the sensitivities one must develop in order to become a good ethnographer in his insightful and humane field methods course in the Department of Sociology at Harvard.

I also owe a debt of gratitude to two institutions which supported me during my fieldwork: to Harvard Law School for awarding me a Junior Fellowship at the Center for Criminal Justice (a fellowship created by Black), which I used while making the initial arrangements for entering the field, and to the Program in Law and Social Sciences of the National Science Foundation for awarding me a Dissertation Improvement Grant (SES-8508349), which supported a good bit of my activities in the field.

During fieldwork, several scholars allowed me to bend their ears about my preliminary findings and in return they offered helpful criticism and support of my efforts. The late Donald Cressey and I enjoyed several long afternoon discussions talking about, in his words, my "adventures with the executive guys." His lifelong interests in corporate crime from sociological and social-psychological perspectives sharpened my sociological imagination in terms of what I was looking for in the field and also led me to quantify some of my findings as best I could. Laura Nader provided invaluable advice as I applied for funding for my fieldwork and as I grappled with making sense of my findings. She also provided me the opportunity to present some of my preliminary findings at a series of ongoing talks by corporate ethnographers sponsored by the Institute for Social Change at the University of California at Berkeley. Throughout my fieldwork, I also talked on a regular basis with Black and White, who urged me not to wait to "think deep thoughts" about my materials before coming out of the field. Just after returning from the field, I benefited greatly from suggestions I received from Pizzorno and Orlando Patterson at a talk I gave in the Department of Sociology at Harvard, and from suggestions I received from the faculty and graduate students at a talk I gave to the Department of Sociology at the University of Virginia (arranged by Black, who had left his post at Harvard Law to become the chair at Virginia Sociology).

Since joining the Departments of Sociology and Communication at the University of Arizona, I have found institutional support in the cause of finishing this book no less generous. I received a semester off from teaching (courtesy of Michael Burgoon, then my department head in the Department of Communication) and a Summer Research Professorship from the University of Arizona's Social and Behavioral Sciences Research Institute, enabling me to concentrate for several months at a time on the analysis and write-up of my field data. William Crano, newly appointed as department head in the Department of Communication, generously upgraded my personal computer system, facilitating the final preparation of the manuscript.

I am grateful to various publishers for permission to incorporate into this book materials that earlier appeared in a slightly different form elsewhere. Chapter 3 and portions of chapters 5 and 6 are drawn from "The Customs of Conflict Management among Corporate Executives," *American Anthropologist* 93 (1991): 871–93; portions of chapter 4 from "The Management of Managers: Disputing in an Executive Hierarchy," *Sociological Forum* 4 (1988) 387–407; portions of chapter 5 from "Conflict Management, Honor, and Organizational Change," *American Journal of Sociology* 97 (1991): 565–621, (c)1991 by The University of Chicago, all rights reserved; other portions of chapter 5 and portions of chapter 7 from "The Private Ordering of Professional Relations," in *Hidden Conflict in Organizations: Uncovering Behind-the-Scenes Disputes*, ed. Deborah M. Kolb and Jean M. Bartunek (Newbury Park: Sage Publications, 1991); and portions of chapter 6 from "Vengeance among Executives," in *Virginia Review of Sociology*, vol. 1, *Law and Conflict Management*, ed. James Tucker (Greenwich, CT: JAI Press, 1992).

Several individuals also deserve special mention for their contributions to this book. By inviting me to coteach the qualitative field methods course in the Department of Sociology with him over a number of years, David Snow taught me the how's, why's, and rhetoric of ethnography. He also taught me by example through his own work, read papers leading up to this book, and read the entire book manuscript itself. Doug McAdam initially introduced me to Doug Mitchell at the University of Chicago Press after reading an early precis I prepared for the book and has taught me that nice guys can indeed finish first and do insightful, first-rate sociology. Woody Powell has over the last half dozen years educated me via his Social Organization Seminar and through his own work about that elusive animal called "organizational theory." He also graciously introduced me to Mitchell and read an early manuscript precis. Michael Burgoon has generously supported me in numerous ways over the years, including reading early papers leading up to this book, spurring me on to raise the caliber of my work a notch higher when I thought I had reached my limit and giving me unique insight into how organizations really work. William Bailey took time out for a young scholar who needed to be educated on the pragmatics of communication. Bailey's influence is implicit throughout this work. Sally Jackson carefully read chapter 3, offering helpful suggestions and comments. She, Scott Jacobs, and Dirk Scheerhorn helped me tighten my thinking about the overall arguments in this book in numerous ways, as well as continuing to provide me immeasurable social and intellectual support. Elisabeth Clemens helped me push my thinking further than I could have achieved alone regarding the knotty relationship between agency and culture. Michael Macy's brilliant insight into social processes helped me straighten out my thinking in a series of e-mail comments and several long discussions at the international sociological meetings in Paris during summer 1993. Renee Storm Klingle provided helpful advice on the analyses in chapter 3 and continues to be a trusted confidant. Curt Madison closely read the entire manuscript and offered valuable comments, as did Paul Dimaggio in a supportive and careful critique for the Press. I thank Doug Mitchell at the Press for his patience, support, and good cheer throughout my preparation of the manuscript.

There are numerous other colleagues and students who have graciously given me their honest reactions to my arguments either through discussion, by reading papers leading up to this book, or by reading portions of the manuscript itself: Mark Aakhus, Alan Aldrich, Chris Argyris, Jean Bartunek, M. P. Baumgartner, Albert Bergesen, Dale Brashers, David Buller, Judee Burgoon, Marc Cooney, Ken

Dauber, Ed Dawson, Frank Dobbin, Mustafa Emirbayer, Paula England, Roberto Fernandez, Kathleen Ferraro, Neil Fligstein, Roger Gould, Karen Hansen, Tyler Harrison, Paul Hirsch, Allan Horwitz, Frank Hunsaker, John Hermann, John Johnson, Charles Kadushin, Rosabeth Moss Kanter, Henry Kenski, Cheryl King Thomas, Deborah Kolb, Michèle Lamont, Eric Leifer, Jim Lincoln, Peter Manning, Diane McTier, Michael Musheno, Mathew Silberman, Ellen Snyderman, Lesa Stern, James Tucker, David Williams, and members of the Arizona Sociology Social Organization Seminar and of the Arizona Sociology Qualitative Methods Seminar.

I also want to acknowledge the enduring support of a longtime friend and of my family. While in the field, I rediscovered my passion for running through my high school and sometime college training partner, Brian Russell. Brian's accomplishments on the track and the roads had long since outstripped mine, but he was kind enough to take me under his wing and teach me again the joy of this primal sport. This may sound like a trite occurrence to those uninitiated in the rites and rituals of a serious runner. But through Brian, I not only got in terrific shape and competed again, but I was able to recapture a part of myself I thought I had lost to a series of debilitating injuries. I also used the running to get some perspective on my fieldwork and to help me sustain rapport with some of the more athletic executives I encountered. My late sister, Alexa Morrill, helped me immensely during my fieldwork, first by opening her home to me as a second base of operations and second by providing some much-needed comedic relief from the pressures of working on the "inside" among corporate executives. Finally, my parents, Ruth and Keith Morrill, provided invaluable material support by encouraging me to use an old garage off their home, which they had converted into a small single apartment, as my base field "tent." This enabled me to bear the expenses of fieldwork and allowed me a secure place to keep thousands of pages of field notes on the delicate matters surrounding conflict among corporate executives. My parents also provided insightful and emotionally supportive sounding boards for my earliest interpretations of my field data. But more than any single thing they specifically helped me with, my parents have continued to provide me with irrefutable evidence that people can live their lives with dignity and integrity, can endure hardship, and can still be optimistic about the future. Thanks!

Tucson, Arizona
March 1994

CHAPTER ONE

INTRODUCTION

Conflict persists at all levels of contemporary corporate life, including the *top*. Yet conflict rarely escapes the boundaries of executive contexts to escalate into large-scale public disputes or firings—the kinds of events that receive widespread media attention. Lawyers, judges, and other institutionally recognized arbitrators or mediators infrequently intervene in executive disputes. Nor do executive disputants often strike formal agreements that prevent the reappearance of individual and group enmities.[1] Rather, the maintenance of normative order in executive life is embedded in the mundane activities of social interaction and privately unfolds much like routine conflict management in less privileged social contexts.

This book investigates these claims with evidence based on two years of intensive fieldwork—semistructured and conversational interviewing, individual and group observation, and the collection of documentation—among 305 top managers and their staffs in thirteen private corporations. The analytic perspective taken here characterizes executive disputants as strategic, but strategic within a world more scripted and structured by *proximate* social contexts than the modern ethos about corporate executives, especially the American ethos, would lead one to believe. What emerges from this analysis is a less heroic but perhaps more realistic vision of corporate executives than we have grown accustomed to in recent times. The sociology and anthropology of conflict management and disputing (e.g., Black 1976; Nader and Todd 1978) focus the inquiry on conflict-in-context and also lead back to themes found in earlier organizational studies by Burns and Stalker (1961), Dalton (1959), and Whyte (1957), as well as more recent contributions by Kanter (1977) and Jackall (1988), about how work settings simultaneously express and shape managerial action. This study also sidesteps some of the traditional concerns of research on organizational conflict—those that focus on the way conflict can be most efficiently handled or used to enhance organizational productivity. The production of normative theory related to the prosocial functions of organizational conflict are certainly laudable goals but may be somewhat unrealistic unless more is known about the indigenous customs of conflict management in organizational contexts.

Throughout this work, *conflict management* refers to the social processes by which people pursue their grievances against one another (Black 1976:105).[2] As in many ethnographies of conflict management, "trouble cases" of "hitch, dispute, grievance, trouble . . . and what was done about it" (Llewellyn and Hoebel 1983:21) make up the raw materials of this study, for such cases allow investigators and readers to observe the temporal unfolding and microdynamics of conflict management, as well as to ascertain statistically "dominant patterns" in numerically large samples (Nader 1990:135). Trouble cases also provide clues for understanding the relations between social contexts and conflict management. Consider, as a first glimpse of executive conflict management, the following trouble-case stories from the tops of three large corporations. All personal and corporate names are pseudonyms for reasons of confidentiality.

Case 1.1 Hanging the Pig Out to Dry (1983–84)

Jacobs, Hawke, and Morris, all vice presidents in Old Financial's western division, believed they had been slighted for some time by their boss, a senior vice president named Manright.[3] By the time Manright had held his position for only six months, he had already earned the nickname "the pig" among his three vice presidents because of his "bloated [overweight] body" and ruddy complexion, and because he publicly took sole credit for their department's recent successes. For two years, Jacobs, Hawke, and Morris unsuccessfully attempted to arrange transfers out of the division and simply grumbled among themselves about the pig's behavior, which, according to Hawke, "was not only incompetent but boastful and belligerent as well."

Manright's superior, an executive vice president named Freeman, had requested that Manright give an update on loan volumes at a divisional executive meeting. Hawke and Morris were responsible for organizing the report. Before the presentation, Hawke and Morris altered the materials Manright would use so that they were incomplete, knowing he would not check them beforehand. Sitting at the conference table awaiting his turn to deliver his report, Manright discovered he had information for only three-quarters of the regions he had been requested to cover. He presented what he had, adding that "he would send the rest in the mail." Freeman enjoined Manright to "review his work more carefully." In addition, Freeman, in the words of one of the other executives at the meeting, "seemed irritated at Manright's 'careless' attitude and expressed his hope that this sort of thing [incomplete reports] wouldn't happen in the future." Manright "impressed" Freeman as a slightly "crude" and un-professional manager. However, this was the first time Manright ever outwardly demonstrated to Freeman any "questionable" behavior. Manright returned to his divisional offices and began to privately make plans to move Hawke and Morris out of the department for their "incompetence," but he never suspected their behavior was motivated by personal enmity toward him. Hawke and Morris learned of Manright's plans through their executive secretaries' "grapevine," and before Manright could act, Hawke left the firm for another bank and Morris arranged a transfer to another division.

At the next divisional meeting, Freeman asked Manright to present a report on his department's "interface" with a divisional marketing plan that focused on areas for which Jacobs and two other subordinates were responsible. This time, Manright directed his executive secretary to check all of the reports before the meeting, and they were found to be complete. But even the perspicacious eye of Manright's executive secretary could not have prevented the subtle action taken this time against Manright by Jacobs. Before attending divisional meetings, it was customary for Manright to meet with his three vice presidents for a final "briefing." With Hawke and Morris now gone, Manright depended solely on Jacobs in these sessions. In Manright's mind, Jacobs typically produced a good "read" of the kinds of questions Freeman and some of the other executives at the meeting might ask Manright. Jacobs spoke a great deal at the meeting, filling almost two pages of Manright's yellow legal pad and several more of Manright's secretary's steno pad with notes on what to expect at the briefing. Jacobs talked and talked, all the while leaving out the crucial questions he knew Freeman would ask. Although Jacobs believed Manright might be "just quick enough on his feet" to answer Freeman's questions, he would not have the answers at his "fingertips" (especially the ones requiring "numbers" about anticipated departmental performance relevant to aspects of the new marketing plan). Manright's presentation again proved unsuccessful because he was unable to answer several questions raised by Freeman. Manright once more faced an angry superior who wondered aloud after the meeting about his subordinate's ability "to anticipate questions and trends in the business." When Jacobs reported on Manright's poor performance during a monthly round of golf with his former colleagues Hawke and Morris, Hawke remarked that "Jacobs really hung the pig out to dry."

Three months after this meeting, Manright visited another division and "boasted" at an executive meeting that "he had to work hard simply to keep his reports [subordinates] from screwing the whole place up." An executive vice president at the meeting later called

Freeman and related his "dismay" at Manright's behavior. Freeman reacted sternly, claimed Manright "had gone too far with his unprofessional style," and quietly assured his colleague that he would "take care of the matter shortly." During the next seven months, Freeman put together a file that contained records of Manright's poor presentations, boastful behavior in the other division, and a "host" of other "offenses" committed over the years. In Freeman's words, "Manright's crudeness and incompetence at our gatherings [divisional executive committee meetings] took on more meaning in light of his recent behavior [in the other division]. He had screwed up; violated a lot of rules about what it means to be a decent executive. So I had him shifted to another part of the division, to head up special projects there; shelved out of the mainstream." And there Manright aimlessly floated earning a great deal of money without much responsibility or respect.

Case 1.2 Green's Misrepresentation (1986)

Green had just been elected partner at Independent Accounting, specializing in tax preparation for financial service corporations.[4] He was eager to capitalize on his new status by aggressively going after several new accounts. Banks, an audit partner, while having lunch with an insurance firm executive whose company he had previously serviced, learned that Green had been referred to the client by a financial services executive in order to prepare taxes for one of the client's subsidiaries, a smaller insurance firm. Green had told the client that he had extensive experience in financial service and insurance taxes, but gave the insurance executive only references from financial services corporations. Banks was careful not to criticize Green when the client asked about the latter's knowledge of the insurance industry. Instead, he suggested the client use a tax partner whose work "he [Banks] knew better" and believed would "better serve the [client]."

Banks was dismayed that another partner would "misrepresent" himself to a client because of the potential liabilities for the firm, and noted that Green's behavior appeared to be an extension of his "boastful style." At no time did Banks confront Green with his objections or mention them to colleagues. Instead, he "simply wanted the matter out of his sight" and "carefully steered himself and his clients clear" of Green by not referring any of his audit clients to Green for tax work. During this time, Banks always accounted for not recommending clients to Green by referring to technical matters. Two years after this incident, however, Green had successfully cultivated a small insurance clientele, and Banks met with him to discuss an "occasional referral relationship." Banks believed that the best action was to keep oneself and one's clients from Green for all but the "most narrowly conceived job where one could keep an eye on Green."

Case 1.3 Redlining in the Parking Lot (1985)

A vice president of sales at Playco liked to think of himself and liked others to call him the "Terminator" because, as he put it, "[he] hunts big game [looks for executives who he can best in arguments at meetings] any way he can."[5] According to several Playco executives, the Terminator's "track record" was not as good as he liked to think, and he frequently allowed the strongest executives to "rape" him [force their opinions on him without rebuttal] in meetings. When he did retaliate, he did so by attacking "pigeons" [weak executives]. The Terminator and his boss, a senior vice president named Greer, each believed the other to be "dicks" [belligerent people] but "flew low" in not expressing their grievances.

One morning, while employees streamed into Playco's main parking lot, the Terminator was unloading briefcases from the trunk of his Lotus sports car when Greer eased his Mercedes by him and asked to see him in his office later that day. After Greer parked his car, the Terminator walked over to his car and said, "Hey, I'm not your dog [a weak, subservient executive]. What the hell do you want to see me for now?" As the two men argued, other issues surfaced, including Greer's accusations that the Terminator openly womanized with company secretaries and with married women at a local health club to which many of the firm's executives belonged. The "catfight," as other executives later called it, quickly "redlined," whereupon Greer shoved the Terminator against the back of his Lotus. The Terminator then grabbed Greer and pushed him to the pavement. A crowd of employees gathered to watch the melee (some even raising bets on who would win). As company security officers arrived on the scene and separated the combatants, Greer threatened to "vaporize" the Terminator. The Terminator left the firm several months later in the absence of visible pressure from Greer. After leaving the firm, the Terminator claimed the accusations and the fight with Greer had severely wounded his "honor" to the point where he believed no one took him seriously at the executive meetings he attended and, as a result, he would be unable to "advance" in the firm.

Perhaps most noteworthy about these cases is the distinctive ways in which the principals handled their problems with one another. A boastful executive has his presentations to his bosses sabotaged by his subordinates and is then shelved as much for his crude style as for his poor public performances (case 1.1). Another executive avoids and shields clients from a boastful younger colleague after the latter misrepresents his expertise. Later, the principals meet to discuss occasional collaborations, although the aggrieved party still maintains his and his clients' distance from the miscreant (case 1.2). Finally, two executives physically fight one another in a parking lot over their dislike of their belligerent stances toward one another. Onlookers urge the principals on as at a prize fight and lay bets on the outcome, framing the altercation in highly colorful language (case 1.3).

These three cases also recapitulate the formal and informal social arrangements at the executive levels of the organizations from which the cases were collected. The culture and rituals of a rigid unitary chain of command at Old Financial shape the interaction in the first case. Jacobs's, Hawke's, and Morris's sabotage against their superior, Manright, unfolds along the contours of their chain of command as does Freeman's disciplining of Manright. Banks's persistent avoidance of Green in the second case reflects the flat authority structure, independence, and culture of restraint that partners at Independent Accounting experience on a daily basis. What appears as pure emotional enmity in the third case is emblematic of a social context of uncertain authority relations and dense departmental alliances arrayed against one another in constant struggle. Executives do business at Playco via open, aggressive confrontation and an executive's "honor" at answering challenges becomes paramount to personal and internal group success.

But this study, grounded as it is in the ethnography of executive action in private corporations, also speaks to more general theoretical issues regarding the isomorphism between social context—interpretive and social structures—and conflict management processes, particularly in formal organizations. As Charles Perrow (1986:132) instructively argues, organizational conflict management stems from "organizational characteristics" rather than individuals. Corporate executives, like all organizational members, undoubtedly have their own personal idiosyncracies, emotional capacities, and interests. However, such individual proclivities occur within the authority structures, the communication networks, and the cultural systems created and navigated by top managers. This theoretical approach, with its supporting empirical materials, thus characterizes routine conflict management as pragmatic action pursued in the workaday world. As such, this approach takes seriously Donald Black's (1976, 1984, 1990) arguments concerning the social-structural bases of conflict management. Yet it is only through heuristic sense making via culture that networks of social relations become imbued with meaning. Social structure and culture therefore operate as two sides of the same coin in the *contextual* approach to conflict management presented later in this chapter.

On an empirical level, this book provides an opportunity to peek into the routines and rituals of corporate executives as they handle the people problems, the slights to honor, the authority challenges, and the rancor typically unseen by those who do not belong to this exclusive club. In this sense, it is a relatively rare instance of "studying up" (Nader 1969) social hierarchies. The book also presents an ambitious attempt to use insights from Black's structural-behavioral approach to conflict management and interpretive theoretical approaches to further move the study of organizational conflict toward more contextually grounded analyses.

Reinventing the Study of Organizational Conflict

Few aspects of formal organizations have been visited and *revisited* as much as conflict.[6] Max Weber's classic work on bureaucracy and Elton Mayo's work on industrial "harmony" in the 1930s put organizational conflict, so to speak, on the map.[7] But empirical studies of organizational conflict, per se, did not gain notoriety until the two decades after World War II, when American sociologists began studying the vast new organizational world the war effort had begotten. Selznick's (1949) study of the Tennessee Valley Authority, Blau's (1955) observations of clerks in government agencies, Dalton's (1959) participant observation of middle managers in a manufacturing firm, Gouldner's (1954) case study of a gypsum mine and processing plant, and White's (1961) sociometric study of a chemical firm became familiar landmarks in organizational sociology. All of these works underscored the role of bureaucracy in simultaneously containing *and* inducing interpersonal and group conflict in organizations. Scholars subsequently used these works as points of departure to study how flexible bureaucratic arrangements (e.g., in some sense "slack," in March and Simon's [1958] term), decision-making processes, and appeal systems could reduce the likelihood and negative effects of organizational conflict (Corwin 1969; Pondy 1967; W. G. Scott 1965). Social psychologists used these works (among others) as points of departure to study conflict management experimentally in the laboratory.[8]

During the 1970s, theorists conceived of organizations as political coalitions which sidestepped the issues of bureaucracy and psychology (Bacharach and Lawler 1980; Pettigrew 1973; Pfeffer and Salancik 1978). The management of conflict came to be viewed from this perspective as the core mechanism through which organizational strategy and change occur, in some ways resembling political-sociological characterizations of conflict in wider society. Largely couched at the paradigmatic level, pluralist strands of these studies view conflict as productive or destructive; the former outcome is more likely when feuding parties negotiate (Kolb and Putnam 1992:9).[9] Interestingly, empirical studies of organizational conflict during this time increasingly became the province of macroanalysts far removed from the actual workings of organizations (Kolb and Putnam 1992).

It is against this historical backdrop that scholars reinvented the study of organizational conflict during the 1980s. This reinvention responded both to the political nature of organizational life and to the range of organizational phenomena little experienced and rarely studied by earlier generations: the increasing volatility of American business acquisition strategies (e.g., Hirsch 1986), the internal complexity of business firms (e.g., Powell 1990), and the upsurge of gender- and ethnic-based conflict in organizations (e.g., Martin 1992a). Accurately representing these aspects of organizational conflict demanded analytic and methodological strategies largely outside the purview of conventional organizational research with a decided turn toward approaches that could capture the stuff of conflict as it unfolded in organizational life (see the review in Barley 1991). Students of conflict management increasingly turned to the anthropology of law and disputing in traditional societies and then to the sociology of informal conflict management outside of the law for their theoretical and methodological inspiration.[10] The resulting studies—what could be called the new ethnography of organizational conflict—strongly suggest that *organizational conflict management often occurs in the crevices of organizational structures, hidden behind the scenes and inaccessible to macroanalyses of organizational politics or conventional survey and experimental methods* (Kolb and Bartunek 1992; Morrill 1989, 1991a, 1991b, 1992a, 1992b; Tucker 1989, 1993; Van Maanen 1992).

Our empirical knowledge of *informal* conflict management in organizations based on conventional approaches may therefore be more limited than a glance at the organizational literature might suggest. This limitation, then, is one specific reason to pursue studies of conflict management in corporations. Even more important, however, such descriptive shortcomings could significantly affect the quality of general theories of conflict management, which may themselves eventually yield considerable normative insight. Thus, it may be crucial to have systematic knowledge about *how* organizational members routinely manage conflict on a daily basis before we engage in large-scale efforts to prescribe how they *should* handle conflict (e.g., Lewicki and Sheppard 1985).

This discussion provides part of the intellectual context of the present study. However, the question remains as to why one should limit one's analysis to organizational conflict management among corporate executives. In other words, why study up?

Why Study Up?

In 1969, anthropologist Laura Nader wrote that social scientists tended to study down rather than up status structures. Innumerable studies, for example, recount the mores, habits, and problems of the less privileged but less often venture into the lair of the capitalist class.[11] Over twenty years later, this trend still holds, especially if one only includes close-up empirical studies, such as those that use ethnographic methods. One might go so far as to advance the proposition that the number of ethnographic studies in a setting varies inversely with the social status of its incumbents. Ethnographic research on corporate executives and conflict management exemplify this general trend.

The few existing ethnographies of executives typically have small samples as well as temporally and socially limited access to the tops of organizations. The most systematic are: (1) Carlson's (1951) study of nine Swedish managing directors during the late 1940s, in which his informants kept diaries of their work activities over a thirty-five day period; (2) Mintzberg's (1973) "structured observation" of five American chief executive officers in medium to large corporations over a five-week period in the late 1960s; (3) Kotter's (1983) observational and self-report study of fifteen "successful" executives drawn from private corporations in the late 1970s; and (4) Jackall's (1988) study of managerial morality at all levels of three large corporations (supplemented by secondary information on a variety of organizations) during the early 1980s. All of these works provide useful insights into the activities, personal motivations, ethical dilemmas, and social backgrounds of executives that will be made use of in the course of this book.[12]

Despite the lack of close-up scholarly studies of executives, their folk-hero status in American society has begotten voluminous popular and prescriptive literatures (Reich 1985). Much of the popular literature fits into what one business scholar calls the "great man school" (Mintzberg 1973:11–12). Such larger-than-life portraits of "great" male executives course through the popular business press (e.g., *Forbes, Fortune, Business Week*), general news magazines (e.g., *Time, Newsweek,*

U.S. News and World Report), television and radio "magazines," and executive memoirs and autobiographies such as Sloan's (1963) recounting of his stewardship at General Motors, Iacocca's (1984) account of his experiences at Ford and Chrysler, and Geneen's (1984) report on his management of ITT. To some degree, all of these sources convey the image of corporate executives as twentieth-century Napoleonic men on white horses. A smiling, confident corporate executive, for example, often graces the cover of nearly every business weekly with an accompanying story detailing how that top manager's personal abilities translated into individual and corporate success. Executives in their memoirs and autobiographies portray themselves as risk takers, mavericks, and visionaries and as hugely successful in nearly all their endeavors. It is as if executive life were a series of one-man plays (and they *are* typically about men) brought to life through the sheer force of the protagonist's will.

The prescriptive literature on executives is no less voluminous and in some instances evokes the same images of executives found in popular media, albeit transformed into general maxims about what "good" managers *do* and *should* be doing at the tops of their organizations.[13] Moreover, the prescriptive managerial literature, like the popular managerial literature, tends to focus on individuals, banishing the interconnectedness of managers with their social contexts to the background or in some cases doing away with it altogether. We thus learn a great deal about individual trees from the prescriptive managerial literature, but less about the forest of which they are a part.

General theory and research on organizations augments these sources of knowledge about executives and certainly has applicability to top managerial behavior, such as that found in the decision sciences (e.g., Cyert and March 1963; March 1988; March and Simon 1958; Simon 1976), organizational sociology (e.g., Fligstein 1990; Hannan and Freeman 1989; Kanter 1977; Moore 1962; Powell and Dimaggio 1991), institutional economics of firms and markets (Williamson 1985), and analyses of the political influence of business elites in wider society (Domhoff 1967, 1970; Useem 1984). As instructive as this scholarship is for studying managers and organizations (as will be apparent throughout this book), it only provides clues to the puzzle of empirical knowledge about executive action as it occurs in the workaday world because most of these works are grounded in data sources somewhat removed from executive suites themselves.

Even less empirical knowledge exists about conflict management among executives than that about executive life in general. Students

of conflict management in contemporary large organizations have focused almost exclusively on the lower and middle levels (Morrill
1991b:871). Even when scholars studying executives address conflict
management, they take a managerial perspective and focus on how
executives can and do repress conflict in whole organizations, excluding how it is handled among top managers themselves (e.g., Barnard
1968; Selznick 1947). This shortcoming constrains our sense of how
high-ranking managers make decisions when faced with delicate and
hostile situations with other high-ranking decision makers.

Thus, research on conflict management also suffers from a lack of
vertical generality—especially in organizations. The reasons for this
last shortcoming can be found in the obvious social power wielded by
executives, which largely insulates them from outside scrutiny. But this
insularity (as well as the small numbers of top managers relative to the
legions of middle and lower managers whom they direct) also makes
for an encapsulated social setting that facilitates observation of the
dramas and subtleties of executive conflict management. In one sense,
most executive contexts can be treated as remote villages: difficult to
reach, but small enough to be studied ethnographically once accessed.

A Social-Contextual Approach to Conflict Management

My theoretical approach in this book draws on two streams of contemporary social science.[14] One stream has its source in the sociology
and anthropology of law, conflict management, and social control, the
pioneers of which were Durkheim (1933 [1893]), Malinowski (1926),
Llewellyn and Hoebel (1941), and Gluckman (1955a, 1955b).[15] The contemporary work closest to these pioneers is Donald Black's *Behavior of
Law*, which advances a structural-behavioral approach to explain how
law varies with its social setting.[16] Sociologists, anthropologists, and
Black himself have explicitly extended and modified this theoretical
orientation beyond legal arenas to study moral orders constituted
wholly or partially outside of the state and to explain how people pursue grievances against one another through extralegal means.[17] A second theoretical stream that emphasizes interpretive structures flows
from work across a variety of fields—cultural anthropology and sociology, dramaturgical sociology, cultural organizational studies, and social cognition. Such structures range from observable symbol systems
and rituals to cognitive frames, schemas, and scripts that enable people to make sense of behavior and competently navigate social contexts.[18]

These diverse theoretical sources create an analytic niche within which compatible insights from structural-behavioral conflict management studies and work on interpretive structures can be interrelated to provide a fuller understanding of how conflict management intertwines with social contexts within formal organizations.[19] Thus, Black's work provides a way to conceptualize general relationships between social structure and conflict management across diverse social contexts. Interpretive approaches provide a theoretical framework to understand how actors in particular social contexts make sense of their grievances and enact local conflict management practices. My approach does not synthesize these two streams of work in the conventional sense. Clearly, the pure theoretical projects contained within these two orientations are incompatible in various ways.[20] As will be seen in the pages that follow, I privilege the proximate (or "local") social-structural underpinnings of context, while recognizing that the existence of structure itself resides in the means by which people make sense of and pragmatically enact structure. In this way, the approach to conflict management that I adopt resonates with theories of organizational behavior that emphasize institutionalized bases of organizational action (e.g., Powell and DiMaggio 1991) and how managerial decision making emerges out of "the social context in which managers operate" (Fligstein 1990:4; e.g., March 1988).

During the last several decades, sociologists have advanced innumerable notions of social context, which vary considerably in terms of the scope and breadth of the milieus in which people find themselves. Some concepts of social context appear as broad brush strokes on the historical canvas, such as Marxist "modes of production," Durkheimian types of "social solidarity," or Weberian "Western rationalization." Other notions of social context contain a sense of what particular individuals or groups experience in terms of proximate patterns of social interaction and the local meanings attributed to such interaction, such as in Goffman's (1983) concept of the interaction order. This second notion of context has emerged as important in the construction of general sociological theory because it focuses attention on the microfoundations of macrosociological theory and provides opportunities for improving such foundations (Knorr-Cetina 1981).[21] The approach thus underscores the need to understand behavior as it unfolds in situ, as well as to compare general patterns in local contexts across larger settings and time. The approach is also particularly appropriate for studying behavior in complex organizations, where people experience local contexts as distinctive bundles of social and interpretive structures expressive of rationalized societal "myths" about how work is to be organized (Meyer and Rowan 1977).

Social Structures

Central to Western societal myths about the social structure of complex organizations is formal structure. Perrow (1986:260) succinctly states the case for the primacy of formal structure in the analysis of organizational life: "The formal structure of the organization is the single most important key to its functioning, no matter how much it may be violated in practice; the violations themselves reflect the constraints of the formal structure." Bureaucracies institutionalize hierarchical divisions of labor and distributions of resources through officially defined spheres of authority (Weber 1946:196–244). The most dominant internal organizational form in contemporary American society is the unity-of-command or "tree" form that specifies that each subordinate be responsible to no more than one superior (Friedel 1967). Unity of command manifests itself most fundamentally in the prerogatives of superiors in performance evaluation and compensation, the allocation of resources, privacy, and access, and the success of ideas (e.g., Lincoln 1982).[22]

But such models and tables of organization really describe disembodied ideologies that come to life only as organizational members enact formal structure via pragmatic communication transactions (cf. Hawes 1974; Kaufer and Carley 1993:97; Thompson 1976). Here again, the animation of formal structure tells only part of the story, for communication among organizational members simultaneously exists both within and without the ideologies of formal structure, creating "informal" chains of transactions or *networks*. The transactions forming such networks take on a variety of properties also useful for the analysis of organizational life. Ties can vary according to the range of activities or types of information that people share. Uniplex ties in organizations are those that involve a single sphere of activities, such as those between organizational members who interact only in purely technical ways or those who interact only in social activities. Multiplex relations in organizations would be illustrated by members who have both social and task-related ties. Ties also manifest themselves in terms of their volume or *density*. Some organizational contexts contain dense-knit (high-density) communication networks in which nearly all incumbents have some sort of interaction with one another. Other organizational contexts contain loose-knit (low-density) communication networks in which people have few interactions of any kind with one another (e.g., Barnes 1969). Dense-knit contexts can further vary according to whether people clump together in coalitions and groups or are dispersed, and whether they are pervasively tied to one another or have few ties.

Communication transactions which animate formal structure and create informal networks have integral relationships with one another (Lincoln 1982; see the reviews in Ibarra 1992 and Monge and Eisenberg 1987). Feld (1981), for example, argues that communication network density is often a function of how institutionalized social arrangements position people vis-à-vis one another. The rationalized conception of the unity-of-command structure suggests a highly specialized division of labor with incumbents' social attention focused on their formal relations. Therefore, one would expect uniplex transactions to exist between superiors and subordinates with the strength of their ties predicated upon the hold of authority on them (e.g., Granovetter 1973). Alternative forms of formal structure not based on the unity-of-command principle, such as the "matrix" (Davis and Lawrence 1977), the semilattice (Friedel 1967), or organizations formally arranged into exchange networks (Powell 1990) create lateral structures which bring people together into diverse groups and activities, and should be associated with denser, multiplex communication networks.

Interpretive Structures and Social-Structural Pragmatics

Organizational members come to make sense of social structures in organizations via interpretive structures that enable them to "define their world, express their feelings, and make their judgements" (Geertz 1973:145). Such sense-making processes occur through the use of cognitive *schemas* that contain descriptive and prescriptive packages of knowledge about contexts well known to actors (Bartunek 1988; Hall 1969; Kellerman 1992; Sackmann 1991:33–45; Tannen and Wallat 1987). Schemas set the scene for what to expect in particular contexts. Cognitive *scripts* lay out the pragmatics for accomplishing situated activities, including the sequence rules for conversation and the ability to cognitively "rehearse" future actions.[23] Schemas and scripts enable people to "acquire" social structure by first providing actors with maps of existing social structures of a context, their relative position or positions in them, and possibilities of social structures yet to exist. Schemas and scripts thus provide a set of *social-structural pragmatics*—strategies for creating and navigating through social structures and role relations (Cicourel 1974:11–41). Individuals learn such pragmatics on the fly, so to speak, from direct experience in their workaday worlds (e.g., Macy 1991:731–32, 1993; Suchman 1987).

Schemas shared by members of a social context are in evidence when people tacitly understand, at some level, the nature and purposes of their interactions without explicitly having to make sense of their every verbal or nonverbal utterance. In this way people come to have a "working consensus" (Goffman 1959) about the routine social contexts in which they interact. Schemas can be imputed directly from behavior, but they are commonly communicated and instantiated in local context via "stories" told among members, as well as stories imported from other contexts. Schemas thus enhance or restrict peoples' ability to tap into other sources of action and meaning, such as the wider culture, and appropriate new meanings for action. Common schemas also enable people to impute meanings to actions that appear unintelligible or chaotic to outsiders. Finally, schemas expand contexts beyond synchronic instances and particular locales, creating spatio-temporal continuities and reproducible interaction—what Scheff (1990:38) calls "extended contexts." The interpretive tapestry woven out of locally shared schemas and scripts, then, provides the cognitive building blocks for the organization of local cultures, hence, local normative orders. If cultures are "tool boxes" (Swidler 1986) for interpretation and action, schemas and scripts may be regarded as cultural tools.[24]

Culture in organizations becomes visible in several ways. First, culture is transmitted via symbol systems that are manifested in rituals, languages, codes, signs, and imageries of all kinds. Second, culture appears in the ways people define themselves and their membership in organizations; what might be viewed as the intersection between social identity imputed by one's organization and self-designated personal identity (Snow and Anderson 1987:1347; cf. Kunda, 1992). At one extreme are instances in which organizational identity completely embraces personal identity. Goffman (1961:180) summarizes such extremes in "total institutions": "Built right into the social arrangements of an organization, then, is a thoroughly embracing conception of the member—not merely a conception of him *qua* member, but behind this conception of him *qua* human being. In telling him what he should do and why he should want to do this, the organization presumably tells him all that he may be." At the other extreme are instances in which personal identity and organizational identity do not embrace one another. In such instances actors attempt to distance themselves from imputed identities, often through their actions as well as disclosures of their beliefs and accounts of their actions (Goffman 1961).

Third, culture expresses itself in perspectives and stories of what Scott (1991) calls "functional fields"—the symbolic and concrete connections among organizations producing, supplying, or regulating similar products or services. This aspect of culture also relates to the way individuals and collectivities use internal cultures to manage uncertainty both in their own contexts within organizations and in the functional fields in which their organizations are embedded (e.g., Thompson 1967). Thus, culture also enables people to make assumptions about the stability and mutability of their contexts; that is, whether what is taken for granted about today's world can be counted on to exist in the same way tomorrow.

Social structures and the interpretive structures that make up culture, then, are conceptually distinct but empirically overlapping phenomena. Organizations cannot exist without shared interpretive structures that through their pervasiveness increasingly give the meanings attributed to behavioral patterns an objective character, while interpretive structures cannot exist for long without "plausibility structures," which root symbols in behavioral patterns (e.g., Berger and Luckmann 1966). Social structure and culture are also enmeshed in one another, each acting on the other via verbal and nonverbal communication transactions. Mutual influence of this sort is especially true for local cultures that arise in particular organizations and that vary considerably across different social contexts within organizations (e.g., in different divisions or departments; see Van Maanen and Barley 1985 and chapters 5 and 6 of the present work). This notion of social context therefore does not necessarily imply uniform normative consensus among interactants. In some settings, people may not have enough commonality regarding the meaning of events to even communicate without great difficulty; at the outset of their interaction they exist in what might be called a "contextual hole." [25] In other social contexts, people may have just enough commonalities to communicate, although such communication produces competing definitions of individual acts, situations, and the context itself. Mutual influences also exist between social context and indigenous conflict management, as the next section discusses.

The Isomorphism of Context and Conflict Management

At the most abstract level, Black (1990:61) argues that routine indigenous conflict management is "isomorphic" with its social context. Conflict management that unfolds between social superiors and social inferiors, for example, "mirrors subordination" (1990:62). High rates of relational mortality, to cite another example, recapitulate high rates of conflict management via avoidance behavior (1990:61). The multidimensional aspects of social contexts—social-tie strengths, the shapes of relational networks, the nature of hierarchies, for example—are reflected in conflict relations. So intense is the isomorphism between conflict management and social contexts that Black (1990) argues pure types of conflict management could be used to identify particular types of social contexts. The question is, *How* does isomorphism of this sort occur?

Just as schemas set the scene for nongrievance social interaction and scripts lay out appropriate courses of nongrievance-related social interaction, so they set the scene for what to expect in conflict relations. Indigenous schemas and scripts of interaction contain a tacit stock of language, imageries, and rituals that provide "local knowledge" (Geertz 1983:167–234) of appropriate conflict management. In this way, the "norms" that govern social relations of all kinds also govern routine conflict management practices (Horwitz 1990:5). As people learn the social pragmatics of indigenous nongrievance interaction, they also gain tacit knowledge of contextually appropriate conflict management schemas and scripts. Actors therefore also "acquire" on the fly the moral orders in which they routinely interact. At the same time, conflict management is not a purely cognitive activity. Obviously, emotional expression frequently accompanies conflict management. But such expressions themselves are typically channeled by available interpretive schemas and scripts for action (Fiske and Taylor 1991:414).

In some contexts, local knowledge translates into ritualized practices associated with conflict management that dramatize and throw in relief routine nonconflict behaviors. For example, modern courts of law dramatize the status differences between judges and disputants, elaborate honor ceremonies symbolizing the equality and respect between disputants often accompanies open vengeance between equals, and negotiations of conflict often require exaggerated etiquette and restrained communication (Black 1990; Koch et al. 1977). Avoidance behaviors may occur with less fanfare as aggrieved parties simply go about their routine activities without ostensibly airing their grievances.

Routine indigenous conflict management, then, is not an isolated behavior or an exotic medicinal dressing that aggrieved parties use to close their social wounds. Rather, indigenous conflict management exists as a constituent component of ongoing social contexts that may or may not resolve grievances. Figure 1.1 summarizes the recursive relationship between indigenous nonconflict scripts, schemas, and behavior, indigenous conflict management schemas and scripts, and in-

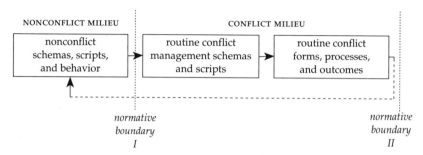

Figure 1.1   Social context and routine conflict management

digenous conflict management actions. To the left of the first normative boundary is daily pragmatic interaction, routine interpersonal relations, and taken-for-granted social institutions. Crossing the first normative boundary in figure 1.1 denotes perceived or actual violations of norms that lead to grievances and the engagement of contextual conflict management schemas and scripts (conditioned at some level by wider culture). The invocation of these cognitive structures lead to routine conflict management forms, processes, and outcomes. The dotted line recursively connecting routine conflict management and routine social interaction is not intended to imply that all routine conflict management ends in resolution. This dotted line simply underscores the isomorphism of routine conflict management with nonconflict social interaction in particular social contexts. As will be seen in the case-study chapters in this book, routine conflict management can continue indefinitely.

Crossing the second normative boundary occurs when conflict management in a particular context departs from local custom. Such normative breaches in the customs of conflict management can occur through accretion, such as when a social context slowly changes over time, spawning recombinations of existing schemas and scripts imperceptible perhaps to the actors involved, but nonetheless bringing fundamental change over extended periods of time. Another way changes in conflict management can occur is via the transposition of conflict management scripts and schemas from one context to another: actors arriving in new contexts may attempt to put into play conflict management schemas and scripts quite different from local customs, and they may succeed. Breaches in the conflict management normative boundary can also occur rapidly through exogenous shocks to particular social contexts. In private corporations, the most common examples of rapid exogenous change would arise from restructurings, takeovers, or mergers, or impending organizational death that begins to shatter local contexts altogether.

The idea of scripted, routine conflict management tends to emphasize the habitual and taken-for-granted nature of social behavior. From this perspective, much of what people do to pursue their grievances is neither rational nor irrational, but nonrational (Merry and Silbey 1984:158). These ideas mesh with behavioral studies of decision making that find managerial action arises less from a "logic of consequentiality" than from a "logic of appropriateness" grounded in indigenous routines (Cyert and March 1963; Levitt and March 1988:320). However, disputants, whether managers or not, do not slavishly obey every cue in their contextual schemas and scripts as they manage conflict. People enact conflict management scripts pragmatically and adaptively according to situational opportunities and constraints just as they enact nonconflict scripts. As Suchman observes, "Actors use the resources that a particular occasion provides—including, but crucially not reducible to, formulations such as plans—to construct their action's developing purpose and intelligibility" (1987:3). Yet, there exists a dualism in such action. Individuals are purposeful in their actions, but such purposes express the social structures and cultural arrangements in which they act (Giddens 1979:49–95; Sewell 1992).

This argument does not imply, moreover, that people have equal access to the cognitive and behavioral tools of conflict management. Quite the contrary. Innate capabilities may enable some individuals to better learn and deploy contextually appropriate conflict management. One's social position may also limit or enable the accessibility of cultural tools and social resources, hence the accessibility of conflict management strategies themselves (Black 1976, 1984). Aggrieved parties of high status acting against social inferiors, for example, have very different scripts and resources available to them than aggrieved parties pursuing their grievances upward. Relationally distant parties experience similar differentials as do people with and without allies at their disposal. Different contexts will also be more or less conducive to various kinds of conflict management. Different contexts thus have different *carrying capacities* for conflict management: the more socially diverse the context, the more diverse the conflict management (Black 1984:17).

Finally, learning the pragmatics of conflict management in a particular social context may often be necessary, but not sufficient, for "successfully" redressing grievances in the conventional sense. Pursuing grievances in appropriate ways merely means adapting one's efforts at conflict management to one's contextual audience. Indeed, one of the lessons from field studies of conflict management is how few conflicts are ever resolved in the conventional sense of the term (e.g., Baumgartner 1988; Black 1980; Kolb and Bartunek 1992; Merry 1979; Tucker 1993).

Up to this point I have used conflict management schemas, forms, scripts, and processes in general and unspecified fashions. In the following sections, I clarify what I mean by conflict management and the interpretive structures related to it. Nearly a century of cross-cultural research on conflict management has resulted in several typologies of the ways people interpret norm violations and pursue grievances. What follows is not an exhaustive typology of all of the aspects of conflict management to which scholars have drawn attention, but a typology that may be particularly useful for studying conflict management in context.

Grievance Schemas

Grievance schemas specifically enable aggrieved parties to interpret injurious events, label norm violators, allocate responsibility for norm violation, and assess the goals and desired outcomes of conflict management efforts (Horwitz 1990:19–22; cf. Pinkley 1990; Snow et al. 1986).[26] Black (1976:4–5) argues that grievance schemas occur cross-culturally in four distinctive master styles.[27] Two styles, the *penal* and the *compensatory*, tend to be more accusatory in their orientation toward conflict management, pointing to the liability that offending parties bear for their norm violations, as well as the notion of winners and losers in conflict management processes. Two other styles, the *therapeutic* and the *conciliatory*, tend to be more remedial, oriented toward the repair of social relations. Implied by Baumgartner (1988), a fifth master schema, which I shall label *indifferent*, specifies norm violation as a nuisance to be put behind the principals with as little fanfare as possible. Each of these schemas is discussed in greater depth below.

A penal schema specifies injurious events as a violation of a specified legal or extralegal prohibition. From this perspective, aggrieved parties view norm violators as voluntary offenders who are accountable for their actions and deserve punishment. Penal schemas are in evidence most commonly in criminal proceedings, but the state does not have sole province over penal conflict management (Black 1983). "Punishment-centered" bureaucracies (Gouldner 1954) illustrate organizational arrangements in which conflict is viewed as an infraction of prohibitions and norm violators are sternly disciplined. Nonbureaucratic groups, such as highly authoritarian or patriarchal families, also respond to normative violations by their members in extremely punitive ways (Swanson 1971), sometimes even specifying death as appropriate for offending members (Veyne 1987).

A compensatory schema renders injurious events meaningful in relation to formal or informal breaches of contracts between parties. In this style, norm violators are identified as debtors who bear the responsibility for repaying their broken obligations either with human services or material resources of some sort. The overarching goal of a compensatory schema therefore focuses on settlement of the broken obligation via payment to the aggrieved party. Civil justice systems illustrate compensatory styles of conflict management. In such systems, the solution to norm violation is typically payment by the principal who is deemed responsible for the breach of obligation (Lempert and Sanders 1986). Just as the state does not solely administer penal conflict management, compensatory conflict management also occurs informally. Interorganizational grievances are typically defined as contract breaches and are resolved via the payment of damages for losses (Macaulay 1963). The handling of war reparations for damages by winners and losers also illustrates compensatory styles of conflict management (Smoke 1977).

Aggrieved parties who invoke a conciliatory schema focus on disruptions in relational harmony. The goal in this style is reconciliation. Conciliatory styles resemble compensatory styles in that both are oriented to toward the repair of some broken obligation. The difference between the two lies in the nature of the obligation. In conciliatory conflict management, the broken obligation is viewed as a breach in a general relational norm. In the compensatory style the breach is in the norm governing the specific performance of a service or services, a difference akin to breaches in generalized versus specific reciprocity (e.g., Sahlins 1974). Institutionalized mediation provides examples of conciliatory conflict management when such procedures are oriented toward reconciling disturbances in relationships between aggrieved parties (Conley and O'Barr 1990:90–95; Witty 1981). Conciliatory conflict management, in which "problem solving" or "compromise" is paramount and finding "integrative" solutions that return relationships between the parties in conflict to some level of harmony, also occurs among families and friends, in romantic dyads, and in small groups of workers (Cahn 1990; Greenhalgh 1987).

A therapeutic schema portrays norm violators as victims whose personalities markedly deviate from accepted standards. This style, like the conciliatory style, focuses away from particular acts, but instead of locating deviation in troubled relationships, finds it in individual psychological aberrations. Unlike either the penal or compensatory styles, then, norm violators in this style are not held responsible for their behaviors. Informal or formal treatment is the solution to grievances, the goal of such treatments being the return of the victim to some sort of normal state. Therapeutic conflict management most often occurs in formal psychiatric or psychological counseling that is applied to disputes in a variety of contexts: families, organizations, friendships, and the like (Horwitz 1982).

Finally, when interpreting conflict from an indifferent vantage point, aggrieved parties label those who provoke grievances as nuisances. This schema emerged from Baumgartner's (1984a, 1988) work on middle-class conflict management and from empirical materials in the present study. The problem to which aggrieved parties respond within this schema are incursions into their autonomy, and viable solutions typically involve some kind of separation from the offending party. Such schemas frequently occur among individuals with transient relationships: suburbanite, neighbors (Baumgartner 1988), traditional hunter-gatherers (Turnbull 1961), and the homeless in modern society (Spradley 1970).

Although some grievance schemas suggest particular kinds of conflict management, a one-to-one correspondence between schemas and grievance pursuits does not necessarily exist. Criminal punishment, for example, may simultaneously be oriented toward retribution (penal style) and rehabilitation (therapeutic style), particularly when prisoners are encouraged to learn skills that will aid their "reintegration" into "law-abiding" society. Likewise, conflict management in families sometimes exhibits several styles at once when it is intended as retribution for offenses committed by children against one another or against their parents, as payment for damages (e.g., when some family possession has been broken by the offenders), and as a means of returning the children's behavior to some acceptable set of social standards. Moreover, aggrieved parties need not invoke an entire conflict management schema when framing their grievances. An individual might frame a grievance as a broken obligation (compensatory), for example, without articulating to themselves or the norm violator the solution for the grievance.

Conflict Management Forms and Processes

Conflict management scripts organize conflict management action into particular *forms* and *processes*. The *form* of conflict management refers to the action that people take to pursue their grievances against others (Black 1984:7). There are countless types of concrete conflict management forms across cultures. Each new study of conflict management, in fact, appears to turn up still more variation in the strategies through which people pursue their grievances.

The *process* of conflict management refers to the way conflict management efforts unfold or, more concretely, who is involved, how people become involved, and the extent of their involvement. It is generally agreed that conflict management unfolds according to the lines of action in a particular case, that is, whether grievances are pursued unilaterally, bilaterally, or trilaterally (Black 1984:7–9; cf. Koch 1974:26–31). These distinctions also correspond to what Nader and Todd (1978:14–15) term the grievance, conflict, and dispute stages of conflict management.

Unilateral grievances involve only one line of orientation or action by an aggrieved party against an offending party. Bilateral conflicts involve two parties pursuing grievances against each other. Trilateral disputing involves third parties who act either as partisans or settlement agents. Trilateral disputing can shift the burden of conflict management away from the principals in two ways. First, the risk of conflict management and the impetus for resolution may be syndicated across a liability group when partisans become involved in a conflict (Koch 1984). Second, decisions concerning resolution can be shifted to a third-party settlement agent such as a judge or an arbitrator (Black and Baumgartner 1983).

The movement from grievances to conflicts to disputes emphasizes the transformation of grievances into triadic resolution procedures. As unilateral grievances are transformed into trilateral disputes, however, the social scope of grievances necessarily enlarges, but does not necessarily lead to resolution (Horwitz 1990:98). This process has been termed *social escalation* to indicate the greater involvement of the relevant social system in each stage of grievance expression (Morrill and King Thomas 1992).[28] *Psychological escalation,* in contrast, refers to increases in excitation of the principals in a conflict (Pruitt and Rubin 1986; Siegel and Fouraker 1960). Conventional understandings of conflict often assume psychological escalation to be the fundamental key to understanding conflict management, particularly peaceful resolutions. Students of negotiation, for example, argue that war is much more likely when nation-state representatives do not remain reasonable and keep their emotions in check during diplomacy (Boulding 1962). Students of interpersonal conflict management imply much the same perspective by arguing that ineffective negotiation or violence is likely when aggrieved parties do not check their emotions (Neale and Bazerman 1991; Zillman 1990).

Social escalation is equally important, however, because different stages in the disputing process result in different options for handling grievances and for outcomes. For instance, a grievance that does not escalate into a conflict can never be negotiated because the offending party may be completely unaware of the trouble. Normative violations contained at the preconflict level may allow grievances to wither away without further difficulties. However, this process need not be linear. For example, when an individual calls the police because of a neighbor's irritating barking dog, the aggrieved party jumps over the conflict stage (assuming the neighbor who owns the barking dog does not have any grievances against the aggrieved) to involve third parties as settlement agents. That same individual who calls the police to secretly complain about a neighbor's barking dog may not obtain satisfaction from the police's visit to the neighbor. Instead of calling the police again (or the animal control board), the aggrieved party may simply tolerate the offending neighbor without the latter's knowledge. The case thus de-escalates to the unilateral grievance stage without ever passing back through the conflict stage.

Conflict management forms can also be distinguished within each of these stages by whether the parties actually engage in direct interaction regarding the grievances between them. Baumgartner (1984a, 1988) distinguishes between two kinds of action in this respect: confrontation and nonconfrontation. Confrontation refers to the direct airing of grievances by one or both principals via communication or physical action. Nonconfrontation occurs when grievances are expressed without direct communication or physical action between the principals.

The choice between confrontation and nonconfrontation is important because it can determine the visibility of grievances to social audiences who might act as supporters or settlement agents, thereby increasing or decreasing the options for resolution. The degree of confrontation in grievance pursuit also influences how conflict management processes and outcomes feed back into their social contexts, either reproducing existing relations or leading to change (Morrill and King Thomas 1992:405). The following sections discuss the isomorphism of two important aspects of conflict management, confrontation and third-party settlement, with their social contexts.

Confrontation

M. P. Baumgartner's (1984a, 1988, 1992) work on conflict management among American middle- and working-class adults and children provides the clearest distillation of one set of social contexts in which confrontational conflict management will likely occur. She argues that nonhierarchical social contexts of loose-knit relational networks will couple with nonconfrontation. Aggrieved parties will more likely opt for confrontation in nonhierarchical tight-knit contexts. In loose-knit contexts, as well, people will interpret their grievances as "bothers," "inconveniences," and "nuisances" mixed with a secondary concern for smoothing over whatever trouble exists between themselves and their adversaries.

Tight-knit networks by definition mean people interact in confined social spaces where confrontation over nongrievance-related issues is a way of life. The atomistic, individuated nature of loose-knit networks induces great expanses of social space. In loose-knit settings, disputants have the social distance and autonomy necessary to withdraw from conflict rather than confront opponents. Second, the weakness of social ties decreases opportunities to mobilize allies who would aid disputants in the pursuit of their grievances, thus syndicating the risks of confrontation. Finally, actors in socially fragmented settings have sparse knowledge of each other's general activities and conflicts. In one sense, disputants in loosely tied networks are treated as "first offenders," which generally leads to less aggressive conflict management than when aggrieved parties have notorious reputations. The opposite prevails in tight-knit settings where multiple communication channels spread information rapidly, especially conflict-related gossip.

Differentially tight-knit networks produce different forms of conflict management as well. In contexts in which nearly everyone is connected to everyone else via interdependent, multiplex relationships, confrontation is likely to take negotiatory forms. In contexts in which people are clumped into tight-knit coalitions, between which exist relatively few bridging ties, conflict management is likely to take the form of vengeance. Disputants may interpret their grievances from a conciliatory stance in pervasively tight-knit contexts and within coalitions, as principals attempt to repair ruptured social relations that enable them to effectively engage rival coalitions. But compensatory schemas dominate conflict management between coalitions via exchanges of material or symbolic resources. If it is difficult to observe the covert conflict management that occurs in loose-knit settings, it is equally difficult to decode the complexity of symbols accompanying conflict management in tight-knit settings either between or within coalitions.

Third-Party Settlement

Black and Baumgartner (1983) argue that some sort of social hierarchy must be present in social contexts in which third-party settlement routinely occurs. Settlement agents draw their abilities to impose outcomes from their status positions in hierarchies vis-à-vis disputants. Of particular importance in applying this idea to organizational conflict management is the degree to which formal structural position confers legitimacy on incumbents to settle disputes. Authority systems bind people into role relations that entitle superiors to legitimately command subordinates. Authority systems also grant formal superiors various resources with which to enforce their decisions, including the ability to back up their authority with institutional forms of coercion (Kelman and Hamilton 1989). In organizational settings, the status conferred upon potential settlement agents by dint of their positions in "informal" hierarchies, such as, for example, those based on gender, ethnicity, or reputation, can enhance, detract, or even replace the ability of third-party settlement agents to intervene into disputes. Here again, the principle of isomorphism is evident in that third-party dispute settlement recapitulates the authoritativeness apparent in downward dealings of all kinds with status inferiors in social hierarchies.[29] When people are so tightly gripped by hierarchy that they become dependent upon it for sorting out their lives and defining their identities, third-party settlement will be most pervasive.[30]

Black and Baumgartner (1983:113) also argue that vertical distance in hierarchies between settlement agents and disputants (taken together) increases the authoritative suppression of conflict, that is, the imposition of outcomes by third parties. The increase of vertical distance, moreover, is also associated with penal schemas of conflict management. Repressive peacemaking, for example, calls for extremely punitive action to be taken by third parties. Disputants are viewed as increasingly in need of harsh punishment as well as jointly responsible for the trouble between them. At the other end of the spectrum, status similarity appears to breed scripts of friendly peacemaking or mediation, and grievance schemas of conciliation and therapy. Relational ties follow this same pattern. To the degree that third parties have weak social bonds with disputants, they will also be more penally oriented. Social intimacy between third parties and disputants appears to be associated with less aggressive and penal forms of settlement, such as friendly peacemaking or mediation.

The foregoing discussion of conflict management and social context can be summarized by the following remarks:

1. Conflict management begins when actors interpret events through the lens of grievance schemas.

2. Conflict management is a process that can be defined according to the lines of action between participants. Such action can be unilateral, bilateral, or trilateral and can also vary according to its directness.

3. Routine conflict management is isomorphic with the structural and cultural properties of its social contexts, as illustrated by the social contexts in which confrontation and third-party settlement are likely to appear.

4. Confrontation will likely occur in contexts without overarching institutionalized hierarchies, but with tightly knit relational networks. The specific form of confrontation will vary according to whether principals are arrayed in tightly knit coalitions with weaker intergroup ties or in pervasively tight-knit relational networks. Nonconfrontation of all kinds will be associated with contexts of loose-knit networks. In loose-knit settings, adversaries are likely to frame their grievances as matters of indifference. Individual adversaries within tight-knit coalitions and pervasively tight-knit networks are likely to frame conflict in conciliatory fashions. Collective adversaries (arrayed in coalitions) will likely frame grievances in compensatory fashions.

5. Third-party settlement will likely occur in institutionalized hierarchies which contain relational distance between potential third-party settlement agents and disputants. Vertical and relational distance between third parties and disputants will vary directly with the penal framing and authoritativeness of settlement processes.

The central questions for the remainder of the book now turn on: What are the parameters of executive social contexts and how do they vary from corporation to corporation? How do executives frame grievances among one another? What are the customs of conflict management at the tops of corporations? What are the implications of the customs of conflict management among corporate executives for understanding organizations and conflict management in general?

CHAPTER TWO

SETTING THE SCENE

Effective reconnaissance into any social context requires several passes, each yielding different types of information that together form a triangulated description of the "lay of the land." The first pass in this chapter focuses on the business levels of the corporations in the study: their sizes, products, and backgrounds. The second pass centers on the social characteristics of incumbents at the tops of these corporations: gender, ethnicity, and education, and the division of labor by social characteristics. A third pass paints a portrait of some of the common themes across all thirteen organizations, including the material splendor and success in executive life, the social insularity and loneliness of being an executive, and constraints on the ability to "lead" large organizations. A final pass into these firms describes the local social contexts of executives, focusing specifically on the hierarchies, communication and personal networks, and cultures therein.

The Corporations

Several different types of businesses, industries, and products are represented by the research sites (with some firms offering overlapping and multiple products or services, hence the total number of corporations for the following categories is larger than thirteen): (1) *construction* ($n = 5$; skyscrapers, energy and communications infrastructure, manufacturing facilities, planned communities); (2) *manufacturing* ($n = 4$; communications technologies, electronics, packaging machines, pharmaceutical and personal health products, retail and industrial packaging, and children's games, learning aids, and toys); (3) *professional* ($n = 4$; accounting/auditing, architecture, management consulting, engineering); (4) *services* ($n = 6$; entertainment, financial, health, insurance, energy); *raw materials* (n) $= 1$; wood).[1]

The corporation sizes also range from Commco, a communications firm with 60,000 employees, 21 executives, and over $8 billion in revenues during fiscal year 1986, to a manufacturer with only 500 employees, 10 executives, and $75 million dollars in revenues during the same

year. The mean number of employees for each firm stands at just under
10,500 and the median at 1,500. The distribution is quite skewed because of Commco's size. Revenues reflect Commco's enormousness relative to the rest of the firms as well. The mean revenue is $1.3 billion
per year but the median revenue is $300 million per year. The sizes of
the executive corps in each firm range from 10 (Container Corporation)
to 76 (Old Financial), with a mean of 23 and a median of 17. Five firms
in the sample reported a profit, 5 firms reported losses, and 3 firms
broke even in 1986. Summary characteristics for the thirteen firms in
the study are presented in table 2.1. Below appear thumbnail sketches
of each firm, briefly focusing on their history, products and services,
and recent activities.[2]

Commco. Commco incorporated before World War II as part of a
large communications conglomerate. The firm provides telephone services, information-processing equipment and services, and infrastructure for residential and commercial electronic communication in several states. The firm divested from its conglomerate in 1984, entering
into a period of rapid change and expansion. In 1982, the firm had
120,000 employees and nearly 40 executives. Less than half of the executives and employees with Commco in 1982 remained in 1986. During
the same period, the company diversified its products and geographi-
cally expanded its services, recording profits for 1985–86. It is publicly owned.

General Utility. A group of entrepreneurs founded General Utility
(GU) in the 1920s and rapidly expanded the areas the firm served in
the first decade after World War II. GU sells natural gas and other
energy sources and provides the infrastructure for energy delivery in
several metropolitan areas. GU owns several smaller subsidiaries
which deliver much the same service as it does. During 1984–86, the
firm began to explore the possibility of supplying infrastructural expertise to several foreign countries in exchange for the rights to import
energy resources to the United States. The firm has been what one
top manager called a "break-even proposition" since the early 1980s,
neither losing nor making much money. The firm is publicly owned.

Playco. Two entrepreneurs founded Playco during the 1940s and pre-
sided over the firm until the 1960s, when the company went public
and began diversifying its products. Playco manufactures computers,
electronic learning aids, and electronic toys and games for children,
and also owns publishing houses, movie studios, computer manufacturers, small chemical companies, and numerous other subsidiaries
involved in various aspects of the adult and youth entertainment in-

Table 2.1   Summary Characteristics of the Thirteen Corporations in
                  the Study

Corporation (Industry)	Number of Employees	Number of Executives	Total Revenues (× $1,000)[a]	Financial Health[a]
Commco (Communications)	60,000	21	8,000,000	profit
General Utility (Energy)	30,000	21	5,000,000	even
Playco (Entertainment)	20,000	43	1,300,000	profit
Old Financial (Savings and Loan)	10,500	76	1,100,000	profit
Smith Brothers (Health/Insurance)	5,000	22	850,000	loss
Hightower (Construction)	2,700	17	750,000	even
Infotain (Entertainment/ Communications)	1,200	15	300,000	loss
Independent (Accounting)	1,000	21	200,000	profit
Bailey (Construction)	1,000	14	150,000	even
New Financial (Savings and Loan)	1,500	16	100,000	loss
Continental Design (Architecture/ Engineering)	1,000	15	100,000	loss
Sunset Group (Health/ Entertainment)	500	14	100,000	loss
Container Corp. (Packaging)	500	10	75,000	profit

Note: Firms are listed in order of gross revenues in 1986.
[a] Data for this variable were gathered from year-end reports for 1986 provided by each corporation.

dustry. The firm recovered from losses incurred during the years just before my fieldwork by returning handsome dividends to stockholders during 1985–86.

Old Financial. The family that founded Old Financial during the 1920s privately held the corporation until the early 1980s, when it went public. Old Financial is a diversified savings and loan with several hundred branch offices, commercial interests, and real estate development subsidiaries. The firm enjoyed moderate profits during most of its history and delivered moderate but steady dividends to its stock-holders since going public.

Smith Brothers. Family Smith founded Smith Brothers Insurance during the early part of this century. The firm remained in insurance until the 1960s, when it diversified into health services by buying several hospitals, health services companies, and health products manufacturers. This rapid expansion and diversification swelled the executive ranks to two and one-half times its mid-1970s levels by 1986. Even so, the firm endured losses during the early 1980s and was forced to sell some of its subsidiaries in the mid-1980s.

Hightower Construction. A single developer founded Hightower during the late nineteenth century. His love of skyscrapers and shipyards focused the firm's attention on those two settings during the first seven decades of its existence. Hightower still specializes in large commercial buildings and also builds manufacturing facilities, shopping malls, and public works. The firm enjoyed profitable years in recent times, but during 1986 broke even.

Infotain. Infotain is a creature of the technology and entertainment developments of the 1970s and 1980s. Originally founded as a spin-off of a large entertainment conglomerate in the mid-1970s, the company severed its ties from its former parent during the early 1980s to offer services in a range of information and entertainment systems. Infotain owns subsidiaries in the entertainment and information industries, and recorded a loss in 1986.

Independent Accounting. A group of accountants chartered Independent Accounting in the early part of this century. Like the other Big Six (formerly Big Eight) accounting firms, Independent audits and does tax work for many of the largest corporations in the world. In recent years, the firm diversified into management consulting, offering services in fields as diverse as personnel training and management information systems. The firm has been profitable nearly every year of its existence.

Bailey Construction. Four executives left an international construction conglomerate during the mid-1960s to found Bailey Construction. The company primarily develops and builds commercial buildings (e.g., warehouse complexes, manufacturing facilities), planned communities, and large public works (particularly in foreign countries). Despite nearly ten years of profits during the 1970s, Bailey fell on hard times in the early and mid-1980s but recovered during 1985 and 1986 to break even each year, drawing much of its revenues from what an executive termed "specialty" foreign construction deals accessible only to Bailey's expertise. The company is publicly owned.

New Financial. Several former savings and loan and banking corporate officers founded New Financial in the 1970s. The company has several branch offices in its local area and became involved in several local and out-of-state real estate developments during the 1970s and 1980s. Despite profitable years during its early existence, the firm suffered consecutive losses in 1985 and 1986.

Continental Design. Two smaller firms merged to create Continental Design during the early 1970s. Much of the firm's business concentrates on the design and engineering of planned communities, housing tracks, and golf courses. Continental grew rapidly during the early 1980s, tripling its 1979 size by 1986 even though it incurred a loss in 1986.

Sunset Group. Sunset Group splintered off from a parent corporation in the early 1980s with an aggressive diversification and acquisition strategy oriented toward capitalizing on what one Sunset executive called the "American health obsession" of the 1980s. The firm began in personal health care products, but by 1986 it owned health clubs and an athletic shoe and clothing manufacturer. Sunset recorded a loss in 1986.

Container Corporation. Container Corporation began as a subsidiary to service the packaging needs of a large agribusiness concern, but went independent in the 1970s. The firm manufactures a number of types of packaging for agricultural products, beverages, and industrial uses. Container Corporation also manufactures, distributes, and services packaging machines of all kinds and turned a profit in 1986.

Executive Demographics

Table 2.2 summarizes the demographics of the 305 top managers in the study. Consistent with Ferguson's (1984), Kanter's (1977), and Moore's (1962) arguments about the monosexual nature of organizational elites, men made up over 90% of the executives in the study. Moreover, female executives are not evenly distributed across all the firms in the study. Five of the thirteen firms do not have women working as top managers. Eighteen of the 23 female top managers in the study work for six of the thirteen firms, the highest numbers of which are at Playco ($n = 5$) and Sunset Group ($n = 4$). Only Sunset Group has what could be characterized as a "concentration" of women relative to the overall number of executives in the firm (4/14; 29%).

Also consistent with the above authors' observations, European-Americans make up the overwhelmingly largest ethnicity at 92% ($n = 280$) in the study. Asian-Americans constitute the largest single Ameri-

Table 2.2 Executive Demographics by Gender, Ethnicity, and Highest Earned Degree

Corporation	Gender		Ethnicity[a]					Degree[b]			
	M	F	E	Af	H	As	F	M	HS	C	G
Bailey Construction	5	—	4	—	25	—	10	100	25	6	2
	(14)	—	(12)	—	(1)	—	(1)	(1)	(2)	(8)	(3)
Commco	7	9	7	—	25	12	—	—	—	4	10
	(19)	(2)	(19)	—	(1)	(1)	—	—	—	(5)	(16)
Container	4	—	3	—	—	12	—	—	12	2	4
Corporation	(10)	—	(9)	—	—	(1)	—	—	(1)	(3)	(6)
Continental Design	5	9	5	—	—	25	—	—	—	—	9
	(13)	(2)	(13)	—	—	(2)	—	—	—	—	(15)
General Utility	7	—	8	—	—	—	—	—	12	9	5
	(21)	—	(21)	—	—	—	—	—	(1)	(12)	(8)
Hightower	6	—	6	—	—	—	—	—	38	5	5
Construction	(17)	—	(17)	—	—	—	—	—	(3)	(6)	(8)
Independent	6	13	7	—	25	12	—	—	—	5	9
Accounting	(18)	(3)	(19)	—	(1)	(1)	—	—	—	(6)	(15)
Infotain	5	4	5	—	—	—	10	—	—	3	7
	(14)	(1)	(14)	—	—	—	(1)	—	—	(4)	(11)
New Financial	5	13	5	33	—	—	10	—	—	3	7
	(13)	(3)	(14)	(1)	—	—	(1)	—	—	(4)	(12)
Old Financial	26	13	25	33	25	25	20	—	—	31	21
	(73)	(3)	(70)	(1)	(1)	(2)	(2)	—	—	(41)	(35)
Playco	13	22	14	—	—	12	30	—	—	13	16
	(38)	(5)	(39)	—	—	(1)	(3)	—	—	(17)	(26)
Smith Brothers	8	—	8	—	—	—	—	—	12	11	14
	(22)	—	(22)	—	—	—	—	—	(1)	(14)	(7)
Sunset Group	4	17	4	33	—	—	20	—	—	8	2
	(10)	(4)	(11)	(1)	—	—	(2)	—	—	(11)	(3)
Total	92	8	92	1	1	3	3	0	3	43	54
	(282)	(23)	(280)	(3)	(4)	(8)	(10)	(1)	(8)	(131)	(165)

Note: By percentage. Figures in parentheses indicate absolute frequencies.
[a] E = European-American; Af = African-American; H = Hispanic; As = Asian-American; F = foreign nationals.
[b] M = middle school (a postelementary school that doesn't award academic diplomas); HS = high school; C = college; G = graduate school. Based on informant self-reports.

can minority group in the study at just under 3% ($n = 8$). The largest minority group in the population are foreign nationals, who comprise 3% ($n = 10$) of the study. African-Americans ($n = 3$) and Hispanics ($n = 4$) were nearly invisible at the firms, both in numbers and influence, as will be discussed later in the chapter. It should be noted that all of the women in the study are European-Americans.

The vast majority of executives in the study are college educated ($n = 296$; 97%), with slightly more executives with graduate degrees than bachelor's degrees. The largest percentage of graduate degrees held by executives, not surprisingly, are MBAs ($n = 107$). Executives without college degrees primarily worked in companies that promote from within, and in particular in the two construction firms, which have a history of promoting tradespeople into executive positions.

Although not included in table 2.2, executive ages ranged from 36 to 72 years of age with a mean of 51 and a median of 53. The women in the study tend to be younger than the men ($\bar{x} = 44$ versus $\bar{x} = 54$). African-American, Hispanic, and Asian-American executives reflect the same educational trends as female executives. All 15 minority executives who were U.S. nationals earned college degrees; 13 of them earned graduate degrees (including seven M.B.A.s and four Ph.D.s). Minority executives' average age ($\bar{x} = 46$) was close to that of women as well. The foreign executives in the study (all men) all had graduate degrees and tended to be about the same age as the average male executive ($\bar{x} = 53$). Concomitant with these age differences across gender and ethnicity were the number of years of executives in their posts. White male executives had much longer tenure in their posts ($\bar{x} = 11$ years) than women executives ($\bar{x} = 3$ years) or minorities ($\bar{x} = 2$ years). Executives with graduate degrees also had far fewer years at the top ($\bar{x} = 5$) than those who had only bachelor's degrees ($\bar{x} = 15$).[3]

Two other aspects of the executive demographics in the study merit attention: the titular levels of executives and functional characteristics of executive positions by gender, ethnicity, and education. The categories for the first set of statistics use the standard titles of vice president, senior vice president, executive vice president (including most chief financial officers), and chief executive officer found in most organizations. The exceptions are Independent Accounting and Continental Design, which are both partnerships. Local titles in these firms were adapted to the more standard classification system in consultation with executives from these two firms.[4]

The categories for functional characteristics are also found in most organizations in the study: finance, legal, marketing, operations, personnel, planning, public relations, research and development, and sales. These categories are self-explanatory except for operations, which is a global classification intended to capture what executives refer to as the "line" businesses of a firm. In some firms, therefore, operations refers to product manufacturing in the traditional sense (as at Container Corporation, Playco, Sunset Group) or the construction of buildings (as at Bailey, Continental, or Hightower). In other organi-

Table 2.3 Executive Ranks by Gender, Ethnicity, and Highest Earned Degree

	Gender		Ethnicity[a]					Degree[b]			
	M	F	E	Af	H	As	F	M	HS	C	G
CEO	5	—	5	—	—	—	—	—	—	5	4
	(13)	—	(13)	—	—	—	—	—	—	(6)	(7)
EVP	6	—	7	—	—	—	—	—	—	5	8
	(18)	(1)	(19)	—	—	—	—	—	—	(6)	(13)
SVP	23	—	24	—	—	—	10	—	—	15	28
	(66)	(1)	(67)	—	—	—	(10)	—	(1)	(19)	(47)
VP	66	91	65	—	—	100	90	—	88	76	59
	(185)	(21)	(181)	(3)	(4)	(8)	(9)	(1)	(7)	(100)	(98)
Total	92	8	92	1	1	3	3	3	3	43	54
	(282)	(23)	(280)	(3)	(4)	(8)	(10)	(1)	(8)	(131)	(165)

Note: By percentage. Figures in parentheses indicate absolute frequencies.
[a] E = European-American; Af = African-American; H = Hispanic; As = Asian-American; F = foreign nationals.
[b] M = middle school (a postelementary school that doesn't award academic diplomas); HS = high school; C = college; G = graduate school. Based on informant self-reports.

zations, operations refers to the delivery of services to clients (as at Smith Brothers or Independent Accounting). Table 2.3 summarizes executive social characteristics by executive titles.

Of the 23 women in the study, only 2 held titles higher than vice president and none held the CEO position. None of the women in the study were in firms in which the SVP and the VP categories were collapsed. An even more striking finding emerges when turning to the ethnicity statistics in table 2.3. None of the minority executives in the study hold titles higher than vice president, except an Italian national at Playco who holds the title of senior vice president in that firm's foreign division.

The relationship between education and title is less dramatic than those between gender and ethnicity and title. Nearly all of the executives without college degrees hold positions of vice president. Nearly an equal number of vice presidents hold college degrees as hold graduate degrees. The middle ranks of the executive levels, senior and executive vice presidents, are largely populated by managers holding graduate degrees. There is nearly an even split between CEOs with and without graduate degrees. Finally, the SVPs and EVPs in the study with graduate degrees tend to be younger than the average executive in the study ($\bar{x} = 43$ versus ($\bar{x} = 51$ for the entire group). Many of these executives come from the most elite business schools in the country

Table 2.4   Executive Function Characteristics by Gender, Ethnicity, and Highest Earned Degree

	Gender		Ethnicity[a]					Degree[b]			
	M	F	E	Af	H	As	F	M	HS	C	G
Finance	11	4	10	—	—	50	—	—	—	6	15
	(31)	(1)	(28)	—	—	(4)	—	—	—	(8)	(24)
Legal	4	9	5	—	—	—	—	—	—	—	8
	(11)	(2)	(13)	—	—	—	—	—	—	—	(13)
Marketing	9	13	9	—	—	—	20	—	—	5	12
	(24)	(3)	(25)	—	—	—	(2)	—	—	(7)	(20)
Personnel	12	48	15	67	25	—	—	—	—	20	12
	(35)	(11)	(43)	(2)	(1)	—	—	—	—	(26)	(20)
Planning	4	—	4	—	—	—	—	—	—	—	6
	(10)	—	(10)	—	—	—	—	—	—	—	(10)
PR	8	22	8	33	50	—	40	—	25	18	2
	(23)	(5)	(21)	(1)	(2)	—	(4)	—	(2)	(22)	(4)
Operations	29	4	28	—	25	25	30	100	25	34	22
	(83)	(1)	(78)	—	(1)	(2)	(3)	(1)	(2)	(45)	(36)
R&D	13	—	13	—	—	25	—	—	—	10	15
	(38)	—	(36)	—	—	(2)	—	—	—	(13)	(25)
Sales	10	—	9	—	—	—	10	—	50	8	8
	(27)	—	(26)	—	—	—	(1)	—	(4)	(10)	(13)
Total	92	8	92	1	1	3	3	0	3	43	54
	(282)	(23)	(280)	(3)	(4)	(8)	(10)	(1)	(8)	(131)	(165)

Note: By percentage. Figures in parentheses indicate absolute frequencies. PR = public relations; R&D = research and development.
[a] E = European-American; Af = African-American; H = Hispanic; As = Asian-American; F = foreign nationals.
[b] M = middle school (a postelementary school that doesn't award academic diplomas); HS = high school; C = college; G = graduate school. Based on informant self-reports.

(Harvard, Stanford, and Wharton, most commonly) and have risen through the ranks more quickly than their colleagues without graduate degrees. This is especially true in the professional firms and in the functions relying most heavily on professional training (e.g., law, marketing, finance, research and development, and engineering).

Table 2.4 contains statistics on executive function by gender, ethnicity, and education. Women in the study are most highly concentrated in the personnel ($n = 11$) and public relations ($n = 5$) functions at the tops of their organizations. A few women also hold executive positions in finance, legal, marketing, and operations. Women in the study did not hold positions in planning, research and development, or sales. African-Americans and Hispanics were distributed among personnel ($n = 3$), public relations ($n = 3$), and operations ($n = 1$).

Asian-Americans held all of their executive positions in finance ($n = 4$), operations ($n = 2$), and research and development ($n = 2$). Foreign executives were most highly concentrated in public relations functions for their firms ($n = 4$). As noted above, the functions that rely most heavily on professional training also contained the most executives with graduate degrees. The functions with the highest ratio of executives holding bachelor's degrees to those holding graduate degrees were public relations, personnel, and operations. Public relations was dominated by executives with bachelor's degrees only. Finally, operations contained the only executive who did not earn a high school degree (a man who had worked his way up through the building trades into the top echelons of his construction firm).

The executives in this study, then, are a socially homogeneous lot: overwhelmingly male, white, highly educated, and middle-aged. Individuals at the very pinnacle of the executive levels share the same social characteristics to an even greater degree than their colleagues at the lower levels of top management. Functional demographics exhibit slight variation as well, with women and minority men concentrated in nonline functions.[5] In the following section I describe some of the common experiences and actions of the executives in the study.

Common Themes across Executive Life

Nearly forty years ago, William H. Whyte (1957) wrote in *Organization Man* that the material benefits of executive life became only incrementally better as one moved up the corporate ladder from the middle to the top.[6] Executives enjoyed a few more creature comforts than their counterparts at the lower levels of management, or as Whyte put it, "the Cadillac, the better address, the quarter acre more of lawn" (1957:165). Income differences between executives and middle managers in this study suggest that just as the gulf between the haves and the have-nots widened in the society as a whole over the past three decades (Wilson 1987), so it widened between what could be called the "have-a-lots" and the "have-somethings." The average executive cash compensation in the study stood at slightly under three-hundred thousand dollars (in 1986 dollars; somewhat skewed downward because of the smaller earnings of top managers in the smaller companies) as opposed to the average middle manager's cash compensation of just under fifty thousand dollars. Compensation also varies within the executive ranks by gender: women earned on average about one-third of the male executive salaries in the study.

Salary only begins to capture the differences between executive and middle-manager compensation. Consider the list below of what some executives refer to as "goodies," which few middle managers had access to or received and for which top managers' corporations paid:

—first-class transportation (e.g., private planes, helicopters, and limos);

—child care for children at exclusive day-care centers;

—vacation homes;

—special office furniture and equipment (computers, health equipment, kitchens, saunas, and Jacuzzis);[7]

—entertainment (e.g., personal season tickets to professional sporting events, theater, symphony, and other artistic events and series);

—miscellaneous items and functionaries (boats, luggage, private chefs, masseuses, private athletic trainers, dog groomers, private security personnel, and "sitters" to keep pets, children, parents, spouses, and relational partners occupied during business trips or when accompanying executives on business trips).

For more than a few top managers, as Jackall (1988) has recently argued, the meaning of work revolved around acquiring and maintaining their access to these kinds of goodies. Executives often talked (or even boasted in quiet and usually subtle manners) about their accomplishments, which usually included some aspect of material wealth.

For other managers, the meaning of their work lay in the simple doing of the work itself. This orientation led to themes in executive work somewhat consistent with some of Whyte's other findings. Most visible is the singular self-absorption of executives with their work, which Whyte (1957:164) argued manifested itself in the inability of executives in the 1950s to distinguish between the temporal and activity boundaries of work life and life outside of work. To put it as one executive vice president in the present study did: "I live, breathe, eat, and sleep my work." As a group, executives estimated that they worked nearly twelve hours a day (counting work "off site," i.e., locations away from their primary offices). Executives rarely use the terms "before work" or "after work," unlike middle and lower managers. Instead, top managers refer to times in their workday as "earlier" or "later" in the day. And earlier typically means between 5:00 and 7:00 A.M. at their offices or an off-site location. Later means as late as 10:00 or 11:00 P.M. A senior vice president offered these remarks: "I think about work all the time, when I'm in the office or off site. I don't feel right unless I'm working on something, planning something, or thinking about a decision of some kind. I can't think of a time during the day or night when I'm not doing something related to work." Notice the blurring of boundaries between work and what in an earlier age might have been called home life as the same senior vice president continues his remarks:

Once I walk out that door [pointing to his office suite door], I don't stop thinking about work. I think about what's going on with work just as much off site at home as here. I've always got stuff with me, whether I'm in a car or on a plane. But I'm most at home when I'm on site in the office, in the saddle. I've got my people here. I've got my life here.

Notice as well that "on site" is where this executive is most at home (as are many top managers). His residence is "off site," while his "life" is in his office. In this sense, the office is the inner sanctum of the executive. This is also evidenced by the physical aspects of executive suites. Some executives in the largest companies in the study had full bathrooms (including showers) and sleeping quarters attached to their offices. Almost all executives had some access to showers and other accoutrements at their offices which would typically be associated with one's residence. Such a blurring of boundaries and roles, however, was not evenly distributed across male and female executives. Nearly all of the twenty-three women in the study reported having to create a sharp boundary between their work and home lives so as not to disrupt both spheres of activity. This boundary typically meant adopting very different interpersonal roles and styles according to whether they were at work or at home. Moreover, they mentioned the difficulty they had "balancing" the interpersonal styles they used at work and, as one informant put it, "the maternal and wifely" roles and styles in their home lives (see chapters 3 through 6 for illustrations).

The social insularity of executives from all but those of like social station and personal staff also emerged as a common theme across nearly all executive informants. Even those executives who spend considerable amounts of time off site with clients (such as at Independent Accounting, Continental Design, or Hightower Construction) mostly interact with other top managers. Executive staffs, moreover, filter much of the information that reaches their executive bosses. Many executives have a staff member, for example, whose job it is to scour the media for information related to their corporations. This staff member then summarizes such information for executives to consume. Staff and clerical personnel also filter virtually all face-to-face access to executives. Gatekeeping procedures extend beyond the executive suites, however, to the locations of their offices at the tops of buildings or, if not in a skyscraper, through a maze of other offices. Security systems through which one must pass functionally and symbolically illustrate the social insularity of executive contexts as well. Corporate headquarters housed in skyscrapers have "executive" elevators that stop only at the executive levels at the tops of buildings. Access to these elevators can be gained only through guards stationed either in a main lobby or in a private lobby adjacent to a main lobby. Some corporations, such as Hightower, do not have guards stationed outside their executive elevators, but instead have a private lobby accessible through an unmarked door that has an electronic numeric lock with a combination known only to executives, their staffs, and security guards. At six of the corporations in the study, X-ray scanners automatically check for concealed weapons or bombs, and guards subject all visitors to the executive levels to extensive searches of their personal belongings.

The insularity of executives thus resembles the insularity from the "outside world" that Goffman (1961) describes for total institutions, such as asylums and prisons, or that Van Maanen (1973) describes for police recruits who are cut off from their old social circles once they become full members of police forces. Listen to this executive talk about the social insularity he experiences:

> I live in a cocoon. I rarely talk to anyone that isn't an executive of some type from some firm. If I'm at work I talk with my staff or other execs. I go to the symphony and I have a box there that I sit in with other top people and their families. I have a box at [the local professional baseball team's stadium]—it's the same situation. About the only time I talk with anyone outside the exec world [making quotation marks in the air] is when I talk with my son's friends at a high school football game or something. But even his friends are mostly from families who have executives in them.

Even cynical executives understand their social insulation from the rest of the world and embrace it as a necessary, even preferred, set of affairs:

> I live in a neighborhood where almost no one in this society can afford to live. I associate with people who almost no one else can associate with. I'm cut off, completely cut off. I sit on a mountaintop with a small group of people and get to look down on the rest of the city. I'm out of touch and I don't care. That's what it takes to do the kinds of things I have to do.

The old cliche "It's lonely at the top" captures yet another theme that emerged among executives. Executive loneliness is associated with one of two factors. In some organizations, there is simply little contact of any kind *between* top managers (see chapter 5 of this book, for example), and the social insularity and long working hours militate against social contacts outside of work. In other executive contexts, loneliness results more from the feeling, as one executive said, "that anything can and will be used against you" (see chapter 6 of this book, for example). The obligation in such organizations is to develop relationships with one's colleagues, but at the same time not disclose information that could either haunt one or one's allies. These two accounts provide some sense of the two different contexts of loneliness:

> I literally don't know any of my colleagues except on work matters and they're pretty much all the people, except for my family, who I have contact with. I'm out there by myself.

> My wife is tired of hearing about work. My kids don't care. I can talk with my colleagues at times, but I have to be careful. Giving them grist for the rumor mill can come back to haunt me so I've got to be careful. I'm really all alone with my work.

Such loneliness also provokes questions in the minds of executives about whether they should continue their long hours:

> Sometimes when I'm working late [at the office] and I look out over the city, I wonder what other people are doing. I've got the money to break into a lot of social circles, to go on great trips with my wife, have the kind of lifestyle that most people would kill for. But here I sit plodding along at the office. Sometimes I feel like the loneliest man in the world and I start to wonder if it's all worth it.

Another theme focuses on what Bennis (1980) calls the "inability" of top managers to lead large organizations. Such inability, he argued, sometimes originates in personal failings but more often arises from the enormity of demands made upon top managers by their organizations and the limited effects of managerial decisions in large bureaucracies. In some instances such demands produce organizational structures that cancel out executives' unilateral authority in their organizations (see chapter 6 of this book, for example). Far more common, Bennis argues that executives come to feel they are powerless to mobilize their organizations for any lasting change from the status quo. That is, they fall prey to organizational inertia. Listen to these top managers express their sentiments about implementing change:

> I went to Stanford for two years to learn the latest in business strategy. Now I'm supposed to put it to use in my organization to get us to change, to get us doing things more efficiently. Right! Everyone always has a million reasons why they can't do what they're doing differently.

You develop the best-laid plans and then people simply don't do it. They fall into their old routines and patterns. But you don't know they're not doing it [implementing the change] until six months later. What a crock! I feel sometimes like we [executives] sit up here on our own and shout off a mountaintop into a canyon that just gives us back echoes. As long as people can send good intentions up the line and don't have to show that they've actually complied with the directive, everything is fine.

A Note on Gender and Minority Relations

When asked, few male executives (29/196, 15%; not every male executive answered or was asked this question) defined the hiring of more women or minorities to the executive ranks as a pressing concern for their organizations. A majority of women executives, on the other hand (14/23; 61%), did express the hiring of more women into the top ranks as a primary concern. For those male executives who did define it as a concern, the most often cited rationale for hiring more women and minorities at the top was real or anticipated legal pressures. At all but two of the firms in the study (Playco and Sunset Group), the abilities of women to occupy the very top levels of the corporation were generally questioned and the overrepresentation of women as vice presidents of public relations or personnel generally embraced. Common remarks by male executives on the inabilities of women to occupy top management positions sounded like this: "They haven't had the experience yet to work at the very highest levels"; "They don't fit in quite yet—we're not accustomed to their presence at the top"; and "Why should I take orders from someone with less experience than me just because she's a woman?" These sentiments capture the flavor of indigenous rationales for the disproportionate representation of women among public relations and personnel executives: "Women have a better touch at certain things like personnel: a nurturing instinct"; "A good-looking woman in PR goes a long way to sell a corporation"; or "We've had a woman VP of PR forever—always some good-looking broad."

It is also interesting to compare the explanations offered by two of the twenty-three women in the study for why women are not more prevalent at the upper ranks in corporations and why they tend to be in personnel or public relations:

I come across a lot of talented women out there who are simply shut out of higher positions. They got hired as the token executive woman and that's it. Corporations aren't set up to promote women beyond the bottom level of the top. The men aren't prepared for it. Organizations don't know what to do with women.

I know I was originally hired by [the former senior vice president of marketing] because he was facing pressure to get a woman back in marketing who was in touch with some of our product lines. Hey, I come out of a hard-core retail marketing background that would teach you anything but a woman's touch [making quotation marks in the air with her hands]. I know they hired some women before me who simply couldn't handle the pressure of this firm, who weren't qualified, who got shot down before they got their guns out of their holsters. That's a big part of the story. Unqualified women get hired to do a job they can't. They get hired just because they're a woman. Firms that are foolish enough to hire women just because they're women get burned because they can't promote them and they don't want a lawsuit on their hands if they fire them. So they're stuck with pigeons and bozos [weak executives] at the vice president level.

The first of these explanations focuses on institutional barriers to the top ranks that also appear in some of the comments by male executives above. The second explanation focuses more on the unintended consequences of what has been more recently called "quota filling" and is also evident in some of the male comments above.

The gist of sentiments regarding rationales for hiring minorities at the top also echoes some of the statements raised above by male and female executives regarding hiring women at the top for certain jobs. The first of these two speakers (both white males) works for an organization that hired an African-American vice president, and the second speaker's organization hired a Hispanic vice president:

This is not some black guy that's three blocks removed from the ghetto who thinks business is about ripping the other guy off and running away. His father was a lawyer and his mother is a painter. This guy's got a head on his shoulders, I tell you. He's an Ivy Leaguer. You would never know he's black if you talked to him over the phone. He's aggressive within bounds, the way we hope all our executives will act.

When we got into the South American market, we needed someone who could talk to those guys in their own language and make them feel confident that we understood what they wanted in a deal. Now you don't need the best engineer in the world for the job, just someone who will work with the engineers, looks good in a suit, can convince the other guys [clients] to go with us, and can be one of the guys. Hernando is that type of guy. He's not that swift on the technical side; not like, say, Joe, who handles some of our other foreign business. But he gets the job done and doesn't cost us any business.

The first executive expresses an oft-cited reason among executives for not hiring African-American executives: they do not conform to European-American executive expectations regarding behavioral or speech styles. The second explanation taps into another rationale: using minority groups to accommodate the needs of particular clients with whom corporations deal. Notice the comments about "fitting in" contained in both of these accounts. In the first instance, one "would never know he's black" (i.e., he could pass as Anglo over the phone because of his speech style). In the second instance, the executive "can be one of the guys." Again, the allusion is to the monoethnic reproduction of executive contexts as argued in Kanter (1977) and Moore (1962).

Such glimpses at executive life undoubtedly leave the impression of rather bleak personal existences amid material splendor and ostensible power, especially if one is a woman or a person of color. Indeed, executives expressed little outward happiness about their work during the times I interviewed and observed them. Material wealth, absorption with work, social insularity, feelings of loneliness, uncertainty, and powerlessness, and unease with and outright discrimination toward minorities and women characterize the themes that arose in different ways across all executive contexts during my fieldwork. It is interesting to note how one manager, with forty years' experience in business and twenty as an executive, reacted to the identification of these themes: "You've [gesturing to me] definitely got the dark side of what it's like to be an executive. I think that in some ways that's a good thing, to let people know it's not all peaches and cream at the top. It can be quite a bumpy road once you get up here."

But what of the positive side of executive life? "Joy," one executive argued, "is not in my vocabulary, but satisfaction and accomplishment are." Nearly every informant in the study claimed to like their job because of the "satisfaction," "accomplishment," "recognition," "challenge," and of course the money that goes with being a corporate executive. Some executives also argued that a key reward to being an executive was the contribution one's organization makes to the well-being of society. A CEO expressed these sentiments most eloquently:

My oldest child at [college] sometimes doesn't think I do enough for the community. She thinks I just tinker with the organization and try to make money. She's right on the second account: I do tinker and try to make money for the business. But by doing that I also serve the community more than any volunteer work I could do or the political crazies she hangs out with. This organization sustains the community by its very existence.

Is this account empty rhetoric prepared for an outsider's ears? Perhaps, but it also may be an exercise in self-persuasion wherein the speaker attempts to "self-rationalize" his own career beyond instrumental careerism (e.g., Jackall 1988). Whatever the answer to the question above, the routine daily experience and moral ethos that executives experience emerges from their activities in the local contexts of their corporations. It is to these local contexts that the discussion now turns.

Local Contexts of Executive Work

As argued in chapter 1, local contexts in organizations consist of various kinds of social and cognitive structures. Three kinds of executive contexts, differentiated by three fundamental elements abstracted from the discussion of rationalized social contexts in work organizations in chapter 1, emerged from the comparative analysis of the thirteen firms: formal hierarchies, communication networks, and perceptions of internal and external (environmental) stability.[8] These three dimensions also appear in a number of classic empirical comparative analyses of organizations (e.g., Blau 1968, 1970; Lawrence and Lorsch 1967b; Perrow 1967). Treated as dichotomous variables (i.e., weak/strong for formal hierarchies, loose-knit/dense-knit for communication networks, and unstable/stable for stability), the resulting matrix of these three variables would yield eight cells. The threefold typology discussed in the next several pages clearly does not represent all possible combinations. The nature of field studies, particularly in contexts which have been rarely accessed by researchers (see the discussion in appendix A about site selection and the trials and tribulations of access), does not allow for the same kinds of neat research designs possible in laboratory or survey research. However, despite the lack of control in the present aggregate comparisons, the typology does contain two managerial contexts expressive of pervasive societal myths about managerial arrangements and a third context which simultaneously breaches these myths, but may represent an emergent myth about managerial arrangements taking hold in many corporations. One set captures Burns and Stalker's (1961) concept of "mechanistic bureaucracy" in which managers work in highly predictable and formal hierarchies.[9] A second set appears closer to what might be called atomistic organizations that comprise largely autonomous work units directed by relatively independent managers, as in professional firms and in some sorts of craft-oriented organizations (e.g., Stinchcombe

1959). A third set contains "matrix systems" that embed managers in dual authority structures (Davis and Lawrence 1977) and to some degree violate the "rules" of work organizations emblematized in the first two types of contexts. In each section that follows, I discuss the routines of each context as experienced by executives. To streamline the discussion, some of the quantitative data supporting the pervasiveness of executive routines in the study appear in several summary tables in appendix B. I also limit analyses and qualitative illustrations of executive interpretations and culture within single executive contexts, leaving such fine-grained analyses to the case studies of representative contexts from each set in chapters 4 through 6.

Mechanistic Bureaucracies

Mechanistic bureaucracies exemplify the received wisdom in organizational design and to a large extent constitute the vast majority of managerial structures in modern society (Chandler 1962, 1977; Lincoln 1982). Institutionalized structures of authority constitute the core of such arrangements within which managers adhere to the prerogatives of superiors as defined by formal chains of command, distinct spheres of influence and expertise, and behavioral predictability. Put another way, executives in these contexts exhibit a tendency resembling what Conley and O'Barr (1990) call a "rule orientation"—so concerned are they with obeying proper bureaucratic procedures (relative to executives in other organizational contexts in the study). Four of the thirteen firms—Container Corporation, General Utility, Old Financial, and Smith Brothers—contain mechanistic bureaucracies at their executive levels.

Formal Hierarchy. Top management superiors in every mechanistic organization formally evaluate executives and other managers who directly report to them in one-on-one evaluation "sessions" or "discussions" that are strictly asymmetrical. Subordinates are infrequently consulted about the performances of their bosses, and if they are, their evaluations have little impact on the content of performance reports.

As evaluation goes, so go promotion and compensation. Promotion is determined solely by superiors in each of these four firms, typically in what several executives called a leapfrog method, in which superiors two steps higher than subordinates to be promoted make the decisions to promote. Compensation is determined in a downward direction, as well, either by superiors singly or with peers in each of the four firms. At the very top, the boards of directors decide cash salaries and bonuses for chief executive officers by voting on the chief's cash salary and bonus, typically after some presentation by the CEO to the board on the company's performance as a whole. Stratification in terms of individual compensation in mechanistic organizations typically follows the contours of the formal chains of command as well. Without exception, managers near the pinnacle of the executive ranks earn more money in cash compensation and benefits than do those near the bottom.

Eighty of the 90 (89%) executives interviewed in the mechanistic firms experienced difficulty specifically articulating the formal criteria for performance evaluations beyond very general levels. One executive took an hour to abstractly lay out the management-by-objectives (MBO) criteria used to formally evaluate executives in his organization, but when asked whether the criteria were really used in actual evaluations, he replied, "I've never seen it used, but it sure is pretty to talk about." Less ambiguous across the mechanistic bureaucracies are the informal criteria for performance. Sixty-two (69%) of the executives interviewed (24 of whom occupied positions higher than vice president) in these four organizations identified the ability to keep in line and keep current with the plans and strategies, and sometimes the whims, of superiors as crucial to positive personal evaluations.

The routines of formal hierarchy also appear in the determination of budgets. In mechanistic bureaucracies, 71 (79%) of the executives interviewed reported they submit budget plans to their immediate superiors within the agendas for such allocations developed by superiors themselves. The remainder of the executives in the four firms followed similar procedures. Superiors subsequently approve or veto requested funds; vetoes typically occur via revision and summary "approval" of the revision proposed by the superior! Very little negotiation typically occurs in these processes and only occasionally do executive subordinates and superiors engage in more than one round of proposal revisions.

Another expression of formal authority in the work lives of executives in mechanistic firms manifests itself in the factors that contribute to the success of proposals related to organizational procedures and production. In these firms, proposals tended to focus on compensation, benefits packages, and marketing strategies. Of the 86 executives interviewed in the mechanistic firms below the rank of CEO, 55 (64%) identify gaining their superior's support as the key factor in the adoption of any proposal beyond their span of control at the executive levels. Thirteen executives (15%) identify the merits of a proposal as key; 11 (13%) identify the proposer's reputation as key to a proposal's success; and 5 (6%) identify coalitions as key to a proposal being im-

plemented. Seventy-seven (90%) of them identify using their own formal authority as the key factor for introducing proposals within their
own span of control.

Illustrations of the impact of formal position on the adoption of proposals include (1) personnel policies resisted for some time by executives suddenly being championed and implemented by the same executives after their CEO publicly supported the policies; (2) elegant
arguments at meetings supporting diversification in particular divisions being cut short by superiors who would bluntly state their opposition to diversification, thereby ending discussion on the topic for all
practical purposes; and (3) innovators who deftly orchestrated coalitions to support their plans having their "legs" cut out from under
them by superiors who would declare particular ideas "dead" or "not
worth pursuing."

Finally, a number of generic monikers that executives use to refer to
their subordinates or superiors were recorded in each mechanistic
firm. Among the most common was the old standby, "boss." Of the 86
executives that have an executive superior, 47 at some time during my
contact with them used the label *boss* to refer to their superiors. Every
single executive of the 86 at some time or another referred to their
superior at some point as "the person I report to" or simply as "my
superior." Other labels for executive superiors indicative of the hierarchical primacy in these firms included several variants of "the guy
who pulls the strings," "who I take orders from," "who decides how I
spend my days," and "who sings the tune I dance to." Other, more
idiosyncratic, labels used by subordinates to describe superiors that
underscore the formal hierarchy in these firms include "Attila the bureaucrat and his administrative herd [a reference to an executive with
a particularly large staff]," "slave driver," and "paterfamilias." Superiors also produced several labels for their subordinates, the most common of which was simply a reference to "my people" used at some
time by 30 of the 40 executive superiors in these four firms. Superiors
also universally refer to their executive subordinates as "the people
that report to me." More personalistic referents included "my gang,"
"my minions," and "my posse."

Communication Networks. Three basic "channels" of information flow
emerged as salient during fieldwork: written, face-to-face, and indirect.[10] Written information flows consist of memos, reports, notes, and
letters sent and received between executives. Face-to-face information
flows include meetings, phone conferences, "one-on-one" conversations, and informal conversations. (None of the executives in mechanistic organizations participated in any sort of electronic mail network

at the time of fieldwork.) Indirect information flows consist of multistep links between senders and receivers, either face-to-face, through written means, or some combination of both.

In a typical week, executives in the mechanistic firms estimate that they have an average of 12.5 communication contacts with their colleagues. Of these contacts nearly half (5.9) flow through written media in the form of memos handled by secretaries or other nonexecutive staff. Somewhat less prevalent are face-to-face conversations and meetings (4.6 per executive in a typical week). Far rarer is what one mechanistic executive called "using the grapevine." Indirect information flows average 2 per executive in a typical week. The outlier in this pattern is General Utility. There, executives report written flows of information that are outstripped by face-to-face information dissemination (an average of 5.9 written flows per executive per week versus 8.6 face-to-face flows) and are only slightly higher than indirect sources of information (an average of 4.6). When executives do opt for face-to-face communication, they tend to do so along the contours of their formal chains of command. This custom is illustrated by the average amount of information flows occurring between subordinates and superiors in a typical work week. Across all four firms, executives estimate that they average 1.7 face-to-face contacts with their peers and 3.3 face-to-face contacts up and down the hierarchy in a typical week. Executives in mechanistic firms also report that 65% of their face-to-face communication occurs within the same work unit (e.g., functions or departments). An additional 21% occurs within interunit task forces, teams, or committees, and the rest occurs between executives of neither the same unit nor interunit committee.[11]

The etiquette of arranging face-to-face contacts also exhibits distinctive asymmetries that vary according to the direction of access (upward or downward) and whether the matter to be discussed is "quick" or "complex." Quick matters require only a few minutes to discuss, perhaps needing a signature or perfunctory approval, or consist of topics already decided in large part through earlier discussions or meetings. Complex matters are those issues requiring more elaborate reflection; the plan of action or even the interpretation of the issues at hand often requires lengthy discussion between top managers. Superiors and subordinates gain access to one another via three processes: by making formal appointments, by making informal appointments, and by spontaneously dropping in to talk. Formal appointments involve calls between executive secretaries, a minimum of a week's advance notice, and a meeting agenda outline. Informal appointments sometimes involve calls between secretaries, but more often than not involve a phone call directly between executives, perhaps only a few hours' or a day's advance notice, and little if any notice of the meeting's content. Spontaneous meetings or "open door" access to executives occurs when superiors and subordinates simply "show up" at each other's offices or call over the phone and start talking about some set of issues without an explicit pretext.

Among the subordinate executives interviewed in these firms, 19% (16/86) use open-door strategies to gain access to their bosses for discussion of quick matters. A much larger proportion of top managers (53%; 46/86) utilize informal appointments to meet with their superiors on quick matters, while the remainder (28%; 24/86) "go through channels" (e.g., secretaries and other staff) to make formal appointments. Nearly all the non-CEO executives in these four firms (95%; 82/86) for whom information could be verified uses formal appointments to discuss complex matters with their bosses.

Conversely, executive superiors appear to have somewhat less compunction about dropping in on their executive direct subordinates, but utilize the informal appointment with nearly the same frequency. Thirty-six percent (16/44—here $n = 44$ because vice presidents do not have executive subordinates) of the superiors gain access to their subordinates without any kind of appointment, 52% (23) of the top managers utilize informal appointments, and only 11% (5) consistently use formal appointments. The complexity of the matters to be discussed dramatically increases the formality of the access process used: 12 (27%) executives engaged in informal access, 31 (70%) top managers used formal appointments, while 1 (2%) top manager opted for simply showing up at his direct subordinates' doors when complex matters were in the offing.

Peer access among executives varies more directly by the complexity of the issue. Excluding executives in firms without formal peers, 26% (20/76) report simply dropping in on their peers without an appointment to discuss quick matters, 55% (42/76) report making informal appointments for quick matters, and 17% (13/76) report accessing their peers only when they had a formal appointment with them. For complex matters, 86% (65/76) of executive peers report using formal appointments among themselves.

Not surprisingly, the content of communication between executives in mechanistic bureaucracies tends to have single focus, save the communication among General Utility executives. Executives at Container Corporation, Old Financial, and Smith Brothers estimate that on average 63% of their communications with colleagues involve narrow technical matters only, 15% involve social issues only (personal issues as well as matters relevant to internal organizational politics), and 22% involve both. This last communicative content was particularly prevalent at off-site meetings, such as in local athletic clubs or on golf courses. General Utility executives estimate that 35% of their communication with colleagues focuses on technical matters only, 23% focuses on social issues only, and 42% mix technical and social issues. It was not uncommon at General Utility, for example, for executives to participate in golfing outings on which business was frequently discussed or to take "family" retreats (typically at the vice presidential level) during which executives would engage in strategic planning or other business-related strategy meetings, as well as leisure outings with their families.

Yet another similarity in the personal ties across the four firms, save General Utility, is the social distance between top managers as indicated by their characterizations of personal relationships with their colleagues. The limited sizes of most executive corps in the thirteen organizations necessarily means that most top managers have at least some passing familiarity with one another. The range of executive personal ties therefore should vary from acquaintance to close friend. Container Corporation, General Utility, and Old Financial executives characterized 67% of their colleagues as acquaintances, 23% as friends, and 10% as close friends. A Smith executive noted this about his personal relationships with his colleagues: "I don't do much socially with my colleagues, except for an occasional lunch. Most of our interaction is in formal meetings or by memo, so there's not much chance of making friends with anyone." This statement also suggests a rather conventional meaning of friendship in these corporations that includes some sort of emotional as well as temporal involvement.

Some of this same meaning of friendship exists at General Utility, but is also mixed with a strong orientation toward what could be called organizational loyalty to one's superiors and subordinates; a strong tie at General Utility is not so much a personal tie as at Container Corporation, Old Financial, or Smith Brothers, but a tie to an organizational member. Many General Utility executives have worked all of their lives with the company, many beginning as nonmanagerial servicemen in the late 1940s and early 1950s. Over three-quarters of the top managers at GU characterize their colleagues as either friends or close friends. Yet many executives admit that their closest colleagues are also their superiors and their subordinates. In essence, their relational networks follow the contours of their formal chain of command. Moreover, formal hierarchy often manifests itself in conversations between junior and senior executives at social gatherings. In such situations, junior executives (vice presidents) address senior executives (e.g., the executive vice president and chief executive officer) as "sir," hesitantly inject comments in conversations with them, and rarely refute their points of view. Such interaction evokes images of Janowitz's (1960) characterization of the uneasy coexistence of personal rapport and deference with formal rank among junior and senior military officers.

Stability. During 1980–86, none of the firms experienced more than one reorganization of its executive ranks, none had more than 8% executive turnover (and that at a constant rate over the seven-year period), few executives in any firm were seriously preparing to leave (at least during the fieldwork period), and only one firm, Smith Brothers, weathered a single serious bid at a hostile takeover. Smith Brothers, in fact, is the only firm that could be characterized as somewhat unstable because of its rapid expansion during the late 1970s. However, in 1984–85 the firm consolidated its growth by selling some of its subsidiaries that were big money losers in the early 1980s.

Executives (86%; 77/90) in these four organizations view their organizations as embedded in highly stable functional fields with well-developed core organizations and technologies. Executives spoke about the stability of their environments by alluding to the lack of "serious" new competition in their markets, few changes in the technologies used to deliver their services and products to constituencies, few changes in their suppliers or distribution systems, few changes in related industries that affected them or their fields, few major changes in regulatory policies, few changes in their firms' policies relative to other organizations (including marketing and joint ventures), and the lack of significant mergers between organizations in their fields. Old Financial and Smith executives proved somewhat outside these tendencies, due to the deregulation of the savings and loan industry in the early 1980s and Smith's aggressive expansion beyond the health insurance industry into health care. I discuss these concerns of Old Financial executives in greater detail in chapter 4.

Atomistic Organizations

Atomistic organizations evoke images of traditional professional firms in the fields of law, accounting, engineering, architecture, and medicine in which lone practitioners ply their disciplines with tightly controlled staffs.[12] The craft orientation in these firms also evokes images of the craft organizations described by Stinchcombe (1958). The paths to these arrangements in the three professional firms resulted from wider struggles over spheres of recognized expertise, societal authority, and professional autonomy (e.g., Abbot 1988; Friedson 1973;

Haber 1991). In other nonprofessional firms with similar structures of work, local political struggles over intraorganizational autonomy, often in response to the lockstep nature of mechanistic bureaucracy, resulted in the emergence of craftlike orientations. The first of these two paths describes the historical development of three of the four organizations classified as atomistic: Continental Design, Hightower Engineering, and Independent Accounting. The second path captures the historical development of a fourth organization in this set: Commco. Commco's atomistic system arose in the aftermath of its divestiture from a large conglomerate and through numerous reorganizations in which executives established the autonomy of their work units in contradistinction to the mechanistic bureaucracy of their former parent corporation.

Nonetheless, each atomistic organization on paper displays formal hierarchies similar to those in the mechanistic bureaucracies, as well as other similarities: well-defined spheres of expertise, sparse personal ties, and internal and field stability (with the exception of Commco). In action, formal hierarchy weakly holds executives in atomistic bureaucracies as suggested by the infrequency of routines and rituals expressive of formal structure. Executives in these firms focus much of their activities on their own work units, practicing an ethic of autonomy and privacy.

At Continental, Hightower, and Independent, executives head work units that focus on particular market niches defined by the specialized services they offer. Such units go by the names of "practices" or "project groups." Within each unit exist numerous groups of nonexecutives who produce the services of each firm and report directly to executives. At Commco, single executives head "profit centers" or "service centers" within which work several layers of nonexecutive managers. Collaborative work between executives in each of the four firms rarely occurs. Reporting relationships between executives either are undefined or don't exist. Executive organization loosely couples in these firms (e.g., Weick 1976), primarily tied through profit sharing, collective liability concerns vis-à-vis clients, and corporate charters.

Formal Hierarchy. In contrast to the top-down evaluation procedures in mechanistic bureaucracies, most atomistic executives perform self-evaluations. These evaluations consist of quantitative rankings that recount revenues produced or costs controlled and are then circulated among executives at each firm for review. Such rankings also include client and nonmanagerial evaluations of executives. Compensation for each executive derives from executive-generated revenues or fixed budgets within their work units. Self-evaluations become the basis for profit-share votes by executives, as well as the basis by which executives are promoted beyond the vice-presidential level to higher offices (e.g., executive vice president). In none of these procedures do CEOs exercise the same degree of unilateral authority as in the mechanistic bureaucracies. They typically ratify self-evaluations as well as votes for compensation in which executives participate.

The processes of promotion in atomistic organizations also differ dramatically from those in mechanistic bureaucracies. Promotion in mechanistic bureaucracies is a matter for superiors, whereas promotion in atomistic bureaucracies comes about via election or outward political process. Once a mechanistic executive obtains high office, return to the vice presidential level rarely occurs, except in cases of conflict management. Incumbency strikingly varies among atomistic executives. Some executives stay in higher offices for many years, winning election after election, or accruing ever-larger supportive constituencies, while others serve their term and then return to their line business. The most obvious reason for such variation is money: there is more money to be made at the line businesses than in high offices. Compensation as such does not vary directly with rank in atomistic firms, but is tied more directly to work unit revenues or cost control. It is therefore not uncommon for executives near the bottom of the executive ranks to earn more money than those near the top.

Earning power of this sort could become the basis for political power in firms as executives demand higher profit shares, accumulate ever-larger staffs, or make claims on altering the overall structures and strategies of the firm. Most executives in these firms generally eschew such courses of action because to engage in such policies would not only detract from their own abilities to generate compensation, but would also violate much of the local customs about how internal corporate politics are to be accomplished. Instead, such material bases typically extend an executive's penetration into their particular market niche and provide insulation for one's own segments from control by colleagues.

Executives have little unilateral authority over budget allocations among their colleagues in atomistic bureaucracies. The most extreme manifestation of such budgetary autonomy occurs among executives at Continental, Hightower, and Independent, whose budget limitations vary directly with their work unit revenues. Commco executives heading profit centers have a great deal of control over their budgets, while Commco executives in service centers typically have relatively fixed allocations unless they are subsidized by governmental funds for infrastructural projects. They therefore depend less upon superiors than upon governmental officials (similar to the way executives at the professional firms depend upon clients for revenues).

Proposals in the atomistic firms tend to focus on technical issues and the management of nonexecutive personnel. In contrast to executives in the mechanistic firms, 71% (37/52) of the executives interviewed in the atomistic firms below the rank of CEO identify the merits of a proposal with an intended impact beyond one's span of control as the key factor in its success, 12% (6) identified mobilizing allies as of core importance, 10% (5) identified the support of one's superior as key, and 8% (4) found the reputation of the originator as ultimately the most important factor in proposal implementation. Within their own nonexecutive staffs, 87% (45) of executives identified their own formal authority as the key factor.

Many executives in the atomistic firms are overtly suspicious of attempts by executives to "pull rank" during discussions of proposals. Executives similarly distrusted and turned away from coalition building in the pursuit of policy change. It is certainly possible that executives ostensibly discussing the intrinsic merits of proposals could simultaneously be experiencing the subtle suasive effects of presenters' or originators' formal or reputational statuses. It should be noted, however, that executives were often unaware of the origins of proposals or those who had particularly high stakes in the adoptions of particular proposals. Unlike mechanistic bureaucracies, proposals themselves emerged as favorable or unfavorable during discussions between executives, rather than particular high-ranking executives being identified as being unfavorably or favorably disposed toward particular proposals.

Formal superiors and subordinates in atomistic organizations rarely use slang for one another that relate to their hierarchical positions. Occasionally executives refer to CEOs as "the old man" or in one case "Methuselah," but such labels have more to do with senior executives' tenure with their firms than with their formal positions. Moreover, executives refrained from labeling people who they formally report to as their "bosses" or even as their "superiors." Likewise, references to "subordinates" and use of such paternalistic terms as "my people" (prevalent among mechanistic executives) did not manifest themselves in any of the atomistic firms. The most frequent monikers used to refer to executives were not nicknames at all, but formal labels denoting their specialties, such as "tax practice partner," "commercial ship project executive," or "divisional vice president of electronic relays."

Communication Networks. Several indices suggest extremely sparse information flows among executives in atomistic firms compared with those among executives in mechanistic bureaucracies. First, executives in atomistic firms recollect an average of 6.2 informational contacts of any kind in a typical week with their colleagues (compared to the 12.5 contacts per week in mechanistic bureaucracies). When information is passed, it generally takes the form of written communiques (an average of nearly 3.9 [63% of messages] in a typical week compared with the 5.9 [47%] per week in the mechanistic firms). Communiques of this sort most often concern technical issues of interest to executives working in the same units. Even rarer are indirect information flows: the average indirect information flow recalled by executives in these firms is less than one (0.7) per week. Many executives, in fact, could not recall receiving or sending information through interpersonal networks.

Another difference between mechanistic and atomistic firms is the amount of face-to-face information flow that occurs hierarchically versus that which occurs among peers. Nearly twice as much peer interaction (0.9 face-to-face contacts as interaction per week) among executives of different ranks (0.5 per week) occurs in the atomistic organizations (although it should be remembered that informants in general recall few instances of face-to-face communication with anyone, save their own staffs or clients). This is the reverse of the relationship between peer and hierarchical communication in mechanistic firms. So uncommon are contacts between executive subordinates and superiors in atomistic organizations that some informants were sometimes unable to estimate the last time they actually talked with their ostensible superior.

What is similar about the communication patterns at the executive levels in mechanistic and atomistic firms is the predominance of face-to-face communication among executives within the same work unit. On the rare occasions on which executives in atomistic organizations do engage in face-to-face communication, they do so with their "own kind," so to speak. In an average work week, informants interviewed in these four firms estimate that 79% of their face-to-face communication occurs with colleagues in their same work unit (practice or division). Less than 15% of their face-to-face communication occurs in interunit committees (such units themselves relatively atypical in these organizations). Another indication of the sparseness of face-to-face communication outside of one's work unit surfaces when executives cannot remember the names of colleagues in other units—a common occurrence during interviews in atomistic bureaucracies. The exceptions to this general pattern occur in atomistic firms (Hightower and Independent Accounting) which have begun business projects that require executives in different divisions to interact with one another on a regular basis. I discuss in chapter 5 an example of such an experiment at Independent Accounting.

Upward face-to-face contacts that do occur tend toward the formal: subordinates in atomistic firms use informal appointments with their superiors (60%; 31/52) or formal appointments (37%; 19/52) for quick matters. Only two executives in these firms routinely practice open-door strategies with their bosses. Every executive for whom information could be verified contacts their superiors to make formal appointments well in advance of discussing formal matters. In contrast to superiors in mechanistic firms, executive superiors in atomistic organizations exhibit much the same formalism as their subordinates in their downward access strategies: 71% (12/17) reported using formal appointments to discuss quick matters with their subordinates, 29% (5/17) reported using informal appointments to do the same, and none reported simply dropping in on their subordinates. All 17 executives report making formal appointments, often more than two weeks in advance, to see their subordinates about complex issues. At the same time, such formality extends to peers: all 52 executives report using some sort of appointment to see their peers regarding either quick or complex issues.

Personal relationships among executives are few and far between in these four firms. To an even greater extent than that recorded overall in the mechanistic firms, top managers in the atomistic firms create and sustain weak uniplex ties among themselves. Across the four firms, executives estimate that on average 70% of their communication with colleagues focuses on technical matters only, 15% of their communication with colleagues is only of a social character, and 16% encompassed some aspects of the lack of personal ties in these firms is the lack of so-called working lunches or what in some firms are called working rounds (of golf). Executives in these firms rarely engage in these activities with one another, although some executives were extremely interested in golf. Many executives, in fact, could not recall the last time they had had lunch with a colleague or been to a colleague's house for dinner.

Two other measures of personal ties further underscore the atomistic nature of these four firms. First, executives on average characterize small proportions of their colleagues in these firms as close friends (8%) or friends (21%). Second, the absence of discernible political coalitions in any of the four atomistic firms suggests yet another marker of the lack of durable relationships of any kind (beyond that granted by membership in the same formal organization). As a result, collective action in support of internal change (already noted above) becomes difficult to organize or sustain.

Stability. Like the mechanistic firms, these four firms also appear relatively stable in their internal arrangements and technologies, with Commco standing as the exception. The other three firms in this grouping, Continental Design, Hightower, and Independent Accounting, experienced nary a reorganization during 1980–86. None of the firms had more than a 4% turnover rate of executive ranks during this period, and few top managers planned to leave. Moreover, none of these firms, including Commco, made or experienced any serious takeover or merger bids. Commco's experience with divestiture in the early 1980s make it an outlier in terms of stability. Reorganizations, noted one senior Commco executive, have become "a way of life" every year since 1984.

The technological stabilities of these firms diverge to some degree as well. Two of the firms, Continental Design and Hightower, continue to offer much the same services and utilize much the same technology to produce those services as they have over much of their histories. Independent Accounting follows this pattern in its traditional accounting and auditing services, but also began expanding its services in its management consulting practice (discussed in greater detail in chapter 6). Commco continues to diversify its information-processing and -dissemination services and also entered and exited several new markets from which it had been formerly barred by law.

Executives in these four firms, save Commco, view their corporations as operating in relatively stable functional fields. As do executivees in mechanistic bureaucracies, executives in these firms spoke of the lack of serious new competitors, changes in suppliers, or state regulation. Most executives also identify a core set of firms in their fields in which they typically place their own organizations. The exception to this pattern again occurred among Commco executives and executives at Independent Accounting in management consulting. Half of the Commco executives viewed what they called the information field as highly unstable because of rapidly developing technologies and the challenge of new competitors. An equal number challenged this assertion by noting that the core technology of the firm remains with telephone services. Independent partners viewed the accounting and audit wings of their "industry" as stable, while the management consulting wing was unstable, primarily because of its successful entry into consulting areas traditionally controlled by more established consulting firms.

Matrix Systems

Unlike mechanistic bureaucracies or atomistic organizations, matrix systems represent relatively recent attempts to consciously redesign the tops of American corporations. *Matrix systems* refers to any effort to "lay one or more new forms of departmentalization on top of an existing form (e.g., to develop a project-by-function grid)" (Burns 1989:350). Such systems are intended to introduce lateral coordinating systems to handle highly complex tasks in organizational fields requiring rapid adaptation. Matrix systems simultaneously place managers in departments (e.g., finance, marketing, supply, operations) and standing project teams focused on specific product lines or services (Davis and Lawrence 1977). These arrangements may seem like a simple redefinition of the line-staff division in any bureaucracy. They differ, however, insofar as traditional line and staff departments still exist in addition to project teams. Moreover, project teams can contain elements of both line and staff. In this system, every subordinate who is a member of a project team has at least two superiors. Conversely, superiors can have two or more sets of subordinates if they simultaneously lead project teams and have conventional responsibilities in their home departments.

The Origins and Diffusion of the Matrix in American Corporations. Little "hard" data exists on the origins and diffusion of matrix systems across American organizations in part because the system has so many labels (e.g., Larson and Gobeli 1987). The earliest uses of matrix systems occurred in the aerospace industry during World War II. Plant managers created standing cross-departmental teams to integrate representatives of various engineering functions during the design of new, complex warplanes. These representatives reported to their original departmental superiors and also to a team leader. In the early postwar period, the technique was scarcely known outside the aerospace industry. Confined to specialized "support" functions (e.g., research and development, engineering), it was viewed primarily as a way to increase the cross-fertilization of ideas among managers without line responsibility.

As the United States government mobilized various technological industries for the "space race" with the Soviet Union during the early 1960s, dual-authority systems spread via personnel who left the aerospace industry to join the initial space projects of the National Aeronautics and Space Administration (NASA). John Mee (1964), then a professor of management at Indiana University, initially wrote about dual-authority systems in the business literature and used the term *matrix* to describe them. At the same time Mee published his piece on the matrix, business scholars and practitioners had begun a full-scale assault on the inadequacies of mechanistic bureaucracy, attacking its depersonalization, inflexibility, and constraints on creativity (reviewed in Bennis 1965; see also, e.g., Perrow 1986: 1–48). In the matrix, many scholars believed they had found the ideal organizational structure to "permit the expression of play and imagination, and to exploit the new pleasure of work" (Bennis 1965:35). They also believed the matrix to be part of the solution to sagging American productivity and decreased international competitiveness during the 1970s.

A few articles on the matrix appeared in the late 1960s and early 1970s in less-visible journals (to mainstream business managers) such as *Journal of Management Studies* and *Management Science* (e.g., Ansoff and Brandenburg 1971; Argyris 1967). As late as 1969, the matrix was still considered something of a "high-tech" fad (Marquis 1969). An informal survey by Perham (1970), in the first article on its use in the popular business press, reported that the innovation was still largely confined to high-tech engineering firms and a few "progressive" service companies. An article in *Business Week* (Fausch 1971) a year later reported the same finding. The matrix did not begin to be adopted until articles extolling its virtues appeared in the mid 1970s in *Harvard Business Review* and *Sloan Management Review* (e.g., Davis 1974; Goggin 1974). Adoption of the matrix found further support in testimonials to its effectiveness by CEOs and other top managers at Citibank, Dow Corning, General Electric, Prudential Insurance, 3M, and TRW, who learned how to implement matrix forms through "organizational development" programs at elite graduate business schools (Davis and Lawrence 1977).

By the late 1970s, the matrix was enjoying "widespread popularity" among American managers (Larson and Gobeli 1987:126). Davis and Lawrence (1977:155–230) reported that matrix forms had been adopted or were being considered in manufacturing, insurance, consulting, accounting, law, securities, banking, retailing, construction, real estate, health, educational, and local, federal, and international government organizations. Despite the biting criticism of the matrix by Peters and Waterman (1982) in their best-selling book, *In Search of Excellence,* the notions of dual authority and lateral coordination inform several types of management systems in use across a wide assortment of organizations in the 1980s and 1990s, including the "flexiform" (Mills et al. 1983) and "dualism" (Goldstein 1985).

Five firms in the study utilize matrix systems at their executive levels: Bailey Construction, Infotain, New Financial, Playco, and Sunset Group. Executives at each firm simultaneously work in traditional functions or departments and in "product" or "project" teams within divisions. Project or product teams differ from task forces in that they have more durable lives, although their life spans are only as long as the product lines or projects on which they focus. Sunset Group, for example, has two standing product lines and corresponding product teams that have existed since the firm's founding. Infotain's product teams have much shorter life spans because of the high rate of product replacement in the firm. Bailey provides yet another example of a matrix system within a multidivisional form. Within its divisions exist functions oriented toward engineering, marketing, sales, law, public relations, personnel, finance, etc. Overlaid on these functions are project teams that have responsibility for particular construction domains such as commercial warehousing or public buildings. Unlike Hightower Construction and Continental Design, then, Bailey's projects are run, as one senior executive put it, "by committees" composed of executives with multiple specialities. Each of the firms has different methods and rules for selecting team leaders. In all of the companies, save Bailey, team leaders are selected from marketing functions; engineers lead Bailey teams.

Formal Hierarchy. Performance evaluation typically occurs between executive subordinates and their multiple superiors. Unlike the bland "businessspeak" used by executives to describe evaluations in mechanistic bureaucracies or atomistic organizations, evaluation meetings go by many colorful names in matrix systems, often evoking a variety of popular genres such as adventures in mysterious lands ("vision quests for bennies [benefits]"), sporting events and television game shows ("sparring for dollars"), or the Old West ("showdowns for compensation"). Such meetings proceed in highly stylized fashions with subordinates charged with first presenting their "case," to which superiors respond. Discussions then proceed without the customary asymmetries between superiors and subordinates as in mechanistic bureaucracies. One executive described such discussions as "tests of will" between all involved in which the parties attempt to "feel the other out" in order to assess their abilities and confidence. In some meetings, executive superiors enter with much the same viewpoint of their subordinate's performance and little substantively emerges from the meetings that would not have occurred without the meeting. In other instances, the principals begin from very different perspectives and a verdict on the subordinate is not reached until one principal (which may be the subordinate) gains control of the proceedings.

A less common ritual of evaluation occurs via what in all of the firms are called "go-between" or "mediated" processes, in which subordinates meet with both of their superiors separately. Superiors then meet privately to jointly come to a conclusion about the subordinate's performance and compensation. Such meetings bear some of the marks of the more common triadic ones, including the constraint on unilateral action and meeting closure marked by the victory (e.g., prevailing viewpoint) of a single executive or pair of executives. An even less common procedure of evaluation occurs via what one executive at Infotain called "mutual sloughing," in which multiple superiors avoid their responsibilities to jointly evaluate a subordinate. Mutual sloughing arises in situations of extreme uncertainty in which it is unclear or underspecified who should evaluate a subordinate or during processes of conflict management in which executives avoid one another (discussed in chapter 6).

Similar to executive work units in atomistic organizations, matrix executives on project teams find themselves responsible for generating revenues for particular products and product lines. However, matrix managers do not enjoy sole responsibility *and* authority over their product teams as executives in atomistic organizations do over their work units (composed as they are of nonexecutive staff). Uneven intersections of authority and responsibility are intended to induce cooperation among executives in different functions, yet they ironically often lead to the formation of coalitions *based on* functional membership. Coalitions also arise across functions in forms that resemble what Stephenson (1990) calls "virtual groups." Virtual groups do not appear on any official organizational chart, often have uncertain durability, may be difficult to specify in terms of concrete members or activities, but nonetheless have efficacy in the sporadic execution of collective action within these firms.

In organizations of uncertain reporting lines and complicated attributions of responsibility for performance, executives without political coalitions may be viewed by their colleagues as out of the "mix" or even as "incompetent." An executive with strong ties to such groups is an executive to be feared and promoted. In this way, a top manager's political skill becomes key to their evaluations either through general respectability or more instrumentally as allies go to bat for a colleague in evaluation meetings.

The matrix creates distinctive ambiguities in budget processes because neither functional nor team-leading executives have responsibility and authority over resources necessary for their activities. Budgetary allocations often take the form of lengthy meetings between groups of executives in functional and product teams. Such meetings take on much the same aura and ritualistic character as evaluation meetings: participants carefully ally themselves with colleagues who they believe will support their positions in meetings and strategically deliver aspects of their arguments during negotiations. Budget meetings rarely end in compromise, but with some group "carrying the day" by achieving their objectives and officially proclaiming their victory via memos distributed throughout the executive ranks and informal communication networks.

Compared to top managers in mechanistic bureaucracies and atomistic bureaucracies, matrix executives believe that successful proposal adoption emerges from coalition building regardless of a proposal's intrinsic merits, or, under certain circumstances, from the reputation of the originator of a proposal. Matrix executives also exhibit a greater variety than the executives in the first two sets of firms in their proposals' substantive issues: executive personnel management (particularly concerned with lines of authority and responsibility), the management of subsidiaries, reorganizations of all or portions of firms, budget processes, and planning procedures. Fifty (69%) of the 72 executives interviewed in these five firms emphasize the overriding importance of allies in proposal adoption, 15 (21%) emphasized the reputation of the author of the proposal, and the rest were evenly divided between gaining support of one's superior and the merits of the proposal itself as key adoption factors.

To a greater degree than executives in either of the other two sets of organizations, matrix executives exhibit a colorful and dense language that they use to label colleagues. Such labels do not, however, vary by formal rank, but conform to the contours of the informal status hierarchies that exist in these firms. The labels also draw from a variety of popular genres. I investigate the communication functions of such linguistic framings at one of the matrix firms, Playco, in chapter 6. A full glossary of such terms appears in appendix C.

Communication Networks. Several indices suggest highly dense information flows among executives in matrix systems compared to both atomistic and mechanistic firms. Executives in matrix systems estimate their flow of written, face-to-face, and indirect messages at just over 27 in an average workweek. Unlike the executives in mechanistic or atomistic bureaucracies, those in the matrix systems send and receive much of their information via face-to-face communication in highly ritualized group and one-on-one meetings (of the sort described above) and less frequently in informal conversations. Executives estimate that face-to-face contacts account for nearly fourteen (13.7) of their total contacts among colleagues in a typical workweek. Written communiques account for 5.4 contacts per week and indirect information flows, 8.7. This last figure is particularly salient when one considers that it is twelve times the average amount estimated by executives in atomistic organizations (8.7/0.7) and over four times the average amount estimated by executives in mechanistic bureaucracies (8.7/2.0).

Matrix executives also spend a great deal of time interacting with peers. Informants estimate that of their face-to-face contacts, nearly eight per week (7.8) are with peers and just under three (2.8) occur up and down the formal hierarchy. As in atomistic organizations, then, matrix executives are more likely to interact with peers than with superiors or subordinates (but with the quantity of face-to-face contacts vastly greater in matrix systems). It differs sharply from the hierarchical emphasis in mechanistic bureaucracies, however. Face-to-face communication in matrix organizations also differs from that in atomistic and mechanistic bureaucracies in its location. Matrix executives estimate that 36% of their face-to-face communication occurs with colleagues in product teams drawn from different units, 24% occurs with colleagues of neither the same product team nor function, and 40% of it occurs within their home units.

Matrix executives utilize formal appointments to an even greater extent than executives in the other two sets of organizations regardless of the direction or content of their communication. Nearly three-quarters of the informants in matrix systems (72%; 52/72) estimate that they use formal appointments to discuss quick matters with their superiors. Another 13 (18%) informants typically opt for informal appointments and 7 (10%) executives simply drop in on their superiors. Virtually every matrix executive uses formal appointments to access their superiors. At the same time, superiors are no less likely to use formal appointments with their subordinates: 71% (24/34) report using formal appointments to discuss quick matters with their subordinates, while 21% (7/34) report using informal appointments, and the rest simply drop in on their subordinates. Seventy-nine percent (27/34) of executive superiors also handle complex matters via formal appointments. The nature of formal appointments in these firms sharply diverges from that found in either mechanistic or atomistic organizations. Formal access rituals among matrix executives neither symbolize deference to authority as in the mechanistic bureaucracies or social distance and autonomy between colleagues as in atomistic organizations. Instead, formal appointments and the formal meetings they beget symbolize the attempt to manage uncertainty between executives embedded in the ambiguous lines of authority in the matrix.

In contrast to the overall character of personal ties among executives in the mechanistic or atomistic firms, matrix executives estimate that in an average week, 19% of their communication with colleagues focuses on technical matters only, 30% of their communication with colleagues is devoted to social issues only, and 51% encompasses aspects of technical and social issues. Interactions among matrix executives that do not involve planning, plotting, or engaging in intrigue with one another rarely occurs. Matrix executives demonstrate particular interest in their colleagues' prospects as future allies or adversaries based on their rising or diminishing reputations in the informal executive hierarchy. Recent defections from or formations of new executive coalitions also pique executives' curiosity during face-to-face interaction.

At the same time, matrix executives on average characterize 42% of their colleagues as acquaintances, 33% as friends, and 25% as close friends. In neither of the other two sets of firms did the close friends and friends categories total together more than 33%. One could be quick to jump to the conclusion that in comparison to the mechanistic and atomistic firms, matrix systems spawn more relational ties as well as communication among managers—in effect, the best of both worlds. Such a comparison denies, however, the meaning of friendship in matrix systems vis-à-vis the other two groups. In mechanistic and atomistic firms, friendship largely exists outside of work and is consummated by prolonged social contact. Friendship tends to be an instrumental relation in matrix systems, comprising specific reciprocity in which the personal fuses with the political. To be a close friend is to be a durable ally, but not necessarily to "like" one's durable ally. This situation occurs with less regularity in mechanistic or atomistic firms, where friendship can be decoupled from organizational politics.

Stability. Matrix executives create and sustain internal arrangements that might be considered hallmarks of "instability" in mechanistic or atomistic firms. Each firm replaces up to 70% of its products every year and constantly innovates with new technologies to produce different products in a variety of markets. To an outsider, moreover, the matrix itself would seem to be a constant source of confusion and uncertainty. Top managers in mechanistic and atomistic firms would find the whirlwinds of meetings and coalition maneuvering chaotic. Nevertheless, some of the unintended effects of the matrix have reintroduced a kind of personal and organizational certainty into them. Chief among these

Table 2.5   Stylized Comparison of Executive Contexts

Focal Characteristics

Mechanistic[a]	—strong hold of formal hierarchy —scalar communication —loose-knit communication networks —stability
Atomistic[b]	—weak hold of formal hierarchy —infrequent communication —loose-knit communication networks —stability
Matrix[c]	—weak hold of formal hierarchy —frequent communication —tight-knit communication networks organized into coalitions —instability

[a] Container Corporation, General Utility, Old Financial, and Smith Brothers.
[b] Commco, Continental Design, Hightower Construction, and Independent Accounting.
[c] Bailey Construction, Infotain, New Financial, Playco, and Sunset Group.

are the ritualized meetings and modes of conflict management (described in detail for Playco in chapter 6) in which nearly all executives participate. These rituals give some sense of order to the internal arrangements of these firms in the absence of traditional unity-of-command prerogatives or relatively independent work units.

Several other organizational markers, however, suggest that these five corporate matrix contexts are somewhat unstable compared to the executive contexts in the other eight corporations in the study. During 1980–86, each of the firms experienced at least two reorganizations of its executive ranks as a result of rapid acquisitions, mergers, and divestitures. Infotain and Sunset Group, for example, reorganized four times in the aftermath of two acquisitions and two divestitures by larger firms. Playco, Bailey, and New Financial each reorganized twice after selling several of their 1970s acquisitions in the 1980s. Playco and New Financial also experienced financial restructurings after particularly unsuccessful diversifications in the early 1980s.

Each of these firms also experienced relatively high rates of executive turnover during 1980–86, ranging from a low of 25% at Playco to a high of nearly 80% at New Financial and Infotain. At Playco, few executives were seriously preparing to leave during the period of fieldwork, but at the other four firms, roughly half of the executive corps talked about how they planned to "parachute" out of their firms should their corporations go "belly up" or be reorganized. Finally, each of these firms reported fluctuating patterns of profit and losses over the first half of the 1980s, and only one firm, Playco, reported a profit for 1986.

The multiple acquisitions and divestitures these five firms participated in as predators and prey led each of them to operate in multiple functional fields. Executives spoke about the rise of new competitors in their industries of origin, the difficulties in keeping up with the technologies in their multiple fields, and the increase in mergers and hostile takeovers directly affecting their corporations. Another indication of field instability can be found in the language executives in these firms use to characterize their fields. Among the metaphors that executives in each of these five firms use to characterize their functional fields are "maelstrom," "thunderstorm," "cauldron of competition," "boiling pot," "stormy seas," and "the jungle."

Table 2.5 offers a stylized comparison of the executive contexts in the study. Each executive context has a central logic to it. Mechanistic bureaucracies exhibit strong formal hierarchies, scalar communication of moderate frequency, loose-knit relational ties among top managers, and behavioral as well as perceptual senses of internal and functional field stability. Atomistic organizations exhibit weak formal hierarchies, sparse communication of any sort among executives, loose-knit relational networks, and behavioral as well as perceptual senses of internal and functional field stability. Matrix firms contrast these staid contexts by exhibiting a weak formal hierarchy born of cross-cutting authority structures, dense communication, tight-knit networks within functions, coalitions, and relative instability compared to the other eight firms in the study.

CHAPTER THREE

PATTERNS OF CONFLICT MANAGEMENT IN THIRTEEN EXECUTIVE CONTEXTS

Extended trouble cases, illustrated by the three cases presented in chapter 1, often contain numerous grievance expressions and issues woven together over time by the participants. Fieldwork yielded 312 extended trouble cases containing 844 grievance expressions undertaken by executives.[1] In the pages that follow, I present aggregate findings for the substance, interpretations, and grievance expressions collected among executives, followed by an exploration of the correlates of these patterns across the thirteen executive contexts in the study.

Grievance Issues

I identified twelve genres of grievance issues that appeared 906 times in the executive contexts under study.[2] The issues and their distribution are: (1) *promotion and compensation* ($n = 197$; 21.7%); (2) *management style* ($n = 131$; 14.5%), (3) *personal life* ($n = 117$; 12.9%); (4) *personalities* ($n = 86$; 9.5%); (5) *individual performance* ($n = 84$; 9.3%); (6) *administrative jurisdiction* ($n = 70$; 7.7%); (7) *resource allocation* ($n = 56$; 6.2%); (8) *organizational strategy* ($n = 54$; 6.0%); (9) *work unit performance* ($n = 50$; 5.5%); (10) *personal appearance at work* ($n = 41$; 4.5%); (11) *unethical behavior* ($n = 12$; 1.3%); and (12) *gender discrimination* ($n = 8$; 0.9%). Except for the administrative jurisdiction and work unit performance categories, these genres reflect how executives themselves refer to grievance issues and categories derived from literature on managerial conflict (e.g., Butler 1973; Lawrence and Lorsch 1967a; Walton 1969).

Promotion and compensation grievances focus on the fairness, timing, and burden (on evaluators and those being evaluated) of decision processes and outcomes related to cash compensation, benefits, mobility up formal hierarchies as well as laterally to different work units. For purposes of this typology, management style is distinguished from performance to focus on the treatment of people in interpersonal and intergroup relations. Personal life grievances focus on how executives conduct their relationships with their families, friends, and significant others, business deals that are unrelated to the organization, affairs, recreational pursuits, and the like. Individual performance grievances appear in guises similar to work unit performance grievances except that they focus on individual executives. Personality grievances are based on individual enimity between the principals without specific reference to other issues. Administrative jurisdiction grievances include actions in which aggrieved executives (either singly or in a coalition) believe their colleagues have overstepped their functional authority or disagree with one another about who has jurisdiction in particular decision-making processes. Resource allocation grievances focus on decision processes and outcomes related to budgets, spatial allocations, and personnel. Organizational strategy includes reorganizing, restructuring, and redirecting the collective goals of the organization (e.g., marketing, mergers and acquisition decisions, and relations with regulators, competitors, suppliers, and the press). Work unit performance grievances are those of superiors who have complaints against their subordinates (collectively) for subpar performance (as expressed in evaluation reports), or executives in work units who believe the process of unit performance evaluation is unfair. Personal appearance primarily focuses on how executives dress both at the office and in informal gatherings related to work. Finally, grievances related to unethical behavior focus on both intraorganizational and interorganizational unethical behavior. Intraorganizational unethical behavior would include using expense accounts in unauthorized fashions (for example, taking a family vacation using the company plane), padding one's expenses with bogus receipts, double billing for expenses, using one's offices for moonlighting, using illegal narcotics, and being arrested (e.g., for drunk driving). Interorganizational unethical behavior includes passing trade secrets to competitors, jumping to competitors with organizational secrets related to production or products, or accepting payments from unions or collaborating companies for favored treatment in joint ventures.

The five most prevalent issues—promotion and compensation, management style, personal life, personalities, and individual performance—do seem to suggest a "personalistic" character of executive conflict management consistent with Kanter and Stein's (1980) arguments concerning the general nature of executive contexts. I should also note that two of the five most prevalent grievance issues, management style and personal life, directly tie to incessant concerns with proper etiquette and pressures to conform to particular normative standards, also consistent with Kanter's (1977) and Moore's (1962) arguments about personal conduct at the tops of corporations.

I should also note what executives in the study did not generally define as unethical. Many male informants did not consider sexual harassment, racism, or womanizing on or off the job as generally unethical, instead typically viewing such behaviors as problems related to management style. Female executives generally considered gender discrimination and sexual harassment not as unethical, but problems related to the entrance of women into executive jobs. Top managers of both sexes also did not consider payments by foreign governments to their organizations or by their organizations to foreign governments for favorable treatment or flouting environmental protection, antitrust, or workplace condition regulations as unethical in themselves. When these issues fuel grievances, executives view them as related to "sloppy" management styles that could create legal "headaches" for their organizations should such conduct come to the knowledge of relevant government agencies. Moreover, those organizations that do have corporate codes of conduct ($n = 6$) for their top executives give more attention to unethical conduct that might decrease profits, such as violating securities exchange regulations that could result in legal fines, than to similar conduct that might increase corporate profits. This finding is consistent with Cressey and Moore's (1983) findings from their survey of 119 corporate codes of managerial conduct.

Grievance Schemas

The bare-bones behavior prompting grievances tells only part of the story about how executives interpret their grievances among one another. When informants would talk about grievance issues or when I observed them expressing their grievances against their colleagues at meetings and in other social situations, they would frame the issues in terms of the kinds of norm violation the issue represented. The distribution of interpretations across grievance expressions is: (1) penal ($n = 216; 25.6\%$); (2) indifferent ($n = 177; 21.0\%$); (3) compensatory ($n = 169; 20.0\%$); (4) conciliatory ($n = 160; 19.0\%$); and (5) therapeutic ($n = 122; 14.5\%$). Issues sometimes have multiple or mixed interpretations, although typically a "dominant" schema emerges as an aggrieved party's focal interpretive lens.

To illustrate how these schemas can transform the meaning of a grievance issue, listen to how one of the most prevalent grievance issues, administrative jurisdiction, sounds through the lens of each of these different schemas from actual accounts of grievance expressions by executives:

penal: "Interfering with my division like that violates the rules of sound management that this company stands for. The EVP should put his butt in a sling for coming over and messing with my people" (Smith Brothers executive).

indifferent: "Yesterday, he [another executive in a different practice] started telling one of my managers how he might better manage one of my project staffs. He's always coming up with little helpful hints like that; such a nuisance. I don't really care what he does. I just wish this situation would end, so we can get on with our work" (Continental Design partner).

compensatory: "He and I have an unwritten agreement to stay out of each other's operations. Then he comes over and tries to tell me how to run my outfit. So now I think it only fair that he let me come over tell him how to run his outfit. Either that or cut me some slack on a project deadline we agreed to, to pay me back for all the trouble he caused me over here with my people" (Bailey Construction executive).

conciliatory: "When she starts dealing with my people and not keeping to her duties it creates a lot of friction between us that needs to be removed if we're going to be able to keep the peace and work with each other" (Commco executive).

therapeutic: "It's not just an isolated incident; he's not normal. He thinks that as an executive he can just set goals and use *my* division *and* his own to achieve them; spray around orders anywhere he wants. The firm ought to send him to one of those management training seminars to get himself straight on how he should conduct himself" (emphasis by the informant, an Infotain executive).

In the first instance, overstepping one's administrative jurisdiction means breaking the "rules of sound management" and deserves some sort of punishment from a higher-up in the firm. The second speaker views his colleague overstepping the boundaries of his authority as a "nuisance," which he hopes will just "end" of its own accord. In the third account, the same issue is framed as a broken obligation that demands some sort of "payback." The account of the fourth executive focuses on the "friction" the jurisdictional overstepping creates and how the friction "needs" to be "removed" for productive work relations to be reestablished. Finally, the speaker in the fifth account calls attention to the abnormality of such behavior and explicitly suggests

some sort of education to return the executive to standards of acceptable behavior.

Conflict Management

Subsequent to or simultaneously while making sense of their grievances, executives engage in a wide variety of actions to pursue grievances linked to the issues above. Table 3.1 contains 33 types of conflict
management actions recorded among executives across the thirteen
organizations.[3]

Five of the conflict management actions listed in table 3.1 contain
44.4% of the total sample: (1) temporary curtailment of social interaction with offending parties within one's unit (avoidance), (2) verbal or
written commands to cease offending behavior immediately (authoritative commands), (3) forgetting about a grievance (lumping/endur-
ance), (4) highly calculated, ritualized, and visible tit-for-tat grievance
expressions (confrontational vengeance), and (5) calling into question
colleagues' behavior and demanding that they participate in some
form of verbal duel to resolve the matter (challenging).

Two of the top five conflict management actions are nonconfrontational and relatively unaggressive. The other three actions involve different types of what Hirschman (1970) calls "voice." One kind of voice
underlies authoritative commands and suggests a common image of
managerial hierarchies in which the prerogatives of superiors dominate the normative landscape. A second kind of voice, represented by
confrontational vengeance and challenging, involve aggressive actions
that would, based on the portraits of executive life painted in previous
studies, seem entirely out of place in corporate suites.

The next six conflict management categories together account for
23.2% of the total sample: (6) what many executives in the study refer
to as "living" with grievances but not acting on them (toleration),
(7) verbally quarreling over grievances (arguing), (8) scornfully and
disrespectfully accusing colleagues of inappropriate behavior in public
(public insults), (9) third-party settlement by colleagues who render
verdicts and solutions to disputes without outwardly taking sides (informal arbitration), (10) arranging a permanent transfer from one's
work unit as a result of grievances against parties in the unit (unit
exit), and (11) publicly finding fault with colleagues' behavior (public
accusations). Here again, one finds more and less aggressive actions
mixed.

The remaining twenty-one types contain 30% of the sample:
(12) leaving one's organization as a result of grievances toward the

Table 3.1 Conflict Management in Thirteen Executive Contexts by Percentage[a]

Action	Frequency	Percentage
(1) Temporary avoidance	105	12.4
(2) Authoritative commands	84	10.0
(3) Lumping/endurance	75	8.9
(4) Vengeance, confrontational	60	7.1
(5) Challenges	51	6.0
(6) Toleration	41	4.9
(7) Arguing	34	4.0
(8) Insults, public	31	3.7
(9) Arbitration, informal	31	3.7
(10) Exit, unit	30	3.6
(11) Public accusations	28	3.3
(12) Exit, organizational	24	2.8
(13) Negotiation	24	2.8
(14) Vengeance, nonconfrontational	22	2.6
(15) Conciliatory approaches	21	2.5
(16) Strategic alienation	21	2.5
(17) Feigned ignorance	20	2.4
(18) Secret complaining	18	2.1
(19) Surveillance	16	1.9
(20) Informal counseling	15	1.8
(21) Peacemaking, friendly	15	1.8
(22) Insults, private	14	1.7
(23) Reassignment	13	1.5
(24) Informal mediation	11	1.3
(25) Peacemaking, repressive	8	1.0
(26) Termination	8	1.0
(27) Liquidation	6	0.7
(28) Physical violence	6	0.7
(29) Consulting legal counsel	5	0.6
(30) Sabotage	3	0.4
(31) Legal action threats	2	0.2
(32) Arbitration, formal	1	0.1
(33) Formal grievance threats	1	0.1
Total	844	100.1

[a] Extended descriptions of these actions in three contexts appear in chapters 4–6.

collectivity or its members (organizational exit), (13) discussions between conflict principals oriented toward mutually agreeable solutions (negotiation), (14) highly calculated, ritualized, and secret tit-for-tat grievance expressions (nonconfrontational vengeance), (15) adopting a posture of reason and cordiality toward offending parties (conciliatory approaches), (16) purposely becoming involved in unso-

cial solitary tasks in the presence of an offending party (strategic alienation), (17) pretending that a conflict never occurred between oneself
and another principal (feigned ignorance), (18) privately expressing
grievances about a second party to a third party (secret complaining),
(19) systematically gathering information about an offending party
(surveillance), (20) advising an offending party on how to return their
behavior to some acceptable standard (informal counseling), (21) third-
party dispute settlement that gently suspends hostilities but leaves the
details of resolution to the disputants (friendly peacemaking), (22)
scornfully and disrespectfully accusing colleagues of inappropriate behavior in private (private insults), (23) transferring an offending party
with or without confrontation to another unit (reassignment), (24)
third-party dispute settlement by colleagues that facilitates negotiation
between disputants (informal mediation), (25) third-party dispute settlement that aggressively suspends hostilities but leaves the details of
resolution to the disputants (repressive peacemaking), (26) firing an
executive (termination), (27) reducing an offending party's work unit
resources until their activities are merely perfunctory to the organization (liquidation), (28) physically attacking a colleague (physical violence), (29) seeking advice about a conflict from a lawyer (consulting
legal counsel), (30) covertly undermining an offending party's activities (sabotage), (31) threatening legal action against colleagues or the
organization, (32) submitting a dispute to a formal outside arbitrator
for settlement (formal arbitration), and (33) threatening to use a formal,
internal executive grievance system. Several features of this distribution bear further discussion.

First, the range of conflict management actions in table 3.1 nearly
mirrors that found in cross-cultural studies (e.g., Baumgartner 1984a,
1984b; Black 1990; Gulliver 1979; Nader and Todd 1978; Roberts 1979).
Despite the wide variation in executive conflict management, it is also
interesting to note what executives do not do to pursue their grievances. I did not, for example, record a single case of homicide and only
six cases of physical violence in the study. From one perspective, such
a finding would surprise few people in modern America. Corporate
executives are not the "types" of people one normally associates with
the forceful prosecution of grievances. Yet the historical record contains numerous examples of persistent violence among people of high
social status, including noblemen in medieval Europe (Bloch 1961), the
upper classes in the contemporary Middle East (Rothenberger 1978),
and middle- and upper-middle-class North American families (Zillman 1990). Thus, the reasons for the lack of violence among executives
may not reside in their elite social status per se, but in the overall fea-

tures of their social contexts, particularly the nature of working in contexts so strongly insulated from other social spheres in which even "deviant" executives are "insiders," unlike nonexecutives. Across a wide variety of social settings, insiders commit violence against one another far less than against those who are considered marginal (Horwitz 1990:104–08). Although the analyses in the following pages will suggest that variation in social distance within executive contexts does introduce corresponding variation in confrontational conflict management, such social distance never reaches a threshold at which violence could become more than an infrequent strategy of grievance pursuit among top managers.[4]

Second, top managers in the study tend to engage in confrontation to handle their conflicts with one another ($n = 424$) virtually as often as nonconfrontation ($n = 420$). Such an overall finding runs somewhat contrary to earlier work on managerial conflict (e.g., Dalton 1959; Walton 1969) that found managers largely unwilling to express grievances against colleagues. These proclivities are not, however, evenly distributed among executive contexts.

Third, executives within an organization in the study rarely resort to legal or other formal means of any kind to handle problems among themselves. Equally scarce are threats to use legal measures or consult with in-house counsel except in a few cases which involve executives who leave the firm under conflictual conditions. Some executives have passing familiarity with "employee at will" legal cases (in which disgruntled former executives have sued their former employers) and case law which govern executive employment; most executives have loosely structured employee-employer contracts. The lack of law in executive contexts is also consistent with the lack of law in middle-class and upper-middle-class neighborhoods where many executives live (Baumgartner 1988). Unlike inhabitants in these settings, however, executives at work display a pervasive concern for the legal consequences of other organizational matters, such as product liability, acquisition strategies, antitrust violations, and potential suits from nonexecutive employees. One reason for the pattern of nonlegal conflict management among corporate executives is simply expressed by one executive who explained that a top manager who does resort to formal measures becomes "tainted" and may have a difficult time in their own firm or in finding a new position.

More fundamental reasons for "lawlessness" among executives can be found in general relationships among social status, social intimacy, informal social control, and the likelihood of legal intervention. Principals who enjoy high status are unlikely to legally manage their conflicts because such intervention, according to Baumgartner (1985:22) "entails a compromise of autonomy and a kind of subordination of the disputants to the outside party or parties involved. . . . the subordination involved may be repugnant unless yet higher-status people are involved as arbiters." In most corporations, in-house counsel do not enjoy the status that top managers do. Nor do most judges or independent lawyers (unless they occupy high court positions or head large law firms). In most cases, therefore, legal officials or lawyers would have lower social status than corporate executives, thus militating against legal intervention.

Moreover, social intimates in general are less likely than nonintimates to use law to handle conflict (Baumgartner 1988; Black 1976:37–58; Lundsgaarde 1977). Just as people of high social status avoid law as a way to preserve their autonomy, so social intimates avoid law to prevent their relational integrity from being compromised. As Black (1976:42) observes, "[A]n intimate's associates may shield him from the law: They are less likely to cooperate with the investigation of his offense; they are more likely to lie for him; they are more likely to hide him. . . . In many ways, then, intimacy provides immunity from law." Although the preceding chapter underscores the variation in social intimacy among executives in the study, their relational distance may never reach a level at which law would become a reasonable form of conflict management.

The overall range of actions contained in table 3.1 suggest that nonlegal conflict management of all kinds flourishes among corporate executives. In general, legal and nonlegal conflict management exist in an antithetical relationship to one another (Black 1976:85–103). This relationship is particularly strong in formal, private organizations because of the internal authority systems which constitute such collectivities. Most organizations go to great lengths to protect their local sovereignty (Coleman 1982; Katz 1977) and as a whole have been portrayed as "beyond the law" (Stone 1975). The social boundaries of executive contexts further protect such sovereignty, removing executives from external authorities in the handling of disputes to an even greater extent than in other parts of private organizations—at least while executives are members of their organizations and their organizations remain intact. Thus, it is not only that executives sit "above the law," so to speak, but that they are insulated from the law by nonpermeable organizational boundaries and the comparative social intimacy they enjoy with each other within their organizations.

Finally, the strategic use of the press and other mass media to combat in-house adversaries (for example, by releasing damaging information about one's adversaries to the press) did not occur in any of the thirteen organizations I studied while I was in the field. The popular press and business scholars occasionally report examples of such grievance pursuits, which are sometimes called whistle-blowing (Ewing 1983). Perhaps the fact that such cases still garner headlines underscores their relative paucity among corporate executives and once again points to the social insularity of executives and their zealous protection of access to their contexts. The foregoing discussion suggests some explanations for the overall nature of executive conflict management, but largely ignore the considerable variation in executive contexts. Within the parameters of conflict management variation described above, what explains how and why executives pursue their grievances? The following sections first examine a number of correlates of conflict management, beginning with the most intuitively plausible and continuing with a brief look at some aspects of interest-based choice theories and cultural-gender explanations outlined in chapter 1. The analyses then focus attention on evidence for the social context approach to conflict management among corporate executives.

Pattern Correlates

Quantitative analysis of the field data required that several of the categories discussed above be collapsed into more parsimonious variables. I collapsed therapeutic and conciliatory schemas into a remedial category and penal and compensatory schemas into an accusatory category, as suggested in Black (1976:4–5). The indifferent grievance schemas did not conceptually fit into either of the two recoded categories and were not recoded. I collapsed grievance expressions as forms, in particular, whether grievance pursuit involved unilateral, bilateral, or trilateral action. I used a third set of classifications for coding whether conflict principals confronted one another via some form of direct action or used indirect means to pursue their grievances. These classifications, then, provide three variables for quantitatively describing conflict management among corporate executives: schema (accusatory, remedial, indifferent), form (unilateral, bilateral, trilateral), and directness (confrontation, nonconfrontation).[5]

Common Sense, Grievance Issues, and Conflict Management

From a commonsense standpoint, it would seem most plausible that the type of issue (managerial style, organizational strategy, etc.) would be a powerful predictor of conflict management (cf. Black 1979b). A number of plausible ad hoc correlates might exist. For example, "individual" issues, such as personal appearance or promotion and compensation grievances, might be handled via bilateral confrontation between the parties involved from an accusatory stance; "group" issues, such as resource allocation, might be handled via trilateral confrontation also from an accusatory perspective. For ease of analysis, I collapsed the grievance issues into a dichotomous category following the examples just provided. Promotion and compensation, managerial style, personalities, personal life, individual performance, appearance at work, and unethical behavior were coded as individual issues. Authority jurisdiction, resource allocations, organizational strategy, and work unit performance were coded into a group category. Statistical analysis yielded nonsignificant results for issue by schema ($X^2 = 4.01$; df = 3; $p =. 27$), issue by form ($X^2 = 3.90$; df = 2; $p = .44$), and issue by directness ($X^2 = 2.37$; df = 1; $p = .13$). These analyses, albeit crude, are somewhat unencouraging for common sense when it comes to systematic associations between conflict management and issues among corporate executives.

Issue Seriousness and Conflict Management

A more sophisticated approach to the linkage between grievance issues and conflict management can be found in the literature on interests and choice. Proponents of this approach argue that conflict issues with seriously adverse consequences for organizations are likely to be handled confrontationally and are the most likely candidates for third-party intervention of some kind. In regard to schema, it is difficult to extract specific predictions from the literature, although Lewicki and Sheppard (1985) discuss within a choice perspective what they call "process control" orientations to conflict management. Managers operating out of "inquisitorial" and "adversarial" orientations to third-party settlement emphasize tight, authoritative process control and the enforcement of outcomes, while those that adopt mediation and "problem impetus" stances place the burden of conflict resolution on disputants themselves. Although they argue that outcome control (the level of authoritative enforcement of conflict outcomes) is a function of seriousness, they do not predict relationships between seriousness and third-party settlement processes. Even so, their discussion of these relationships suggests that more serious issues will draw inquisitorial–adversarial process control, while less serious issues will draw mediation–problem impetus control.

When I began this project I did not originally plan to examine interest hypotheses. However, during the fieldwork, managerial conflict literature regarding questions of rational choice increased at a rapid rate. Moreover, informants themselves sometimes emphasized rational choice approaches in lengthy statements about their personal philosophies of conflict management. As a result, I asked informants about the seriousness (in terms of the impact on organizational functioning) of the recounted and observed trouble cases. In general, informants defined as serious conflict issues those that involved significant company financial investments and losses, unethical behavior (again, committed against their organizations), long-range planning, promotion, and executive compensation.

In the absence of more rigorous or reliable quantitative measurements of seriousness, I coded it as a dichotomous variable encompassing serious and less serious conflict issues. The accusatory variable approximates Lewicki and Sheppard's (1985) inquisitorial and adversarial process orientations, while the remedial variable captures the lower process control orientations. Escalation relates to the concerns of choice scholars of conflict management regarding third-party settlement (e.g., Walton 1969). Finally, confrontation/nonconfrontation captures the choice notion of confrontation as "direct engagement" between the principals found in Walton (1969:6) and Bergman and Volkema (1989).

Statistical analyses again yielded nonsignificant results for seriousness by schema ($X^2 = 1.14$; df $= 2$; $p = .57$), seriousness by form ($X^2 = 0.68$; df $= 2$; $p = .71$), and seriousness by directness ($X^2 = 1.01$; df $= 1$; $p = .31$). These relationships were further explored by holding constant the financial health of the organization. It might be reasonable to assume that in organizations losing money, issues perceived as serious might be considered even more in need of attention, requiring an accusatory perspective (e.g., inquisitorial and adversarial process control), social escalation to third parties who could quickly settle matters, and confrontation between principals. Again, statistical analyses yielded nonsignificant findings for seriousness by schema ($X^2 = 2.01$; df $= 2$; $p = .37$), seriousness by form ($X^2 = 1.26$; df $= 2$; $p = .53$), and seriousness by directness ($X^2 = 0.83$; df $= 1$; $p = .36$).

These results suggest that sole reliance on interest explanations, at least as couched in some of the organizational conflict literature, may be overly optimistic. At the same time, the findings were obtained under conditions of little control and less precision than one might like for a "fair" test of these ideas. As such, they should be viewed as tentative and suggestive of future research directions. They are also counterintuitive from the perspective of conventional wisdom regarding how "serious" issues affect the way people handle conflict. But they are not without precedent in organizational analysis. Psychologist Irving Janis (1989), for example, argues that the widely held assumption that *unimportant* conflict among leaders results in "seat-of-the-pants" decision making and nonconfrontation among the principal players is false. His work corroborates the findings above: even conflict involving organizational crises, which could directly lead to the death of an organization, often involves efforts at nonconfrontational conflict management and decision making oriented toward interpersonal rather than organizational concerns.

To argue that organizational health–oriented rational choice is a poor predictor of conflict management in situ is not to argue that choice perspectives and language are absent from executive life. Some executives espoused beliefs about conflict management consistent with the interest perspective, while the majority of executives talked about precepts and accounts of conflict management that emphasized concerns other than organizational health and efficiency. It is interesting to note the type of executive prone to espousing the interest perspective: the youngest and those who had most recently been educated at elite business schools—where, not surprisingly, rational choice theories predominate (March 1988). Those farther away from such institutions (in terms of experience) may be more prone to make sense of their actions within their local social contexts, drawing on local schemas and scripts for decision making and conflict management. If these speculations have merit, they also imply that a wide crevasse may still exist between the *lived experience* of managerial decision making and most formal education *about* managerial decision making.

Individual Level Analyses

Age and Education

Analyses of individual level characteristics[6] and conflict management yielded nonsignificant results for age (split above and below the median age of 53 for informants as "older" and "younger" executives) for schema ($X^2 = 0.17$; df $= 1$; $p = .68$), form ($X^2 = 0.96$; df $= 2$; $p = .62$), and directness ($X^2 = 1.06$; df $= 1$; $p = .30$). Analyses of education (coded as secondary school/high school, college, and graduate) also yielded nonsignificant results for schema ($X^2 = 3.07$; df$= 4$; $p = .55$), form ($X^2 = 4.88$; df $= 4$; $p = .30$), and directness ($X^2 = 2.26$; df $= 2$; $p = .32$).[7]

Table 3.2   Conflict Management Form by Gender in Thirteen
                  Executive Contexts

	Gender		
	Male	Female	Total
Unilateral	54	29	52
	(423)	(19)	(442)
Bilateral	28	25	28
	(217)	(16)	(233)
Trilateral	18	46	20
	(139)	(30)	(169)
Total	92	8	100
	(779)	(65)	(844)

Note: By percentage. Figures in parentheses indicate absolute frequencies. $X^2 = 31.50$; $df = 2$; $p = .00$; $C = .19$

Gender

Analyses of gender yielded nonsignificant results for schema ($X^2 = 3.97$; $df = 2$; $p = 14$) and directness ($X^2 = 4.26$, $df = 2$, $p = .12$). A weak statistically significant relationship emerged for gender and form as table 3.2 suggests.

Further analyses revealed that the three forms appear not to be equally used by males. Specifically, male executives appear to engage in unilateral grievance expressions more than bilateral or trilateral forms, although the differences between male usage of the different forms is not quite statistically significant ($X^2 = 3.97$; $df = 2$; $p = 14$). Table 3.3 suggests an even weaker statistically significant relationship between gender and directness. There was no evidence of any pronounced preference for confrontation over nonconfrontation among males ($X^2 = .128$; $df = 1$; $p = .72$). But such evidence did emerge for female executives for form ($X^2 = 4.95$; $df = 1$; $p = .03$; $C = .28$) and for directness ($X^2 = 3.93$; $df = 1$; $p = .05$; $C = .25$).

At first glance, these findings do not imply a decided preference for nonconfrontation as a way to protect relational connections, as suggested by Tannen (1990) and earlier by Gilligan (1982). Nonconfrontation therefore may not be a routine part of the repertoire of indigenous conflict management for the 23 female top managers in this study. But the picture of male and female executive conflict management is more complex than the percentage differences and weak statistical relationships contained in tables 3.2 and 3.3 appear to indicate.

The rates of conflict grievance stories that I collected from interviews with men and women were 3.1 for women versus 4.2 for men.

Table 3.3   Conflict Management Directness by Gender in Thirteen
                  Executive Contexts

	Gender		
	Male	Female	Total
Confrontation	49	63	50
	(383)	(41)	(424)
Nonconfrontation	51	37	50
	(396)	(24)	(420)
Total	92	8	100
	(779)	(65)	(844)

Note: By percentage. Figures in parentheses indicate absolute frequencies. $X^2 = 4.26$;
$df = 1$; $p = .04$; $C = 0.7$.

In the field, women spoke less freely about their conflicts during initial
interviews than men, who often volunteered their conflict experiences
during first interviews (in some corporations even with a kind of bra-
vado). Female informants rarely talked about their conflicts until a
much greater rapport developed between us, typically during second
interviews or even further beyond the first few encounters. The reluctance of women to talk about their grievances, conflicts, and disputes
during initial interviews does conform in part to Deborah Tannen's
observations. Women did appear reluctant to recount their experiences
of trouble with their male or female colleagues. And when they did
offer stories of conflict, *they would often narrate confrontations with offending parties that included the role of powerful partisan supporters on their
side.* Moreover, this tendency among female executives is consistent
with findings regarding gendered stories of disputing from contexts
far removed from the tops of private corporations. Goodwin (1993)
found, for example, that working-class African-American boys and
girls (ages 4–14) tell differing stories about disputing: boys tend to
focus on immediate settings with the teller as the confronter of the
principal adversary in the story, while girls tend to talk in terms
of coalitions ("two against one") who will confront adversaries in
"the future." Indeed, Goodwin argues that the establishment of such
alignments among girls is key in bringing forth future confrontations
over grievances and in reproducing girls' notions of social organization.

   Thus, my claim is that female executives appear to experience *both*
connection (acting in coalitions) and confrontation in excess of that
engaged in by their male colleagues in the study. Yet, this claim also
raises questions about the nature of the self-report data used in this

portion of the study, recent studies about the temporality and use of third parties in male and female conflict management, and the special conditions under which female executives are brought into the tops of corporations. My claim rests on the underlying assumptions that (1) female and male executives view "confrontation" and "nonconfrontation" similarly and (2) male and female grievance schemas contain the same interpretive lenses. Indeed, it could be that women have a much different sense of what it means to confront people, such that many episodes of conflict management in which direct contact occurred between female executives and their adversaries were defined by women not as "grievance-related confrontations" but as some form of "problem solved directly and cooperatively." My interview data, however, do not suggest such divergences and may even underscore the degree to which female executives in the study are socialized into the *male* worlds they inhabit. The following representative quotes from a female and a male informant suggest the similarities in interpretation of confrontation and nonconfrontation.

> *Female informant:* When I confront someone it means that I express myself forthrightly, don't pull in any punches. Now we might fight or we might negotiate our differences, but it's direct without holding back. That's the way you've got to do it if you as a woman want to be seen as a strong.
> *Male informant:* If I confront someone, I sit right down and talk to the person, get it all out on the table even though it's tough to do sometimes. It's just full speed ahead, lay it on the line.

The first account, particularly, suggests the unique conditions (relative to men) under which women work at the tops of the corporations in this study and in corporate America more generally.

Kanter (1977:230–37) found that small token numbers of female managers often produce narrow identities for women in which incumbents are viewed and come to enact distinctive roles. Three of these roles express traditional stereotypes of women: the "mother," the "seductress," and the "pet" (or "one of the boys") roles. She also argues that a more contemporary role, the "iron maiden," refers to women who do not fall into any of the other three roles. Iron maidens, according to Kanter, cast women as "tougher" than their male colleagues. Nearly all of the 23 female executives in my study talked about how they believed they had to be "stronger" than their male colleagues and that they could never let their peers "see them cry." A female executive in the study put it like this: "It's not just about being smarter than the men, although I guess that has something to do with it. A woman in upper management has to get people to fear her. You do that by being tougher than the men, to show them that you are not afraid to mix it up with them and will never back down." The archetypal illustration of this role can be seen in the behavior and perceptions of one executive known as the "Princess of Power" at Playco (discussed in greater detail in chapter 6). According to her male and female colleagues, the Princess is the toughest "SOB" in the firm, who makes and breaks weaker male colleagues with the "snap of her fingers." The Princess often engages in confrontational conflict management as well: aggressive arguing, challenges, direct negotiations, and confrontational vengeance with the aid of supporters.

At the same time, female executives noted the differences in their on-the-job conflict management and their home demeanor. As support for the managerial role-relation effect on conflict management, listen to these two female executives:

> Most of these bozos around here couldn't imagine that in my own home I make peanut butter and jelly sandwiches for my kids, I try to get along with my husband—be really supportive, cooperative, and not get in his face about stuff. If we have problems, we might discuss it or just let it disappear without really talking about it. They probably think I just kick ass and take names at home. Well, sometimes I *do forget* where I am. Sometimes you just take the workplace right into the home because you spend so many hours at work. I remember a family meeting once that I ran like I do one of my committees. The whole family started yelling at me to stop being a manager and just be mom. That shook me right out of that tough-guy manager thing [emphasis by the informant].

And:

> There is a very large difference between being at home and being in the office. At home, I don't have the feeling of being in a glass bowl and having to really take on all comers. In the office, I've got no choice. I've got to use whatever resources I've got to push ahead and that means getting on people directly about things.

Thus, one explanation of the propensity for female executives in the study to confront their adversaries could lie in the likelihood of women's adopting the iron maiden role both in their routine nonconflict behavior, in their conflict management, and in their accounts to me of their conflict behavior. In this sense, female executives' stories about conflict may tap into what Mills (1940) called the "vocabulary of motives" that people use to explain their actions to themselves and others.

In the case of female executives, part of their vocabulary of motives is rooted in tokenism and the narrowly proscribed roles available to them at the tops of their corporations. One could also plausibly argue that the stories of conflict management I collected from female executives simply reflected their attempts to justify their actions by noting that they did not act alone, that supporters also saw their "side" of the dispute and acted on their behalf, thus legitimating their confrontational actions. However, I observed seven different female executives engage in highly confrontational behaviors with their colleagues (all but one adversary a man) during fieldwork. I also collected numerous stories from male executives and clerical personnel about female confrontation, both of which suggest that female executives' accounts of confrontation were not merely impression management for an outsider, but actually reflected some set of routinized behaviors. More to the point: *being* an iron maiden may *mean* confronting one's adversaries.

Kolb (1992) further suggests that what may be taken as a female *voice* emphasizing harmony and behind-the-scenes nonconfrontational peacemaking may actually be a function of female managers' subordination to male managers in most organizational hierarchies. In essence, a woman's voice is a subordinate's voice.[8] Yet Kolb's argument may be tempered by other structural factors that account for conflict management tendencies by female managers. One of these structural factors may be the sense of abandonment that Kanter (1977) suggests many female managers who are in extreme minority positions experience while enacting the iron maiden token role. Iron maidens, unlike the other stereotypical roles female managers enact, rarely receive protective or sympathetic responses to their problems from their male or female colleagues. Confrontation, then, may act as something of lashing out at world in which they feel deserted. Many of the 23 women in the study did discuss feeling "isolated" in the managerial ranks relative to the variable levels of social ties their male colleagues experienced.

Confrontation by female executives over and above that of their male colleagues may also be related to other unique structural conditions of the female executives in this study. All 23 women talked about the crucial role that older male mentors played in their ascendancy to the top ranks of their organizations. Mentors in these contexts function as sponsors, sometimes as counselors, to their protégées, and would often be the only strong voice arguing for the promotion of a female executive into the top echelons. Male informants talked about the role of mentors, but also told stories of "going it alone" up the corporate ladder and "splitting" with their mentors. All but two female executives in the study still worked in the same corporation as their mentors. A female executive talks about her experiences:

> There were no women at the top before I got here. I needed someone to vouch for me, to bring me along and convince the other executives that I was worth the risk. Sanders [a senior executive in her firm] did that for me. I became his project and I helped him too, made damn sure I took an interest in his activities. Now that doesn't mean he defends me outright when I go after someone or that I can cry on his shoulder when things get tough, but it does mean that I *always have a powerful supporter waiting in the wings* [emphasis added].

What this top manager implies, at least for the 23 women in this study, is that male mentors function as a ready ally when problems arise with colleagues. To support this contention, consider that of the 30 grievance expressions that female executives escalated to the trilateral stage, 23 involved individuals whom female executives identified as "mentors" or "sponsors" acting as either supporters or settlement agents. Female executive disputants in this study therefore find the sponsorship system, which both enables and constrains their pathways to the top, is a resource in their disputes with other executives, particularly men.

To further bolster my argument, consider the general relationship between confrontation and access to allies found in the cross-cultural literature on conflict management. Men *and* women with ready access to reliable allies demonstrate a decided preference to confront adversaries across a wide variety of social contexts. M. P. Baumgartner (1988:97–98) discusses this general relationship:

> Without supporters to help in the management of their conflicts, people are more likely to forgo direct confrontations. Evidence from [other] settings indicates a close relationship between the availability of support and the vigorous prosecution of grievances. . . .
> Whether and to what extent disputes will be settled by negotiation, for example, depends greatly on the ability of the aggrieved parties to recruit an "action set" to help them. . . . In ancient Athens, fraternities and clubs which assisted their members . . . stimulated recourse to professional advocates.

It appears, then, that tokenism, social support, and gender orientations interact to play crucial roles in explaining gender differences in conflict management among corporate executives. Two of these factors—tokenism and powerful allies—may especially compel women to confront offending parties and escalate their grievances to disputes more often than their male colleagues. Even so, the use of "built-in" allies, as one female executive noted, cuts both ways because it can translate into "dependence on male mentors" just as continued recourse to powerful allies by men and women in a variety of contexts does. The cost for female executives relying on male mentors as allies may be higher, however, because it taps into and may perpetuate the hierarchical relationships that exist between most male and female executives at the tops of large corporations. Thus, as the gender composition of top managerial ranks changes and as female managers' pathways to the executive levels change, I would expect female executives' tendencies to aggressive confrontation to change also.

These preliminary analyses also provide empirical evidence that social context plays a crucial role in how conflict management unfolds among corporate executives. Specifically, aspects of executive contexts may accentuate gendered conflict management schemas and scripts (e.g., Goodwin 1993), producing tendencies of women to simultaneously value and preserve relationships (with allies) while calling on those very same relationships in their confrontational grievance pursuits against colleagues. In the following sections, I quantitatively examine associations between context and conflict management.

Social Context and Conflict Management

In chapter 1, I argued that grievance schemas and forms couple with contexts in distinctive ways. Disputants are likely to frame their grievances remedially in pervasively tight-knit contexts or accusatorially in contexts dominated by coalitions with few social ties between them. Loose-knit contexts are likely to be associated with schemas of indifference. Moreover, confrontation is likely to occur in social contexts that combine relational network density and weak institutionalized hierarchies. The accusatory framing of grievances is likely in contexts containing strong institutionalized hierarchies, as is the transformation of grievances from unilateral to trilateral forms, particularly third-party settlement. Although the grounded typology presented in chapter 2 does not allow for a controlled assessment of these claims, it does allow for a consideration of the coupling of conflict management with empirical contexts.

Table 3.4 contains the grievance schemas associated with each of the three types of executive contexts. Overall, the relationship between context and schema is moderate (X^2 = 228.59; df = 4; p = .00; C = .37).[9] These findings suggest that accusatory schemas are most prevalent in

Table 3.4   Conflict Management Schema by Type of Executive
                      Context

	Mechanistic	Atomistic	Matrix	Total
Accusatory	63	20	59	46
	(182)	(63)	(140)	(385)
Remedial	30	34	37	33
	(87)	(108)	(87)	(282)
Indifferent	7	46	4	21
	(20)	(146)	(11)	(177)
Total	34	38	28	100
	(289)	(317)	(238)	(844)

Note: By percentage. Figures in parentheses indicate absolute frequencies.

the mechanistic bureaucracies and matrix systems. Indifferent schemas appear most readily among executives in atomistic organizations. Remedial schemas appear in a little over a third of the executive grievance expressions in atomistic and matrix contexts, and in just under one-third of the grievance expressions in mechanistic organizations. In mechanistic bureaucracies, executives frame grievances as deviations from explicit standards grounded in formal authority. An accusatory tone also pervades the interpretation of executive grievances in matrix systems. But top managers in matrix firms do not invoke formal authority to pursue their grievances, instead drawing from their own reputations generated via the constant exchange of accusatory grievances within the firm. Top managers in atomistic organizations depart from the accusatory schemas that prevail in mechanistic and matrix contexts, largely making sense of their grievances as nothing more and nothing less than nuisances or bothers to be dealt with as quietly as possible. Executive grievances, therefore, come to be systematically colored by the proximate social contexts in which they occur. To be sure, executives do not frame their grievances in lockstep with their colleagues, but these analyses underscore the idea that more variation in grievance interpretation exists across executive contexts than within them.

Systematic aggregate patterns of conflict management among corporate executives further emerges for conflict management form and executive context as presented in table 3.5. This table suggests that conflict management forms are distributed unevenly across executive contexts in the study ($X^2 = 114.31$; df = 4; p = .00; C = .26). Specifically, table 3.5 suggests that mechanistic and atomistic contexts contain far more unilateral forms of conflict management than do matrix systems, which contain a greater prevalence of trilateral forms. The fact that top

Table 3.5   Conflict Management Form by Type of Executive Context

	Mechanistic	Atomistic	Matrix	Total
Unilateral	60	61	32	52
	(174)	(192)	(76)	(442)
Bilateral	24	31	28	28
	(69)	(98)	(66)	(233)
Trilateral	16	9	40	20
	(46)	(27)	(96)	(169)
Total	34	38	28	100
	(289)	(317)	(238)	(844)

Note: By percentage. Figures in parentheses indicate absolute frequencies.

managers in atomistic and mechanistic contexts use similar lines of action to pursue their grievances does not mean they share similar contents of action. In mechanistic bureaucracies the modal grievance expression is the authoritative command delivered by superiors to subordinates, whereas the modal grievance expression among executives in atomistic organizations is temporary avoidance. Both of these contexts differ from matrix systems, in which executives confront one another in highly ritualistic fashions with the support of partisan coalitions. In matrix systems, executives most often practice some strict form of vengeance in which paying adversaries back for previous transgressions is paramount.

The data in table 3.5, however, do not shed light on questions about the social conditions under which unilateral grievances and bilateral conflicts are transformed into triadic settlement processes—in effect, which contexts are most closely associated with sending problems "up the line" for resolution by superiors. To answer these questions, I broke down trilateral conflict management into two categories, following Black and Baumgartner (1983): settlement (relatively neutral intervention into a conflict by a third party with the purpose of resolution) and partisanship (the intervention into a conflict on behalf of one side by a third party). Table 3.6 contains the results of these analyses. A statistically significant and moderate relationship emerged between trilateral form and executive context ($X^2 = 16.90$; df $= 2$; $p = .00$; C $= .32$). As one might expect, mechanistic bureaucracies exhibit a greater propensity to engage in settlement than partisanship, with informal arbitration and peacemaking by executive superiors among their subordinates the most prevalent forms of action taken. In contrast to these patterns, top managers in matrix systems display a decided tendency to transform their grievances into partisan trilateral forms, drawing on

Table 3.6   Trilateral Form by Type of Executive Context

	Mechanistic	Atomistic	Matrix	Total
Settlement	63	44	28	40
	(29)	(12)	(27)	(68)
Partisanship	37	56	72	60
	(17)	(15)	(69)	(101)
Total	27	16	57	100
	(46)	(27)	(96)	(169)

Note: By percentage. Figures in parentheses indicate absolute frequencies.

Table 3.7   Conflict Management Directness by Type of Executive
            Context

	Mechanistic	Atomistic	Matrix	Total
Confrontation	55	32	69	50
	(160)	(100)	(164)	(424)
Nonconfrontation	45	68	31	50
	(129)	(217)	(74)	(420)
Total	34	38	28	100
	(289)	(317)	(238)	(844)

Note: By percentage. Figures in parentheses indicate absolute frequencies.

standing support groups found most often in their departments and engaging in disputing in cross-functional meetings. Executives in atomistic firms, as table 3.5 indicates, display the least propensity to engage in trilateral forms of either type.

In addition, all four mechanistic bureaucracies had formal grievance procedures at the *executive levels* in place when I was in the field and executives in one of the atomistic organizations (Commco) were considering implementing a formal grievance procedure as well. Such procedures typically involve some kind of formal arbitration, with the president and or CEO acting as a settlement agent. I collected only one actual usage of such procedures (at Old Financial; discussed in chapter 4). None of the other firms in the study had operating formal grievance procedures at the executive levels.

Finally, analyses of the relationship between conflict management directness and context also yielded a moderate relationship ($X^2 = 106.58$; df $= 2$; $p = .00$; C $= .36$). As table 3.7 suggests, executives in atomistic contexts are more likely to engage in nonconfrontation, while executives in matrix systems are more likely to engage in confrontation. A one-way analysis of directness and context in mechanistic bureaucracies yielded nonsignificant findings ($X^2 = 3.11$; df $= 1$; $p =$

.08), but consistent with expected patterns: nonhierarchical loose-knit executive contexts are associated with nonconfrontation, while tight-knit contexts are associated with confrontation.

The patterns of conflict management described in these analyses, then, suggest three different normative orders of corporate executives. An *authoritative* order is commonly found in mechanistic bureaucracies, where formal authority pervades the handling of conflict.[10] It is characterized by accusatory grievance schemas and unilateral acts of authority in the pursuit of grievances. When trilateral acts do occur they are more likely to take the form of settlement than partisanship. This executive order resembles the normative orders found at the middle and lower levels of most private or public bureaucracies, such as the punishment-centered bureaucracy described by Gouldner (1954) and organizations that rely on coercive control for compliance characterized by Etzioni (1961). Atomistic organizations offer a second normative order characterized by unilateral nonconfrontational actions often executed within a schema of indifference. Such an order captures what Baumgartner (1988) calls *moral minimalism*. In this context, order is secured as much by what people do not do to pursue their grievances as by what they do. Finally, matrix systems display yet another executive normative order, the *reciprocal*, in which executives publicly and ritualistically confront one another with the aid of supporters to exchange grievances. Conflict management in these contexts evokes images of the highly differentiated managerial subsystems studied by Lawrence and Lorsch (1967b) in which confrontation prevails.

In subsequent chapters, I present case studies of these three orders. The three organizations selected highlight the dominant features of each type of context and order, although subvariation in each also exists. As such, I treat each of them as a "semi-autonomous social field" in the anthropological sense that each is a "small field observable to the [researcher] . . . which can generate rules, customs, and symbols internally, but that also is vulnerable to rules and decisions and other forces emanating from the larger world by which it is surrounded" (Moore 1974:54–57). In chapter 4, I describe and analyze the authoritative order among executives at Old Financial. In chapter 5, I turn my attention to the minimalist order among Big Six partners at Independent Accounting. My last organizational case study focuses on the reciprocal order at Playco.

CHAPTER FOUR

MODERN TIMES: AUTHORITATIVE CONFLICT MANAGEMENT IN A MECHANISTIC BUREAUCRACY

You ever see that old Charlie Chaplin film, Modern Times? *It's about people living their lives like machines; people becoming machines. That's what it's like at Old Financial. The machine in our firm is the corporate hierarchy. No matter how high you get in the organization, you have to live by the chain of command, not get out of control, control your reports [subordinates], all the while trying to get to the next slot.*
—executive vice president, Old Financial

Old Financial's contemporary executive context is a product of two periods of rapid growth during the last fifty years. The first occurred during World War II, when the company, then barely three decades old, expanded from its original business in private savings and home financing to providing financial backing for large-scale housing projects for military personnel and defense plant employees. The second period of growth began in the early 1970s and continued into the early 1980s. During this period, Old Financial diversified its services into real estate development and investment, mortgage banking, insurance, property management, and commercial lending, as well as extending its operations into several states. By the middle 1980s, nearly ten thousand employees and seventy-six executives generated over one billion dollars in yearly revenues for Old Financial.

The firm's corporate headquarters occupies several floors in a gray glass-and-steel office building near the center of a large metropolitan area. The main lobby to the building contains two entrances: one for the flagship branch office of Old Financial's oldest concern, banking, and a second that opens into a large foyer with several elevators. The elevator farthest away from the foyer's entrance stands out because of its mahogany-covered doors and gold piping. A uniformed guard sits outside this elevator to clear visitors and to call ahead to the executive levels to "prepare the way" for visitors. Inside this elevator one also finds mahogany paneling and the company logo subtly woven into the burgundy carpet that covers the elevator's floor. The elevator panel contains only three buttons: ML (main lobby), E1 (executive level one), and E2 (executive level two). The elevator skips the thirty-three floors between the main lobby and E2. For those who travel to the executive levels, the floors between the top and the ground floors are known simply as the "chasm," where the "lower" managers, staffs, and other workers "plug" away at their "dreary" jobs.

This elevator, a private elevator that travels only between the two executive floors, and a sweeping spiral staircase connect the two floors. The ceilings of both floors are high and there is open space as far as the eye can see. Where there are no windows, heavy mahogany doors lead into private executive offices and conference rooms, all out of sight from the main floor. Little adorns the walls or the floor spaces of either E1 or E2. Glazed windows filter the sunlight, further darkening the hues of the floor and the walls. The outside windows do not open and a vaguely musty scent hangs in the air.

Facing the E2 elevator landing some thirty feet away, a lone "receiving" secretary sits at a large wraparound desk. She rises to introduce herself simply as Mrs. Raditz to anyone disembarking from the elevator. An imposing figure, Mrs. Raditz stands five foot ten, is of northern European descent, and is in her late forties. She wears a dark dress and a diamond pendant bearing the Old Financial logo. A waiting area with large leather couches and a table on which sit magazines, newspapers, and company propaganda is directly behind her. There are no other secretaries or desks in sight. There are no sounds, save for the occasional muted telephone ring at Mrs. Raditz's desk. One has the feeling of being in an immense carpeted warehouse.

Private secretaries (always women) usher visitors from the main waiting area behind several closed doors to executive offices, which are stratified on the executive floors by formal rank. E2 houses junior executives who often have small conference rooms (in addition to the large ones in the center of each floor) and large baths adjoining their offices. Each executive on E2 has at least one "head" secretary and a clerical staff of two or three people. All head secretaries (called "lead personal assistants" or LPAs) are female. E1 offices have private baths, private conference rooms, and in the cases of the most senior executives, private kitchenettes with a chef on call from the executive dining room. Executives on E1 also have multiple layers of secretaries who sit in adjoining rooms that one must walk through in order to reach an executive's private office.

Private executive offices vary in size and location. The most junior executives occupy inside offices on E2, while the most senior of the junior executives (particularly those ready to make a move up the hierarchy) occupy corner offices on E2. A similar pattern exists on E1 for more senior executives. In every executive's office, one finds large mahogany desks with overstuffed leather chairs. The size of the desk and the chair also varies according to location; executives with E1 corner offices have the largest desks and chairs. Every office also has some area designated for private meetings either by a round conference table or an arrangement of couches and reading chairs. One finds much the same personal effects in each executive office: family portraits, a few books and reports visible on shelves, and an occasional advanced degree diploma and personal computer in younger executives' offices.

Most executives are of northern European stock, male, and in their fifties (see table 2.2 in chapter 2 for Old Financial demographics). Male and female executives tend to be tall, the men near or over six feet and the women near or over five foot eight. Whether male or female, all executives wear dark suits, dark shoes, and white shirts or blouses. Executive secretaries reflect these demographics and dress tendencies as well, except all are female.

Consistent with their conservative dress, Old Financial executives display studied, almost stiff control of their bodily movements or as one executive noted, a "buttoned-down" style. Old Financial executives never hurry or saunter as they walk to and from their offices on E2 and E1. They stride in an even, measured pace. This style carries over to executive speech as well. In conversation (and ethnographic interviews), executives speak in measured sentences with confident assurance of what they are saying. Greetings among executives on the main floor reflect the same buttoned-down style, rarely lasting more than one conversation turn, with each turn rarely more than a few short, measured sentences:

"Hello there, Jim. Marketing going fine, I hear."

"Yes it is. We must get in some golf some time. May I have my secretary call yours to arrange a round?"

"Sounds splendid. Let's arrange it."

Inside the Mechanistic Bureaucracy at Old Financial

Old Financial's local executive context manifests itself most clearly in its unambiguous reporting lines and explicitly defined authority jurisdictions—the kinds of formal structures that are found in many economic enterprises (Chandler 1977; Williamson 1975) and that particularly exemplify mechanistic bureaucracies (Burns and Stalker 1961). One senior executive described the overall climate of Old

Financial's executive context: "We're not big on surprises here or politics. My idea, and I think a lot of other executives who have been here awhile will agree, is to go through channels. Make sure your boss knows what you're doing [and] try to set up procedures and rules [that] are reliable and accountable."

The corporation is divided into western, eastern, and central divisions (see figure 4.1) that are remarkably similar in internal organization. Each division is headed by an executive vice president–divisional manager who in turn has five senior vice presidents who report directly to him (there are no female division managers). Senior vice presidents often have a number of divisional vice presidents and managers without executive titles who report to them. Two of the divisional offices are based in other states, away from corporate headquarters. Sitting atop the divisions are four senior executive vice presidents who make up the "corporate level" of the firm and are responsible, respectively, for marketing, subsidiaries, finance, and branch management. They report to the president–chief operating officer, who in turn reports to the chief executive officer–chairman of the board. Divisional managers report to the branch management senior executive vice president. Senior executive vice presidents report directly to the president. Old Financial also has a number of executive and senior vice presidents at the corporate level who report directly to the president. Executives in these positions are involved with long-term planning or finance activities. There are also a few corporate vice presidents who focus on marketing, administration at the corporate level, public relations, and corporate philanthropy.[1]

Old Financial's recent diversification brought with it a phenomenon largely unknown in its local context prior to the 1970s: executives who did not climb up the firm's hierarchy from the branch-office level to the executive ranks, but were hired laterally into the firm. About one quarter of the corporation's top managers constitute what Old Financial executives call "imported talent." Even so, most imported talent come from other financial institutions and are quite familiar with Old Financial's buttoned-down culture.

Hierarchies

Formal Authority. As suggested above, formal rank matters a great deal at Old Financial. Formal evaluations clearly express the efficacy of formal rank and play key roles in legitimating promotions as well as salary bonuses or decreases. As in other mechanistic bureaucracies, superiors are uniquely charged with evaluating the subordinates

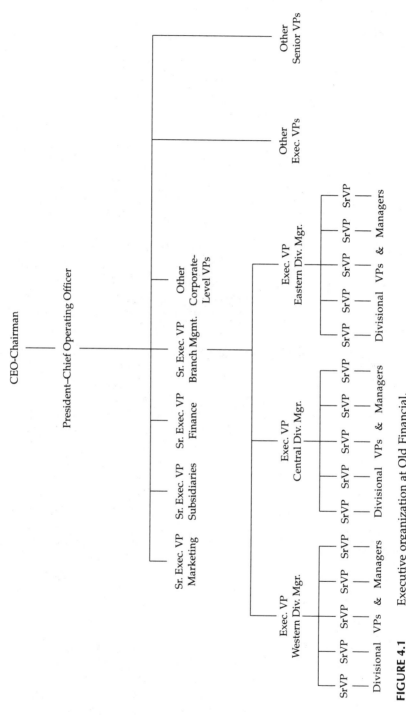

FIGURE 4.1 Executive organization at Old Financial.

within their authority jurisdiction. Superiors do most of the talking during evaluation meetings, using evaluation meetings as an opportunity to tell executives their general expectations for them and the company as a whole. Evaluations involve quite elaborate interaction rituals, as described by this executive vice president who reports directly to the chief executive officer:

> Our evaluations occur at the end of each calendar year; for us that's in July. It's the same pattern every year I've been here: His secretary calls mine to make an appointment. That call is supposed to trigger my year-end report to be sent up to his office, but usually I've already done that because I know what's coming. He already has my year-end report on my activities when we meet. We meet in his office den for an hour or so—he has these overstuffed leather chairs with a coffee table set up, very cozy; brandy, cigars, the whole bit. He starts out talking about how *I* think I've done on my goals for the year. I never really say anything. I just listen to him talk. I do the same thing with my direct reports. What he always stresses, what we always stress at Old Financial is whether we've done our job and followed orders. We never really get to specifics; the numbers are in the report. Besides, I never look at the numbers when I evaluate my people, he doesn't either. He can read as well as I can. That's how it happens and that's what we get evaluated on. At some point, he says that he's covered all he wanted and he ends the meeting. End of evaluation.

An Old Financial senior vice president provides a similar account of a quicker evaluation ritual lower in the executive hierarchy:

> He [the EVP to whom the speaker reports] calls the meeting. It lasts about twenty minutes max. He goes over what he understands my department accomplished during the year; nothing too specific, just sticking with the generalities. He talks about what he wants out of the division the coming year and what he wants out of the company the coming year and that's really it. I don't really say much. Oh, I might clarify something if it's unclear, but I don't say much. You're in and out in twenty minutes.

These accounts vary from the "official" management-by-objectives (MBO) criteria used to evaluate Old Financial executives: profit contribution, managerial effectiveness, community and social service, and a residual set of goals left to the discretion of the superior. Nearly all of the executives at Old Financial had difficulty articulating the formal criteria for their performance evaluations. Most remarked that such evaluations were "not well spelled out," based on general "contributions" to the "bottom line," or even "hazy."

This finding corroborates an important element of executive evaluation that Kanter found in her corporate field study: "The further away from first-line involvement with operating tasks, the more managers seemed to be aware of increasingly vague performance criteria" (1977:60). The *informal* criteria for performance evaluation at Old Financial, however, suffer from few ambiguities. To satisfy a superior, a subordinate must keep in line with the chain of command and specifically keep current with the plans, the strategies, and sometimes the whims of superiors. One way to keep current is to "scout around" for "pet projects" in which one's superiors are engaged. To be unprepared to talk in an informed way about a superior's ideas does not go unnoticed by superiors. The experience of an executive vice president illustrates how such criteria appear during evaluation:

> An important part of performance that is graded around here is whether your people are in the mix. By being in the mix, I really mean knowing what I'm up to, what I'm planning. One of my senior vice presidents is really out of the mix on most of the stuff I'm doing. I can't ever run an idea by him on something that we're engaged in. That kind of stuff comes up in an evaluation. It's core.

At the same time, superiors looking down the managerial hierarchy often regard evaluation meetings as trivial confirmations of what they already knew about their subordinates given the asymmetries of information flow up and down the executive hierarchy. Listen to this superior (a senior executive vice president) describe evaluation meetings:

> When I evaluate my people, I know what they've done and what they haven't done. I set up the meeting and define our agenda. It's one-on-one. Nothing that manager says to me is going to alter how I think he's done. Hey, you don't have to read a spreadsheet to know how a man is doing. I watch my people all the time. That's the difference, even at this level in the business: I've more information about what they're doing than they do about what I'm doing.

Respectability. The executive ranks at Old Financial are also stratified according to the "respectability" of top managers. Respectability at Old Financial consists of the interaction between an executive's competence (e.g., ability to stay within budget or meet business and personal goals) and their moral character (especially the perception as one who

does not "stab people in the back" and does not "play politics"). As in
interfirm relations (see Macaulay 1963), then, an executive's "good
name" is crucial to their intrafirm pursuits.

Gender and Ethnicity. Gender and ethnic hierarchies also exist among
Old Financial executives. Of the 76 executives at Old Financial, 3 are
female (see table 2.2); all 3 are of northern European descent, all either
have or are studying for advanced degrees, and 2 of the 3 work in
some form of personnel or planning functions. Two of the women were
hired laterally from other financial firms because of their expertise in
some of the "new" businesses into which Old Financial recently entered. A third woman began her career at Old Financial as a secretary,
worked her way up to LPA, and then the corporation paid for her to
attend college and eventually earn an M.B.A. All 3 of these women
believe that they are "unique" in their abilities to live in what they
called a man's world. Consistent with my argument in chapter 3 about
the role of male sponsorship in female executive mobility, each of the
three women had strong male sponsorship and maintained those ties
at the time of fieldwork. Despite their high status relative to most
women working at Old Financial, all of the female executives recognized that there was little chance they would ever be promoted much
beyond their current positions. One female executive summarized the
condition of female executives at Old Financial with a mixture of resignation and quiet resentment:

> It's simply the way things are. I can't change the whole system. I've
> got two things against me: I'm not in the mainstream of the firm and
> I'm a woman. Sometimes I get mad about it, but I've got to remem-
> ber: my mother couldn't have even gotten close to this job. She was
> college educated. Maybe my daughter will go further. One thing is
> for certain: things will have to be quite a bit different for that to hap-
> pen. Many of the men I work with aren't that happy that I'm here.
> I've broken into their club. Well, that's tough. I'm here to stay and
> so are other women breaking into the top.

Nonwhite executives have similar minority status at Old Financial.
Of the 76 executives, there is 1 African-American, 1 Hispanic, 2 Asian-
Americans, 1 born in India, and 1 Malaysian. All of these executives
are male with advanced degrees. None work at higher than the vice-
presidential level. All work in some area in either personnel or planning. For most of the executives in the firm, these 6 are nearly invisible
because they work, as one white executive put it, in the least "mainstream" parts of the firm. None of these executives had line branch

management experience either. Moreover, 2 of them had been with Old Financial several years and had been passed over for promotion more than once. One of these two cases, discussed in a subsequent section, resulted in the passed-over executive's threatening to use the formal executive grievance system and to take legal action against the firm.

Scalar Communication and Interpersonal Relations

Executives report that much of their information about company affairs comes from their superior or subordinates in meetings or memos. Lateral communication is typically formal as well. As noted above, superiors enjoy a certain leeway in accessing the worlds of their subordinates. Superiors can directly drop in on a subordinate whereas the reverse rarely occurs (except occasionally when newly hired executives from other firms violate these unwritten rules). If they do drop in on a subordinate, they may engage in what might be called "search behavior": small-scale oral investigations instigated to learn of their subordinates' latest activities and performances.

As at the tops of most stable corporations, executive secretaries often develop deep personal loyalty to their bosses, particularly if they have climbed the corporate ladder with them (Kanter 1977:67–103). Such is the case at Old Financial, where nearly every executive who attained their executive position from internal promotion carried at least one LPA with them to their current rank. Executives hired into the firm also often bring their secretaries with them. As a result, Old Financial executives can deploy their trusted secretaries to engage in search behavior. An LPA describes how search behavior typically unfolds:

> Say I call Riley's [a senior vice president] LPA to inquire whether he is coming to executive luncheon [held once per month for senior executives in the executive dining room]. Mrs. Barnes [Riley's LPA] tells me that he's flying out of town for a one-day trip to one of the regional headquarters and probably won't be back in time to attend. Now I know that Mrs. Barnes is very capable and would never let Riley out of town so he would have to miss executive luncheon. Something's up and it's not good if he has to leave corporate [headquarters] to check something out of town. I pass this on to my boss, who then keeps this in the back of his mind. My boss may even have me call back and get more information.

However, LPAs of subordinates are not oblivious to the information-gathering functions of their bosses' bosses' LPAs. Subordinates' LPAs may even try to obfuscate what they know about their bosses' activities if they have particularly strong loyalties to them. A brief conversation between an LPA and one of her assistants illustrates how such protection occurs and the tightrope that an LPA walks while engaging in such behavior. In this episode, an LPA (to an executive vice president) tried to prevent her boss's boss's LPA from finding out that her boss had called several emergency meetings with his subordinates because a large real estate development deal had gone "sour" with local participants. This conversation occurred just after a phone call between the two LPAs:

> LPA [with a concerned look]: I know that she knows something is up, but can't quite put her finger on it. They couldn't have heard anything definite up on E1.
>
> ASSISTANT LPA [hovering over the LPA's desk]: You know she'll go running to Craven [the senior executive vice president] and say that something's up.
>
> LPA: Yeah, except that I made it out like he [her boss, the executive vice president] was in a meeting all morning with some of his managers [preventing him from attending a short meeting with his superior]. She knows he has meetings like that all the time because they're working on that development out in Colorado. I can probably keep her going for another couple of days before she really starts trying to find out and I have to look a little smarter than I do now.
>
> ASSISTANT LPA [smiling]: Hey, hear no evil, see no evil, say no evil. You can't keep tabs on the guy every minute.
>
> LPA [with a frown]: If he [the executive vice president] doesn't get that mess straightened out soon, I'll have to say something. I don't want to look like I don't know what my own guy is doing.

In general, LPAs working for executives of different ranks display much of the same communication patterns characteristic of Old Financial executives. On many occasions, while waiting to see an executive for a formal interview, I eavesdropped on LPAs calling or receiving calls from secretaries of the executive informant's superiors. Such calls were invariably scripted with extremely deferential behavior on the part of the subordinate's LPA toward the superior's LPA. When a subordinate's LPA would initiate the call, she would typically first encounter a receiving secretary who passed the call on to her boss, an LPA. The sequence of these conversations would generally take the form of initial polite requests by the subordinate LPA followed by several affirmative uh-huhs to statements from the superior's LPA. The subordinate's LPA would also typically ask when the LPA's boss had free openings for an appointment. One LPA commented, "For me it's almost like talking to my boss's boss himself. She [the superior's LPA] is up there with him. I don't report to her or anything, but in a way, she's my boss too."

Executive meetings tend to be quite formal and choreographed according to a written agenda. Superiors dominate conversational turntaking in meetings, with subordinates designated to lead particular portions of meetings when called upon by their bosses. A twenty-year veteran of the executive ranks offers these observations about meetings and the process by which written agendas are constructed:

> Prior to a regularly scheduled meeting, a boss who knows what he's doing will talk with his subordinates, maybe even set up meetings with them to talk about what's going to be covered in the meeting. He already knows what he wants to cover, but he checks it out with his subordinates so there are no surprises and so no real decisions have to be made in public that he can't control. A good meeting is smooth. People say their bits and there's no spiraling off on tangents and getting lost. If they do, the head man reins them in pretty quickly. I've only seen a few meetings where things got out of control and nobody was in charge. An out-of-control meeting is a quick way to be seen as incompetent in this firm.

Again, one sees the allusion to the precise mechanistic orientation of Old Financial executives. All actions must be controlled from above in tight fashion. One also sees how Old Financial superiors use the asymmetries in their access to information (relative to their subordinates) to maintain their public reputations of being in control.

Asymmetries between superiors and subordinates also occur in written communication. First, more memos (almost ten times as many) travel upward than downward. Second, the qualitative content of executive communication differs among superiors and subordinates. Upward communication tends to be informative *and* covertly rhetorical. Conversely, superiors are overtly rhetorical in their downward communication and less informational. An example of the differences in the contents of upward and downward communication was related by this senior vice president of branch management in dealing with his superior, an executive vice president division manager:

> We had a branch that I wanted to close. The place was in an older part of [a city] and wasn't doing very well. We had a newer branch nearby that could serve the needs of the older branch's customers. It would be too expensive to make the older branch state-of-the-art. I

could have written a memo that argued for closing the old branch, but I didn't. I had my staff make up a report using several sets of data—cost accounting, depreciation of the building, customer profile—you name it, it was in there; lots of pretty graphics from our new graphics software, nicely bound cover, the works. I sent that up to the EVP. It said what I wanted it to say—Close the old branch down—without saying it in so many words. [Smiling as he tells this part of the story.] Led the EVP right to the decision to close the sucker. It's a different story when he wants to get something done. One time he wanted to close a branch that had been a flagship at one time for a small bank we acquired a few years ago. He writes a one-page memo telling me to start disentangling ourselves from the branch after the new year. No figures, no nothing, just do it. Obviously, if I know what's good for me, I don't write a memo like that to him. It's simple here, really, at Old Financial; different rank, different way to get things done.

When subordinates do attempt face-to-face influence on their superiors, they begin privately in formal one-on-one meetings or during formal lunches and, if the superiors are receptive to their ideas in these encounters, their tactics culminate in public multimedia presentations at formal executive committee meetings. Private resistance, on the other hand, typically leads to discontinuation of the persuasive attempts by the subordinate. Such presentations function as a forum with which to galvanize the partisanship of superiors. Public presentations by subordinates of policy proposals enable superiors to assess how well proposals will play on a "live stage." As one senior vice president observed about upward persuasive communication:

You've got to know how to stroke these guys. We're not down in the mail room, you know. People at this level are quite sophisticated, but you need to get them on your side. There's not really anything like a grass-roots movement here at Old Financial. You need the higher-ups to carry the message into the highest reaches of the corporation. Without them, you're dead. No matter how good the idea is, it won't go anywhere unless your boss buys into it.

Superiors directly rely on their authority to gain compliance and support from their subordinates for proposals and plans (as illustrated above by the senior vice president of branch management's observations on written vertical communication). Moreover, public presentations by superiors are not attempts at conversion, but statements of how a policy *will be* pursued and attempts to reinforce policies with which subordinates have already complied. Lateral influence attempts take on some of the same qualities as upward influence and have the partisanship of superiors as a crucial element.

One might expect that the close attention paid by superiors and subordinates to one another's activities would breed a few strong interpersonal ties among Old Financial executives. The reality is that there are personal ties among Old Financial top managers, but these are few and far between, as one executive explains below.

> Some of us have been in this business nearly forty years now and we certainly know each other. I wouldn't say there are many friends though. You see, you can work with a boss and you get to know him as a colleague, how he deals with corporate issues, what his managerial philosophies are, but you don't necessarily get to know him as a friend.

Implicit in this statement is a pervasive feature of social life at Old Financial: social attention focuses vertically between *offices* rather than between *incumbents*. Among executives who "grew up" in Old Financial, there is familiarity, but few close friendships. Executives new to Old Financial find even fewer personal attachments, generally keeping to themselves and finding their friendships outside of the firm. A newcomer had this to say about affiliative ties among top managers at Old Financial, "Yeah, I keep up on what my reports are doing; I know what the CEO is up to, what's on his agenda. But my friends aren't in the firm."

Internal Stability and Field Perceptions

Despite its recent growth, the core of the Old Financial executive levels remains relatively stable. The top leadership of the firm can trace its roots directly to the corporation's founders. None of the "imported talent" hold key positions in the executive hierarchy; most were hired to direct operations out of the firm's core businesses. Although the firm continues to diversify its financial products, much of its business remains in home financing, whether of individual consumers or moderately sized real estate developments. Together these business lines account for over eighty percent of Old Financial's total revenues. At the same time, Old Financial executives have voiced concerns about becoming too "entangled" with large commercial financing, although such enterprises enabled the firm's first great growth period in the 1940s and 1950s. Many Old Financial top managers believe the kinds of businesses searching for funding during the 1980s and 1990s can expose Old Financial's investors and stockholders to higher risks than are advisable. Some of these differences of opinion festered into disputes among Old Financial executives and are discussed in subsequent sections.

Authoritative Conflict Management

Old Financial executive grievance issues also vary according to the target of the grievance and tend to correspond in nearly one-to-one ratios to conflict management actions. Of the ninety-four grievance issues recorded, superiors expressed grievances against their subordinates over a variety of managerial style issues, including what executives call being "rough with the secretaries" and "not being aware of a superior's vision" (i.e., plans, goals, or decisional premises). Superiors also base their grievances against subordinates on work unit performance problems, such as not meeting unit goals or backsliding from previous years' performances, and poor individual performance, in particular "not meeting personal goals." Administrative jurisdiction issues are the basis for yet other problems that Old Financial executives call "sticking [one's] nose in other managers' decisions" or "overstepping one's authority." Despite the lack of personal interaction among Old Financial executives, superiors do on occasion sanction subordinates for what they label "open womanizing" (as compared with more discreet "affairs"), "drinking too much," or generally "acting in a manner unbefitting an Old Financial executive." Finally, superiors sometimes "call [subordinates] on the carpet" for personal appearance ("dressing too loudly" or "dressing in a risque manner [applied to women]").

Subordinates express grievances against their superiors for "cheating" them out of bonuses, "passing them over" for promotions, or giving "unfair" year-end evaluations. Resource allocations also generate grievances against superiors. Subordinates, for example, refer to "getting the heart ripped out" of their budgets and "unjust" staff reductions. Like their bosses, subordinates also take issue with their superiors for management style indiscretions such as "taking credit where credit is not due" or being "slave drivers." Disagreements over organizational strategy prompt still other grievances, often referred to by subordinates as "leading the unit astray" or not "seeing new opportunities."

Peers express grievances over such issues as administrative jurisdiction—for example, "trying to give orders where [one] has no authority." Management style provides still more grist for conflict among peers and includes difficulties such as being "uncooperative" or being a "bear to get along with." Peers also raise grievances against one another as a result of different perspectives on organizational strategy. "Not having a clue about organizational goals" or "taking units in the wrong direction" are typical of the ways that executives talk about such grievance issues. Some of these issues would sometimes translate into private accusations of unethical behavior committed against the corporation. Finally, female, but not male, executives voiced some generalized grievances about the general "attitudes" of men toward them (captured in the remarks quoted in the previous section).

Grievance issues that focus on personalities are nearly absent among Old Financial executives, but present in the larger sample. One of the reasons for the absence of purely personality-based grievances may lie in the lack of social intimacy among the majority of Old Financial executives. The tight embrace of role identities by Old Financial executives in the mechanistic bureaucracy may further provide little opportunity for the development of such grievances.

As with all social behavior at Old Financial, the executive hierarchy casts a distinct shadow on the pursuit of grievances among top managers, delineating distinctive scripts of conflict management according to the direction of grievances. One constant in these scripts is their typical grounding in a penal schema. Grievances initiated by superiors sometimes develop into conflicts, but rarely evolve into disputes; that is, they rarely escalate to third-party settlement agents or the public arena. Executive superiors display a marked attempt to, as one executive remarked, "keep the lid" on problems within their spans of control by simply ordering a subordinate to cease objectionable behavior. Should this not satisfy the aggrieved superior, disciplinary sanctions of some sort may be applied. Grievances initiated by subordinates are even more rarely escalated to the conflict or dispute stage. Subordinates typically tolerate behavior they define as inappropriate by their bosses or respond to it through other nonconfrontational strategies. In contrast to these scripts, disputants who hold the same formal rank are much more likely to have their conflicts take on a public nature and escalate into disputes settled by a third-party superior.

Gender-related grievance expressions appear to vary less by formal position than by gender itself. For male executives, gender-related conflict is virtually a "nonissue," as one male executive noted. Most female executives simply tolerate their grievances of this sort just as subordinates of either sex do in the corporate hierarchy as a whole.

Table 4.1 contains the frequency distribution of the nineteen types of conflict management actions collected among Old Financial executives. Below, I describe how grievances, conflicts, and disputes unfold

Table 4.1   Conflict Management among Old Financial Executives by
                 Percentage

Action	Frequency	Percentage
Authoritative		
commands	20	22.5
Toleration	13	14.6
Lumping/endurance	8	9.0
Arbitration, informal	6	6.7
Informal counseling	6	6.7
Temporary avoidance	5	5.6
Reassignment	5	5.6
Secret complaining	4	4.5
Conciliatory approaches	3	3.4
Peacemaking, friendly	3	3.4
Peacemaking, repressive	3	3.4
Liquidation	2	2.2
Termination	2	2.2
Sabotage	2	2.2
Exit, organizational	2	2.2
Negotiation	2	2.2
Arbitration, formal	1	1.1
Formal grievance threats	1	1.1
Physical violence	1	1.1
Total	89	99.7

in the executive context of Old Financial using a representative sample
of the trouble cases collected from the firm.

Downward Actions

Authoritative Commands/Informal Counseling

Verbal or written authoritative commands are the most common
type of conflict management action by superiors against subordinates.
They typically consist of directives to subordinates to alter some aspect
of their behavior immediately and without question. Superiors embed
their grievances in their "rights" to take action for the good of the
company within their spans of control. Case 4.1 describes very well
the process by which superiors enact written authoritative commands.[2]

Case 4.1 Riley's Case (1982)

Riley, the branch management senior vice president for the central
division, oversees nearly fifty branches. He had cultivated an infor-

mal relationship with two branch managers whose branches are
part of the western division, but very close to the border of the central division. Two of Riley's branches are nearby, so Riley would
sometimes fly into Central City (the regional hub for the area) to
meet with his branch managers and play golf with the two branch
managers he had befriended in the western division. The three men
had become well acquainted and one of them even called Riley
from time to time for advice on "management matters." Drake, Riley's direct superior, learned of Riley's ties to the two western
branch managers through Riley's LPA and became concerned that
Riley's counterpart in the western division might interpret Riley's actions as a "power play" or at the very least perceive them as an inappropriate incursion into another division. Drake therefore sent Riley
a memo directing him to limit his visits to Central City and his golf
outings with the two western branch managers to the annual executive golf tournament. After sending Riley the memo, Drake released
a memo to his peers in the division that detailed the "burgeoning"
expenses in terms of time and money which site visits had cost Old
Financial over the previous year but did not mention anything about
Riley's situation.

   As a result of the cost increases, Drake was instituting new policies on site visits which would cut down the amount of time divisional executives spent outside of the office. Riley never spoke directly about the matter to Drake. From Riley's perspective, he had
not "done anything unethical or out of sorts"—he had not been accused of unethical behavior—but in the next year he followed
Drake's new field-visit guidelines to the letter, including sending
one of his vice presidents to make all the field visits in Central City.
He also discontinued all but occasional "official" correspondence
with the two western branch managers.

Case 4.1 also illustrates the elaborate interaction rituals Old Financial superiors will follow in order to communicate to their colleagues
that their units are running smoothly and that they have control over
their direct reports. As such, Old Financial executives do not appear
to engage in a practice generally known in business organizations as
carbon copying. This strategy involves sending copies of a directive to
colleagues to make known a deviant colleague's transgressions and the
corrective action taken in response to them. Carbon copying, as one
executive noted, would only "raise eyebrows" and could cause other
executives to wonder whether the source of the memo in fact wasn't
the "real problem."
Sometimes superiors informally counsel their most able subordi-

nates following verbal or written commands. When this occurs, the language used can become tinged with a therapeutic schema as the superior attempts to explain paternalistically to the subordinates how they can "get on the right track." Such a strategy is seen in the following case.

Case 4.2 The Harsh Vice President (1984)

Samuelson, a senior vice president, believed that one of his best direct reports, a vice president named Dalton in charge of data management for the division, was unduly hard and aggressive with his staff. Because the corporate mainframe computers were several floors below E2, Dalton had an office on E2 and another on one of the middle floors of corporate headquarters. Stories had percolated up to Samuelson that Dalton worked "all hours of the day" in his midbuilding office and that he often yelled at his staff when things went awry, expecting each of his staff to work as hard as he did. According to Samuelson, Dalton's actions were "out of bounds with the Old Financial way of management." As Samuelson put it: "It's fine to work long hours. Who among us doesn't? But one can't expect the lower employees to work as hard. And one can't especially yell at them if they don't." Samuelson had once himself gone out of bounds by directly telling Dalton to stop being such a "hard-ass" with his reports. After issuing those orders, Samuelson met with Dalton for a long lunch at a private club away from corporate headquarters and advised him how he could motivate his subordinates without being so "harsh." Dalton held fast to his beliefs about how hard his staffers should work but also believed, in his own words, that he had "lost some perspective." The two periodically met for lunch thereafter to discuss Dalton's progress in his attempts, in Dalton's words, to "make over" his management style more in line with the Old Financial way.

Grievance-related informal counseling also involves sending subordinates to management-training seminars, college night courses, and drug and alcohol rehabilitation centers. In such cases, Old Financial superiors typically talk about how they and the organization "saved" the miscreant in question. In some instances, executives are in fact "saved" and return to the organization to their same jobs. More often, executives return to jobs with their duties redefined and their jurisdictional scope diminished; they have been taken out of what executives call "the mainstream."[3]

When superiors fail to obtain satisfaction through authoritative commands or the occasional informal counseling, they often turn to a variety of disciplinary sanctions, including reassignment to positions of lesser responsibility within their span of control, transfer of resources from one subordinate to another, or termination from the company. These strategies typically occur somewhere in the operational twilight between confrontation and nonconfrontation. Sometimes offending parties are directly confronted with their "offenses" and then action is taken. At other times, offending parties are confronted in muted ways with grievances followed by further conflict management action. At still other times, offending parties, as one senior executive put it, "never know what hit them."

Obviously missing from this repertoire of downward negative sanctions is a strategy commonly used by supervisors at the middle and lower levels of most organizations (e.g., Etzioni 1961): temporarily reducing compensation or, as it is commonly known, "docking one's pay." It appears as though reductions in personal compensation for any reason are relatively unknown as a grievance- or nongrievance-related practice at Old Financial. Ironically, as some of the cases and discussion in the following sections illustrate, the targets of conflict management actions can even receive increases in their personal compensation.

Reassignment

When subjected to reassignment, subordinate executives are removed from their current positions and placed into positions with less mainstream responsibility, or as one Old Financial executive put it, "shelved." This form of punishment occurs within spans of control and can be accomplished with little fanfare. It is usually reserved for talented "newcomers" who have developed reputations of being particularly capable, but who are believed by their superiors to be particularly *incapable* at the moment, or for older "veteran" executives who have become less useful to the corporation. An example of a young executive's reassignment can be found in the following case, in which a top manager's personal life and individual performance provided the basis for downward grievances.

Case 4.3 Getting Organized (1980)

At age 34, Cramden had risen to senior vice president in charge of "special operations projects" in the eastern division, a position primarily reserved for inexperienced junior executives who needed "seasoning" and were expected to advance rapidly up the corporate hierarchy. Cramden always imbibed more than a few glasses of white wine at lunch. "Keeps me facile," he would tell his LPA. In the afternoon, he might stop off on his way home from headquarters at a favorite watering hole for a few more. On business trips, he also enjoyed his wine: in the airport, on the plane, at meals, and at social gatherings. At home, he often fell asleep after dinner, typically with a half-empty glass of port in front of him. Cramden's superior, Norton, was impressed with Cramden's potential, but also wary of his drinking: "He was continually late with reports, sometimes very uncommunicative, and never seemed to know what the status of things were; never had a sense of where I was taking the division. He always talked about needing to get 'organized.' It became a private joke among myself and some of the other SVPs that getting organized meant getting drunk. It made more sense to move him to a position where he could do less damage, clean up his act; perhaps not be so *organized.* That way, if I decided to let him go, it wouldn't cause such a stir" (i.e., be that visible).

Norton never directly approached Cramden with his grievances, but transferred Cramden to an administrative post "to learn that end of the business." Cramden also received a slight pay increase "to compensate him for his added responsibilities". Cramden stayed in his administrative post for another year until he finally left for a new position and a pay raise with another large financial services corporation.

Case 4.3 demonstrates a reassignment that became obvious to other executives in the target's division, but involved nonconfrontation between the two principals. The case also illustrates that such action, albeit punishment, occurs with a minimum of visibility to social audiences within or without the corporation and may also carry a weak therapeutic tinge to it.[4] In other cases, aggrieved and offending parties may outwardly portray reassignments as promotions and "new challenges" to "rejuvenate" one's career. Moreover, the targeted executive actually agrees with the reassignment and may be completely unaware that it stems from grievances against them.

Case 4.4 A Challenging Pasture (1986–87)

Chilton, age 62, had worked for Old Financial for most of his adult life. As senior vice president of branch management in the western division, he often had to "hustle" to keep up with his duties, but he more often than not met his goals and kept pace with his EVP, Bobson. For a few years, Chilton had felt particularly challenged by some of the new developments in the firm: diversification, new subsidiaries, computerization of much of the corporation's record keeping. Sometimes, he longed for a simpler time when Old Financial focused on what he called the "mom-and-pop customer." He also felt "out of touch" with the branch managers and divisional vice presidents. Twelve years his junior, Bobson had for some time believed Chilton's time as a "productive" member of the executive echelon had "come and gone." He also believed that Chilton's unfamiliarity and unease with the firm's new businesses and his increasing reticence to "buy into" the firm's computerization made him a "liability." Bobson did not want to simply demote Chilton for fear that such action would be seen as too "cavalier" for a veteran executive who had worked so long for Old Financial. Bobson knew of Chilton's desire to stay "in touch" with the core part of the firm's oldest business, its branches. So he approached Chilton with a "challenge" to take on as a "special assignment" a particularly unproductive cluster of eight branches in a picturesque but remote section of the western division. Bobson had once proposed that the firm divest itself of the eight branches, but no other firms appeared interested in acquiring them.

Bobson approached Chilton during a long lunch at corporate headquarters by inquiring what Chilton, who directly supervised the "troublesome" cluster as part of his duties, thought should be done about them. Bobson also asked Chilton if he had any "hard-charging" vice presidents who might be willing to take on the assignment of improving their "long-term viability." The conversation continued for some time until it became clear to both men that the only executive "qualified" to try to turn the branches around was Chilton. Chilton seemed eager to take on the assignment but also concerned about how he would maintain his duties as SVP of branch management for the entire division. A plan was devised such that Chilton would temporarily "share" some of his duties as SVP of branch management with the much younger Conley, also a senior vice president, then working in marketing.

The move was made nine months later, with Chilton reassigned and Conley put in place. Chilton gradually faded out of the decision-making processes at the divisional and corporate executive levels until he retired to the life of a casual rancher three years after his reassignment.

Some superiors also use reassignment to expose a subordinate's "weaknesses." Through this exposure, a superior can gather more information on the subordinate's "offenses." This strategy also enables superiors to structure "discoveries" of incompetence so as to minimize accusations by higher-ups of "poor judgment about anticipating trouble." In such cases, superiors sometimes deploy subordinates as "watchdogs" against another of their subordinates without the target's knowledge until well after the strategy achieves its intended effect. In the aftermath of this type of reassignment, in fact, one of three outcomes usually occurs: targets are terminated, they leave Old Financial, or they simply tolerate their "difficult" reassignment. The last outcome occurred in case 4.5.

Case 4.5 The Setup (1985)

Harris, the senior executive vice president of finance and CFO, believed that Hogarth, one of his senior vice presidents, had reorganized the company's internal audit unit such that it was incapable of "performing" as it was intended. Harris believed Hogarth thus "violated sound management principles" in reorganizing the unit. At the same time, Hogarth "trumpeted" his newly reorganized unit at executive committee meetings as the "wave of the future" in corporate financial control. Given the "small aura" Hogarth had built around himself, Harris believed he had to subtly reassign Hogarth to another set of activities and also have the internal audit unit reorganized again. Harris decided the safest plan would be to arrange for Hogarth to work with some of the "hottest young executives" (whom Hogarth had never interacted with) on a special finance task force Harris created to review Old Financial's entire management information system. Harris knew the strategy was risky because the task force could have an important impact on decision-making processes in the firm. At the same time, he had personally handpicked two of the senior vice presidents on the task force and he knew how they would react with Hogarth once they had sustained interaction with him. Harris hoped such interaction would render some "hard evidence" of Hogarth's shortcomings so that he could permanently reassign him or "move him out of the company" if necessary.

Before he reassigned Hogarth, Harris lunched with two of the SVPs with whom the soon-to-be-reassigned executive would deal and told them that they might need someone with Hogarth's background on the task force. Even so, Harris let the two executives know that Hogarth "occasionally" made "less than optimal" decisions and that the two SVPs should be wary of this. Implicit in Harris's instructions to the two SVPs was the injunction to pass on any "misgivings" they might have about Hogarth directly to him (Harris) and not share any of the information with anyone else. One month after the task force began to meet, Harris began receiving calls from one of the SVPs thanking him for warning him about Hogarth. For several months thereafter, Harris received calls about Hogarth's "problems." Now armed with concrete and reliable evidence that Hogarth did indeed have deficiencies, Harris began talking with one of his peers about how he might have to "move" on Hogarth to get him out of mainstream responsibility. Some months into the task force's work, Hogarth learned from his LPA (who herself learned of it through the secretarial grapevine) that he had been "set up" by Harris and that one of the task force members was feeding Harris "damaging" information.

Hogarth became infuriated, but never confronted Harris. Hogarth observed, "By the time I found I had been set up, what was I going to do? March in there and tell Harris where to get off? No, I have a career in the firm, what was left of one anyway, to protect. I just lived with it. It's not my fault that Harris couldn't see what I had done for him." And live with it Hogarth does in a narrowly prescribed span of control working with a small piece of the firm's management information systems.

Liquidation

Yet another type of subtle discipline involves the "liquidation" of an executive's formal resources, or what one top manager called "sucking a department dry." Within this strategy, an executive's unit gradually receives staff reductions, budget cutbacks, and decision making limitations that finally make much of what the unit does perfunctory to the overall operations of the firm. At the same time, the offender's superior may overtly complain about the weakened unit's inability to meet productivity goals or even increase the unit's goals. In this way, liquidation can function either as a punishment after offending behavior has been committed or, as in some cases of reassignment, to create the bases for more severe disciplinary sanctions. Moreover, liquidations typically occur over long periods of time compared to other conflict management processes. Consider case 4.6:

Case 4.6 Kill the Ads! (1983–87)

The rumpled shirt, the loosened tie, the large blue-gray bags under his eyes, and the jittery movements always gave Rogers the look of a man who had drunk too many cups of coffee. Unlike any other Old Financial executive, Rogers liked to, as he put it, "roll my sleeves up and get my hands dirty with the work." Rogers, a senior vice president of corporate marketing in charge of advertising, had championed an advertising campaign in 1983 that flooded a variety of local media. After the ads had run for several weeks on television and in the newspapers in one of Old Financial's divisions, that division's marketing department produced a survey that indicated that customers using its branches believed by a two-to-one margin that the campaign portrayed the company in an atavistic light. At the end of the same quarter, the finance department of the same division produced figures indicating that its rate of new account openings had steeply dropped from the previous quarter during a time of the year when the division had historically done well. Although difficult to prove, two senior executive vice presidents, not including the SEVP of marketing, Yates, believed the dip in new accounts could be attributed to the ad campaign. Yates himself did not believe the ad campaign could be responsible for the drop in new accounts, but he could not deny that customers appeared disenchanted with the campaign.

Yates sent Rogers a written order in all capital letters to "KILL THE ADS!" (with a postscript to investigate how they could be "incorporated" into a different campaign after they had been yanked from television). Yates's memo, according to Rogers, "chapped my ass." Rogers continued his regular duties for nearly two years before being turned down by Yates on a request for three new ad manager positions in 1984. Yates then asked Rogers for "budget reductions" of fifteen percent in each of the subsequent two years. Simultaneously, Yates kept the "heat" on Rogers by demanding that Rogers decrease the time between his presentations on other ad campaigns and take over the other public relations duties for the firm. Rogers continued to try to meet these demands despite his depleted staff and budget (the latter reducing Rogers's ability to farm out some of the advertising work to external agencies). Finally, Yates sent Rogers a memo that stated that he had contacted several agencies about taking over much of Old Financial's "big advertising needs" in the future. Yates further enjoined Rogers to reduce his staff in preparation for acting only as a "liaison" between the SEVPs, the CEO, and agency representatives. According to Yates, "Our advertising and public relations were a mess, starting with that damn ad campaign Rogers put together back in '83. A good ad executive should have known better than to invest so much in a risky campaign. We have a rule about how much exposure the corporation can have on new ad campaigns and Rogers broke through that ceiling plain and simple. It's like breaking the law. You screw up and go to jail. Rogers's prison was having his unit sucked dry; less budget, no new positions, that sort of thing. I talked with him and told him what he had done and that I'm the boss and I make the decisions."

Rogers was privately resentful of the liquidation, knowing that his career at Old Financial had been "stunted" to say the least. But he continued working at the firm with dramatically diminished responsibilities, trying, as he put it, "to make the best go of it I can."

Termination

Severe disciplinary sanctions in the executive hierarchy involve confrontation of a deviant with their "offenses against the company" and termination. Such actions frequently occur with what Old Financial's president calls "attempts to save the executive's public dignity" in that the offender is allowed to resign rather than be officially terminated. Moreover, termination is often accompanied by extensive documentation about the top manager's deviant behavior in order to prevent legal retaliation by the discharged executive. Documentation of this sort is also used as a threat to coerce the subordinate to resign. These records are assembled by the employee relations executive who may also sit through termination sessions (along with a member of Old Financial's legal staff) as a witness to the proceedings. Termination sessions are in fact the only time that the legal department appears to be involved in conflict management among Old Financial executives. Even so, such interventions occur when offending parties, are, as the employment relations officer put it, "out the door." A case in point occurred at the highest reaches of the managerial hierarchy at Old Financial.

Case 4.7 Taking the Reins Too Firmly (1978–82)

Graves's power at Old Financial flowed directly from his status as a relative of one of the founders. He had started at Old Financial as a teller "to get experience and learn the business from the ground up," as he put it, and over several years had climbed his way up the hierarchy to the corporation's highest office, CEO and chairman. Nisbet, the president and chief operating officer, had been with the firm for more than three decades, having started as a branch manager and then slowly moving his way up. The two men's careers met at the pinnacle of the firm in the early 1970s, when both were executive vice presidents, and they came to the summit of that pinnacle in the late 1970s, when they assumed the top two spots in the firm. During a three-year period, Graves and Nisbet engaged in continuous conflict over their corporate responsibilities. From Nisbet's perspective, Graves managed the firm "too close to the till," meaning that he micromanaged the firm in every one of its activities. Graves believed that one of a CEOs prime tasks was troubleshooting and that his authority allowed him to intervene where he chose.

Graves also believed Nisbet to be too "hands-on" and "controlling" in his management style toward him.

For three years of their "partnership" Nisbet tolerated Graves's interventions, although privately he believed that the firm was being harmed by them. In a long private meeting in 1980, Nisbet carefully approached Graves about how the latter's interventions were "undermining" Nisbet's authority in the company. During this same meeting, Graves complained that Nisbet had taken "the reins of the company too firmly in his hands." After this meeting, Graves began systematic documentation of Nisbet's "recalcitrance," "erraticness," and "poor judgment" in performing his duties. After gathering the desired evidence, Graves then claimed to Nisbet that he could document the latter's "insubordination" and that he was prepared to go to the board. Graves then asked Nisbet to take early retirement, which Nisbet did, but only after a "buyout" worth several million dollars, some of it paid upon his resignation and the rest deferred over a several-year period.

Occasionally, superiors terminate subordinates prior to building records of their offenses. This prompts a strategy known at Old Financial as "backtracking": the creation of normative documentation after an executive has been terminated. Only one such case occurred during my investigation.

Case 4.8 Sex, Drugs, and Buffy (1985)

Campbell, a divisional senior vice president of administration, was arrested late one Saturday night for reckless driving in a company car while under the influence and in possession of narcotics. Also in the car at the time of his arrest was a partially clad and intoxicated woman initially identified only as Buffy, but who later turned up with a long criminal record for solicitation and narcotics possession. Campbell's lawyer posted bail for him that night. The next day he called Campbell's direct superior, Pope, and requested a meeting between Pope, the president, Campbell, and himself that afternoon. Pope declined the meeting, having already spotted a newspaper story about the case in the Sunday paper. He suggested they meet in the president's office on Monday once "everyone had their wits about them." The group met and Pope suggested that the publicity generated by the incident made it "impossible" for Campbell to continue in his present position without tainting Old Financial's business reputation. Pope also suggested that the firm was ready to be generous in "severance pay" so that Campbell could get "back on his feet."

Pope had an Old Financial lawyer draw up and deliver a resignation letter with the terms of the severance agreement, which Campbell signed at the meeting. In the weeks that followed, Pope also
had one of Campbell's subordinates (who had been moved up into
Campbell's position in an "emergency promotion") build an extensive record containing numerous "discrepancies" and "irregulari-
ties" in Campbell's performance on various projects over a several-
month period.

Pope noted a few months after the dossier on Campbell had been
prepared, "You can never leave any loose ends in a case like that.
Anyone looking over that dossier could see that we were dealing
with a guy who was ready to go AWOL, to explode. Letting him go
on such short notice was reasonable."

Despite the fact that case 4.8 escaped Old Financial's organizational
boundaries, involving outside authorities and visibility, note how Pope
continued to direct the proceedings, with the president also present
in order to communicate to Campbell and his lawyer that Pope was
operating with the backing of the highest reaches of the firm. This case,
like the vast majority of downward grievance pursuits in the authoritative order at Old Financial, unfolded within the rule-oriented rhetorics
and rituals of formal authority. If downward conflict management unfolds in the hard light of the formal hierarchy, upward grievances unfold in its shadows. So dark are these shadows that many upward
grievances never see the light of day of any kind. Moreover, many superiors are not aware that their subordinates harbor grievances against
them or that they are the targets of upward, covert actions, even when
they are pursued tenaciously and aggressively by their subordinates.

Upward Strategies

Toleration, Avoidance, and Exit

When subordinates face difficulties with their superiors, they most
often react with inaction, tolerating whatever they find objectionable
about their bosses (e.g., Baumgartner 1984a:83–84; Merry 1979); sometimes this process is referred to as *endurance*. Subordinates often hold
longstanding grievances against their bosses, secretly hoping that they
will be punished in some way for their transgressions.

Case 4.9 Fooling Around in Finance (1983)

Harris, the CFO, had been married for twenty-six years. He was also
known to be dating some of his female clerical staff in violation of

the unwritten company rules against such behavior. Despite his direct reports' disdain for his behavior, they neither brought the matter up to their boss nor contacted the CEO or president about his conduct. Some of Harris's subordinates developed elaborate fantasies in which Harris' trysts were discovered and he received his just deserts by being hit with paternity suits or being "ruined" by being "written up in the newspaper." One subordinate even recounted a recurring "daydream" that Harris would be discovered by an avenging husband who would shoot Harris dead, thus punishing him for his deeds.

None of these punishments ever befell Harris. Instead, as one of the offended put it, they "just let things take their own course. Harris is a highly respected leader in this company. You can't just assassinate a fellow's character for this kind of behavior." This case never evolved beyond the grievance level, and eventually was "accepted" as one of Harris's "bad" personal habits.

Subordinates also engage in a range of temporary avoidance and exit strategies to manage their grievances and conflicts with superiors. Subordinates often use their LPAs in the service of such strategies, throwing up what one executive called a "wall of unavailability" in front of their superiors. Case 4.10 illustrates this kind of temporary avoidance in response to authoritative commands.

Case 4.10 Infinite Hold (1985)

Riggs had his own way of doing things: He drove a foreign sports car (most other Old Financial executives preferred Lincolns or Cadillacs), he wore brown suits (most other Old Financial executives wore black, gray, or navy suits), and he preferred a hands-on management style in everything he did. Riggs directed insurance subsidiaries and reported directly to Mills, the senior executive vice president in charge of all subsidiaries. Riggs traveled far more than any other senior executive, meeting with subsidiary directors and visiting field sites. Mills often found Riggs's traveling superfluous and believed that Riggs spent too much time micromanaging rather than looking at the "big picture" of the overall "business direction" for Old Financial insurance subsidiaries. Mills believed this even though the "numbers" indicated that subsidiaries under Riggs's control were returning handsome quarterly earnings.

Nonetheless, Mills ordered Riggs to cease much of his traveling and to devote more time to planning and acquisition. Mills's directives, as Riggs put it, "irked" him. Riggs complied by reducing his meetings in the field with subsidiary directors. Simultaneously, he made direct meetings between himself and Mills more difficult to arrange. Whenever Mills's LPA called to arrange a meeting between Mills and Riggs, Riggs instructed his LPA to place Mills's LPA on what he called "infinite hold" and then afterwards to provide a lengthy account for the hold that would indicate the amount of activities occurring in Riggs's office. She was then instructed to "dance around dates" proposed by Mills's LPA, to ask Mills's LPA to call back so that tentative meeting dates could be confirmed with Riggs, and to reschedule meetings with Mills whenever possible. Such avoidance was easy to accomplish because Riggs's LPA was particularly adept at providing convincing accounts in the unruffled Old Financial communication style that justified scheduling difficulties based on Riggs's "intensified efforts" at acquisitions and planning.

Grievance-based exit from Old Financial also occurs in nonconfrontational manners.

Case 4.11 A Courageous Stand (1984)

Keesing, a senior vice president in the eastern division, left Old Financial after repeated unsuccessful efforts over a four-year period to convince Downs, his EVP, that the division should concentrate more of its efforts on financing new high-tech firms in the midst of a rapidly expanding local electronics industry. Keesing complained in an interview that Downs agreed that the numbers supported getting into the high-tech financing market and that Keesing had the experience to make the venture "go," yet Downs would not take a "courageous stand" and commit to the strategy for fear that it might not be the direction Downs's superior wanted to go. During the four-year period, Keesing never complained to Downs or expressed his grievances to other colleagues. Finally, he resigned from Old Financial because, as he told Downs during a formal exit interview, he could not pass up an opportunity to join a bank that was already heavily into high-tech financing.

Keesing privately confided that "Downs flew in the face of a sound business opportunity. I couldn't work anymore for a manager like that and a firm that moved at glacier speed like Old Financial. These guys are violating the mission statements we all wrote about sound business policy. It's a violation of the business policy of the firm itself!" (emphasis by the informant).

Case 4.11 demonstrates how executives can live with their grievances for years without taking action because of their structural positions vis-à-vis their superiors, yet still frame their grievances penally. Short of leaving Old Financial, executives find it difficult to arrange unit transfers out of their divisions as a way to permanently avoid their

superiors within the firm. Because superiors within authority jurisdictions are solely responsible for personnel decisions, an executive subordinate wishing to transfer would have to "go through their superior"
to do so. As a result, as this senior executive vice president put it, "You
often have to live with the harsh realities that life in a big corporation
is not a bed of roses. You may simply have to hope that one day you
will be promoted out of the bad situation or that your boss will be promoted."

Together with cases 4.7 and 4.8, case 4.11 also illustrates how "push"
factors are necessary but rarely sufficient to lead an Old Financial executive to resign from the firm. Lucrative opportunities outside the firm
or severance packages must coincide with motivating grievances for
executives to leave Old Financial. In any event, avoidance of any sort is
rarely admitted to by practitioners to targets. Accounts of scheduling
difficulties can continue indefinitely, all behind the veil of civility pervasive among Old Financial executives. Such civility even inheres
when executives leave their firms under adverse circumstances (such
as in case 4.11 above), when exit is only portrayed as a good "career
opportunity" for the aggrieved party. Despite the prevalence of nonconfrontational upward conflict management actions, subordinates
also express upward grievances with more open strategies.

Conciliatory Approaches

On occasion, subordinates confront their superiors. Even then, they
rarely take a forceful stance, and confrontation may have very little
effect on the behavior of the superior. When they do confront their
superiors or receive downward complaints, subordinates are quick to
try to resume outwardly normal relations via "conciliatory approaches" (Baumgartner 1984a:86–88) with their superiors or even establish closer personal ties than existed prior to their troubles. Executives enact such approaches in highly ritualistic ways, calling them by
such names as "treading a fine line," "creeping into the lion's den," and
a term that is the same as a conflict management form first discussed
by Blake and Mouton (1964), "smoothing." In all of these variations,
subordinates "prepare" a superior by multiple apologies or lavish
lunches at which the subordinate may often focus on talking about the
superior's latest plans, all the while trying to interject, when appropriate, some of their own plans for increasing productivity. At the same
time, Old Financial subordinates who express their grievances during
conciliatory approaches report simultaneously harboring desires directed toward punishing their superiors in some manner, rather than

simply interpreting wrongs committed by the superior as some tear in the social fabric in need of repair as in a conciliatory schema. Conciliatory approaches as practiced by Old Financial subordinates thus represent conflict management where multiple schemas are sometimes in operation or where behavioral scripts depart from the corresponding schema being used by the aggrieved party. As a result, conciliatory approaches carry great risks for subordinates should they "leak" out their desires to punish their superiors. Consider the conciliatory approaches in case 4.12.

Case 4.12 Soothing an Angry Boss (1985)

> An executive vice president named Marask became upset when he received an "angry memo" from his superior, Reale (senior executive vice president of branch management), demanding that he immediately forward late revenue reports for several branch "clusters" in his division to the corporate branch management offices at headquarters. Marask complied and sent back a note along with the reports, apologizing for the delays and arranging to have lunch with Reale the next time he visited corporate headquarters. At the lunch, Marask apologized again for his tardiness with the reports and explained that he had "no one to blame but himself." He then explained that one reason the reports had been late was that the procedure used for reporting revenues was new that month. Many of the branches in the division were not yet tied into the firm's computer network and had to mail their data to divisional headquarters. He also told Reale that he was a bit "taken aback" by his memo, but that he understood how Reale felt. He further asked Reale if he could "hold up" on the memos and "bear" with him over the next couple of months while everybody adjusted to the new system. Marask urged Reale to call him directly if there were any further problems, adding that they should try to work as closely as possible during this "transition."
>
> Privately, Marask believed that Reale should have his year-end bonus suspended for being so "impatient" with him. In an interview, Marask confided that it was "inexcusable" for a "good" superior not to "understand" the hardships that he was experiencing with the new system. Marask added, "A good superior backs his people up. This kind of behavior is way out of bounds."

Conciliatory approaches can also occur with the aid of supporters. Some supporters are drawn wittingly and unwittingly from the ranks of the large clerical staffs that surround executives. Other supporters may be senior executives who do not work within a subordinate's span of control but who played key roles in sponsoring the subordinate into the executive ranks. As generally argued in chapter 3, the latter kind of social support was pervasive among female executives in the overall sample and among male executives who have strong mentoring relations with senior executives. Both kinds of supporters may be deployed in "softening" tactics which often lay the groundwork for later conciliatory approaches.

Case 4.13 With a Little Help from My Friend (1984–85)

Fuller began as a staff executive secretary at Old Financial. Through her own perseverance and abilities, as well as the sponsorship of her former boss Yates (now the marketing SEVP (see case 4.6), she had risen to senior vice president of administration in the central division. In each of the previous three years, her superior, Drake (see case 4.1), had not rated Fuller in the highest evaluative categories during year-end evaluations. Fuller privately believed that Drake was a "sexist" who still considered her a "glorified" secretary. She claimed that she brought the central division's personnel practices "out of the Stone Age," redesigned the executive compensation system, and had also participated in several companywide planning committees which in turn had benefited the central division. Yates and Fuller were still regular lunch partners whenever Fuller visited corporate headquarters, and their conversations would sometimes naturally turn on Fuller's relations with Drake. After her third consecutive year of "moderately" positive ratings by Drake, Fuller directly asked Yates at lunch what he honestly thought of her performances since she had become an SVP. Yates pondered the question for a moment and then responded with one word, "stellar," followed by a detailed assessment of her abilities relative to those of her "competitors." After Yates's comments, Fuller responded, "It's too bad Drake doesn't see what you see." Yates then suggested to Fuller that she approach Drake carefully about the evaluations and ask for some help in "getting over the hump." (Fuller had already done this after the first year she believed she was slighted.) Yates then suggested that Fuller pass through her LPA to Drake's LPA some "news" about a new EVP slot that was being created at the corporate level to direct Old Financial's strategic planning efforts. The slot would directly report to the CEO and have access to the board. Although he "leveled" with Fuller that the CEO had his eye on an SVP of finance for the slot, Yates also believed that Drake might believe that Fuller would be a viable candidate because of her background in corporate planning. Drake would also realize that Fuller's knowledge of the new position must have come directly from Yates, thus reinforcing Drake's knowledge of her personal tie to a powerful sponsor. Fuller enacted the strategy (although her LPA overstepped the bounds of the ruse by stating that Fuller had "applied" for the position). Fuller then followed up this tactic with several lunches with Drake in which she asked for counseling from him in order to make herself a more effective executive. In the ensuing months, Fuller noticed that Drake came to rely on her more during divisional executive meetings and also discussed with her at lunch whether she might be interested in becoming senior vice president of branch operations if that slot opened up. Fuller remarked a few months after the initial actions in this case had largely ended that it had been a "harrowing" experience and would continue to be so until she could get out from under Drake's control. Until then, she was glad to have "a little help from her friend" whenever it was needed.

Fuller's tie to Yates (particularly as it was expressed in their pivotal lunch conversation) functioned in a number of ways in this case. It reinforced and legitimated Fuller's belief that Drake had slighted her during year-end evaluations. It also syndicated the risk that Fuller ran in confronting Drake. In one sense, Fuller no longer confronted Drake alone, but with Yates backstage, a situation about which Drake would no doubt be aware because of the information he received through his LPA prior to his lunches with Fuller. Moreover, the circulation of information regarding Fuller's candidacy for a position with a direct report to the president also enhanced Fuller's respectability. It meant that she would approach Drake from a higher informal status position than she might have otherwise occupied. Thus, Yates's social support appears to have facilitated confrontation in case 4.13, yet Fuller's confrontation still followed the normative contours of other upward conflict management in its carefulness, civility, and appeasement.

Secret Complaints

Not all executives react to objectionable behavior by their superiors through toleration, avoidance strategies, or conciliatory approaches. When subordinates develop longstanding grievances against their bosses, they may complain to their LPAs, executive subordinates, families, friends away from work, or professional therapists. Conflict management of this type has generally been termed *secret complaints* because they are typically unknown to the offending party (Baumgartner 1984a:88–90) and may develop into gossip if they are diffused through a social network. Although executives may use their secret complaints occasionally to mobilize allies, they more often are simply "letting off steam" or using secret complaining as a form of gossip to judge parties without their knowledge (e.g., Merry 1984). Complaining secretly to members of the firm, however, has its costs. LPAs or managers may use such privileged information against the complainant at a later time or may "accidentally" circulate the complaint through the company until it reaches its target. For such reasons, executives report family life often provides the "safest" haven for secret complaining about conflict at work. Dual-career couples, however, may be especially disadvantaged when it comes to using their families to air secret complaints. Listen to this executive's comments about secret complaining at home:

> My husband and I used to work for the same firm, but in different ends of it. We were both vice presidents. When we came home, we felt like we could never get away from the business. I would complain about something somebody was doing and he would do the same. It was a never-ending cycle. Now we work for different firms and at least the players have changed. I almost look forward to parties to see some of the asses that Phil talks about. I sometimes envy my colleagues who don't have a working wife [sic]. They can come home to a safe haven, to someone who doesn't know their world firsthand and let it all out, get a sympathetic ear and someone on their side. Sometimes I wish Phil would retire and just write that novel he's always been threatening to do. It might be healthy for both of us!

Sabotage

Less frequently, subordinates act against their superiors in a manner resembling sabotage (see generally Baumgartner 1984b). Such tactics often involve supplying a superior with incomplete or inaccurate information for presentation at a meeting of the superior's peers or superiors. Although only two grievance expressions of this sort were recorded during fieldwork, Old Financial executives speculated that the practice might be more widespread than my data reflect because top managers did not want to admit that they had ever participated in it or contemplated such action. Local terminology for sabotage reflected this aversion: "dirty tricks," "black operations," or "back stabbing."

As can be seen in case 1.1 in chapter 1 ("Hanging the Pig Out to Dry"), sabotage can act as a tacit appeal for support in the face of a persistently annoying or conflictive superior. Executive subordinates who pursue this course of action hope to "wound" a superior directly and induce closer or retroactive scrutiny of their boss's actions, thereby increasing the likelihood that their superior will be "justly punished." The saboteurs' superior's superiors unwittingly do their bidding and, as in case 1.1, leave the saboteurs themselves less open to recrimination from above. At the same time, skilled superiors in the executive hierarchy protect themselves from sabotage through the use of their LPAs. As one executive remarked:

> You're a fool in this firm if you don't believe that a direct report could come after you like that [i.e., with sabotage]. It's true that Manright [referring to case 1.1] set himself up. A manager can bury his subordinates' noses in the mud only so many times. And then to brag about it, well . . . [shaking his head in disbelief]. But he would have known some of what they [Manright's subordinates, Hawke, Morris, and Jacobs, as well as his superior, Freeman] were doing if he had a dependable LPA who kept up with what was going on and was loyal to him. Hell, she probably despised him too.

Lateral Strategies and Third-Party Settlement

Grievances against peers sometimes remain at the predispute stage and are resolved by a unilateral or bilateral curtailment of social interaction. Avoidance, however, can entail certain costs for its practitioners (e.g., Felstiner 1974), particularly when they are interdependent. Among Old Financial executives, the costs most often involve the inability of the aggrieved to complete tasks because of information or expertise needed from an avoided colleague. Disputants may also have been assigned a joint task to complete and are officially enjoined from separating.

Many grievances between peers escalate to conflicts via the exchange of authoritative commands. Such commands obviously have little efficacy, sometimes providing light comedy as the principals continue to issue orders without their intended target responding at all, except with orders of their own. Such conflicts easily "spin out of control" with authoritative commands among the principals becoming more vitriolic until they escalate the matter to a common superior for settlement. When executives in cross-divisional conflicts do not have a common superior, informants report that superiors generally support their subordinates in conflict. At the same time, not a single informant could remember an *actual case* of intradivisional support in intergroup conflict management. When I raised this anomaly with a veteran senior executive he responded with:

> Back your reports. A good man will do it. I don't know what people have told you, but it doesn't happen that much here. I know firms

where it does happen. First of all, people really don't have all that much to do with one another across divisions. If one of your guys does get into it with someone in another division, the first instinct I guess is to shut it down no matter how you do it. We don't get a lot of people going out on a limb here. That's not the way we do business here.

"Shutting down" a dispute between subordinates usually does not mean third-party settlement because of the aspersions such visible actions could cast on the settlement agent's ability to keep his "flock in order." When settlement does occur within spans of control, it most often takes the form of quick "peacemaking." Less common is informal arbitration (simply called "arbitration" by Old Financial executives) and even rarer is the use of formal grievance procedures. In general, peacemaking suspends whatever open hostilities exist between the principals, while not taking issue with any of the underlying causes or responsibilities for the dispute (Black and Baumgartner 1983:98–99, 106–07; see also Lewicki and Sheppard 1985; Walton 1969). In informal arbitration, on the other hand, settlement results from a review of evidence, the assignment of responsibility for various acts committed by the disputants, and the declaration of winners and losers (Black and Baumgartner 1983:102–04; see also Mentschikoff 1961).

Peacemaking

Peacemaking most often occurs spontaneously at Old Financial executive meetings. The chair of a meeting, usually a direct superior of those in conflict, intervenes between the disputants with a few words such as "I think this discussion has gone far enough"; "Perhaps this issue is better left to a meeting between you two [referring to the principals, but can refer to more than two antagonists]"; or simply "Let's move on."

However, disreputable executives who attempt peacemaking often fail in their attempts, as case 4.14 demonstrates.

Case 4.14 The Hip Shooters (1985)

Downs, EVP of the eastern division (see case 4.11), was regarded by his subordinates as a "weak" executive—a manager who did not make timely decisions and would not back up his subordinates in their dealings with other executives. When Downs made decisions, it was usually without consulting his subordinates about it even when such decisions affected them directly.

In 1985, a conflict developed between two of Downs's direct reports, White and Fiske, about whether Old Financial should jump "feet first" into the rapidly expanding real estate development business in the western division. According to White: "At the time there was a lot of talk in the industry about these massive real estate deals being put together in the West with little regulation that could encumber investment, so it seemed like a gold mine. We were all set up do it. But I had some information that indicated that one of our largest competitors was going to move in on us. So it seemed simple. We move a few months earlier and try to round up some big deals. But Fiske, our finance guy, is really fiscally conservative; too conservative in reality. He didn't think we should commit so many eggs to one basket." Fiske believed White to be a "hip shooter . . . incapable of putting risk in proper perspective." At a divisional executive committee meeting, the two executives each attempted to direct the other to "stand down" from his position. According to Fiske, "I resisted bowing to White's pressures. I was incensed that he was telling me how I should ready finance for this move [into large real estate deals]." According to White, Downs stepped into the conflict and "says cool it. . . . This guy [Downs] hardly knew what Fiske and I were talking about. Talk about me hip shooting. Downs was hip shooting, only he was firing blanks. We kept right on with our discussion. And Downs didn't say another word."

White eventually "jumped rank" by going over Downs's head to Reale, the SEVP of branch management (see case 4.12) about the dispute. As unusual as this strategy is among Old Financial Executives, it succeeded in that Reale paid close attention to Downs's activities and "interviewed" several of Downs's subordinates at secret lunches and secret meetings. White also replaced Downs eighteen months later after Downs was reassigned to a corporate position in special projects.

Ironically, White faced increasing pressure from the Old Financial board of directors to limit the corporation's involvement with several large real estate deals. Some members of the board believed that one of Old Financial's subsidiaries, a real estate development firm, should be most involved and the "mainstream" parts of the firm should stay in the background in large-scale development.

Less often, peacemaking occurs in more time-invested and subtle processes in which third-party executives attempt, as they put it, to "redirect" a dispute to a more "productive situation." Such intervention thus resembles what Black and Baumgartner (1983:99–100) term *friendly peacemaking* because of the care taken by the settlement agent to establish a mutually beneficial peace. These cases usually come to the attention of a superior through the appeal of one of the principals or through the superior's LPA. In some instances, subordinates approach their superiors for "advice" on how to handle a "difficult peer." An appeal for advice may then evolve into a request to be separated from the subordinate's antagonist. Under such conditions third parties may have what Old Financial managers call a "three-party" with the principals at a lunch in an attempt to suspend hostilities. As one executive noted, three-parties are not intended to "work everything out" among disputants, but only to get the principals back on "terms" so that they can take care of the problem themselves.

Peacemaking that is far more hostile toward disputants, termed *repressive* by Black and Baumgartner (1983:106–07), also occurs among Old Financial executives. Unlike friendly peacemaking, executive settlement of this sort often ends with both disputants being reassigned to duties "out of the mainstream"; in effect, they are jointly punished for their dispute. As one executive put it:

> If you have two people who are in a snit, sometimes you just shut it down without caring what happens to the managers [the principals]. That happens when you see there's no hope of saving the people involved. The situation [dispute] just has to end or else your colleagues will start thinking you can't handle *your* job [emphasis by the informant].

Informal Arbitration

Informal arbitration also occurs in response to lateral executive disputes. It differs significantly from peacemaking in that evidence is systematically presented by each disputant, and the third party declares a winner and loser. Case 4.15 illustrates the process at Old Financial.

Case 4.15 Cash Flow (1986)

Allworth, a senior vice president of corporate planning, and Naber, a senior vice president in corporate finance, engaged in conflict during several weeks over whose model was more appropriate to use in forecasting cash flow through Old Financial's branch offices during an upcoming fiscal year. Allworth's model yielded higher expected cash flow than Naber's, which could seriously affect the rest of the company's planning effort, including its pending budget. During the dispute, the parties issued several "heated" memos ordering each other, as one executive put it, to "cease and desist." Naber threatened to take the matter before the board of directors and at one point even threw a stack of data printouts at Allworth in the latter's office. The president intervened, without either principal's requesting it, prior to a senior executive meeting to discuss budget allocations for the next three years. He had seen drafts of the models and supporting materials several times. Even so, he visited the disputants in their offices and requested a final draft of their models so that he could make a decision on the matter and announce it at the meeting. He made a decision after a meeting with Harris, the CFO (see case 4.9), who concurred with the president that the firm should adopt Naber's model because of its sounder grounding in the "customary stance" of the firm. The president met privately with each disputant to tell them of his decision. During his meeting with Naber, he gently "scolded" her for her behavior toward Allworth (according to Naber and the president). At his meeting with Allworth, the president suggested that Allworth devote his energies to strategic planning and "leave the finance to finance." The president then announced his decision at the next executive committee meeting and further announced it in a corporate-level memo. Allworth regarded the decision with some disdain but never openly challenged it. Naber was privately irritated by her "scolding" but kept her grievances to herself.

Despite the fact that subordinates outwardly accept such interventions and outcomes in informal arbitration (particularly if they involve reputable superiors), they are usually shunned by disputants who consider them a public "blow" against their ability to handle their own responsibilities. Naber commented on the dispute in case 4.15:

Nobody wants to have your boss intervene and shut down a problem between yourself and another colleague. Allworth was in over his head. He had stepped over his jurisdiction to begin with. He needed a slap in the face. He shouldn't have been allowed to put forth such a stupid model. There were some other things going there about the role of corporate planning in finance and I hate to say this, but the fact that I'm a woman may have been threatening to Allworth.

For his part, Allworth added:

It was a little embarrassing to have the president arbitrate between us. The situation with my colleague [Naber] spun out of control. My God, I couldn't believe that an Old Financial executive could throw something at me. She was totally out of bounds. It had to go up the line or else we might have had a budget stalemate on our hands. I knew that I was dead meat with Naber's ties into the CFO's office.

The president wasn't going to take on all of finance [Naber and CFO Harris].

Other executives in the firm reacted quite negatively to this dispute because both executives, as one senior manager put it, "stepped well over the boundaries of appropriate executive behavior." According to the president:

> The situation with Naber and Allworth was quite serious from a personnel standpoint, from an organizational standpoint. I applied some very gentle sanctions to both of them. In another firm the president might wade in and send both of them someplace far, far away, or even terminate them. But we don't do that at Old Financial. We're cautious here, some would say a little stodgy. We handle people's money and you have to be careful in all facets of the business, whether it's personnel issues or planning or whatever.

Formal Grievance Procedures

Consistent with their mechanistic bureaucracy, only one formal grievance has been filed by one Old Financial executive against another. This occurred approximately one year before my fieldwork. In most cases involving nonexecutives, the employee relations executive acts as an ombudsman (fact finder) or an arbitrator between disputants. At the executive level, this role is filled by the president. Most executives, in fact, are disinclined to resort to the procedures and some are even ignorant of their availability. Reasons for their reluctance range from "not wanting to be seen as scarred" (i.e., developing a bad reputation within the company) to being afraid of being "put on the shelf later" should they file against a superior (i.e., engendering reprisals from a superior in the form of a reassignment). In one case a subordinate used threats of formal filing with informal tactics to harass his superior.

Case 4.16 Make My Day (1984)

Armitraj, a vice president born in India, was denied a promotion from divisional vice president of planning to senior vice president of planning. Armitraj believed he had been, in his words, "the victim of racism" by Gates, his superior, because Gates had consistently given him low ratings in his year-end evaluations despite the fact that Armitraj believed he had displayed "superior" performance in his duties.

Armitraj let it be known through his LPA that he was considering filing a formal grievance against Gates. He also missed several meetings that Gates scheduled with Armitraj, each time having his LPA call at the last moment with a justification for his avoidance. Finally, Armitraj confronted Gates to voice his grievances. Gates was agitated because of the "wounding" his reputation had taken from the rumors about his "difficulties" with Armitraj. But he listened without making a sound and then responded to Armitraj's grievances by suggesting that Armitraj was well within his rights to file a grievance. Gates then added that such a filing would "make his day" because he had nothing to hide and perhaps the filing would clear up any "misconceptions" Armitraj held about his abilities. Armitraj contacted the employee relations officer to seek information about filing a formal grievance against Gates. Although he collected several documents explaining the procedures, including the grievance form itself, Armitraj never filed a grievance after being told by close colleagues in the firm that it might damage his reputation to the point where it would be impossible to function effectively within the corporation or find gainful employment with another firm. According to Armitraj, he "never intended" to file, but wanted to "scar" Gates's reputation. Approximately six months after this incident, Armitraj left the company for a competitor. Gates spent several months attempting to repair his reputation, not as a "racist," but as an executive who could not contain management problems within his own span of control.

As seen in case 4.16, threatening to use formal grievance procedures can wound a superior or even dramatize a subordinate's claim, but such tactics typically do not lead to subordinate "wins." Only one case was uncovered in which an executive filed and had a case decided through the formal grievance procedures since their inception. Nearly every informant called this case "shocking" because of its unusual nature relative to routine patterns of conflict management at Old Financial. Similar to case 4.15, an executive superior's poor reputation appears to have contributed to the escalation of the conflict into a formal dispute. Note as well how the third-party settlement agent takes more of a conciliatory stance in the aftermath of the dispute toward the "plaintiff" and more of a penal stance toward the "defendant" even though he settles the dispute in favor of the defendant.

Case 4.17 Downs Strikes Again (1985)

"Downs strikes again," Garrety claimed to have remarked after he read the official summary of his year-end evaluation letter in which it was also noted that he was unlikely to receive a bonus. Downs (see cases 4.11 and 4.16) had denied Garrety, one of his direct reports, a year-end bonus which four other peers in his division received. After reading his denial letter and inspecting the rankings, Garrety made an appointment with Downs to question the validity of the rankings and to note his "valuable" contribution to divisional projects. In response, Downs sarcastically urged him to "file a grievance against me if you really think it's unfair."

Garrety did just that. He went to the employee relations officer, Bowen, to request materials on the company's formal grievance mechanism. After two conversations with Bowen about the implications for one's career of filing a formal grievance, Garrety was still unpersuaded that he should not file, stating in an interview: "Bullshit, I didn't care what might happen. Downs was not right and he is a weasel. I filed anyway." Garrety filed the grievance, which was in turn sent to Downs for his signature. Downs returned the form with several copies of Garrety's evaluations and his own summary of the dispute. The two "briefs" contained essentially the same information with the exception of the quantitative data supplied by Downs supporting his denial of Garrety's bonus. Bowen also sent memos to the disputants detailing how the procedure would be structured and scheduled. Approximately two weeks after the initial filing, the president received copies of the case materials from the employee relations officer.

A settlement session was scheduled for one week after the president's receipt of the materials. It would bring together Downs, Garrety, Bowen, and the president as an arbitrator. Neither disputant requested that counsel or a colleague be present at the meeting (as is allowed by the formal procedures), although Garrety apparently contacted his lawyer prior to formally submitting his version of the dispute. Before the settlement session, Bowen remembered trying to act as an intermediary between the disputants. He hoped, as he put it, to "talk some reason into the junior executive's [Garrety] head . . . let him know that it didn't look good for him." Bowen also hoped that the matter wouldn't go "public" in the firm for fear that it might raise some "red flags" in the minds of other senior executives or even the board of directors about how he was "running the ship." In the end, Bowen decided that he had better get the matter settled before "lawyers" got involved and it "really looked bad" to his subordinates and the board. At the settlement session, the disputants verbally presented their cases to the president. Garrety spoke first and emphasized the "shaky basis" on which his yearly bonus had been denied. His arguments rested on the vagaries of the rankings and his undocumented "contributions" to the division. Downs then argued his side, citing the data on which the rankings were based and emphasizing that some of the areas in which his subordinate ranked low were based on personal goals agreed upon between the two of them. Despite their "objective look," Downs admitted the evaluations largely represented his own subjective judgment of Garrety's performance. The president listened to both sides and did not immediately render a decision. Two weeks later the president sent a short written statement to each of the executives finding in favor of Downs. At no time during his deliberations did the president consult in-house counsel. The statement argued that the "data" presented by Downs had been persuasive. He also urged each disputant to see him privately to "round out the matter."

When he met with Downs, the president cited several mistakes that Downs had made in the case, which escalated it to a formal grievance. When he met with Garrety, the president expressed his "hope" that the incident would induce Garrety to demonstrate he was capable and deserved "special recognition in the future." Two months after the case officially ended, Garrety left Old Financial. Downs speculated that Garrety might try to prepare some sort of suit against the firm, but three years after Garrety's exit, Bowen had not been contacted by Garrety or his lawyer.

Concluding Remarks

This chapter describes conflict management in a mechanistic bureaucracy. In most instances, grievances are framed accusatorially (particularly in a penal schema), and less often as therapeutic or conciliatory exercises. Sometimes, these schemas are mixed, creating onstage behavior very much at odds with executives' offstage desires regarding their grievances. Downward grievances are generally handled via authoritative commands and a variety of disciplinary sanctions, while upward grievances are typically endured or offending parties merely avoided. Occasionally, persistent problems with superiors result in subordinates' leaving the company, engaging in covert sabotage of their superiors' activities, or even appealing for settlement from a higher-ranking superordinate. Both upward and downward grievances carry with them heavy ritualistic baggage that communicates the nature of the formal authority to all those involved. Much of the meaning of such rituals is implicit when grievances and conflicts occur between incumbents, one of whom is an immediate subordinate of the other. Grievances between peers within the same span of control frequently escalate to full disputes and are ultimately settled in some way by a third-party superior. Overall, then, it appears executive disputing at Old Financial varies according to its participants' ranks.

These findings conform to the more general results from the aggregate analyses of the four mechanistic bureaucracies in the study. The findings also conform to the general conditions hypothesized in chapter 1 to be associated with third-party settlement, and suggests some conditions under which confrontation will occur in social hierarchies.

Even so, from one perspective it would seem unlikely that formal rank or, more generally, an executive's position in social space (Black 1976, 1984) could explain so much of the variation in their disputing. Some organizational researchers argue that the tops of modern organizations differ from lower levels because they are less bureaucratized (e.g., Kanter and Stein 1980:12). Yet some of these same authors also argue that as traditional corporate management becomes more rationalized, the tops of some organizations have become more "objectified and formal" (Kanter 1977:54). My findings tend to support the latter view, with the important caveat that, similar to interorganizational affairs where managerial reputations shape disputing and its outcomes (Macaulay 1963), executive reputations also play an important role in determining how executives handle intraorganizational conflict. As at lower and middle managerial levels, executive hierarchies formally empower superiors to direct the affairs of their subordinates in the name of the organization to which they belong, especially where a superior's jurisdiction is unitary and well demarcated (see, e.g., Blau 1955:207–28; Butler 1973).

The relationship between unitary jurisdictions in institutionalized hierarchies and authoritative conflict management holds for a broader array of social contexts than the elite levels of modern business organizations. Across a wide variety of hierarchies, the tie of subordinates to one jurisdictional authority strengthens the hands of their superiors to handle their disputes authoritatively. In ancient Rome, for example, fathers were ultimate arbiters in familial affairs. Rarely challenged, they could legitimately ordain death for their sons for unbecoming behavior (Veyne 1987:27). The decline of jurisdictional sovereignty in the European manorial system is associated with the decline of third-party settlement of serfs' disputes by their lords (Bloch 1961:359). In modern India, disputants in low-status castes are expected to submit their cases to dominant caste members for settlement (Cohn 1967). Although the social organization of executive work appears generally less authoritative than these examples, formal relations at Old Financial create the necessary conditions for superiors to handle grievances, conflicts, and disputes involving subordinates within their jurisdictions authoritatively and with very little outside interference. Moreover, executive superiors are largely autonomous in terminating subordinates over whom they have responsibility; the ultimate sanction behind their authoritative responses to conflict. Recent research on organizational communication among business managers also demonstrates that superiors use more assertive influence strategies than their subordinates (Kipnis et al. 1980). The opposite holds for upward conflict management. As with subordinates at the lower levels in organizations (Pondy 1967; Putnam and Wilson 1982) and subordinates in all types of unitary jurisdictions, executive subordinates are generally disinclined to grieve their superiors confrontationally and, instead of having direct access to the resources of formal authority and power, at best must rely on subtle strategies that enroll high authorities without their knowledge into their grievance pursuits. These arguments together with the findings from this chapter suggest four hypotheses regarding routine conflict management:

4a. Downward conflict management actions in institutional hierarchies with unitary jurisdictions will be exercised and overtly accounted for using the rhetoric of formal authority.

4b. Upward conflict management actions in institutional hierarchies with unitary jurisdictions will be exercised covertly and accounted for overtly using the rhetoric of formal authority.

4c. Downward grievances in institutional hierarchies are likely to be framed within a penal schema.

4d. Upward grievances in institutionalized hierarchies are likely to be covertly framed within a penal schema, but outwardly framed within a conciliatory schema.

The foregoing hypotheses may seem like so much common sense, but their implications are far from intuitive given the conventional wisdom about how bureaucratic hierarchies operate. Superiors and subordinates can both use formal authority as a resource in pursuing their grievances and can both draw from the legitimacy of formal authority in explaining the processes and outcomes of conflict management. The use of formal authority by superiors and subordinates to manage conflict differs dramatically in terms of availability and agency. Superiors by definition have formal authority readily at their disposal to both execute and account for their conflict management actions against subordinates. Subordinates, in contrast, have a much more difficult time accessing formal authority for upward conflict management. Subordinates must create the conditions under which their immediate superiors draw attention to themselves from higher-ups who can use their formal authority to levy downward negative sanctions. Moreover, subordinates use formal authority differently than superiors to account for conflict management actions. Whereas superiors typically justify their own agency in such matters by explicitly referring to their formal authority, subordinates will typically use formal authority to distance their direct involvement in the downfall of their immediate superiors. In case 1.1 ("Hanging the Pig Out to Dry"), for example, Jacobs outwardly maintained to all but a few confidants that the higher-ups who decided to shelve Manright had "legitimate" reasons for shelving him, but he did not know the "specifics" of their rationales. From the perspective of Jacobs's public account of the case, Manright was simply a casualty of impersonal formal authority rather than any actions Jacobs himself had taken.

Jurisdictional authority supplies the necessary but not sufficient conditions for the perpetuation of the authoritative order observed among Old Financial executives. Merely holding formal rank over one's subordinates does not ensure the legitimacy and deference necessary to handle a conflict without engendering subordinate recalcitrance, public scrutiny by colleagues, or a reduction of respectability. One's legitimacy, even in highly bureaucratized social arrangements, also derives from one's normative status, particularly one's respectability (e.g., Black 1976; Granovetter 1985).

This is true cross-culturally in a number of social contexts with institutionalized hierarchies. Historically, the leopard-skin chief of the African Nuer relied upon a combination of formal political authority (as an elder and leader) and personal respectability (as a peacemaker) to influence settlement among those in lower age ranks (Evans-Pritchard 1940). Similarly, the respectability of political leaders among the Waigali of Afghanistan enhances their success at dispute resolution among members of their constituencies (Jones 1974). Even in contemporary America, political leaders who enjoy the professional and moral respect of their constituencies have more success in settling business, neighborhood, and community disputes within their districts than politicians of lesser repute (Karikas 1980).

Respectability gained through professional excellence or by positively violating the social expectations of adherence to formal authority in institutionalized hierarchies can even protect superiors who display moral flaws in their personal character. The same holds true for subordinates. Highly reputable subordinates, in fact, enjoy special leeway in their normative affairs. Again, this effect of respectability is not confined to the executive suites, but is part of a wider sociological process. It appears, for example, that respectability significantly affects whether a perpetrator's acts will be considered unethical by other managers at the lower and middle levels of modern organizations (Baumhart 1961; Cressey 1953; Fulmer 1971; Morrill, Snyderman, and Dawson 1994; Posner and Schmidt 1987). Respectability can also affect upward grievance expressions in that highly respected subordinates are more likely to confront their superiors without fear of recrimination. These findings and arguments suggest three more hypotheses that relate to the interaction of formal status within institutionalized hierarchies and an incumbent's respectability:

4e. The power of superiors in institutional hierarchies to directly impose outcomes in grievance expressions, conflicts, and disputes with subordinates is based on the interaction between formal position and respectability.

4f. The power of subordinates in institutional hierarchies to resist the imposition of outcomes in grievance expressions, conflicts, and disputes with superiors is based on the interaction between formal position and respectability.

4g. The likelihood that subordinates in institutional hierarchies will openly express grievances against their direct superiors varies directly with their respectability.

The findings also suggest that there is not an automatic relationship between social status and the likelihood of third-party settlement as implied by Black and Baumgartner's (1983) arguments summarized in chapter 1. Respectability also impinges upon the likelihood that superiors will embrace the role of a third-party settlement agent. As implied in the cases above, executive superiors may attempt to dissuade subordinates from escalating conflicts to them for settlement because of reputational concerns for themselves. If settlement does occur, superiors are likely to take control of the proceedings in highly authoritative ways to quickly end the session or sessions rather than opting for lengthy rounds of negotiation or mediation according to a widely reported finding in organizational conflict studies (Kolb and Sheppard 1985). Stated more formally:

4h. The likelihood that superiors in institutional hierarchies will act as third-party settlement agents will vary indirectly with their perceptions of the loss of reputation such proceedings will entail.

The descriptions, cases, and accounts in this chapter also imply that formal position grants superiors certain advantages over subordinates in maintaining favorable normative status. Goode (1978:305) elaborates more generally on this point in relation to task evaluation:

> Superordinates can enter the work space or performance space of subordinates, but the latter must ask permission to enter the work space of superordinates. Superiors have the right to read the memo-

randa subordinates write and receive, but they keep to themselves the memoranda they send upward or receive from their superiors or subordinates. Teachers read the examinations of students, foremen look at the output of workers, and overseers watch the performance of their slave or native laborers, but the latter do not usually have much opportunity for checking the efficiency or intelligence of the former.

This certainly holds true in the mechanistic bureaucracy of Old Financial executives. Executive superiors at Old Financial use these conditions to help them sustain respectability in the eyes of their subordinates and peers. Much of the time this consists of shielding information from their subordinates that might indicate that they had not been fairly treated or not opening up decision-making processes at executive meetings. It may also necessitate suppressing information about losing a dispute. The normative informational asymmetries between superiors and subordinates at Old Financial are further aided by their communication patterns. Much of their communication transpires through official memos, at formal meetings, and in written reports. Although executives fortunate enough to have well-placed and highly skilled LPAs in the secretarial communication networks of the firm do appear to thrive on informal communication, asymmetries exist in the distribution of such secretarial "resources." Secretarial talent tends to be snatched up by higher-ups, leaving junior executives to less skilled LPAs or to try to keep talented secretaries whom they trust. Moreover, LPAs working with junior executives share many of the deference patterns of their bosses; that is, they tend to be deferential to their bosses' superiors' LPAs. As might be expected, the majority of written documents passed vertically do not contain information relevant to normative matters or even other specific activities of executives. This argument suggests a final hypothesis:

4i.   The perpetuation of authoritative order within institutionalized hierarchies depends in part on the privileged position superiors have in manipulating their normative status.

Hypothesis 4i may also explain why peers rarely settle their conflicts authoritatively, succumbing to intervention from above. They most often have neither the formal nor the informal status to unilaterally impose outcomes, and their largely scalar communication further constrains the development of cross-linkages that could induce negotiated outcomes (e.g., Black 1990; Gluckman 1967).

To be an executive at Old Financial means, as one senior vice president bluntly put it, "to follow authority and to be authority." Thus,

Old Financial executives find themselves looking up and down their formal hierarchies and strongly embracing their social identities as executives in the authoritative order of a mechanistic bureaucracy. The routine workaday world of the Old Financial executive unfolds with slow, machinelike precision in peace as in conflict.

CHAPTER FIVE

SILENT HIVES: MINIMALISTIC CONFLICT MANAGEMENT IN AN ATOMISTIC ORGANIZATION

What's it like working at Independent Accounting? The thing that comes to mind are little silent beehives. Young associates hover around their managers and partners working as hard as they can, doing this and doing that, running off-site, flying a red-eye here and there. Partners aren't much different. A lot of the work is done behind closed doors; it's really quiet here. Partners aren't a bunch of killer bees out of control stinging each other or their associates. Not like some of the firms I work with.
—senior partner,
Independent Accounting

The members of the Big Six accounting firms trace their origins to the nineteenth century, when American industrialists first turned to nascent professional audit firms for help in the financial management of large business organizations.[1] The Big Six currently provide audit, tax, and management consulting services for the largest private corporations in the world, thousands of public organizations, and miscellaneous other organizations requiring the services of certified public accountants. Like other Big Six firms, Independent Accounting's core businesses are in commercial audit and tax services. During the past two decades the firm expanded slowly, but steadily, into management consulting, offering services in information management, organizational design, personnel management, and high-level management training. Unlike other large corporations, Independent Accounting is owned and directed by "partners," who make up its top management ranks. More than 10,000 employees and the several hundred partners at Independent produced over $1 billion in yearly revenues by the middle and late 1980s. At the largest regional office (at which I collected the data for this chapter), 21 partners directed nearly 1,000 employees who generated $200 million in revenues for Independent Accounting in 1986.[2]

Independent's largest regional headquarters occupies several floors near the top of a glass skyscraper. Independent's building has a two-floor public lobby, with windows on all sides. Two large metal mobiles hanging down from the ceiling some fifty feet off the ground dominate the air space. A revolving art exhibit fills one end of the second floor near several long escalators connecting the two lobby levels. Independent partners rarely see the main lobby because they use a private lobby with an express elevator that links their private part of a vast subterranean garage with the floors housing their private offices. The entrance to their private lobby is unmarked—a security precaution, for although there is video surveillance of the entrance, there are not any humans in sight. The executive lobby also has a combination door handle on it that requires several codes. Visitors to Independent's offices use the upper floor of the main lobby and must check in with security personnel who sit outside of a bank of elevators.

The elevators from the main lobby bear a remarkable resemblance to those that partners use: they are both paneled in dark wood and have dark carpeting and are somewhat plain. The main-lobby elevators stop at the "receiving lobby" on the lowest of Independent's ten floors (other firms lease the remaining forty-odd floors that make up the rest of the building). The ceilings of the receiving lobby are low, but the lobby floor stretches out perhaps fifty feet from the elevator, past another security guard, to a receiving secretary opposite the elevators. The walls are covered by dark wood and the floors are covered with a rich, chocolate-brown, medium-length carpet. Wall-mounted brass lamps provide the only light in the receiving lobby—there are no windows to the outside world. Several overstuffed dark leather couches, matching black marble coffee tables, and a few magazines neatly arrayed on a single black table occupy the space nearest to the receiving secretary. The executive elevator opens on any of the ten floors on the side of the building opposite the receiving lobby. As one Independent executive put it, "Our elevator gets us to the guts of the place. Other people have to be inspected first."

Security guards bear responsibility for inspections of visitors and stand at a counter facing the main elevators on the lowest of Independent's ten floors. One must present identification once more and state with whom one has an appointment before being granted access to a receiving secretary who sits at a large black console. Beside her is another secretary with a small headset that enables her to use the switchboard without her hands. To the right of the console are two large black shiny double doors that lead into the firm's work spaces. The heavy scent of perfume wafting around the console battles for air supremacy with pipe and cigarette smoke.

One hears few noises while sitting in the receiving lobby, save the announcement of a new visitor by the security guard, the scratching of a pencil across a pad of paper held by a visitor waiting for an appointment, or the soft footsteps of another secretary. Few people pass through the double doors leading to the "guts" of the firm. Secretaries appear and disappear through a smaller black door on the opposite side of the console. Secretaries, however, always escort visitors through the double doors.

Entering the double doors ushers one into an immense room illuminated by banks of fluorescent lights embedded in the ceiling. A maze of workstations and cubicles stretches out as far as the eye can see. But there is still little noise, except for the clacking of typewriters, adding machines, computer keyboards, papers being shuffled, and hushed conversations. Nearly all of the people working in the cubicles wear black or dark gray suits. Few wear their suit jackets; some have the sleeves to their shirts or blouses rolled up. Nearly all appear to be white and in their twenties and thirties. There appears to be an even mix of men and women. Occasionally, a man or a woman walks out from one of the private offices or meeting rooms that line the sides of the floor to ask a question of someone working in a cubicle. Sometimes, groups of young people can be seen rushing from one of the private offices or meeting rooms carrying papers, binders, and large briefcases.

Most of the offices lining the edge of the floor are cramped with house "staffers" who report to partners or their immediate subordinates. Some of the offices, however, are somewhat set off from the others by the size of their doors or their positioning on the corner of a floor. On nearly all of the floors, secretaries sit within cubicles in front of these offices; these cubicles are set up so that the secretaries within can see both the nearby smaller cubicles and the private offices in front of which they are positioned. Inside these larger cubicles work partners' secretaries (all women, all white), who, as one partner put it, act as "sentries" outside partners' private offices. The secretarial desks are sometimes quite elaborate and have consoles similar to that found in the receiving lobby, as well as typewriters, filing systems, stacks of papers, and personal effects. Sometimes, a partner's private office juts out toward the center of the floor and a private secretary will sometimes be able to position herself in such a way as to have two walls to her back, while still maintaining an unobstructed view of personnel working in nearby cubicles. The idea, as one secretary said, "is to make it difficult for other [people] to see you, while making it easy for you to see them." Near each secretary is a small waiting area with leather couches without the usual "waiting" magazines or, for that matter, many visitors waiting.

One is never unaccompanied from the receiving lobby to a partner's private office. A receiving secretary or staffer brings visitors to the appropriate private secretary, who then deposits the visitor inside a partner's office. The insides of private executive offices are nearly identical. They all have one entire wall composed of floor-to-ceiling windows. A partner typically has a large burgundy teak desk at one end of their office, with a dark round meeting table, chairs, and several tables at the opposite end of their office. Nearly every surface in a partner's office is covered with papers (mostly in stacks). Offices are also equipped with multiple bookcases that contain shelves of large technical books, binders, and other books. Small pictures of a partner's family usually rest on a table behind their desk along with awards and sometimes an advanced degree diploma. Many partners have typewriters, personal computers, and computer workstations that hook into the firm's mainframe computers. Every partner's office has a private bathroom, but one does not find kitchens, saunas, or other such accoutrements common in other executive contexts (compare chapters 2 and 4). Nor does one find a private, in-house executive dining area at Independent.

Independent partners tend to be of Northern European stock, male, and in their forties and fifties (see table 2.2 in chapter 2 for their exact demographics). Male and female partners tend to be of average height, the men near or over five foot ten and the women near or over five foot five. Whether male or female, all partners wear dark suits, dark shoes, and white shirts or blouses. Like the personnel found working in the cubicles on the floors, many Independent partners look somewhat disheveled, with their jackets off.

It is rare to see partners conversing in the open space of the floors, to see partners emerge from one another's offices, or even to see them greet one another as they pass on the main floor. One rarely sees a partner lingering anywhere in sight. Most partners arrive at their offices before 7:00 A.M. and leave well after 6:00 P.M. unless they have business off site or at one of their "remote" offices in another city nearby. Some partners, in fact, are hardly ever seen except for the beeline they make from the elevator to their offices and back. In interviews and meetings partners talked at an equally hurried, almost frenetic pace, and occasionally offered somewhat elaborate explanations of firm business (particularly of technical issues).

Inside the Atomistic Organization at Independent

Independent Accounting is organized into three main "practices" that reflect its core services: tax, audit, and management consulting.

In each practice exist loosely defined "industry specialities" (i.e., in insurance, banking, computer manufacturing, etc.). The firm is also divided into several highly permeable geographic regions (in terms of partner mobility) headed by an executive committee composed of partners from each practice. Each of the twenty-one partners working at Independent's main regional office have multiple "associate" staffs working under them comprising the entry-, lower-, and middle-level ranks below the partnership. Several hundred clerical and temporary personnel also work in conjunction with associate staffs.

Production at Independent occurs via one-on-one professional-client interactions called *engagements*. The audit of an engineering firm's assets prior to its purchase by an oil company, the preparation of taxes for a large commercial bank, or the design of an information management system for a manufacturer are typical engagements. Engagements vary in length from a few weeks to several months. They also vary from "one-shot" deals, such as the design of an automated payroll system by management consulting partners, to multiyear "repeat" engagements exemplified by yearly tax preparation.

Hierarchies

Formal Authority. The official "spine" of the firm is a formal hierarchy that begins with partners who do not hold a management title other than "partner," continues up to partners in charge of industrial specialties, through *practice partners* in charge of tax, audit, and management consulting, and finally ends at the managing partner. Among the practices, management consultants officially report to those in audit and tax, who have the final say in large-scale transfers of personnel and other resources across practice lines to consultants. In this way, partners in the traditional practices retain some formal control over those partners in consulting. These simple structures are replicated at the national level at Independent's world headquarters, as well as at all of the firm's offices which contain all three practices. Below the partnership exists a strict hierarchy composed of associates that begins at the entry level and continues up a number of ranks through "senior associates" and finally to "manager," the rank just below partner.

The managerial hierarchy below the partnership resembles aspects of a mechanistic bureaucracy in that reporting lines are strictly defined, and superiors unilaterally evaluate their subordinates. At the top of the associate hierarchies are partners to whom managers report. Associates hold a formal rank in the managerial hierarchy below the partnership but de facto work for partners who lead engagement staffs. There are few associates who "free-lance" from partner to partner. Indeed, one of the signs that an associate has not "caught on" (become integrated) in the firm is their lack of work ties to a partner or group of partners working in an industry specialty. But such ties do not usually translate into personal ties. Strict boundaries separate the partners from the associates. Some partners even refer to their associates as making up a "stable of talent" or as their "private stock of workers" to denote their "ownership" of associates and the lack of status of associates.

Newly elected partners enter a world quite different from the one they knew as an associate. "Offices" within the partnership (e.g., practice partner) are rotated among partners, with partners often reluctant to serve their terms because of the deleterious effect such responsibilities can have on their own revenues from engagements. Moreover, reporting lines rarely operate as in mechanistic bureaucracies. As Zebrewski, a thirty-year veteran of the partnership, explained:

> Up here [in the partnership], we operate our own little firms. I don't have to ask the managing partner for anything and he doesn't have to ask me for anything. Sure, we share the costs of mass media advertising. If you hold office, you have a responsibility to make sure the practice is running smoothly. Most of the time, though, it's very hands-off. We share liability costs too; that sort of thing. That's why we're in the firm in the first place. We also have access to some of the best and brightest young people coming out of school to fill our staffs. But [we partners are] quite independent of one another. It's not like some bank or manufacturing firm where when the senior VP or president comes on the floor, everyone starts whistling the same tune he does. We whistle our own tunes here. Everyone can cut it on their own. That's what it means to be a partner.

The lack of formal evaluation of subordinates by superiors, a hallmark of mechanistic bureaucracies, further underscores this partner's observations. Partners engage in self-evaluations, after which they prepare a dossier that can be read by any partner in the firm and that will be used in determining yearly profit shares. Dossiers typically contain breakdowns of billable hours and other data pertinent to goals set by partners themselves. The only outside evaluation documents in partner evaluation dossiers are evaluations of partners completed by managers and clients on each partner after engagements. Most managers— the highest-ranking associates—do complete evaluations on their partners, and many clients perform perfunctory evaluations or send letters lauding their partner's efforts. In practice, neither associate evaluations nor client evaluations have much impact on partner self-evaluations, as evident in these two disclosures by Independent partners: "I look at the evaluations from associates, sure. But they all tend to look the same. I've never seen one that wasn't favorable. If I'm an associate, am I going to get on my partner about the way he's handling an engagement? I don't think so." And: "Paper evaluations from clients don't mean much. Clients who don't like the way you handle them move to another firm. A partner knows he's doing a good job because his clients stay with him."

Most partners are extremely careful in constructing the quantitative components of their self-evaluation dossiers (e.g., billable hours, etc.) because they know their colleagues will be privy to them. Partners cavalierly regard the nonrevenue aspects of dossiers, including a modified management-by-objective section, as "useless." Most partners described the only meaningful evaluations as those they administer privately to themselves. One Independent partner, Vega, described his self-evaluation process as a "gut check":

> I open up the drapes in my office so I can see the city, and I think about what I've done over the past year. If my gut starts to ache, then I know I've had a bad year. If my gut feels good, then I might light up a cigar and enjoy the moment. The billable hours are the key. All the rest is just business school mumbo jumbo.

Other partners echoed these kinds of sentiments and recounted similar personal self-evaluations.

Officially, partners send their dossiers to their practice partners for review; the practice partner then forwards them to the managing partner. Nevertheless, although practice partners and the managing partner review dossiers on case-by-case bases, they rarely take any sort of action as a result of their reviews. As the managing partner noted: "At this level, these people are really beyond review. They evaluate themselves and if they have a problem they'll figure it out on their own."

Respectability. Hierarchies built upon gradients of respectability also appear relatively weak among partners. The very fact of being elected to the partnership means more than having one's technical competencies scrutinized and evaluated favorably. Banks, a longtime partner, argued:

> When you become a member of the partnership, you become a member of an exclusive club. A manager has to have technical expertise to be a partner. Almost as important is their character, moral verve, to be elected. I can't think of an Independent partner who I don't respect. That doesn't mean some of our partners don't some-

times make mistakes. But every partner is a substantial person; worthwhile people.

The importance of moral character among partners extends beyond the firm, however. Listen to Independent partner Hornish comment on moral character among Independent partners:

> Independent Accounting partners are owners, not employees. That position carries with it a lot of responsibility. It's more than that, though. As partners, we have a responsibility to the public in our duties to see that the financial matters of firms are handled professionally, ethically, and competently. If we don't select people who are morally upstanding and professional, the whole business goes up in flames, and some of this could have a ripple effect beyond us to the major corporations we handle.

Thus, from the perspective of most partners, the moral identities of their colleagues are somewhat identical. Most partners view themselves and their colleagues as highly respectable by the very dint of *being* partners.

Seniority. Although hierarchy built on respectability per se is not very prominent among partners, seniority, and the image of wisdom that it conveys, does stratify partners to a greater degree. Evidence for this can be seen in the deference junior partners show to senior partners and in the reverential tone used by junior partners to talk about senior partners. Junior partners also report that at meetings senior members typically receive more time to speak should they desire it. As Giles, a partner for five years at Independent, noted:

> If you're in the business for twenty or thirty years, you've seen it all. That kind of experience is something we value at Independent. You have to give senior people their due, let them speak and listen to them. They don't always have the answers, but they do have insight into the business. It's something you can't train and you can't buy. You have to live it.

Gender and Ethnicity. Few partners at Independent Accounting fall outside of the typical white-male social demographics common to most corporate executives. Of the 21 partners in the main regional office, 3 are women (all white), 1 is Hispanic, and 1 is Asian-American. As do many female executives in other firms in the study, all 3 female partners at Independent have strong mentoring relationships with male senior partners. In other firms, such mentors can sometimes unilaterally or with the support of another powerful executive bring their candidates into the executive ranks, but ascension into the partnership at Independent requires an affirmative vote from partners. Mentors must campaign on behalf of their candidates. Listen to this male senior partner's experience:

> To become a partner you have to be known as an associate. Getting that recognition can be really difficult if you're a woman. A lot of men in this business have never worked with a female partner. They don't even consider them. A lot of the best women drop out before they are ready for the partnership. If you spot a hot woman associate, no pun intended, you've got to really fight and convince your colleagues of her candidacy.

The difficulties for women, however, do not end once they are selected for the partnership. Although partners generally do not work closely with one another (see the section below), some male partners nonetheless have occasion to interact with their female colleagues. The accounts of male-female interaction conform to the general findings about the iron-maiden stereotype Kanter (1977) found in her observations of female managerial role identities. Listen to these male partners comment about their female colleagues: "You know this is the 1980s when you look around the room and see women in suits and they aren't carrying steno pads. These women we have are rough customers, I tell you. They don't back down from anyone. They have to be because they're the mavericks." And: "*Combative* is the word I might use to describe the women partners I've encountered. They spoil for a fight wherever you find them. You can be riding the elevator and get into it with one of them [emphasis by the informant]."

Interestingly, female partners view their behaviors in much the same way, and with similar rationales: "I work in a man's world. They're always looking for the screwup, the mistake. So I have to be on my guard and be ready to stand my ground. If I make mistakes, then it will be difficult for women associates to be elected [to the partnership] in the future."

Despite this sense of partial responsibility for the ability of women to be elected to the partnership, none of the female Independent Accounting partners invested heavily in the notion that they could sponsor women into the partnership themselves or ever become the managing partner of the firm. As one female partner remarked: "They let me into the boys' club, but that doesn't mean they will let a woman be the leader of the club." Some of the sentiments toward sponsorship can be explained by the newness of women in the partnership: as junior partners, they do not wield as much "clout" as older senior partners. At the same time, the lack of a sponsorship orientation among female partners must also in part be ascribed to the overall effects of resistance to having women in the partnership.

It is difficult to generalize about ethnic relations when so few partners are non-Anglo. The two minority partners in the firm also benefited from strong mentorship, although both made partner in less than average time because, as one senior partner put it, "They were so good that if we didn't act fast they would get snatched up by a competitor." Neither executive recounted "differential" treatment by colleagues, although, again, neither had been partners for very long.

Sparse Communication and Weak Ties

The silent-hive metaphor also captures the general lack of interpersonal and organizational "noise" to which partners are exposed, particularly in tax and audit. Tax and audit partners send few memos among themselves, interact little on a face-to-face basis, and have few meetings (see tables B.1 and B.2 in appendix B for overall quantitative support of these generalizations among Independent Accounting partners).[3] Tax and audit partners infrequently call on one another as allies in any sort of decision-making process (corroborated by tables B.7 through B.9 in appendix B). A tax partner summed up this tendency thus: "We just don't do social activities with one another. We retreat to our own worlds whether it's at work or at home." An audit partner put the lack of interpersonal ties more bluntly: "I don't really even work with these people. Why should they be my friends?" Even on those occasions when partners do collaborate, these engagements resemble joint ventures between autonomous staffs more than group mergers. Tax and audit partners in these circumstances agree on the specific tasks they and their staffs will perform, and they retain control of their own associates.

In management consulting, however, partners have begun to engage in more of what they call teamwork. On nearly every measure of social interaction, including information flow, face-to-face communication, and formal meetings, management consulting partners display far denser communication patterns than their colleagues in tax and audit. Nor is it uncommon for management consulting partners to form multipartner engagements or to meet and participate in recreational activities (typically golf or tennis). In joint engagements, management consulting partners often blend their staffs so that they function as a single unit, rather than maintaining their separateness as among the tax and audit practices. One management consulting partner who had begun in the tax practice described the differences between the two contexts within the partnership:

I would go for months without even saying hello to one of my tax colleagues. Here [in management consulting] we talk a lot more and work together on projects. Don't get me wrong. We still don't buy completely into the whole teamwork thing. This is not some sensitivity-training center we're running here. We are all [Independent] partners after all. We all have our own engagements except for the ones we work jointly on.

Despite the increased density of interaction among management consulting partners, the partnership overall is an atomistic social context in which partners are largely disconnected (cf. Sproull and Kiesler 1992) from one another in terms of communication and social ties; this is a common finding among accounting partners (Wolf 1981).

Such atomization extends to communication networks among secretaries and associates as well. Associate communication networks reside within engagement staffs and their social attention focuses up and down the formal hierarchy within those staffs. Secretaries confine most of their attention to the sphere of activities in which their partners and associates interact unless there is a specific reason to "snoop" around into other partners' or associates' business. A partner's secretary explains:

My boss has so much going on, especially when he's off site [at a client's business], that it's all I can do to keep everything rounded up in good order. Sometimes you'll have a secretary that gossips and tries to find out things for her boss that he might not be able to find out about. Most of the time that kind of dope [information] doesn't matter much. Our guys really aren't dealing with each other on most engagements, they're working with their associates, clients; competing with guys in other [accounting] firms so it doesn't pay to keep tabs on them unless they're up to something that directly affects your boss, like some sort of trouble between them. Then, you might get a little more friendly with one of the other executive secs [secretaries] or you might go to lunch with people and get the news. Can't do it too often, though, or people will stop talking with you.

As this secretary's statements suggest, secretaries can be of strategic importance during conflict management processes, a fact that is explored in later parts of this chapter. More generally, this secretary points to the sparseness of communication and social ties of any kind among partners.

When partners do venture forward to make contact with their colleagues, they often do so via formal appointments, regardless of the formal rank in the partnership or seniority of the colleague with whom they wish to meet. Most striking about the process of appointment making at Independent is the complexity of rationales that executive secretaries use when making an appointment. On the eleven occasions on which I heard executive secretaries (three secretaries in tax, two in auditing, and two in management consulting) making appointments for their bosses, the secretary nearly always launched into several-minute soliloquies justifying to her counterpart the need for the appointment. It is certainly possible that these were performances for my benefit. However, associates, staff, and partners themselves confirmed how elaborated such rationales can be. As one partner noted:

> We don't meet that much around here, so when we do, there has to be a meeting of the minds. I have great respect for my partners, but there's a lot of people who are not gifted with communication skills. It takes a while for them to get an idea across. Technical people are like that sometimes. I'm like that.

Indeed, partners recounted the same tendency toward elaboration in the few formal meetings where groups of partners would interact, particularly when one partner attempted to sell colleagues a new idea. In these instances, partners typically took what many referred to as a technical tack, demonstrating that the strategy proposed (for example, for training associates after their initial orientation training or for dealing with client assets in specific industrial specialties) had already become a proven method in their engagements.

The lack of identifiable allies is also an especially salient part of the atomistic social context created and lived in by Independent partners in the traditional practices. Partners in these practices experienced some difficulty recalling instances in which colleagues had mobilized them on behalf of some "cause" (except for the promotion of an associate to partner) or had called on them in the management of conflict. Nor could partners easily recall associates being deployed across engagement lines to pursue conflict agendas with other partners. A junior partner bemoaned the lack of collective action among Independent's tax and audit partners: "We couldn't get partners to work together to unload the bank vault on the first floor—even if they let them split up the money after they finished. But we could probably get some movement if we let each partner go down there on his own and get all that he could."

To bring the above descriptions to life, consider a typical day experienced by Phil Dolan, a partner in the tax practice, as excerpted from my field notes:

> Dolan is an eighteen-year veteran of Independent and for the last ten years he has been a partner. He is forty-four years old. He ar-

rives at Independent by 6:00 A.M., greets me in the executive parking garage in an area reserved for visitors to Independent, and parks
his Lincoln Towncar in an area of the garages reserved for partners.
The private elevator takes us to Dolan's office. He barely acknowl-
edges two partners riding the elevator with us. From the elevator we
walk to Dolan's office. I sit down and begin poring over notes and
questions I want to ask Dolan as the morning proceeds. By 7:00
A.M. he finishes reviewing notes he made into a mini–tape recorder
the previous day. The notes concern an upcoming bid to become
the regular tax consultant of a natural gas supplier. He then calls the
president of a client in the east (for whom he "saved" millions
through an engagement with the client's subsidiary) and "personally" RSVPs to an invitation to the wedding of the president's youngest daughter. Dolan's administrative assistant, Laura, arrives at 7:00
A.M. Fifteen minutes later, Laura brings Dolan's morning mail, neatly
organized into three stacks of ascending urgency, and coffee for
both of us. She reminds him of a meeting with an engagement staff
at 8:00 A.M., a client meeting at 10:00 A.M., another engagement
meeting at 11:00 A.M., and a meeting with another client at Dolan's
South County office at 3:00 P.M. He skims the stacks, finds a magazine, and thumbs through it while he sips his coffee. Ten minutes before eight, Dolan reviews some files for his engagement meeting.
He opens his door at eight to find several associates carrying files
and other materials. He reminds them that a "student" interested in
the goings-on of an accounting firm will be observing the meeting.
One associate (a manager who I later learn is second in command
of the "staff") walks to a personal computer at one end of Dolan's offices and inserts a floppy disk. The other associates are seated at the
meeting table near the computer. The manager begins talking about
data that have appeared on the computer's screen. The meeting
lasts for one hour. The group confines its talk mostly to a question-
and-answer format with Dolan asking the questions until Dolan
raises two issues which he says "have not been dealt with systematically." The group focuses its attention on these questions and the
computer spreadsheet is forgotten. The meeting ends at 9:15 with
Dolan assigning various tasks to the staff. Dolan asks his manager to
stay behind after the rest have departed and tells him to "keep his
eye on Brown [another associate who] didn't seem to know what
was going on again."

    After the manager has left, Dolan goes to another stack of files on
his desk and begins reading them prior to his 10:00 meeting. He
pauses and talks to me about the meeting. A discussion ensues
about the backgrounds of the associates. Dolan asks that I step out
for the meeting with the client due to the confidential nature of the

anticipated discussion. I sit on a couch near Laura's desk outside of
Dolan's office. The meeting ends a few minutes after ten, and Dolan
is met by a harried-looking associate who "must" speak to him
about a tax engagement that has taken some "unexpected turns."
Dolan confers with the associate momentarily in the hall and then
returns to his office to prepare for his 11:00 meeting. The meeting
takes the same form as the 8:00 meeting and it ends by 12:00 P.M.,
whereupon Dolan and I go to lunch at the restaurant on top of Independent's building.

At lunch, we discuss a range of topics: my impressions of Dolan's
associates, his oldest daughter's plans to enter college in the fall,
and his strategy for "selling" a client he is to meet in his South
County office. Dolan jokingly apologizes for the lack of "action" I
witnessed during the morning, but observed that "that's what it's
like around here." Lunch ends and Dolan and I return to his office
to pick up some materials prior to driving to the South County office. The drive lasts one and one-half hours, during which Dolan receives a phone call from Laura on his car phone about another prospective client who wants to meet Dolan in another city to discuss a
possible long-term engagement. Arriving at the South County office
at 2:45, Dolan greets his secretary, Janice, who says the client will
be thirty minutes late. Dolan spends the extra time working on a
draft of an engagement report for another South County client. The
client arrives and I am allowed to stay. Dolan greets the client
warmly and explains that a "young student" will be sitting in on the
meeting. The client smiles and shakes my hand. We all sit down.
Dolan asks some questions about the client's firm and then talks
about similar engagements he currently has. The meeting ends at
4:00 with the promise by the client that he will get back to Dolan
by the next week. Dolan and I drive back to the main office, where
I parked my car. During the drive, our conversation ranges from
sports to music to Dolan's being unable to remember the name of
another partner which is "on the tip of my tongue. . . . I think we
once played golf at the tourney we tried to get going in the firm, but
who knows. I haven't seen the guy since. He still works here
though." The day's observations end at 5:30 P.M.

Dolan's typical day is emblematic of the habituated behaviors that
most partners at Independent experience.

Internal Stability and Field Perceptions

Quietly mining functional fields for individual clients, Independent
Accounting partners held steady in their market positions for decades,
leading to highly consistent perceptions of internal and field stability.

Partners, as one senior partner put it, still "expect to grow up and die in the business." Partners did sometimes talk about the possibility of mergers among the Big Eight (which did occur in 1989). The partners most favorable to mergers worked in management consulting and considered themselves more forward-looking than the others. They believed that the time had come for Independent Accounting to go "head-to-head" with the largest "pure" consulting firms and that management consulting, particularly in the information-processing field, was where the big money could be made in the audit/accounting business. From the perspective of partners in the management consulting practice, the sun would eventually set forever on Dolan's typical day. Such a prospect disturbed partners in tax and audit, as much because the firm would have to depart from the work that partners knew best as because it would mean a revolutionary transformation in the organizational context in which partners worked. These divergences appeared most distinctly in the customs of conflict management among audit and tax partners, on the one hand, and partners in management consulting, on the other.

Minimalistic Conflict Management

On a day-to-day basis, Independent partners find fault with their colleagues for issues similar to those that executives in the larger sample do. There are some divergences in the patterns of grievance issues pursued. Unlike authoritative orders, in particular, the direction of grievances up and down the partnership's formal hierarchy within practices makes little difference for the substance of issues raised. Issues vary horizontally between the more traditional practices, tax and audit, and what some partners call the new kids on the block, management consulting. Moreover, only a few issues fuel interpartner grievance expressions in the traditional practices. In these practices, partners raise complaints about each other related to individual performance, such as "losing accounts to competitors" or using "problematic accounting principles." Trouble among partners also arises from management styles that are too "flamboyant," not "grooming" associates properly, or being "self-indulgent" in one's communication at executive meetings. Interpartner grievances occasionally turn on ethical questions about their colleagues' "stealing clients" or "padding expense accounts."

Management consulting partners, in contrast, exhibit a wider array of grievance issues. Most dominant in their grievance pursuits against colleagues are issues pertaining to organizational strategy, or as one management consulting partner put it, "where we're going and why."

Administrative-jurisdictional "battles" over "staying out" of each other's engagements and accounts fuel still other conflicts and disputes. Unlike their peers in tax and audit, these partners also have grievances based on personal appearance, as when partners look like "hired help" instead of "owners" by wearing informal clothing to the office (e.g., blue jeans, shirts without ties on Saturdays, light-colored suits). Individual performance grievances among management consulting partners hinge on nearly identical concerns about "losing accounts" and being technically "with it" as in the more established practices. Grievances raised against behavior labeled as unethical take on similar hues among management consulting partners as in tax and audit: partners occasionally raised complaints about a colleague's handling of their expense accounts or "honing" in another partner's clients without the latter's permission. Finally, grievance issues related to management style among management consulting partners substantively differ from those in tax and audit. Whereas tax and audit partners focus such grievances around the treatment of associates and clients, management consulting partners focus such grievances on the "openness" of interpartner "communication." These issues typically address partners' "inabilities" to effectively communicate with colleagues with whom they have joint engagements or being "total lone rangers," as in the more traditional practices.

Finally, troubles between partners in the traditional practices and those in management consulting exclusively revolve around management style, organizational strategy, and administrative jurisdiction (authority). Grievances of the first sort tend to concentrate on what partners in the traditional practices call "running at the mouth" tendencies among partners in management consulting. This style issue, so one tax partner argued, involves more than haltingly elaborated rationales into which partners launch when explaining an issue, but "cuts to the core of who we are." He continued: "They [management consulting partners] spend a lot of time over there talking about this and that. Sometimes I think it's just a social club. They're always arguing and carrying on. It reaches the level of being unprofessional in my opinion. They should shut up and get on with their work."

Administrative jurisdiction issues focus on the formal authority relations between management consulting partners and those in tax and audit. Central is the "right" of "CPAs" in the traditional practices to maintain their dominant position in directing the firm and controlling the majority of its resources. Consultants believe they should be as independent of interference from CPAs as CPAs are from management consultants.

Organizational strategy issues cut directly to the core of the firm by raising questions about the future mainstream activities that Independent Accounting will conduct. As noted earlier, management consulting partners have increasingly created engagements composed of teams of partners (particularly in information systems design). Part of these "undesirable" changes, from the perspective of tax and audit partners, is the fact that in recent years the number of management consulting partners who grew up in the firm are dwindling to the point that many partners predict less than one-third of the partners in management consulting throughout the firm will have started at Independent as associates. For their part, management consulting partners fear the opposite: that the firm is not moving fast enough to take advantage of the opportunities in the general area of information management and processing. They accuse tax and audit partners of being too conservative and too wed, as one management consulting partner put it, to "the old ways of doing things."

Largely outside the locus of visible grievance issues within the partnership are issues pertaining to hiring practices, sexual harassment, and minority issues. Partners would typically respond to the paucity of such grievances by noting that the road to partnership at Independent does not discriminate according to race or sex, but depends on ability. However, one partner echoed Kanter's (1977) and Moore's (1962) statements about the "homosexual reproduction" of executive social characteristics in his statements about the relationship between so few grievance issues of these kinds at the partnership and the lack of women and minorities among Independent partners:

> Let's face it. We've got an exclusive club here. It's a men's club, a white men's club. I imagine that will change in the future, but for right now in the 1980s that's what we have. In answer to your question about race and sex conflict, we don't have it because we don't have that many minorities and women. Come back in ten years and you may see more.

Conversational interviews with partners in 1990 partially bore this prediction out. As one partner put it:

> People [e.g., men] are beginning to be concerned about what they say and what they do. We have more women on board and the atmosphere has changed a bit. I think the way partners treat each other—men and women I mean—is more up in the air now than at any time in my twenty years at Independent. It's still pretty sleepy here, though. It's not that different from ten years ago when I first became a partner.

Table 5.1 Conflict Management among Independent Accounting Partners by Percentage

Action	Frequency	Percentage
Temporary avoidance	24	31.2
Toleration	11	14.3
Strategic alienation	11	14.3
Informal counseling	5	6.5
Lumping/Endurance	5	6.5
Public accusations	5	6.5
Conciliatory approaches	4	5.2
Surveillance	3	3.9
Exit, organizational	3	3.9
Negotiation	3	3.9
Reassignment	2	2.6
Informal mediation	1	1.3
Total	77	100.1

Many of these issues are framed as nuisances that partners attempt to quickly put behind them in order to resume their routine work. Indifferent schemas pervade most grievances within the partnership with ancillary interpretive schemas taking conciliatory and therapeutic perspectives. As such, grievances among partners infrequently escalate into conflicts and almost never to disputes. The exception to these patterns occurs in conflict between the traditional and consulting practices, where a mixture of interpretive schemas and scripts drawn from their respective local contexts manifest themselves in their routine conflict management. Table 5.1 presents the distribution of the twelve types of conflict management actions collected among Independent partners. The following sections are organized according to the social context within the firm in which grievances arise: within the traditional practices of tax and audit, within management consulting, or between the traditional practices and management consulting.

Trouble in Tax and Audit

The least visible way that partners in tax and audit pursue grievances among one another is via toleration. In general, toleration involves inaction by an aggrieved party but recognition that whatever is at the basis of a grievance or conflict still exists (Baumgartner 1984a:83–84). Partners recalled specific situations or explained cases that I witnessed by using expressions such as learning to live with their colleagues' "eccentricities" or "problems," for example, or not letting "stupid things" around the office committed by other partners disturb their work. A case involving appropriate auditing techniques illustrates such actions:

Case 5.1 Depreciation Hell (1986)

Bailey and Hornish had both been audit partners at Independent for five years. They had worked together once as associates and decided to work together again on an audit of a large utility firm about to be acquired by another firm. During Bailey's previous work with Hornish, he had remembered having doubts about the depreciation accounting procedures Hornish preferred. Whereas Hornish championed methods that computed depreciation using a traditional "age-life" method (based on the depreciation of an organizational asset over its lifetime), Bailey preferred a "unit-of-production" method, which takes into account the downtime of production facilities. Bailey especially believed that the unit-of-production method should be used in the current audit because a recent downturn in the local economy had led to many of the utility's facilities' standing idle. In what he called his "darker moments," Bailey even suspected that Hornish had "cut some sort of deal with the utility to use the age-life method to inflate their assets" prior to the acquisition.

As he and the associates working on the engagement inspected the utility's records and facilities, Bailey firmly believed the age-life method to be "problematic." But he allowed Hornish to frame the determination of depreciation using the age-life method. These actions created what Bailey called a personal hell for himself because it was difficult for him to entirely disbelieve his darker interpretations of Hornish's actions.

In this case, then, Bailey allowed Hornish to continue with his method during the engagement without direct challenge.

When tax and audit partners pursue grievances against colleagues, they most often do so via temporary avoidance (for general discussions of this concept, see Baumgartner 1988; Felstiner 1974). Avoidance of this sort involves curtailing interaction with offending parties in quite subtle ways. Partners would often refer to temporary avoidance as "shunning," sometimes using more colorful monikers such as "keeping out of partner's way until the dust settles" or "going underground for a while." Avoidance tactics involved moving one's parking space in the executive garage away from an offending party, spending more time off site, walking the opposite direction when in the presence of an offending party, and pretending to be engrossed in conversation with someone else when an adversary approaches. Case 1.2 ("Green's Misrepresentation") in chapter 1 illustrates avoidance in the audit practice that involved quite elaborate actions by the aggrieved party, Banks, to avoid his colleague, Green. In most cases, temporary avoidance takes on far simpler forms, as illustrated in case 5.2.

Case 5.2 Urgent Missions (1984)

The quarterly tax practice meeting typically lasts about two hours, during which partners discuss a variety of organizational issues relevant to the practice. Gough, a portly individual who delivered each of his ideas as though he were puffing out cigarette smoke, was known to take up at least twenty minutes with what partners called his "own agenda." His agendas translated into lengthy pontifications about the state of the accounting profession, the direction of the firm, and the "education" of associates.

For several meetings running, Johnson, another tax partner, would be "called away" from the meeting on urgent business during Gough's "soliloquies." Sometimes, Johnson's head secretary would enter the room with an urgent call for Johnson to talk to a client (always a legitimate excuse in the partnership for withdrawal from almost any internal activity). At other times, Johnson would mention to the practice partner, Wilson, just prior to the meeting that he would have to be leaving before the conclusion of the meeting in order to speak with a client. At all times, Johnson profusely apologized for *his* "bad manners" because he had to leave midmeeting. Johnson privately admitted to finding Gough a bore who simply disrupted meetings and once having gotten hold of the floor nearly always attempted to direct conversation back to his agenda. Johnson also observed that Gough's speeches nearly always began about twenty-five to thirty minutes into the meetings. As a result, Johnson could time his departures to occur before or during Gough's talking. Johnson preferred to leave when Gough was "just getting going" because Gough, according to Johnson, would become oblivious to his surroundings and rarely even notice when Johnson (or anyone else) hurried out of the room on an "urgent mission." It should also be noted that Gough and Johnson had always been and continued to be on good terms, according to both parties.

Although many cases involving avoidance are so subtle as to be practically undetectable by outsiders or the target of the avoidance, in some cases, such as case 5.2, partners construct "cover stories" for their avoidance to draw attention away from grievances. In case 5.2, Johnson covered his avoidance through apologies to Gough and others who might be affected by his absence at the meeting.

Cover stories also facilitate the rekindling of relations with offending partners and, during or in the aftermath of avoidance, constrain the snowballing of old cases into new ones with different themes or into open conflicts and public disputes directly involving partners other than the principals. This is consistent with what partners want for themselves and their colleagues: to be left alone to handle their trouble without interference, without visibility, and without open hostilities.

Temporary avoidance can last for several months before ending with a spontaneous rekindling of social relations. Other cases involving partners who have had some previous interpersonal tie demonstrate bilateral temporary avoidance that lasts for only a few days or even hours. Such was the situation in the aftermath of a particularly bitter competition for a client. In the week that followed, the two partners would avoid eye contact when in the same room, or one would pretend to be on the phone when the other walked into his office. At the end of the week, the two partners were seen laughing about a lopsided loss that a local professional basketball team had inflicted on another team the previous night.

Tax and audit partners also engage in other actions that may occur subsequent to toleration or provide a prelude to avoidance. Even then, such tactics may be attributed to nongrievance-related factors by their targets or others on the sidelines. Consider this nonconfrontational conflict management in presence of an offending party:

Case 5.3 The Pipe Cleaner (1985–86)

Dales and Simpson are regular participants at the tax practice's quarterly marketing meetings. These meetings can be valuable to partners for developing new clients and for "pitching" their services in line with the firm's overall advertising strategies. Dales and Simpson have been partners for seven and twelve years, respectively, but, like many partners, do not have much contact except during these meetings. For six straight meetings, every time Simpson began a long oration on marketing strategy, Dales, who found Simpson a "bag of wind and a nuisance," began an elaborate process of cleaning and loading his pipe. Dales would continue this process for as long as Simpson spoke, after which he would finally light his pipe. He would then stare out the window of Independent's forty-third floor executive conference room engrossed in smoking his pipe as though no one else were in the room, often with his body nearly turned away (in a swivel chair) from Simpson. All the while, Simpson would not outwardly react to Dales's lack of attention.

Subsequent interviews with Simpson revealed that he simply tolerates what he calls Dales's "rude" behavior; Simpson allows Dales to be rude in exchange for continuing to talk. In general, this kind of private conflict management is similar to Erving Goffman's (1967:113) notion of "alienation from interaction" in which individuals during interaction "spontaneously become involved in unsociable solitary tasks." Among Independent partners, these behaviors can function purposively to express some sort of grievance about another's behavior. It therefore might be labeled "strategic alienation." Its other manifestations in the sample include carefully stacking and restacking computer printouts or drawing intricate patterns on paper while colleagues are talking. For some partners, these behaviors are nervous habits. When such activities express a grievance toward a colleague, however, they become strategic alienation.

Yet another part of the routine conflict management repertoire among tax and audit partners is what they call surveillance: the systematic gathering of information by aggrieved parties about those against whom they have grievances. Partners also refer to these actions as "watching" or "keeping tabs on an offender." In such cases, surveillance may seem like toleration to offenders and uninvolved observers, as is illustrated in case 5.4.

Case 5.4 Keeping Tabs (1985)

McClellan and Fowler, both in tax, run huge engagement staffs who service some of the largest petroleum concerns in the area. McClellan for some time believed that Fowler was, in McClellan's words, "underutilizing a talented young associate" named Hage and not properly "grooming" her for the partnership. McClellan began to keep tabs on Fowler's use of Hage through a variety of means: through one of his secretaries (who sometimes struck up conversations with members of Fowler's clerical staff), through an associate on Fowler's staff who had been Hage's college classmate, and through some friends of his in the petroleum industry who knew several members of Fowler's staff. McClellan and Fowler interacted at meetings and even occasionally lunched as though the grievance never existed. Finally, the grievance withered away as McClellan moved on to other activities.

As might be expected, surveillance is somewhat difficult to enact among the partners because of their sparse social ties. In all three instances in which this tactic was used, partners used what few indirect means of surveillance they could muster.

Even rarer among tax and audit partners is exit from the firm as a result of conflict. I uncovered only one case of resignation among tax and audit partners. Partners generally remarked that this strategy is a method of last resort used only in response to persistent problems with colleagues. As one partner put it in response to my questions about resignation: "If a guy has a beef with people in the firm, he can just not deal with them. It takes an awful lot of problems for a partner to leave the firm. People don't usually leave the firm, even those who don't perform. Once you're a partner you can work out things in some way." The partner's description of the conditions under which exit occurs appears to reflect the one example I collected among tax and audit partners. But even when faced with leaving the firm, note the indifferent frame that this aggrieved partner used to orient himself to his grievances:

Case 5.5 I'm Sick of This Place and I'm Leaving (1987)

Colehahn began working at Independent fresh out of college in the mid-1950s. He was elected partner in the early 1960s and proceeded to build a solid set of engagements in several entertainment industries. By the late 1960s, Colehahn had become "bothered" with some of his colleagues as a result of management style and individual performance issues, specifically Colehahn's belief that several of his older colleagues were "deadwood" and should retire.

Because of these grievances, Colehahn arranged a transfer to another large Independent office, where, after ten years of infighting with partners in tax and other parts of the firm, Colehahn transferred yet again to another regional office. The same pattern ensued and six years later, Colehahn again transferred.

By the late 1980s, Colehahn, now nearing his middle fifties, looked back on the conflict management he had engaged in and to which he had been subjected at Independent: "I always tried to put the problems I've experienced behind me wherever I've been in the firm. Just get on with the work: that's my motto and I think the motto of most of my colleagues. It's not like some of the scenes I've watched at some of my clients: people raising their voices to one another, threatening each other. It's not at all like that here. No sir. It's deadly silent. You notice at meetings that when you speak, people look out the window, light their pipes, get called away to another meeting *all the time* [emphasis by the informant]. After a while, no amount of money can keep your sanity in a place like that. People shunning you; you shunning them. I know. I did it for thirty years. It's a nuisance to work in a place like this and I'm leaving. I don't really care what happens to Independent Accounting. For the first time in my career I don't know what tomorrow will bring, but I do know it will take me away from Independent Accounting forever." Colehahn left Independent with little fanfare, ostensibly to open up a small accounting firm in a neighboring state.

Confrontation among Management Consulting Partners

The basic themes of nonconfrontation, restraint, and subtlety apparent in the repertoire of conflict management actions in cases 5.1 through 5.5 also appear among management consulting partners. To this repertoire, however, management consulting partners add a variety of confrontational forms: "one-on-ones" (a kind of negotiation), informal peer counseling, open accusations, and what partners call "replacement": the removal of a partner from their regular duties. Moreover, partners in the management consulting practice punctuate their conflicts with more definable outcomes rather than simply letting grievances simmer underground until they wither away. Case 5.6 illustrates a one-on-one between management consulting partners.

Case 5.6 Scavenging (1985)

When a partner moves to a different branch, decides not to service a client any more, or retires, questions arise about who among the other partners will be allowed to seek out the newly freed clients for their own. Managing partners may be consulted by the disengaging partner but never become involved in settling the issue. Instead, partners make direct claims to the disengaging partner based on their expertise with similar kinds of clients. Partners call this process *scavenging.*

Williams was retiring from Independent after more than ten years as a management consulting partner. Two younger partners, Dokes and Freidberg, had previously worked together as associates and partners on large engagements. They continued to have a working relationship on two engagements, but they handled the majority of their engagements independently of one another. They both wanted Williams's two largest active clients. Both partners met several times with Williams during a two-month period, often taking the older partner to lunch and breakfast (breakfast meetings are common at Independent). Knowing Williams's fondness for sailing, Dokes also hosted Williams and his wife on a weekend sailing trip to some islands just off the coast. Freidberg treated Williams to a weekend at his resort condominium at a nearby golf resort. Each of these outlays prompted grievances by the two younger partners against the other. In interviews, each claimed the other had overstepped the boundaries of appropriate behavior and argued that his own behavior had been in response to the other's actual or anticipated behavior. For a few weeks after their weekend soirees with Williams, neither Dokes nor Freidberg spoke to the other, communicating through their associates about a joint client. They also visibly averted eye contact and did not speak to each other at a Halloween party for Independent partners' children thrown by the wife of another partner. During this time, Williams confessed he felt "awkward" about the situation but simply avoided both men while considering giving the clients to a third partner, Halsted, whom he had not yet contacted. Finally, nearly four months after the scavenging had begun, and with Williams still undecided about whom to give the clients to, Freidberg had one of his associates relay a message through Dokes's associates that he wanted to have a one-on-one lunch with Dokes to talk over some "important matters." They met the following week. Freidberg described the meeting as "cordial," while Dokes commented that neither of the two men ever accused the other of anything, "but talked over what had happened and how to get the most out of Williams's clients."

In the end, they agreed to approach Williams with a joint offer to handle the clients together. They did so and Williams agreed to give them the clients. They also agreed that in the future the most experienced partner in a particular specialty (demarcated by industry) should have the first shot at clients. By this time, however, Williams had talked to Halsted, who expected to receive the clients. Upon finding out that Williams had given Dokes and Freidberg the clients, Halsted became upset but neither confronted nor avoided Williams. He simply did nothing.

At the heart of this case is a process which the anthropologist P. H. Gulliver (1979:3) identifies as an "exchange [of] information and opinion . . . argument and discussion [to] propose offers and counter offers relating to the issues of trouble between two or more parties." The agreement reached at the conclusion of the negotiation in this case, it should be noted, is explicit in its relevance to the grievances at hand as well as in laying out rules for handling similar situations in the future—qualitatively different from the implicit bargains created via nonconfrontational tactics.

Much of the negotiation among management consulting partners occurs as addenda to other activities, which allows the principals to mask (to their colleagues and themselves) the fact that they have problems with each other and, as in nonconfrontational grievance pursuits, treat such problems as nuisances to be handled as quickly as possible. Quick negotiations often occur at the end of phone calls about other issues, at the conclusion of meetings in the hallways, or even at the few parties the firm has. Two of the three negotiated conflicts were collected from among management consulting partners. The one exception involved two partners who had joined Independent from another firm in the audit practice. In all of the cases in which negotiation occurred, the principals avoided or tolerated one another to some degree prior to negotiating.

The next two cases demonstrate the limits to which management consulting partners go in mandating changes in the behavior of their colleagues. Case 5.7 illustrates peer counseling in the service of returning the partner in question to an "acceptable" managerial style. In case 5.8, peer counseling facilitates replacement. Despite the actions in these two cases, management consulting partners expressed reluctance to counsel their colleagues even at another's request because it would overstep the boundaries of proper interpartner etiquette.

Case 5.7 The Boastful Partner (1984)

Jimson had recently made partner due in no small part to his mentoring by Vega, an older partner in a nearby office on the same floor. As they greeted one another each morning, Jimson repeatedly boasted about his latest engagements and laughingly added that "a new era had dawned" in which Jimson would mentor Vega on how to deal with clients. Vega tired of these "pronouncements" and soon began hurrying into his office when he saw Jimson coming down the hall and closing the door muttering something about having to make a phone call.

After two months of this behavior, Vega bid good day to Jimson in the hallway one morning and asked him to step into his office. Once inside, he congratulated Jimson on his success during recent months and commented that when he (Vega) had a "run of particularly good success, he sometimes felt a certain intoxication." He then asked Jimson if he ever felt the same thing. Jimson replied with a chuckle that he had felt very confident and maybe a bit "cocky" with his recent accomplishments. Vega ended his five-minute conversation by telling Jimson that one of the distinguishing marks of an Independent partner is a "reserved and professional perspective."

"Too much confidence," Vega warned, "could lead one to arrogance and ruination." He then suggested that Jimson let his "accounts speak for themselves through client referrals and year-end [profit] shares." Jimson partially heeded Vega's advice by curtailing his boasting when Vega was within earshot but continuing it with some of his junior associates.

Case 5.7 also illustrates how the age hierarchy that exists between partners sometimes appears in their conflict relations. Although partners are universally civil and deferential to their colleagues, older partners sometimes enjoy some additional leeway and deference when confronting their younger colleagues. Indeed, younger partners (with less than three years as a partner) all agreed that they would generally ignore counseling if it came from an age peer. While they were not willing to grant senior partners extreme latitude in their interaction, they did allow them to, as one partner put it, "get away with more" while managing conflict.

Case 5.8 presents one of two cases in the sample where other partners became directly involved in disciplinary action against another partner for lack of performance. Even here, the restrained and covert qualities of the conflict management repertoire among partners is apparent. This case also illustrates highly strategic collective action on the part of the partners involved as well as a blurring of the boundaries between formal and informal grievance pursuits.

Case 5.8 The Partner Replacement (1984)

Samuels seemed to drive away as many clients in the management consulting practice as he generated. He had joined the firm several years earlier than Smith, the managing partner, and MacIntyre, the head of the management consulting practice, but had played an occasional game of golf with each since he had made partner. While playing golf one day with Smith, MacIntyre, and Lindsey (a member of the management consulting practice), Samuels began talking about his recent woes with a large savings and loan information system design that he had just lost to a rival Big Eight firm. Samuels spoke at length about the pressures of dealing with savings and loans in the aftermath of the deregulation of the industry in 1982 and how some of the older partners in the firm had a "stranglehold" on some of the financially stable savings and loans and banks despite not having serviced them as clients for some time. Partners were sometimes said to keep clients "dormant until such time as they might service them." This practice, Samuels argued, left the weaker financial institutions to younger partners "who might have a harder time collecting fees and maintaining a relationship with the client." Smith listened to Samuels and asked him several times what he thought should be done to ameliorate the situation. Samuels suggested some sort of policy to give every partner a chance at "good clients." He also suggested to Smith that he might need a leave of absence from the firm to sort out some things for himself.

In the clubhouse after their game and after Samuels and Lindsey had left, Smith discussed Samuels's leave with MacIntyre, who recounted several instances he knew of (some from his associates who were "keeping tabs" on Samuels) where Samuels had mishandled accounts. They agreed that Samuels's proposal "made sense for the good of the firm and the partner." After their discussion on the golf course, MacIntyre mobilized some other partners in the management consulting practice to be prepared to step in to handle Samuels's engagements should Samuels decide to take a leave of absence. The next week, Samuels, MacIntyre, and Smith met and discussed Samuels's situation. They agreed that Samuels had faced undue pressure in the newly changed financial services industry and that problems with his family (namely, the arrest of his son on narcotics possession) may have contributed to his troubles with clients. Smith urged Samuels to take a three-month leave effective during the summer of that same year (nearly four months later). Samuels also insisted that he himself be allowed to draw up a plan about who would replace him on his accounts during his absence.

Samuels, who was 53 at the time, took his leave but never returned to the firm. His engagements were taken over by other partners in the practice. Instead, he opened a small consulting firm in another part of the country and slipped into semiretirement. This prompted Smith to issue a memo in which he argued that the "spirit" of the firm recognized that partners were bound to pursue whatever clients they wished within the boundaries for proper etiquette. He also drew up procedures for partnership leaves in similar situations.

A notable aspect of this case is the ease and speed with which MacIntyre was able to mobilize other partners in management consulting to "pinch hit" for Samuels. A tax partner commented that his practice could never have arranged a replacement so smoothly because most other partners would have been disinclined to get involved. Interestingly, tax and audit partners also found the speed with which other partners stepped in for Samuels somewhat "appalling." One partner in audit went so far as to describe the aftermath of the case as a "feeding frenzy." Management consulting partners, in sharp contrast to the traditional partners, framed their handling of the case as another example of their "teamwork." Such wide differences in the interpretation of the same behaviors, in fact, helped fuel the growing intergroup conflict within the partnership between the CPAs and the consultants.

Interpractice Conflict Management

Nearly all Independent partners believed the biggest challenge faced by the firm in the 1980s and into the 1990s would involve relations between the "consultants" in the management consulting practices and the "CPAs" in tax and audit. The development of management consulting partners as major players in the firm meant that new markets and opportunities presented themselves to Independent Accounting. The possibilities for referrals, for example, between the practices seemed boundless, as one senior partner noted:

> Think about it. I do taxes for a large client who wants to automate all of their internal accounting processes: financial, stock, personnel, you name it. I know that firm [the client] like the back of my hand. And I can refer my client to my colleague in management consulting who can design the system for them. I can be a consultant myself on the project. These kinds of deals are worth millions over the long haul. It's a match made in heaven.

From a purely technical perspective, many partners agreed that the match of management information systems and the practices in the firm did make good business sense. From other perspectives, however, the match proved far from heavenly. As early as the 1970s, the Securities and Exchange Commission had already attempted to dampen the expansion of large audit firms into management information systems by publicly urging them to confine most of their business activities to auditing. These policy considerations stemmed from the opportunities for bias and the constraints on objectivity accountants might display when auditing clients whose financial systems they had themselves designed or had been designed in their firms (Stevens 1991). Another external source of trouble arose from the competition from established consulting firms who not only openly bested Independent for clients, but also lured highly qualified consulting partners away from the firm.

The most severe problems posed on a day-to-day basis by having both consulting and auditing ventures in the same firm did not relate to scrutiny by the SEC or competition from large consulting firms. They stemmed from internal relations and stylistic differences between the practices. In effect, what Big Six firms in general, and Independent Accounting specifically, faced were increasingly common occasions for intercultural communication between partners in the traditional practices and those in management consulting. Case 5.9 illustrates some of the core grievance issues and one set of responses to those issues among Independent CPAs and management consultants.

Case 5.9 The City Information System (1983–86)

In 1983, Independent Accounting consulting partners contracted to design a large management information system for a municipality. The engagement came to be known among all partners simply as the city information system or more commonly as the CIS. All told, the CIS could generate in excess of seven million dollars and take about two years to complete. Because the CIS would require some amounts of time from almost all of the management consulting partners, partial time commitments from CPAs in tax and audit, and more associates than were available in the consulting practice, more than a few partners in tax and audit were skeptical of the commitment.

Smith, the managing partner (see case 5.8), believed that the firm "couldn't ignore this opportunity," but also shared the concern that the consulting practice might be "in over its head." He further noted that since the consulting practice had "pitched" the CIS at a meeting of the partners in late 1982, he had been to more meetings between CPAs and consultants in two years than in his entire twenty-year career at Independent. The protocols at these meetings, according to Bailey (see case 5.1), fell into highly predictable patterns: multimedia presentations by consulting partners about aspects of the CIS or its various contracts and subcontracts, followed by a very quiet "discussion" period during which CPAs would ask a few pointed questions, occasionally pontificate about why, from a "technical" standpoint, some of what the consultants proposed seemed "risky," and then ratify the consultants' request to go ahead with negotiations on CIS. As Smith put it, "We've made a commitment to be a major player in the information processing business. The CIS marks our entry into the field as a major player."

But this marker also sparked fear and private grievances among CPAs that the CIS "interfered" with the mainstream of the business and that Independent might eventually become nothing more than a "consulting" firm comprised of "snake oil salesmen" selling informational "elixirs" to all comers. A more fundamental issue lay at the heart of these grievances: who would have the ultimate power and authority in the firm, CPAs or consultants. Green (see case 1.2) articulated this grievance most succinctly by arguing in a private interview that the CIS could "put the consultants in the driver's seat" in the firm and take away the autonomy that CPAs had had to do what they wanted without interference. A second source of consternation for CPAs centered on what they called the consultant style. As Simpson (see case 5.3) put it, "They're always jabbering—and the incessant meetings, they can't get enough of them. All they want to do over there is take each other out to lunch."

During this same period, members of the consulting practice also harbored secret grievances against the CPAs or, as they derisively called them, the "bean counters." MacIntyre (see case 5.8), himself a CPA by training and a tax partner before heading the management consulting practice, argued that there is "bean-counter mentality" that induces "a fear of change." MacIntyre further elaborated this point: "It's a different world in tax and audit than consulting. They work alone. We have to work together. The CIS is taking the whole effort of the firm. That's never happened before."

Independent ultimately undertook the development of the CIS. It required far more time and resources than had been forecast by management consulting, and as a result several CPAs worked unusually closely with consultants, as did associates from tax and auditing. These sporadic contacts further deepened the rift between the two groups. In line with MacIntyre's concerns, consultants privately complained about the time it took CPAs to make decisions about committing resources to the CIS, about the CPAs' disdain for meeting when collective decisions were needed, about the reserved, stoic nature of the CPAs in meetings, about having to go to the CPAs for approval on CIS, and about how CPAs did not raise complaints about issues, but instead didn't return phone calls or would boycott meetings. Consultants also complained about CPAs' unilaterally reassigning associates off of the CIS to their own engagement without notifying the consultants in charge of that part of the engagement. MacIntyre again: "The CIS may ultimately mean hundreds of million dollars to Independent if we can pull it off. And these guys [CPAs] don't seem to want to be part of the action. They just want to keep up their old businesses. We should be able to procure what we need when we need it, not be beholden to them for our engagement staffs."

The CPAs, on the other hand, steadfastly maintained throughout this three-year period that the consultants had introduced a measure of "disorderliness" and "greed" into Independent unprecedented in the firm's history. Their grievances also continued to touch on the amount of meetings that consultants required.

Amidst the avoidance tactics by CPAs and the more confrontational urges by consultants, Foster attempted in 1984 to be a peace-maker among the principals. Foster was himself a tax partner and confided that he privately "dreaded" having to run a meeting de-signed to troubleshoot. As he put it, "I have a lot of skills but run-ning court isn't one of them." MacIntyre, Smith, and Strodt (of audit) were not receptive to Foster's intervention even though each of them admitted to being tired from the "rocky road" of the CIS en-gagement. Nonetheless, Foster eventually was able to persuade them to meet with him after several months of individual meetings with each of them. The four men met for a lunch meeting at which Foster attempted to facilitate discussion of some of the issues that all agreed were hampering the smooth completion of the CIS. Foster re-ported that the meeting did some "good" because it brought the CPAs out of their "shells." He also noted that during the meeting all three executives still seemed to resent his intervention and politely but firmly resisted some of his suggestions at new procedures in as-signing personnel. The meeting ended with promises by the three to meet with one another and discuss the matter further.

Strodt and MacIntyre did eventually meet (after Strodt canceled several scheduled meetings with MacIntyre) to further iron the mat-ter out. Smith did not meet with MacIntyre and as a result tax associ-ates played less of a role in the CIS than did audit associates. All three partners privately expressed their respect for Foster's efforts but admitted they were uncomfortable with his attempts at peace-making. As MacIntyre noted, "It's highly unusual in this firm to have any kind of meeting like we had. People just don't get involved in other people's affairs. I know I wondered, and so did Strodt, what Foster had up his sleeve on this one." What the principals most feared was that Foster might attempt to get closure on the jurisdic-tional aspect of the dispute without letting the principals formulate a plan themselves. Ultimately, Independent completed the CIS despite the cost overruns (which totaled several million dollars) and delays in part related to disputes between the CPAs and consulting.

As of 1990, the grievances that were woven into the fabric of this case persisted across a number of large information management en-gagements at Independent. The management consulting practice had also grown precipitously, nearly doubling its size, while tax and audit have grown only slightly. Despite the relative consistency in grievance issues, there were signs as the 1990s began that the nonconfrontational tactics of the CPAs were giving way to a new, slightly more confronta-tional style. Although still restrained, CPAs appeared to be adjusting to the endless rounds of meetings as well as their newfound interde-pendence with the consultants.

Packed into case 5.9 are tensions similar to those that emerged throughout the Big Six during the 1980s. Some firms managed the struggle between consulting and the traditional practices by increasing the autonomy of management consulting so that consultants did not report to CPAs. At other firms, consultants split off their practices to start new firms wholly dedicated to consulting (Stevens 1991). By 1990, Independent had taken neither of these courses of action, although consultants talked among themselves about the possibility of a permanent split between CPAs and consultants.

Concluding Remarks

To be a partner at Independent Accounting means having autonomy in one's actions vis-à-vis one's colleagues, being socially distant from one's colleagues, and symbolizing one's professional station in the firm by handling conflict without confrontational or authoritative overtures. These patterns are most extreme among tax and audit partners and less so in the management consulting practice. Partners in the tax and audit practices routinely engage in efforts to deny, avoid, and endure trouble with their colleagues in order to minimize the probability that grievances will be pursued in any but the most oblique and truncated fashions. Partners in management consulting display the same general propensities, but also evidence a greater willingness to deal with their conflicts openly, particularly through negotiation.

Conflict management among management consulting partners illustrates a normative order closer to the reciprocal order within functions and coalitions in matrix firms. Conflict management in this order occurs via positive reciprocity, resembling Anselm Strauss's (1978) sense of organizations as social tapestries woven out of negotiated agreements. Intergroup conflict between the tax and consulting practices displays a blend of schemas and scripts exported from the intragroup contexts most familiar to the participants, although here too a reciprocal order is emerging as partners in the traditional and management consulting practices become more interdependent. Finally, trouble between partners of sizable age differences displays some tendency to be defined as an opportunity for informal counseling by more senior partners.

In general, the structuring of work into independent engagements reflects general professional "freedom . . . to practice one's craft without interference, advice, or regulation by others" (Freidson 1970:98). Partners in the consulting practice, without the ties to the accounting profession, may be breaking away from this master ideal. Even so, continued adherence to such arrangements may more accurately reflect historical and rhetorical processes begun long ago, as public accountants carved out space for themselves as a profession with particular jurisdictional boundaries in the societal division of labor (Abbot 1988). The autonomy Independent accountants reserve for themselves is the perpetuation of a master ideal about how professional work is to be accomplished and regulated. All of these findings conform to the general arguments in chapter 2 on the contextual conditions associated with nonconfrontation. More interesting, however, may be what happens in social contexts conducive to unilateral or bilateral nonconfrontation when people attempt third-party intervention.

The formal hierarchy among partners only weakly stratifies the partnership and also appears to discourage the submission of disputes for judgment by third parties, which might diminish open conflict. Submitting a dispute to a third party generally entails a reduction of the disputants' autonomy, in effect a relinquishing to the third party of some or all of the ownership of the conflict by its principals (Christie 1977). Although I collected only one instance of third-party intervention at Independent (case 5.9), it does illustrate what happens when parties of relatively equal social status do attempt to engage in triadic conflict management. In case 5.9, the disputants resisted the third party's suggestions for resolution and also believed that the third party had a hidden agenda which could adversely affect the outcome of the dispute. Such struggles do not always occur in contexts in which there are greater power and status differentials between disputants and third parties. Although greatly disadvantaged people sometimes resist the imposition of conflict outcomes by superiors (e.g., Baumgartner 1984b), in a variety of settings wide differences in social status contribute to third-party settlement marked by the deference of disputants to the authority of the settlement agent. Such is typically the case in modern courts of law, but also historically and cross-culturally in tribal moots and other disputing forums (Black and Baumgartner 1983; Yngvesson and Mather 1983). In the mechanistic bureaucracies in this study, disputants displayed a marked deference toward third-party settlement agents who held formal authority over them unless those agents had particularly sullied reputations. These arguments and findings suggest two hypotheses:

5a.   The closer the social status between disputants and third-party settlement agents, the greater the likelihood of struggle between disputants and third parties over control of the dispute.

5b.   The salience of hidden agendas attributed to third-party settlement agents by disputants will vary inversely with the differences in social status between disputants and the third party.

These hypotheses, then, suggest some caveats to the often-argued position in conflict studies equating third-party settlement with peaceful resolution. If the third-party settlement agent enjoys very little social status over and above that of the disputants, attempts at third-party settlement may actually exacerbate hostilities as the disputants become more suspicious of the third-party's actions. In this sense, the focus of grievances may shift from the principals to the settlement agent, in turn creating another dyadic conflict.

To the degree that work among all Independent partners is structured around autonomous engagements, all partners participate in the minimalist order by pursuing their grievances nonconfrontationally. Yet, as argued earlier in this chapter, management consultants place greater emphasis on team projects and being team players. Management consulting partners also have the weakest links to the accounting profession (although some consultants are CPAs), and so the historical emphasis on independence in their work is less pronounced than among their brethren in tax and audit. Indeed, what the partners in tax and audit fear most is the decreasing social and physical distance among partners, which from their perspective leads to increases in confrontationally expressed grievances and confrontational conflict management. Interdependence and multiplex ties do indeed increase rancor in social groups, but also paradoxically increase the opportunities for conflict resolution via positive reciprocity in negotiation processes. Anthropologist Max Gluckman (1967:23) noted that customary multiplexity and interdependence tend to "multiply" the "occasions which breed quarrels among [people]," but also "unite where [they] divide, cooperation and conflict balancing each other." Stated more formally:

5c.   Interdependence and multiplexity increase the likelihood of open grievances among aggrieved parties.

5d.   Interdependence and multiplexity increase the likelihood of negotiated conflict management *and* resolution among disputants.

Tax and audit partners thus fear the loss of a minimalist order in which they are, in the phrasing of the anthropologist Robert Edgerton, "alone together" (1977) with their colleagues. In its place, partners in the traditional practices fear the rise of a normative order in which interdependent ties among members are arrayed in coalitions—a kind of negotiated order in which avoidance is difficult and the restrained, professional etiquette to which they are accustomed is scarce. Despite the changes under way among Independent partners, they have not begun to enact the changes that top managers experienced during the last two decades in firms which rapidly diversified and self-consciously experimented with nontraditional management structures. The next chapter investigates an exemplar of just such an experiment.

CHAPTER SIX

BRAVE NEW WORLD: RECIPROCAL CONFLICT MANAGEMENT IN A MATRIX SYSTEM

We're not some namby-pamby manufacturer with neat chains of command or some hotsy-totsy law firm. It's a brave new world at Playco. It's pure action here. We're sharks circling for a kill. If someone takes a bite out of you, you take a bite out of him. It's not very pretty, but it can be fun if you're doing the biting.

—vice president, Playco

Playco's fortunes rode on a narrow set of product lines focused on children's toys and games for thirty years. Then, in the 1970s, Playco self-consciously reorganized its executive ranks with matrix management and aggressively participated in several corporate acquisitions and divestitures. As a result, its product lines dramatically diversified and by the mid and late 1980s, Playco owned and operated businesses in a variety of entertainment industries, including film production and distribution, publishing, software, and computers. Playco also expanded its production facilities and markets into several overseas locales. In 1986, twenty thousand employees and forty-three executives generated in excess of one billion dollars in yearly revenues for Playco.

Acres of blacktop parking lots (called the "moat" by Playco employees) bordered by electrified barbed wire fences surround Playco's world headquarters. Within the moat are yet more acres of single-storied bungalows (called "islands") linked to one another by covered causeways. Jutting up from the bungalows stand twenty stories of green glass and steel—the "tower." A brisk walk from a parking space near the electric fence to the tower takes nearly five minutes.

In front of the tower fly flags of several countries as well as what look to be thin, brightly colored banners. On a typical day, the walkway to the main entrance is thick with people of all descriptions walking and talking in dyads and small groups. Some are dressed in dark-colored suits and dresses. Others are dressed casually in blue jeans, overalls, sport jackets, shorts, and the like. Many are carrying large portfolios or models of products they hope to sell to Playco. Finally, there are children with guardians walking between the main tower to the surrounding lawn.

The talking ("buzzing") of the people outside the tower grows louder the closer one gets to the entrance to the main lobby. Just inside the front of the main lobby sit two men and two women in a reception station that contains a bank of phones, a personal computer, and several large leather-bound books marked Appointments on the top of each page. To the right of the reception station is a door marked Private that is propped open. A quick glance through the open doorway to the private room reveals that it is filled with television sets and three uniformed guards watching the sets.

A large knot of people, all trying to talk to the receptionists, crowds around the station with urgent-sounding requests. An elementary school teacher herds a group of small children into the lobby and inquires about the location of the marketing department test room G-4. A nervous man with several oversized portfolios does not have an appointment, but is sure a manager in design whose name he obtained from a friend will want to see him. A woman who identifies herself as Laura's mother loudly demands in a high-pitched, nasal voice to know why the test department did not choose her daughter (whom she lifts up onto the reception station) to test a series of learning aids for preteen children. At the same time, men and women with employee passes walk briskly past the reception station, sometimes waving to the receptionists, and sometimes too engrossed in conversation with others to wave. Beyond the reception station is an expansive waiting area, carpeted with bright blue carpeting and filled with couches of various colors arranged in U shapes. Pictures of Playco products adorn the walls. In one end of the main lobby, several plaques and pictures denoting employees and managers of the month and year hang on a special "Wall of Fame."

Every visitor to Playco must check in with the reception area, have their name checked off on the appointment book by one of the receptionists, have a confirmation call made on their behalf to the Playco employee they are visiting, and receive a visitor's badge. Employees have numerous other entrances they can use to access their offices. Executives have a private entrance and elevator as well in order to avoid what some call the circus in the main lobby.

The uppermost floors of the tower house the "flight deck," where Playco top managers (save those in personnel) work and from which a "thousand ideas are launched" to bring "fame and fortune" to the corporation. Executive offices on the flight deck are all arranged on the edge of each floor, with one side (or two sides if on the corner) composed of glass and the interior looking inward toward the large work spaces on the floor. Some offices approach garishness in terms of the amount of leather, precious metals and other objects of art, exercise equipment, and number of adjoining private rooms. Other offices are nearly Spartan, containing only a mahogany executive desk and leather high-backed chair, a round meeting table, and a few other personal effects (such as family portraits and pictures of significant events).

Adjacent to each executive suite is a single office occupied by a female executive secretary. Clustered around some executives' suites are offices occupied by lower executives and middle managers in the same department or division. The membership of such clusters comprise what is called an executive's "gang," "crew," or simply "people" (as in "my people"). Beyond those offices are even more extensive clusters of work stations occupied by lower managers and clerical staff. Floors are divided by function, with marketing and finance sharing the very top floors of the flight deck and the remaining functions occupying the floors below. Personnel executives occupy a single-story bungalow adjacent to the tower.

Most Playco executives are of northern European stock, male, and in their fifties (see table 2.2 in chapter 2 for the exact demographics). Male executives tend to be tall, the men near or over six feet, but female executives tend to be of average height, near or over five foot six. Executive dress varies considerably. Male executives typically wear suits and sport coats, but some abhor what they call "establishment" attire and wear everything from blue jeans to overalls. Female executives typically dress formally in suits, dresses, and high-heeled shoes. The frenzied activity of the main lobby is reproduced on the flight deck. Playco executives seem to be in constant motion as they stride to and from their offices and meeting rooms, typically with other people in tow as they walk and sometimes rallying people from the clusters around them with a shouts of "Let's meet people" or "Here we go, crew, there's wars to be fought, battles to be won." In conversation (and formal interviews), Playco top managers speak in clipped sentences, often using colorful metaphors to express their ideas. A typical exchange of greetings among executives as they pass one another on the flight deck often contains metaphorical references to competition and conflict always delivered in a swaggering style:

"Iron Man, I hear you're dueling today. Good luck."
"You know me, I love the smell of fresh meat."
"Kick the shit out of those bozos."

Executive Social Organization and Conflict Management Patterns before 1975

To understand the contemporary executive context at Playco, one must place it in historical context. Before 1975, Playco's executive core consisted of twenty-one top managers organized into several departments. There were only three ranks: vice president, senior vice president (who headed departments), and the president/chief executive officer of the firm. A unitary command system ruled the executive echelons, creating unambiguous and scalar reporting relationships. A long-time executive described the executive levels at Playco as "staid" and "laid back." Another described the internal arrangements of the firm during this period as "highly bureaucratic with a touch of playfulness." In many ways, then, Playco could be described as a mechanistic bureaucracy before the mid 1970s.

The substance of executive conflict during this period focused around four broad issues: diversification of Playco's product lines, production scheduling, the gradual removal of the founders of the firm from central sources of power (one chaired the board of directors, while the other occupied the presidency), and what several executives referred to as "personality conflicts." The following accounts by two executives who have worked with Playco since the 1960s strongly suggest that authoritative management of conflict pervaded the executive ranks at Playco in the mid 1970s. One recounted:

> We used to have conflicts between departments: engineering and design. In those days, the president always settled them, when the two department VPs couldn't get a grip on it. But it was all done very quietly, behind closed doors. You wouldn't dare shout at one of your colleagues. It was a different world then. There was also a lot more discipline within the departments. I remember being a young VP and working for this complete horse's patoot of a SVP. I would never even think about challenging him like the way VPs challenge their SVPs in the firm today. I had to change in the eighties. I had to get with the game myself; get more aggressive, take people on in public. It took awhile. I sometimes think it hurt me; not getting with the game until a few years ago.

The other stated:

> The only public conflicts I remember happened when the founders
> bowed out of the firm in the early seventies. There were some don-
> nybrooks over that. We [the speaker and two other senior execu-
> tives] were hired to help them run this itsy-bitsy firm that had grown
> into a multinational corporation over [a] thirty-year period. We
> wound up running the firm. Hey, I sat around here grumbling about
> [the founders] for years before anything came out in the open. The
> same thing with personal issues I had with colleagues. All of the
> stuff you see on a daily basis around here now just didn't happen
> back then. Divisional managers [senior vice presidents] kept their
> shops clean; people kept to themselves. Sure, there were problems,
> conflicts between top execs. But it got settled quietly.

Other executives and consultants working in or with Playco before
1975 echo these sentiments. Conflict management took particular
forms according to its downward or upward direction as in other unitary managerial hierarchies (Dalton 1959; Morrill 1989; see chapter 4).
Conflict management among Playco executives also exhibited certain
ceremonies (Trice et al. 1969) marking its occurrence and conclusion.
A consistent ritual was that of removing a conflict from the public view
and handling it as quietly as possible behind closed doors as the first
executive quoted above noted. When approaching a superior in a conflictive situation, subordinates tended to make special appointments
to see their superiors alone and tended to rehearse the presentation of
their grievances so that they would not offend their superiors. More
often than not, such presentations were cut off by superiors who settled the matter unilaterally after briefly listening to their subordinates'
opening remarks. The superior would then return their subordinates
back to their regular duties to "work out the details" of the solution.
Superiors with complaints against their subordinates would usually
call those subordinates into their office for a quick meeting to clear
up problems. Although some executives reported "rehearsing" their
presentations to subordinates, most argued that such actions tended
to occur without much thought about how they would specifically
present their grievance. Accounts of peer conflicts contain consistent
references to private conflict management and intervention by superiors acting as third-party settlement agents, again emblematic of an
authoritative order. The next two sections of this chapter describe the
dramatic organizational changes that occurred at Playco during the
late 1970s and early 1980s.

Inside the Playco Matrix

The Origins of the Playco Matrix

Playco executives first implemented their matrix in the mid 1970s following the participation by several of its executives in midcareer management programs at two graduate business schools. A long-time senior vice president remembered:

> We had read about the matrix in *Harvard Business Review* and believed it might invigorate our top management, especially related to product development. So, a few of us went to an OD [organizational development] seminar to learn about it. It sounded complex although it also sounded like we needed it.

In fact, many executives initially resisted the matrix because of their perception of the uncertainty its dual-authority structures would create. A vice president of personnel recalls:

> We had a hell of [a] time convincing our people to give it a try. What with the changes in industry going on, a lot of people thought they might lose their jobs; that the matrix would replace them or something. People wanted to hold on to their old ways of doing things. For the first couple of years, it was chaos. Nobody knew who to report to or who was responsible to whom. Everybody was really uncertain about the future.

One measure of the initial uncertainty faced by Playco executives in the matrix derives from files of the administration department containing "operating procedure memos" issued to executives about their new responsibilities in the matrix. In 1976, the first year of the matrix, fifty-five general memos were found detailing executive reporting lines and responsibilities. Many of the fifty-eight general memos in 1977 corrected earlier memos regarding authority and task responsibility. In each successive year such memos decreased gradually until they ceased in early 1982.

As Playco executives struggled inside the corporation to manage the uncertainty of their jobs, the American economy came to grips with significant changes in corporate acquisition practices, particularly what came to be known as hostile takeovers. Hostile takeovers occur when "more than 50% of the shares of a large, publicly held corporation are purchased by another over the loud, public protestations of the target company's management, board of directors, and/or minority shareholders" (Hirsch 1986:801). Playco engaged in several "friendly takeovers" (with the full knowledge and consent of shareholders and management of the target firms) and a few unsuccessful mergers; it also warded off two hostile takeovers and two friendly offers between 1975 and 1987. Executives at the firm considered friendly takeovers a legitimate business strategy, especially the way they "play the game." As the Playco chief executive officer put it, "We've worn white hats [as the good guys would in an Old West movie] in the takeover game. We're not [Carl] Icahn or Texas boys [in reference to particularly ruthless takeover entrepreneurs]."

By the early 1980s Playco had emerged as a firm with domestic and international divisions. The executive ranks were further divided into eight functions—operations, research and development (R&D), marketing, sales, finance, administration, engineering, and product planning—that are crosscut by seven product teams. This formed a product × function matrix (Davis and Lawrence 1977) in which product teams and functions are formally equal in decision making in the organization.

Hierarchies

Formal Authority. The "office of the president" represents the highest reach of the executive ranks and has four offices: the presidents of the domestic and international divisions, the chief executive officer, and the chairman of the board, who is infrequently involved with the daily affairs of the company. Departments contain two executive ranks: vice president and senior vice president.

Product teams are responsible for the company's products from conception to distribution. Some teams are responsible for a single product, such as a best-selling learning aid; other teams are responsible for an entire product line, such as games for children six to nine years old. Vice presidents of marketing typically lead product teams, and one representative from each of the company's departments (except administration and finance) sits on each of the product teams. In most instances, executives fill out the membership of a product team, although "managers," the rank just below vice president, may also be included. Several factors determine the membership of product teams: an executive's reputation, task expertise, friendships with product team members and leaders, and individual interest in becoming a member of a particular team.

Playco vice presidents typically report to a senior vice president and a team leader. Senior vice presidents report to one of the presidents or to both a president and the chief executive officer, and they may sit on a product team in which they are also a "follower." An example of such a situation would be when a marketing vice president leads a team that includes, among other executives, a senior vice president of engineering or sales. Such situations create extremely uncertain lines of authority in which formal superiors may cancel the authority of one another out, thus leading to constant managerial conflict—a common occurrence in many matrix systems (e.g., Barker et al. 1988).

Ambiguities in the formal executive hierarchy manifest themselves whenever top managers of differential ranks interact. Vice presidents do not "lie down and play dead" when confronted with the formal authority of a senior vice president or president, and senior vice presidents are wary of "stepping on the toes of powerful vice presidents." Such interactions among executives of differential ranks as well as the same ranks take on highly competitive and confrontational characters. Listen to this Playco president describe the matrix:

> Everyone is more or less on the same plane in the matrix; that's the idea and we've been able to maintain most of that philosophy in the firm. So you've got to treat people with respect. You can't simply drop in and expect to get the time of day from a colleague. I can't snap my fingers and have a vice president in my office; not unless I want trouble.

Executive responsibilities often place top managers in formal structures with different standards and goals, a situation that creates differential allegiances in terms of authority and time commitments. Under these conditions, department heads, officially charged with the evaluation of their direct subordinates, find it difficult to apply meaningful evaluative criteria. It is equally difficult for any one superior to unilaterally evaluate subordinates. The rituals of evaluation thus take on very competitive natures in which superiors and subordinates demonstrate their mettle via informal influence during face-to-face meetings. "It is important," noted one Playco executive, "that you stick to your guns in a performance meeting. The meeting isn't over until somebody has carried the day." Note that it is *not* assumed that a formal superior will carry the day, only that *someone* will. *How* one "jousts" in arguing one's case for promotion or a compensation increase also becomes intertwined in the criteria for judging good individual and collective performance. A Playco senior vice president put it thus:

> You [a superior] look for the fellow's ability to present his case, who he knows, what he knows about what's going on. In these meetings you get an up-close and personal feel for the guy's abilities. The numbers don't mean shit unless you know something about who's

generating them. Numbers don't mean anything without knowing what's in a person's head, what they have to offer personally to the [business] effort.

Playco executives also call budget meetings "jousts" in which executives "battle" for supremacy of their opinions. A senior Playco executive provided this colorful portrait of budget processes:

> It's like the inner city in here. We don't have central authority. The police have pulled back. It's just the gangs banging each other for control. I worked at a place [a more mechanistically organized cable television company] where you had power plays and politics, but the senior vice president or the CEO had final say. They could put through what they wanted and people mostly followed orders. They could wade into a meeting and simply allocate resources. It doesn't work that way here. You have to bring your people with you in a meeting and fight it out, show you're a tough SOB who won't cave in when there's trouble. Nobody has power in this firm without allies and respect.

Respectability. This last statement underscores the importance of reputational hierarchies at Playco. In an organization of ambiguous and uncertain formal authority, respect helps guide executives' loyalties and decisions. For Playco executives respectability is "honor" or the "strength" an executive demonstrates with forceful rhetoric as they express their ideas in public meetings. Because the functions and code of honor among Playco executives are bound up integrally with routine processes of communication and conflict management among Playco executives, it will be discussed in more detail in subsequent sections of this chapter.

Gender and Ethnicity. Among the forty-three executives at Playco, five are female, a higher absolute number of female executives than at any other corporation in the study and over twice the average rate of female executives across U.S. corporations (Fierman 1990; Segal and Zellner 1992; see chapter 2). Nonetheless, women are obviously in the vast minority of executives in this corporation. Moreover, at the time of fieldwork, none had progressed beyond the vice presidential rank.[1] The tendencies toward highly aggressive behavior noted in chapter 2 for female executives in general are particularly pronounced at Playco. The women "swagger" more than the men and, as will be seen in the sections that follow on conflict management, have in some instances earned reputations as the most feared top managers in the corporation.

The same does not hold true with ethnic minorities at Playco. Three of the four minority executives were foreign nationals whose duties often took them away from the world headquarters for months at a time. As a result, many of these executives did not participate as fully in the day-to-day affairs of the firm as their colleagues. The one minority executive at Playco who was not a foreign national held a position in planning.

Coalitions and Networks

Playco executives exhibit decided patterns of dense interaction. Executives send relatively few memos to one another (relative to the average number of memos sent among executives in the entire study), but interact on average over twice daily and have numerous meetings (see tables B.1 and B.2 in appendix B for overall quantitative support of these generalizations among Playco executives).[2] Moreover, it is not uncommon to see Playco executives in small groups walking through the main lobby to lunch and congregating outside their offices. One of the core functions of the communication networks among Playco executives is as a medium of gossip through which executives continually update themselves about theirs and their colleagues' reputations. Executives also use gossip to assess the trustworthiness of allies and potential allies in coalition building and maintenance.

Coalitions are most often based on functional membership (for quantitative support of this assertion, see tables B.7 and B.8 in appendix B). Coalitions, like reputation and rhetorical skill, play important roles in a manager's success or failure at influencing decisions because of the ambiguity of formal authority in the matrix. Every executive I interviewed at Playco commented on the importance of having groups of allies. Listen to this Playco top manager talk about the importance of having "friends" in a matrix system:

> In every organization you need friends. If you don't network you won't be able to get anything done at all. But in most organizations you also have rank, which helps more than a little in most situations. In this type of an organization, you can't rely on rank to get you through. You live in a world of interdependence where people need you to get through the day and you need them. Being a friend means backing another guy in tight situations, not ratting on a colleague, stuff like that. There's a scene in *The Godfather,* I think, where Don Corleone says to some guy after the guy does him a favor, kills someone I think, that "now we are friends, when you have a problem I will help you." I do something for you and you do something for me. That's the way it works here. You don't make it in this

kind of an organization without friends, friends who owe you something.

Nowhere is the importance of coalitions more important than in executive meetings called to discuss policy proposals. Playco executives describe their meetings as "moments of truth" during which their ideas are "shot down" or "victorious" based on one's rhetorical skill, honor, and the support of their allies. A poignant example of the importance of allies can be found in this story by a Playco senior vice president:

> One summer just after I joined Playco, I proposed that we have a visitor's procedure between product teams in the firm—like I had seen at [another matrix company] so that every executive could have a chance to see what it's like to work on different product lines; a way to get everyone on the same boat in terms of the concept of the firm and what we're trying to do here. So I wrote this puppy up and presented it at an executive committee meeting. I usually go around and make sure I've got some backup in a meeting. This time I didn't and all of a sudden I'm taking hits from all sides on this thing as a big waste of time, financially infeasible, etc. I was out there all alone with no one guarding my flank. It was like walking into an alley where a whole gang of thugs is waiting for you. I bailed quickly I tell you. Burying that proposal six feet deep wasn't deep enough: the stench still got into my office. The funny thing is that some months later three of my colleagues proposed the same thing. This time it flew. I finally figured out I had blown it by going out on a limb alone on the thing without any backup. I never made that mistake again.

Another telling measure of the density of social interaction among Playco executives is the extent to which top managers mix business and pleasure in their dealings with one another (see table B.8 in appendix B for quantitative support of this claim). Interpersonal relationships are the stuff of coalitions in which the political and personal are fused. As one executive makes clear: "All of my best friends in the firm are my closest allies in the firm. Friendship is really political here. If you've got allies you've got friends. If you don't have friends, you don't have any allies."

To flesh out the texture of executive communication and interpersonal relations at Playco, consider a day in the life of R&D senior vice president Bill Stennet, taken from my field notes:

> Stennet is 44 years of age and a ten-year veteran of the executive ranks at Playco, having held the title of SVP for five years. Stennet

and I greet each other in the executive parking lot at Playco at 7:00 A.M. Stennet closes the door on his Cadillac and hurries to the executive entrance of the tower. We board the executive elevator, quickly ascend to the eighteenth floor, and are met by Jill, Stennet's administrative assistant. She hands him several small pieces of yellow paper, each with some notes jotted on them. Stennet ushers me into his office, which is in a corner with floor-length windows on two sides of the room. Stennet sits at a large mahogany desk with his back against one wall. He has a round conference table across the room from his desk as well as a small sink and private bathroom. Pictures of Stennet and others with large fish in their hands adorn the walls. A picture of his wife and three children sits on his desk.

He begins speaking to me in an excited manner: "See these [referring to the yellow pieces of paper]. Each one has to do with some meeting I have to go to or a message to call someone in R&D. I've got a product team meeting to go to at nine this morning. Two guys there are going to duel it out on whether we should go total glitz on presenting our product line this year [at an industrywide trade show] or not. Another one is a message from the president of domestic; another is a reminder from some personnel fool that I need to get him the evaluations of the vice presidents in R&D. I can trash that one; it'll take two weeks to talk to their product team leaders to get any data to put into a report." He continues to recount the rest of the yellow papers, noting that each one requires that he interact with another executive, middle manager, or managerial group. Stennet calls one of his vice presidents to ask him whether he is ready for his "duel" with a member of the vice president's product team. The two talk about how best to present the vice president's argument. Jill returns at 7:30 with Stennet's mail, which he does not look at and leaves in a stack on a side table near his desk. Ten minutes later, Brown, another vice president in R&D, enters Stennet's office to alert him that the "Princess of Power" [the senior vice president of marketing] is going to be "gunning" for him at a meeting later in the week with the president of the domestic division as a result of some earlier "skirmishes" [disagreements] between a vice president of R&D and a vice president of marketing. Brown and Stennet decide to discuss strategy on how to "beat" the Princess in the meeting.

Jones, a middle manager from engineering, has been waiting at Stennet's door while Stennet finishes with Brown. Before Jones can speak, Stennet tells Jones that if Bobson [Jones's superior in engineering] wants to talk with him he should come himself and that he doesn't speak to "errand boys." Jones leaves hurriedly. Stennet then asks Jill who he is to meet at 10:00 A.M. Jill launches into a description of three "hired-gun artists" who want to "pitch" new product ideas. Stennet agrees to keep the date and asks that Jill ask Levine, another R&D vice president, to attend the meeting and Sara, another of his secretaries, to take notes during the meeting. At 8:10 A.M., Stennet leaves the office to walk to the personnel department to attend a presentation by the senior vice president of personnel on restructuring executive retirement benefits at the firm. The presentation has three other executives in attendance and includes slides comparing the present plan with the new plan. Stennet leans over to one of his colleagues and whispers, "What a bunch of horseshit. I don't know why I do these favors [i.e., come to such meetings]. They could have sent us a memo on this one."

Back in the office by 9:15, Stennet is greeted by Jill, who tells him that Gordon [the Princess of Power] wants him to call her back and that Levine may be too busy to attend the 10:00 A.M. meeting. Stennet sets his jaw and enters his office, asks me to make sure the door is wide open, and to listen to the "fireworks." Stennet calls Gordon, says hello, and begins listening. After a few minutes, he says, "Look, if you want to go to war on this one, fine. Fine, you do that. Look, don't get so hot. See you at the meeting, bye." Stennet explains that he and the Princess are going to duel at the meeting regarding the primacy of marketing in setting "conceptual product delivery" deadlines for product teams. He then adds that she "gets too hot under the collar about these things." Stennet receives another phone call from a middle manager in a model-making unit in R&D who is a "fishing buddy." Stennet and the caller talk for a few minutes and set a time to go fishing the next Sunday. Stennet then calls Levine and says, "If you can't come, you can't come. Stop by this afternoon to look over some of their [the artists'] stuff. Hey, can you make it this Sunday to fish? OK, we'll talk this afternoon." The phone call ends.

At 9:50 A.M., Jill and Sara enter Stennet's office to announce the early arrival of the artists. Sara goes to Stennet's kitchen to make coffee and then seats herself slightly away from the round meeting table. At 10:00, Jill ushers the artists into Stennet's office. After exchanging pleasantries, Stennet asks the artists what they have for him. They unfurl a large portfolio of product sketches. One of the artists talks for fifteen minutes about the sketches, after which Stennet asks him specific questions about how the artists believe the products fit in with existing product lines at Playco. The meeting lasts through lunch, which Stennet has ordered from the executive dining room through Sara. At 1:00 P.M., the meeting ends with Stennet assuring the artists that he will give serious consideration to their ideas. The artists seem pleased and leave all-smiles.

One could continue to recount Stennet's day until its conclusion at 7:00 P.M., but the lines of action drawn in the portrait above would be much the same: frenzied interaction via phone and in meetings.

Internal Stability and Field Perceptions

To an outsider or an executive from a more staid context, the pace of work, the ambiguous lines of authority, and the stress that one encounters among Playco top managers would indicate an unstable context as well as unstable individuals. Moreover, product replacement runs nearly 90 percent per year, which results in product teams being continually reorganized to develop new products and lines. Yet there is an order to Playco executive life that does not revolve around the staid machinations of mechanistic bureaucracies or the etiquette of professionalism, but rather the notion of what it means to be an honorable manager: forthright, honest, supportive of allies, and willing to confront enemies.

Playco executives frame their interorganizational relations in much the same way as their internal relations. They use colorful, action-oriented metaphors to describe their functional fields as "Wild West towns," "the jungle," or "highways without lanes or stop lights." This last metaphor underscores a common complaint among Playco executives that other firms do not play by the same "rules of the game" as they do. These complaints do not, however, appear to emanate from any generalizable set of rules that corporations adhered to prior to the 1980s. Rather, the rules of the game executives refer to emanate from their own framings inside their organizations. A Playco president commented:

> You go into these deals thinking that you're dealing with honorable people and you get stuck. I think this is the liability of working in a firm like ours. We deal so much with each other every day. We come to know what to expect and how to get what we want from each other. We tend to take those same ideas outside of the firm and we are amazed to learn that not everyone plays by the same rules.

This executive also implies that a relatively stable set of social expectations exists at Playco to which executives are expected to adhere in their relations with one another. The next sections explore how these expectations revolving around honor are articulated in executive conflict management at Playco.

Reciprocal Conflict Management

Like conflict in other organizations with matrix management (Barker et al. 1988; Butler 1973; Stinchcombe 1985), much of the conflict among top managers at Playco centers around issues of administrative juris- diction and organizational strategy, or, in the words of the executives themselves, "who's supposed to do what, how soon, and where." Such conflicts typically involve differences between product team leaders and department heads over what executives term "vision"—the heads manage the demands of many product teams while product team lead- ers, in the words of a department head, "only worry about their products."

The allocation of resources (such as money, office space, and person- nel) within the company also fuel interpersonal and intergroup ten- sions at the executive level. As noted above, many executives attempt to place subordinates with whom they most often work in offices near them. This practice prompts conflict because executives, trying to build similar spatial "empires," find themselves outflanked by their colleagues. Still other executives fume at personnel reductions, espe- cially if they face increasingly difficult group goals but have fewer em- ployees or smaller budgets to meet them.

The simple scheduling of meetings can cause executive conflict as well. Top managers often remarked during interviews about how "in- sulted" they feel when colleagues cancel meetings without reasonable notice or simply do not attend scheduled meetings. One executive commented, "We waste more time around here trying to find meeting times. It takes a bozo to miss a meeting without calling."

Conflict sometimes occurs over what top managers term "ethical is- sues": acceptance of gifts from suppliers or vendors, fabrication of travel receipts, or pilfering from the company stores for private use. Conflicts also arise over managerial style. One example concerned a president who frequently delivers "barbed quips" to his opponents at executive meetings. According to another top manager:

> He has to learn to express his opinions, strongly, even if they are opposed to whatever is on the floor, and not be so sarcastic. He should treat his people [subordinates] more openly. But I guess it's just a defense mechanism. It's hard to be shot at when all there is to shoot is some quip you've thrown out.

Some executives are also accused of another stylistic flaw which execu- tives often call "risk aversion." Such was the case when a president criticized a senior vice president for the latter's unwillingness to take the lead in a quality control program that might initially generate cost overruns for a new product, but could save the company millions of dollars in the long run.

Executives also regard the mixture of aggressiveness and excessive "emotional involvement" a highly inappropriate managerial style, particular for female executives. Gordon, the aforementioned Princess of Power, illustrates this tendency. An informant explained that Gordon sometimes violates executive etiquette:

> Sometimes in meetings, she hammers at you, and gets real emotional about it; lets things get to a personal level. Most of the time she keeps it together. But you never know when she's going to redline, when things will get out of hand. It's one thing to be direct, to defend yourself in a strong manner, and quite another to be so emotional.

It is interesting as well to note what topics rarely cause executive conflict at Playco: gender issues related to fair treatment or hiring practices, legal consequences of company practices, stealing ideas for new products from colleagues, and the quality or social value of new products. When these issues do become the bases for conflict, executives are especially prone to focus on *how* the principals pursue their grievances, rather than the substantive content of the disputes themselves.

Honor among Executives

Whatever the issues involved, Playco executives place great importance on personal reputation and public esteem—honor in handling conflict with their colleagues. At Playco, honor constitutes the core of managerial culture. Playco executives often speak of an executive's honor by reference to their "style," characterized as either "weak" or "strong," or whether they wear "white hats" or are "white knights," denoting their herolike status. Less honorable executives are often referred to as "black hats" or "black knights," denoting a more deviant (in some cases, villainous) status. The origins of executive honor at Playco can be dated to the firm's first corporate acquisition in the mid-1970s. A senior vice president recounted:

> Everyone [executives] seemed to be talking about [hostile] takeovers; white knights this and black knights that; how some takeover players played the game dirty [were not "up-front" in their takeover bids]. The art of the takeover became big conversation at parties and at the office. . . . We began talking about the "art" [using his

hands to make quotation marks in the air] of the meeting, getting promoted, dealing with each other; especially fighting with each other. Now it consumes us.

Another executive casts more light on the social identity of an honorable Playco executive: "What is a strong executive, a guy who wears a white hat? A tough son of a bitch, a guy who's not afraid to shoot it out with someone he doesn't agree with; who knows how to play the game; to win and lose with honor and dignity."

And the "game" at Playco, like many codes of honor (Bourdieu 1965:211; Hoebel 1967:188; Rieder 1984:138; Wyatt-Brown 1984:372), demands that challenges to one's decisions or behavior by worthy opponents be aggressively answered in a calculated fashion, and that one's colleagues recognize this concern for riposte. In this way, honor is, as Pitt-Rivers generally notes, the "value of a person in his own eyes, but also in the eyes of his society" (1965:21). To be honorable, then, means to follow a particular code of conduct and to have claim to the esteem of others and superiority over those who deviate from the code. At Playco, honorable individuals and groups often translate their status into decision-making power and greater opportunities for gaining resources and building trust. The informal status conferred by executive honor thus displays less ambiguity than formal titles in the matrix. Highly honorable executives' statements at executive meetings (regardless of content) receive more respect and outward consideration by their colleagues than those of less honorable executives. Formally low-ranking but highly honorable executives are, as the executives say, "brought into" important decision-making processes by members of the office of the president. The company trusts those of great honor with the most sensitive executive tasks (such as negotiating with foreign governments about building manufacturing or distribution facilities). Honorable executives usually receive requested product team assignments. Executives even ask their highly honorable colleagues to facilitate executive conflict management. A thirty-year veteran at the company commented on this aspect of honor among Playco executives: "Unless people [executives] see you have some notches on your gun, you're not going anywhere in this company. You can't back down here. You can't ambush people or shoot them in the back. Everyone knows real fast what color hat a manager wears in this organization."

Yet task performance does not always translate into honor. A product team known as "the wild bunch" typifies this tendency as described by Playco's chief executive officer: "That team has been successful with our home computer lines, but they're a bunch of outlaws. . . . In what way? They don't understand how we do business

Table 6.1   Conflict Management among Playco Executives by
                    Percentage

Action	Frequency	Percentages
Challenges	17	16.5
Vengeance, confrontational	14	13.6
Insults, public	12	11.7
Feigned ignorance	9	8.7
Secret complaining	8	7.8
Negotiation	7	6.8
Toleration	7	6.8
Vengeance, nonconfrontational	6	5.8
Arguing	5	4.9
Conciliatory approaches	4	3.9
Temporary avoidance	4	3.9
Physical violence	2	1.9
Informal mediation	2	1.9
Lumping/Endurance	2	1.9
Exit, organizational	2	1.9
Informal mediation	1	1.0
Termination	1	1.0
Total	103	100.0

at [Playco]. There are appropriate ways and inappropriate ways of fighting. The members of [the wild bunch] never learned that. Their days are numbered here."

The subsections that follow analyze how Playco executives handle conflict. First, I examine conflict among honorable executives, then conflict among executives of lesser repute. Table 6.1 contains counts of conflict management actions collected during fieldwork at Playco.

Conflict Management among Honorable Executives

The transformation of what Playco executives called conflict management "behind closed doors" during the 1970s into public contests of honor parallels the transformation of corporate acquisitions through symbolic imagery into a "high-stakes drama and spectator sport with a full panoply of characters cast as heroes and villains" (Hirsch 1986:814). Playco executives generally use the imagery of "valiant efforts" and "failed gambits" to frame what they call honorable or strong conflict management. The Playco imagery used to describe honorable conflict also draws from the more respectful aspects of chivalry, Old

West, sports, and warfare genres, which are used in popular language to describe hostile takeovers and are also used at Playco in reference to the company's entertainment product lines. Table 6.2 presents a listing of the terms used by Playco executives sorted into genre groups and their takeover derivations.

Behaviorally, Playco top managers pursue their grievances against each other with a moralistic "tit for tat" (Rieder 1984:133) or "reciprocal aggression" (Black 1990:44) characteristic of vengeful conflict management among honorable disputants everywhere. As argued earlier, codes of honor generally specify the rules of challenge and riposte, including when, where, and with whom vengeance should occur. The social identities of the aggrieved party and the foe is particularly salient. Only weak subordinates, as several executives noted, back down from defending their decisions even when challenged by their superiors, and only weak superiors fail to press their claims against recalcitrant subordinates—at least until compromising with them. To protect or advance one's honor, only worthy opponents can be challenged or responded to in a dispute. This prerequisite assumes that the principals recognize each other as honorable (and are aware of their overall reputations in the company) and that with the exception of interdepartmental conflict (discussed below), top managers wait until a strategic public occasion to issue their challenges or responses. Worthy opponents therefore know and follow the rules of the game, generally play well (even if they lose), and abide by and accept the consequences of their outcomes. Those who do not play the game well are to be avoided lest they contaminate the reputation of honorable and higher-status executives. Table 6.3 presents the processual character of honorable conflict management actions and their appearance across three important social contexts in which they occur at Playco: within departments, within product teams but between principals of different departments, and between principals of neither the same department nor the same product team.

Although reputations are mutable at Playco, early labeling as a black hat tends to follow an executive throughout their career at the firm. In this sense, one's initial reputation can act as a self-fulfilling prophecy. Behaviors one would find unusual in honorable executives, such as emotional outbursts or covert action, come to be expected from dishonorable Playco executives. Even identical behavior, such as arguing, carries with it different labels reflecting the status of the disputants. Arguments are "skirmishes" among honorable executives and "catfights" among less honorable top managers. At the same time, honor-

Table 6.2   Genres of Playco Conflict Imagery by Takeover Derivation

Genre	Playco Imagery	Takeover Derivation[a]
Animals	catfight	—
	dogs	—
	dogs on a leash	pigeon
	pigeon	pigeon
Body/health	amnesia	—
	dick	—
	gas attack	—
	strong	—
	temporary amnesia	—
	weak	pigeon
Chivalry	black knight	black knight
	duel	shoot-out
	exec in distress	—
	honorable	white knight
	Princess of Power	—
	second	—
	sleeping beauties	sleeping beauties
	white knight	white knight
	Wizard	—
Navigation	jumping ship	—
	life vest	—
	pirate	pirate
	raid	raid
Relations/sex	crying	—
	patching up	wooing
	rape	rape
	waltz around	dancing
Science	meltdown	—
	redline	—
	vaporizing	—
Sports	blindsiding	—
	cheap shot	—
	failed gambit	—
	hunting big game	hunting big game
	playing the game	ball is in play
	serious player	takeover player
	target	takeover target
	valiant effort	—
Warfare	burning fighter	—
	declaring war	—
	killing an idea	barricade
	fighting fire with fire	—
	flak vest	war
	flight deck	—

Table 6.2 (continued)

Genre	Playco Imagery	Takeover Derivation[a]
Warfare	flying low	wounded list
	hand grenade	—
	peace talks	—
	roadblock	—
	small bursts of fire	—
	war	flak
	withdrawal	—
	wounded list	—
Western	ambush	ambush
	black hat	—
	bullets	flak
	bushwhack	ambush
	call out	—
	cavalry	—
	outlaw	—
	reserve	—
	shoot-out	shoot-out
	sit down	wooing
	white hat	—
	wild bunch	—
Miscellaneous	art	—
	bozo	—
	hiding	—
	Iron Man	—
	Italian lira money	—
	order	Russian rubles
	playing by the rules	playing the game
	skirmish	—
	sucked in	—
	Terminator	—
	Texas boys	big-hat boys

[a] Takeover imagery terms derive from Hirsch (1986). Not all Playco images correspond with takeover imagery.

able executives enjoy a certain leeway in explaining and having their behavior explained should they deviate from the code of honor.

If honor provides the overarching rules of the game for Playco executive disputes, the social distance between honorable disputants determines how those rules are applied in particular cases. Social distance generally increases the aggression between principals (defined here as the degree to which a disputant attempts to achieve a desired outcome at the expense of an adversary), the length of disputes, and their scope

Table 6.3   Conflict Management among Honorable Playco Executives

Work-Unit Membership of the Principals	Initial Exchanges	Secondary Exchanges	Probable Outcomes
same department (case 6.1)	skirmish	sit down	patch up
same product team (case 6.1)	call out	duel/shoot-out	withdrawal, patching up, or rescue by a white knight
different product team and department (case 6.3)	call outs and hand grenades	war	war, rescue by a white knight, peace talks, or jumping ship

Note: For case 6.1 types, $n = 7$; for case 6.2 types, $n = 11$; for case 6.3 types, $n = 6$. $N = 24$. For definitions of terms see appendix C.

in terms of the number of individuals involved (on this general effect, see Koch 1974:91–158; Rieder 1984:146–48). Where the principals are more socially intimate, such as in the situation of departmental colleagues, the reciprocity of their actions is less exact, less controlled, but also less aggressive and more likely to end in a mutually agreeable outcome. Conflicts among departmental colleagues not only weaken departmental solidarity, which may be crucial in interdepartmental feuds, but also threaten the department's collective honor, so important in maintaining its status relative to other departments. For these reasons, departmental colleagues (especially department heads) attempt to prevent a dispute from escalating beyond the private confines of their department. Because of the ambiguities in command created by the matrix, departmental colleagues' influence remains limited to persuasion. Such persuasion is most effective when departmental colleagues have offices near one another, where they can use their intimacy as a resource with one or the other principal. Social distance also affects the imagery used by principals in framing conflict management. More intimate principals tend to use more nuanced imagery in describing their own and their opponent's actions, and the imagery they use is less aggressive than that used for interdepartmental conflict. The narrative below offers a representative illustration of the interdepartmental conflict management pattern in table 6.3. It begins with an argument between the principals. Rather than escalating into a more aggressive pattern, the principals negotiate a compromise to their conflict.

Case 6.1 The Gifted Vice Presidents (1984)

Representing Playco in dealing with foreign companies is always
tricky business. In one instance, two highly regarded operations
vice presidents, Spelling and Roberts, received gifts from a supplier
during a trip to the supplier's Southeast Asian country. The gifts, intended to strengthen the relationship between Playco and the supplier, included expensive jade jewelry for the VPs' wives and Rolex
watches for the VPs themselves. Spelling and Roberts knew they
would have an argument with their senior vice president, Turner,
over accepting the gifts. Yet, as Roberts pointed out, "We took a
greater risk not taking them and losing face with [the supplier]." The
vice presidents also knew Turner would take a strong stance in handling the matter because he wears one of the "whitest hats" in the
firm. An argument erupted between Spelling and Roberts and
Turner when they told him of accepting the gifts. Turner demanded
they return them, claiming they had put the company at legal risk.

Spelling and Roberts were quite confident that their colleagues
recognized the ambiguities of doing business abroad and at the very
least the information would not escape the organization and reach
legal authorities. They were more concerned that the department
not be viewed, in their words, as weak and torn by indecision. After
talking with departmental colleagues about the importance of resolv-
ing their dispute, the principals had a "sit down" to "patch things
up." Turner agreed to visit the country and meet with Playco's suppliers. Until then, Spelling and Roberts would refrain from accepting any more gifts from suppliers.

Case 6.2 illustrates what Playco managers refer to as "meeting
duels," before which the principals punctuate their challenges and ripostes with more patience and what Rieder observes in general for
honorable conflict management as "a quality of calculation . . . the wily
sizing up of a rival's mettle" (1984:145); the disputants argue until the
proposals or ideas of one of them are, as the executives say, "killed"
and the bearer of the vanquished idea "withdraws." Case 6.2 illustrates
interdepartmental conflict within a product team and also underscores
an important principle among Playco executives: the way an executive
wins is as important as the way they lose. Victors rarely claim complete
defeat of an opponent. To do so would be to insult the honor of the
vanquished and, in the process, dishonor themselves. Even executives
who do not win, but who play by the rules, maintain a part of their
reputations and can more easily restore their honor in a future contest.
At the same time, the imagery used by executives to frame interdepart-

mental disputes versus that used in intradepartmental conflicts is more aggressive. Such variation conforms to the aggressive imagery used to describe socially distant actors relative to the business mainstream in highly publicized hostile takeovers (Hirsch 1986) and generally by international disputants to describe socially distant opponents (White 1965).

Case 6.2 The Target Date Duel (1985)

Executives on the same product team often split into smaller groups to decide issues relevant to the team as a whole. Three executives—the marketing team leader (Harris) and the executive representatives from R&D (West) and sales (Holmes)—decided to meet separately from their team to devise a set of target dates for the development of a new set of products. West agreed to arrange meetings with Harris and Holmes and attempted to do so over a three-week period. Each time he scheduled a meeting, either Harris or Holmes canceled at the last minute. In the meantime, West quietly gathered the data necessary to organize the plan by himself because he knew he "was dealing with a couple of the strongest people on the product team and he had to be ready" if they proposed their own plan. He announced at a regular team meeting that he would not be caught by surprise by his colleagues and would put together a plan of his own. Facing Harris in the meeting, West announced that he would have nothing to do with a plan proposed by her or Holmes if, as he phrased it, "they had the balls to talk." Harris and Holmes decided that they might be able to "put some notches in their own guns" if they shot West's proposal down. Harris responded to West's challenge by walking to his office the day after the meeting and, in the middle of a meeting between him and three other managers, told West "that they [Harris and Holmes] were insulted that he had gone ahead without their participation, and would present a plan of their own." These challenges and counterchallenges indicated a "duel" would occur at the next team meeting. Besides carefully preparing their presentations, each of the principals prepared themselves through rituals common in such situations. All of the principals wore their lucky ties (or "power bow" in Harris's case) and "flak vests" (not commonly worn on a day-to-day basis) to fend off "bullets" from the opposition. They all spent extra time at their respective health clubs: taking more time in the sauna, having a massage. They also spent considerable time talking to their departmental colleagues about how they would comport themselves during the presentation. The rest of the team knew of the duel via an agenda circulated three days before the meeting.

At the start of the duel, an uninvolved team member spun a gold fountain pen flat on the meeting table; the principal to whom the ink end pointed was allowed to choose the order of presentation. The pen pointed toward West, who elected to present last. Holmes acted as Harris's "second" by handing out copies of the plan to team members and handling all of the visual aids. West used an R& D middle manager as his second. At the conclusion of each presentation, West and Harris began a give-and-take of questions, criticisms, and rebuttals, each careful not to interrupt the other. During this part of the duel, Harris's rebuttals and criticisms grew weaker until she sat mute in response to two lengthy questions by West. West, on the other hand, grew stronger; his criticisms and rebuttals to Harris became more forceful each time he spoke. The other team members remained silent until, as the operations representative put it, the "jousting" concluded. In the aftermath of her two-minute silence to West's final points, Harris tore up her copy of her and Holmes's plan, signaling her acceptance of West's plan. Holmes then collected the copies of his and Harris's plan from the rest of the team and instructed a secretary to feed them into a paper shredder. After the meeting, the combatants ritualistically shook hands. None of the other team members spoke until after the duel, at which time the meeting moved on to other agenda items. Later, West told the observer that, although the team had not accepted his colleagues' plan, Harris and Holmes answered his challenge "strongly." "After all," he concluded, "they're strong players. They couldn't just sit there and do nothing after I called them out."

In disputes between principals who do not work in the same product team but reside in "strong departments," matters that might seem trivial to an outsider—the remodeling of one wing of corporate headquarters, whether the company should fly the flags of representatives of foreign governments when they visit a company installation, and the location of assigned parking places for executive secretaries may escalate into a collective feud between departments and their allies. In all of these cases, the lack of social links between the disputing departments means there is little social pressure to end hostilities and great social pressure to attack in honorable ways. Executives therefore find it nearly impossible to end interdepartmental conflicts without the aid of third parties who intervene to bring about some sort of settlement (white knights who "rescue executives in distress"). Here again the matrix weakens the ability of third parties to constrain or resolve hostilities because of ambiguous and overlapping chains of formal authority. As in interdepartmental conflict, such intervention is limited to persuasion.

Third-party supporters, however, may have the opposite effect on interdepartmental disputes, spreading them to many departments and product teams. The solidarity among marketing and operations executives, for example, engenders the expectation of automatic partisanship in interdepartmental conflict involving one of their own. In less cohesive units, such as sales, partisanship is highly tenuous, and defections to the opposition are not uncommon. Case 6.3 illustrates the modal patterns of conflict management among executives who do not work in the same unit and who work in departments with staunch allies.

Case 6.3 Shoot-out at the Marketing Corral (1985)

Executives at Playco earn colorful nicknames, such as the aforementioned Princess of Power, Iron Man in operations, and the Wizard in R&D. Early one year, the Princess of Power became the head of marketing and introduced a new general marketing plan for the company. Playco traditionally concentrates its production in a five-month period. With several months of marketing surveys showing Playco's home computer products leading the way, the Princess of Power wanted to extend production to nine months per year to capitalize on expanding markets in Australia, Southeast Asia, and Europe. As head of operations, Iron Man believed this plan would jeopardize the quality control systems he had personally championed in the company's manufacturing facilities, systems that had become industry standards. The Princess of Power and Iron Man had never sat on a product team together, so when they met twice with members of the office of the president to discuss the nine-month plan, they spent most of their time, as Iron Man observed, "simply trying to understand each other." At some point in these meetings, Iron Man became annoyed with what he called the Princess of Power's "small bursts of fire" about operations' lack of support for the marketing plan. He felt that she treated him like a "horse put out to pasture who didn't know a demand function from a hole in the ground," while "she did not understand, nor want to understand, what the hard constraints on manufacturing related to quality were." The Princess of Power believed Iron Man was "inflexible" and "out of touch with the direction the company had to go."

At two subsequent meetings the principals exchanged very direct complaints along the lines described above. By the fourth meeting, the Princess had grown tired of Iron Man's "roadblocks" and, in her words, "carefully questioned whether [Iron Man's] questions were in the company's own interests or his own." Iron Man waited several minutes until the Princess had finished her complaints about his reactions to the plan. He then stood up and, in his words, "threw her a couple of hand grenades by looking her in the eye and saying that [he] would not allow her to kill every idea he brought up in public." The Princess then stood up and said, "If you want a war, we'll give you a war."

The ensuing months witnessed the outbreak of war between operations and marketing and their supporters: several presentation shoot-outs between marketing and operations executives and managers as well as the mobilization of members of other departments on behalf of the principal departments. During the dispute, the vice president of administration, Johnson, known as a white knight who rescued executives in distress, intervened with two other white knights, the president of international affairs, Sims, and the Wizard, to reduce the "wounded list." These attempts proved initially unsuccessful, but eventually resulted in a two-day off-site set of "peace talks," which nearly thirty executives and managers attended. The meetings produced a truce between the factions and a private dinner between Iron Man and the Princess at which, according to Johnson, "they agreed to disagree on a variety of matters."

While these analyses and illustrative cases portray the modal realities of conflict management among Playco executives, there is, as the Playco managers say, a seamier side to political life at the top of the corporation that involves only those executives labeled as less honorable.

Conflict Management among Less Honorable Executives

Less honorable executives most clearly indicate their lower status by not responding at all or responding in inappropriate ways to grievances by colleagues. They allow colleagues to verbally "rape" them, simply tolerate their opponents by "flying low," participate in covert action to inconvenience opposition departments through "raids" (nonconfrontational vengeance), or avoid inflamed conflicts by "parachuting out of burning fighters" (when they should see them to their end and "ride them down").[3] Table 6.4 contains the patterns of conflict that are labeled less honorable by Playco executives.

The imagery of conflict used by executives to describe the conflict

Table 6.4   Conflict Management among Less Honorable Playco
                    Executives

Work-Unit Membership of the Principals	Initial Exchanges	Secondary Exchanges	Probable Outcomes
same department (case 1.3) (case 6.4)	flying low or catfight	flying low, hiding, or redlining	amnesia, jumping ship, or vaporizing
same product team (case 6.5)	waltzing around	temporary amnesia, gas, hiding, crying, and/or meltdown	amnesia or jumping ship
different product team and department (case 6.6)	call out	temporary amnesia, crying, or bushwhack/ ambush/raid	amnesia or jumping ship

Note: For case 6.4 types, n = 5; for case 6.5 types, n = 6; for case 6.6 types, n = 4. N = 15. For definitions of terms see appendix C.

management among less honorable executives also highlights that group's violations of the code of honor at Playco. Whereas honorable colleagues portray their opponents in worthy lights by referring to them as white hats or serious players, less honorable executives talk about their adversaries as "dicks" or "sleeping beauties." Moreover, honorable executives commonly label their less honorable departmental colleagues as "pigeons" or "bozos" and their arguments as catfights rather than the more value-neutral skirmishes.

The intradepartmental patterns of executives labeled as less honorable are illustrated in case 1.3 and case 6.4 below. Case 1.3, it will be recalled, simmered nonconfrontationally for some time before it redlined into a "meltdown" (a physical fight) between two executives in the parking lot near the tower. There was no clear winner of the fight, which was gently broken up security guards. In that case Playco executives did not deplore the physical fighting. Rather, they deplored that it occurred outside the boundaries of the code of honor and within the view of "common employees." During fieldwork, for example, two boxing matches were arranged between executives at a local gym in order that they might, as one executive observed, "work out their differences." Case 6.4 involves a similar pattern to case 1.3—the principals' initial nonconfrontation evolves into loud, out-of-control arguing. However, unlike case 1.3, case 6.4 ends with an outcome in which both principals deny that they had ever had a conflict.

Case 6.4 Catfight at the Finance Corral (1985)

A number of issues divided Hicks and Agean of finance. They had earned advanced degrees from rival universities, and when one of their schools lost to the other in a sporting event, the winner would frequently place a banner over the door of the loser or make loud jokes in his presence about the "pitiful" abilities of his team. Both had been hired at the same time, and both desperately wanted to climb up the corporate ladder toward the office of the president. Each regarded the other as a weak executive and, at every turn over their seven-year term with the firm, each attempted to prove his superiority over the other. Neither Hicks or Agean ever learned how to play the game at Playco with anything but less-than-modest skill. As a result, they were viewed as "bean-counting bozos" by their more honorable colleagues.

Hicks and Agean each believed that the other "brownnosed" Bell, the chief financial officer, in dishonorable ways. Hicks claimed that Agean would "wash the guy's car if asked," while Agean claimed that Hicks would "balance Bell's [personal] checkbook." This trouble surfaced when Bell chose Hicks to fill a special finance position being created in engineering (to examine how this case blended into another, see case 6.6 below). Hicks knew that by being considered for the position, he had gone "one up" on Agean. To make sure Agean understood the meaning of Bell's choice, Hicks continually related the move during discussions in meetings that Agean attended. Agean did not retaliate, although privately, he felt "insulted" and called Hicks a "dick completely without honor." Finally, during a meeting, Agean interrupted a Hicks "speech" on the role of finance in engineering by aggressively asking how the engineering position was relevant to the discussion. Hicks responded aggressively by asking Agean if he wasn't bothered by something else. The two men began shouting at each other at such a rapid rate that neither could hear the other speak, according to another executive at the meeting. Both men rose from their chairs and continued shouting for several minutes until they seemed to grow tired and gradually simply "burned themselves out." None of the other executives at the meeting attempted to intercede.

Unlike the heroic tales that circulate among the managerial ranks in the aftermath of an honorable duel, only jokes circulated about the finance catfight. For example: "What's the difference between a loser and finance vice president?" "I don't know." "None." Another went like this: "Did you hear that Hicks and Agean finally had it out in finance?" "No. Who won?" "Nobody, they're both losers." Such jokes made their way to the principals and, needless to say, neither executive wished to make his role in the conflict visible. In meetings with their more honorable colleagues who sometimes jokingly referred to it, they pretended not to know what they were talking about.

Social distance has the same general effects on conflict among less honorable top managers as it does on their honorable colleagues. Intradepartmental conflict among less honorable executives is less aggressive, is shorter, and has a narrower scope than that which occurs interdepartmentally. The imagery used by less honorable disputants to describe socially distant opponents is also more aggressive and accusatory (in the sense that principals attempt to garner zero-sum wins with their opponents). Case 6.5 illustrates interdepartmental conflict between less honorable executives. Note that this case begins as one might between two honorable executives. However, it quickly evolves into several nonverbal grievance exchanges, including "temporary amnesia" by one principal of the other's complaints, "crying" about the conflict by both principals to confidants, "hiding" by one principal to avoid the other, and finally a "meltdown."

Case 6.5 The Wild Bunch (1986)

The wild bunch is a product team responsible for computer learning aids for children. In one situation, planning vice president Pound believed operations vice president Ingle to be unsuitable to present their team's new products at what Playco managers termed a "product send-off" (a presentation attended by hundreds of Playco employees to preview new products before they go into production). At two weekly team meetings, Pound and Ingle "waltzed around" about the latter's suitability to present. At a third meeting the following week, Ingle turned away from his colleague and noticeably frowned as though he had had a "gas attack." He then interrupted Pound in midsentence with a loud, lengthy comment. Subsequently, both Pound and Ingle went crying to friends, but never confronted each other. Pound hid from team meetings for two weeks because, as he put it, he "couldn't stand to be in the same room as that dick." Rumors began in the company that Pound feared confronting Ingle.

Two weeks after the initial incident, at another team meeting, Ingle interrupted Pound loudly again and Pound responded by raking his hand across the burgundy teak meeting table, pushing his and two other colleagues' materials to the carpet. Pound and Ingle then had a meltdown, pushing each other and swinging their fists. The meltdown lasted several minutes, spilling out into the hallway, where a security guard watched for two or three minutes before breaking it up. Inside the meeting room, two colleagues continued talking about another issue, and two others were laughing. The principals suffered several bruises and clothing tears.

Word of the fight quickly spread through the company. Pound commented in the aftermath that he "couldn't let that dick get away with pretending not to listen to me again."

Whereas honorable disputants can mobilize departmental and cross-departmental allies to attack enemies at meeting duels, less honorable executives command neither the loyalty nor the trust to do the same. The scope of less honorable executive conflict management enlarges in unpredictable ways as executives become allies (get "sucked in") because, for example, they happen to work near a conflict management action. Respectable third parties do not generally intervene to settle such disputes either, because of the same trepidation one would have, an executive noted, in intervening in a fight between rabid dogs: "You never know what's going to happen, even if it's your own dog. You could get bit yourself." The narrative below illustrates this process. Note that it begins with a "call out" (as in interdepartmental conflicts between honorable executives). Yet its path deviates from the honorable way when the principals engage in numerous covert actions ("raids" on an opposition department, or "ambushes"—also called "bushwhacks" or "cheap shots"—against individual adversaries) and, like in intra- and interdepartmental product team disputes, allow their grievances to peter out without a public and ritualistic resolution as they tire of the conflict.

Case 6.6 The Finance Raid (1985)

Two of the executives known for their covert conflict management (who wear black hats in the firm)—Bell, the chief financial officer, and Tweedle, the president of domestic affairs—became embittered over Tweedle's attempt to transfer Hicks (see case 6.4) to engineering to create a new position: vice president of engineering cost control. Financial executives do not meet regularly with product teams but are ultimately responsible for all cost control. Tweedle viewed the transfer as an experimental attempt to integrate finance with the product teams. Hicks would remain a member of finance, have an office in engineering, and meet, when appropriate, with one or two product teams. Bell believed Tweedle had ulterior motives: "This is a chickenshit ambush on my decision power in corporate financial affairs. Tweedle tried to do this last year by taking more formal control for the domestic budget. Now this. Hicks would end up reporting to Tweedle."

Bell called out Tweedle at a meeting of the office of the president to "lay out his whole strategy for integrating finance into the product teams." Tweedle did not respond at the meeting or subsequently, suffering temporary amnesia by denying to close colleagues that there was any problem between him and Bell. Hicks's reassignment occurred as Tweedle planned. In the ensuing months, Tweedle ignored Bell's many memos questioning the transfer and spread rumors that he and Bell had worked out an agreement for Hicks's transfer and that Bell's word was worth as much as an "Italian lira money order" and perhaps he "did not have all his dogs on one leash."

The dispute escalated during remodeling at headquarters when Tweedle approved plans for temporarily moving finance executives to a building adjacent to the tower. Without advance notice to finance, the move occurred on a weekend. When finance executives arrived the following Monday, they discovered the move and that several important computer tapes and data printouts from an internal audit they had just completed had been thrown away. Tweedle knew that Bell had personally championed the now-disrupted audit. Speculation ran high in the company that Tweedle had involved himself directly in throwing away the data when he had stopped by headquarters for two hours during the move. Tweedle expressed his temporary amnesia by maintaining that he had nothing against finance, although he admitted to some that the move would upset the sleeping beauties in finance, who were believed to be enamored with their own abilities but ignorant of their negative reputation among other top managers.

Bell stopped his memo writing for two weeks following this incident as his staff attempted to reconstruct the data from older backup tapes. In the meantime, Bell suspended all financial data reports to teams developing domestic products. Bushwhacks such as these continued for nearly two years until Tweedle and Bell tired of the battle. Tweedle and Bell eventually jumped ship, and Hicks became interim chief financial officer until a national search could be done for a new CFO.

Concluding Remarks

One could argue that Playco's growth into a multinational corporation during the 1970s and its high product replacement rate (which decreased in the 1980s) could have led by themselves to the conflict management patterns at Playco. One could also argue that the imagery

Playco executives use to frame their conflicts derive solely from their products lines: games and learning aids that encompass the themes of chivalrous duels, Old West shoot-outs, and science fiction warfare. Indeed, only twenty-eight of seventy-four Playco conflict images derive directly from hostile takeover imagery (see table 6.2). Yet the very same themes in these product lines—the "bread and butter" of the firm as one executive put it—existed for over thirty years before the firm's restructuring with the matrix and the advent of the hostile takeover. Despite all of these factors, the culture of honor among Playco executives did not exist until the 1980s. Conflict management prior to the 1980s had a decided authoritative character. Thus, many of the local symbols that Playco executives draw on to frame their conflict into compensatory contests of honor existed, but they did not have a plausibility structure associated with them until the transformations brought about by the matrix. By the same token, the imagery of the hostile takeover would not have had the impact on executives if it did not coexist with the particular plausibility structure at Playco. If the language of the hostile takeover represents the institutionalization of a symbolic dimension of a macrosocial change in intercorporate American business (Hirsch 1986:821), the experience of executives at Playco illustrates the impact of symbolic and structural dimensions of matrix structures and hostile takeovers inside corporations. It is first to the plausibility structure of Playco honor that I now turn, and I follow with an examination of the functions of Playco honor at the organizational and individual levels. I conclude the chapter with some speculations on the implications of intracorporate executive honor and vengeance for the study of executive inertia, control, accountability, and decision making.

The Plausibility Structure of Honorable Vengeance

The findings of this chapter largely corroborate the arguments made in chapter 2 concerning the relationship between accusatory schemas of conflict management, confrontation, and communication networks arrayed in coalitions in the absence of hierarchy. Beyond these general explanations lie more specific explanations about the structural conditions under which vengeance and codes of honor arise. Once again I turn to Donald Black's work on cross-cultural conflict management.

Black (1990:44–47) argues that highly predictable and ritualized conflict management framed by codes of honor is common among relatively equal disputants who have sustained, mutual access and who have standing groups of supporters they can easily mobilize on their behalf, but who are not socially intimate or functionally interdependent. Taken together, these factors constrain disputants' choices of conflict management. The more a setting contains these social characteristics, the more likely it will contain a predominance of reciprocal vengeance ordered by codes of honor (1990:62).

Equality (in terms of resources and authority) means that disputants are constantly struggling for some sort of symbolic capital vis-à-vis their opponents. This induces the swift address of affronts by a challenger lest one gain an inferior reputation (Berscheid et al. 1968; Peristiany 1965). Egalitarian settings also contain few third parties who command the resources or deference necessary to settle disputes. Those third parties that do exist in such contexts typically rely upon their personal influence over the parties to suspend their hostilities. Conflicts are therefore rarely transformed from dyadic confrontations between principals to triadic settlement processes (Koch 1974). Where standing groups exist, the risks of confrontation can be syndicated across group members. As a result, groups, rather than individuals, may be even more willing to openly reciprocate grievances against opponents (Thoden van Velzen and van Wetering 1960). Finally, relational distance and functional independence between coalitions reduce the likelihood of common interests (especially exchange relations), which both disputant groups may want to protect and which can engender more restrained conflict management (Colson 1953; Gluckman 1967).

Playco executives experience all of these conditions simultaneously as they navigate their matrix and departmental authority systems. As described earlier, Playco top managers find themselves in a relatively egalitarian system: the crosscutting authority in the matrix and departmental hierarchies tend to cancel each other out. The uppermost levels of the corporation, the office of the president, contains four top managers of relatively equal formal status and with complex and ambiguous reporting lines to their subordinates. Thus, even at the top of the corporation, the possibility of third-party settlement is highly constrained. Executives also have easy access to each other by being housed in the same building and by attending frequent meetings with each other. Yet most executives still tend to confine their informal interaction to departmental colleagues, reserving much of their interdepartmental interaction to formal meetings. When executives speak of the necessity of informational interdependence among colleagues, they primarily refer to that among their intradepartmental colleagues. Many executives, therefore, can call upon departmental colleagues as allies in disputes and other affairs. The fact that more ritualized challenges and ripostes occur in interdepartmental conflict conforms to general propositions that relational distance, functional independence, and a high capacity for collective action are found whenever disputants engage in honorable vengeance. Also found in settings where honor is the symbolic currency of conflict is behavioral predictability at the individual and social organizational levels.

Small Wins and Individual Uncertainty

In a world where the corporation could be "taken over at any minute," as one Playco top manager put it, in which corporations are increasingly restructuring their operations, executives realize their substantive decisions can become instantly meaningless because of the actions of unknown investors or shareholders. One of Playco's presidents commented that "to worry about a single decision and how it's going to affect the firm is foolish. We can't really control what the market does, what the shareholders do, or what some yahoo investor with big money wants to do [in the case of a hostile takeover]. So you might as well try to affect the things closest to you."

In social-psychological terms such behavior tacitly adopts the strategy of "small wins . . . controllable opportunities that produce visible results" (Weick 1984:43). Actual restructuring and its threat in companies that have experienced takeovers have eroded organizational loyalty to the point where small-win strategies often manifest themselves as managerial free agency (Hirsch 1987:107–08): a lack of focus on corporate goals and the continual consideration of viable employment with organizations other than one's own. Playco executives breathe the air of takeovers, have witnessed their effects on companies that have been so acquired, but have successfully fended off takeover attempts themselves. Although Playco executives have not experienced high turnover rates, as indicated by the lengthy tenures most of them have with the firm, they have adapted to this increasing nihilism toward corporate loyalty by focusing on their own fates as expressed ritualistically through small-win strategies in their culture of honor.

Social Similarity and Organizational Uncertainty

Honor not only allows individuals to maintain a sense of balance and efficacy within the volatility of American business, it also operates as an organizational culture control to reinforce social similarity relative to outside groups. This is particularly salient at a time when more women, however slowly, are joining the largely male domains of the executive levels, specifically at Playco. The functions of social similarity persist among Playco executives through executive honor. Playco's code of honor defines a particular "masculine" standard to which viable members of its relevant community must adhere. Like codes of honor everywhere, it is the key link between self and community, defining appropriate institutional roles for incumbents (Berger et al. 1973:86). Honor at Playco defines who is to be trusted; it helps executives predict what their colleagues will do in a setting that might otherwise seem like a maelstrom of ambiguous authority and continual dramatic confrontation. The unnerving experience of conflict is framed as a contest of honor with the roles of the principals and their supporters carefully defined. Honor therefore provides an evaluative criterion for executives that operates outside of the official criteria but can more easily be used in dealing with colleagues. Honor also defines a particular worth and virtue for the individual that enhances the prestige of more formally conferred markings, such as earnings or formal organizational rank. To be honorable is to achieve a social identity in distinction to one's colleagues.

This is why less honorable executives are avoided by their more honorable colleagues. Honorable Playco executives fear being contaminated by associations with less worthy individuals, particularly during disputes. They also fear the unpredictability of their less honorable colleagues far more than the familiar challenges of their honorable colleagues. Ironically, less honorable executives possess a more valuable form of capital than their honorable colleagues: unpredictability. Yet, in imperfectly imitating the routine conflict management of their honorable colleagues, less honorable executives become impotent in transforming this capital into power by framing their behavior in relatively predictable patterns.

Implications of Intracorporate Honor

The contrast between the matrix system at Playco (as well as the other three firms in the study that experimented with various forms of matrix management at the executive levels) and mechanistic and atomistic firms is striking. As a result, the hypotheses tentatively offered below are more far-reaching than those offered at the ends of the previous two chapters. The first three of these are directly grounded in the Playco case, while the last two are more speculative in nature.

Dramatic, confrontational conflict management does not necessarily equate with organizational chaos and disorder. To summarize these arguments more formally:

6a.   Ritualized conflict management ceremonies provide stability and predictability in organizational contexts of high uncertainty and ambiguity.

In essence, this hypothesis implies an often forgotten and painful lesson about conflict: that stable conflict relations, albeit aggressive, distasteful, and even violent, are themselves a kind of normative order. Some conflict schemas and scripts, such as those in the minimalist order analyzed qualitatively in the previous chapter, intuitively appear to be associated with order because grievances are nonconfrontational. The rancor observed in such an order is low. Mechanistic bureaucracies seem integrally linked with order as well because conflict management acts as a damper on public disputing and because of the wider cultural hegemony that bureaucratic solutions to organizational conflict enjoy in American society. When scholars and laypersons turn their attention to confrontation, particularly aggressive self-help such as that at Playco, the assumption is immediately made that such behaviors are emblematic of social disorganization or even senseless (e.g., Black 1983).

In mechanistic bureaucracies superiors use the prerogatives of their formal position to visit control in the daily routines of their subordinates. In atomistic organizations, direct control at the top is nearly impossible to achieve because of the low visibility and independence among top managers. If control exists, it occurs through tortuously slow and hardly accountable minimalist grievance pursuits. In organizations like Playco, control emerges out of the system of conflict management.

6b.   Intracorporate reputation and honor ceremonies can be sources of control and information for top managers over their executive subordinates.

This hypotheses is suggested by Eccles's (1985) arguments that managerial conflict among subordinates can be used by superiors as a source of information, thus increasing their ability subtly to control subordinates' behavior. Control can also result from managerial conflict as managers police each other's actions, ensuring, as Eccles argues, that "both are using resources as efficiently and effectively as possible" (1985:215). The public nature of the art of honorable vengeance makes it a perfect source of information for top management at Playco. Playco's chief executive officer, for example, noted that he need not practice Peters and Waterman's (1982) "management by walking around" because information abounded regarding winners and losers in recent managerial duels. The fact that Playco executives gauge reputations in order to appropriately challenge their colleagues and respond to challenges also ensures a great deal of mutual monitoring.

The empirical materials presented in this chapter, however, also suggest that control and information obtained in this way can cut several ways. Benefits from conflict and intracorporate vengeance in particular depend on three crucial issues. First, such benefits will result only if executives are driven not only by conflict games but also by substantive issues of importance to the health of their organization. At Playco, ritualized conflict games mean a great deal to executives aside from the substantive issues at stake. Consider, for example, the importance placed by the participants in cases 6.1 through 6.3 on how they fought their conflicts, how they would be perceived by their colleagues, and whether they won, rather than on what they fought about. In cases 1.3 and 6.4 through 6.6, winning was the only thing, to quote Vince Lombardi's old cliche; the standards of the game, much less its content, were not paramount to its participants. As a result, it is unclear what kinds of standards the participants will uphold in executive settings conducive to intracorporate honor and vengeance—standards related to the game itself or those related to bottom-line efficiency however measured.

Second, the amount of public conflict (as suggested in remarks by Playco executives comparing mid 1980s conflict management at the firm with that which occurred in the mid 1970s) may lead to further uncertainty and even a sense of powerlessness by top management. The complexities of crosscutting authority relations at the executive levels may constrain translating knowledge of executive activities into timely action. Moreover, members of the office of the president are sometimes constrained to act on the information they garner lest they become involved in a protracted and potentially damaging (to their honor) conflict.

Finally, the informational and control benefits of intracorporate, honorable vengeance depend upon whose perspective one takes in assigning its costs and returns. The office of the president at Playco could benefit from the public nature of conflict in the culture of honor. At the same time, the benefits to the participants of vengeance are harder to assess. Certainly, one may gain skills at managing conflict in an honorable way. If the diffusion of matrix forms and hostile takeovers have created similar conditions in other large firms, then these skills may have some transferability. This is an open question beyond the scope of this book. Moreover, one may even enjoy the "biting" if one wins one's disputes as the executive quoted at the outset of this chapter suggested. However, the materials herein suggest that some executives thrive in the world of challenges and ripostes at Playco, while others find it difficult to play the game or even perform their duties because, as one vice president put it, they "are always looking over their shoulder."

A third implication of this study relates to the previous one but with specific ties to executive accountability and decision making:

6c.   Intracorporate reputation and honor ceremonies act as a check on the obsfucation of accountability in executive decision making created by the matrix and the language and practices associated with hostile takeovers.

Matrix systems promote the syndication of risk by entire executive corps as groups of high-level managers embedded in complex authority relations, rather than individual managers, are responsible for decision making. In such a structure, it is difficult to trace decisions to any one manager; most decisions must be traced to some group process within or between product teams or departments. Hostile takeovers similarly obfuscate managerial accountability by creating ambiguous lines of corporate control from executives to their own corporation. The turbulent sea of hostile takeovers provides executives with convenient fall guys for poor decision making—stockholders, boards of directors, unknown corporate raiders—all of whom, in a broad sense, syndicate the risk of decision making for corporate executives. Honorable vengeance provides one check on this because of its public nature. The necessity of maintaining one's honor within the corporation requires executives to tout their own prowess at vanquishing opponents, thus making themselves more visible as principals in decisional outcomes.

Scholars and practitioners have long argued that matrix management is extremely difficult to implement (Davis and Lawrence 1977). Less often discussed is the process of changing a matrix system to another kind of managerial structure (such as back to a unitary command structure). Black (1990:47) calls the social setting in which vengeance persists a "stable agglomeration" because its participants are often "frozen together" in endless patterns of negative reciprocity framed by honor. Such a scenario captures the behavioral patterns at Playco and suggests yet another implication:

6d.   Over time, the negative reciprocity engendered in matrix systems tends to increase internal organizational inertia.

Playco's chief executive officer noted in a 1989 interview that the managerial system designed to promote flexibility and change, the matrix, may itself be nearly impossible to change once it has been in place over a period of years. In that interview, he expressed some dismay with twelve years of the matrix because it seemed to make executive relations "more drawn out." When asked if the firm would ever consider restructuring the executive ranks into a traditional hierarchy, he speculated that the matrix was so firmly entrenched that it would be impossible to replace in the absence of a takeover or merger.

As many sociologists of organizations have argued, to understand large corporations one must consider how multiple sets of managerial interests and structural factors interact to produce organizational outcomes (Fligstein 1987, 1990). To be sure, Playco executives do think about substantive organizational productivity, but, like the upper middle classes in general (Lamont 1992), these concerns are mixed with, and often superseded by, concerns about how their behavior will immediately be viewed by their colleagues, and whether their behavior will enhance or dissipate their social standings as people of worth and virtue. Playco executives keenly feel these pressures—more so than the pressure to substantively produce for the firm's bottom line.

CHAPTER SEVEN

CONCLUSION: ORTHODOXY, CHANGE, AND IDENTITY

Caught in the ordinary milieux of their everyday lives, ordinary men often cannot reason about the great social structures—rational and irrational—of which their milieux are subordinate parts. Accordingly, they often carry out series of apparently rational actions without any idea of the ends they serve, and there is increasing suspicion that those at the top as well—like Tolstoy's generals—only pretend they know.

—C. Wright Mills

My intent was to explore, examine, and explain patterns of conflict management among corporate executives. In so doing, I also hoped to comment more generally on conflict in corporations as well that which occurs beyond the confines of formal organizations. My findings largely substantiate claims about the private and informal nature of executive conflict management made in the opening pages of chapter 1. The findings are also favorable to the contention that local social contexts and indigenous customs of conflict management are isomorphic. This book thus stands as something of a counterpoint to the prevailing tendency to view decision making by managers and disputants of all kinds as consciously rational and optimal, if not for their corporation and society (e.g., Chandler and Hikino 1990; Williamson 1985), then for themselves. Indeed, implied by my arguments and observations is the question of the conditions under which executives consciously and rationally act in the interests of their own corporations, and more generally the conditions under which all disputants consciously pursue their grievances in instrumental fashions. Executives, like all disputants, purposively manage conflict (as the preceding chapters demonstrate), yet they do so within the normative parameters of their local contexts. In particular, local customs of conflict management shape the possibilities for dispute processing that individuals imagine when they begin to make sense of a grievance and think about how to pursue it. The customs of conflict management provide, at the executive levels, the foundations for each corporate normative order, which exists as a semi-autonomous social field relative to its larger environment.

Beyond its private and informal nature, executive conflict management cannot be characterized by a single dominant pattern. Two sets of widespread executive contexts in American corporations represent well Melville Dalton's (1959:263) insight that corporate managers "are so busy hiding conflict that [they] quake when [they] must simultaneously deal with it and pretend that it does not exist" (1959:263). In both mechanistic bureaucracies and atomistic organizations, conflict is largely hidden and conflict management for the most part becomes an affair set behind closed doors—in the mechanistic bureaucracy in order to demonstrate competence at managing one's subordinates and in the atomistic organization in order to demonstrate proper professional etiquette.

Conflict management in mechanistic bureaucracies is constituted in its authority structure and varies according to the ranks of its participants within the chain of command. Whatever the issues involved, executive superiors typically attempt to handle their grievances against subordinates unilaterally from a penal perspective by simply ordering their subordinates to cease their objectionable behavior or by engaging in some informal form of disciplinary action. Subordinates pursue grievances quite differently. They typically endure objectionable actions by their bosses, living with their grievances for some time prior to acting on them. Although subordinates also tend to frame their grievances against superiors penally, they commonly pursue such grievances by secretly complaining to confidants within or outside the firm and by attempting to avoid contact with the offenders. Occasionally, subordinates resort to more nefarious means of pursuing grievances against their superiors by covert means, such as sabotage. When subordinates do confront their superiors they outwardly engage in careful, conciliatory approaches, often secretly wishing they could punish a wayward superior. Executives of the same rank who are in conflict typically refer their problems to the next-higher common superior for settlement. Very few instances of negotiation occur in mechanistic bureaucracies (and none among executives of differing ranks). Although formal grievance procedures exist at the executive levels in some of the mechanistic bureaucracies in this study, they are rarely used except as a desperate threat or as a precursor to legal action by aggrieved executives exiting the corporation.

In atomistic organizations, official rank has little influence on the kinds of conflict management in which adversaries engage. Overall, executives are highly autonomous and have weak ties with one another. Top managers in such settings primarily avoid one another as a means of expressing and pursuing grievances. An executive's seniority in the firm has some impact on their ability to impose outcomes in conflict situations, but the restrained and minimalist framing of conflict management remains relatively constant. The conflict management imagery associated with these patterns focuses on "professionalism." Conflict management is viewed as an unnecessary and dirty aspect of organizational life and a professional manager is one who is above confrontation and above using whatever authority they have to impose an outcome. Professionals repress their grievances and ignore the grievances of others.

But order among executives is not simply a function of the conventional societal myths about how to organize managerial work. Matrix systems, which have become relatively popular alternatives to the first two kinds of executive contexts, exhibit orders maintained without the sure spine of unitary chains of command or the flesh of professional etiquette. In matrix systems conflict management occurs via positive and negative reciprocity, which tend to open up conflict processes rather than suppressing them as in mechanistic bureaucracies or atomistic organizations. All of the matrix systems in this study overlaid project teams over existing functional units. While weakening the formal authority of superiors, such arrangements in many instances strengthened the solidarity of functional units as they operated as coalitions in intergroup disputes. Intradepartment conflict management tends to unfold via positive reciprocity expressed through negotiations, resembling to some degree the vision of organizations as "negotiated orders" (Strauss 1978). This same tendency was noted at Independent Accounting within the management consulting practice and as an emergent property of conflict management between the traditional and consulting practices at Independent Accounting. Even so, executives negotiate far less than they engage in other forms and processes of conflict management, except under very special circumstances in which formal authority relations are largely relaxed and interdependence among managers is unusually high—just the sort of conditions that occur in matrix contexts. Product team meetings at Playco, for example, become the terrain on which negative reciprocity in the form of vengeance games occurs between disputants and functional partisans. Thus, one of the lessons from interdepartmental disputing at Playco—perhaps all of the matrix systems in this study—is that normative orders in organizations, albeit somewhat rough-hewn, can be maintained via negative reciprocity as well as positive reciprocity in the absence of strong central authority (cf. Taylor 1982).

These characterizations as well as the longer descriptions and analyses from which they are drawn provide the reader with portraits of contexts at a certain time and place. In regards to this objective—case studies of particular contexts—Snow and Anderson write that "such studies capture social processes and actors in configurations of relationships and perspectives at a specific time. But social configurations change" (1992:303–4). Indeed, the three firms described at length in chapters 4 through 6 have changed in the years following my fieldwork in them.

In the late 1980s and early 1990s, Old Financial found itself mired in the worst financial industry crisis since the Great Depression of the 1930s. Old Financial's environment has grown turbulent and uncertain as numerous savings and loans have been reorganized, disbanded, or merged. The firm has thus far weathered the numerous savings and loans closures by reinventing itself as a bank and selling off some of its subsidiaries. Authoritative conflict management at Old Financial still persists, although parts of the corporation's executive levels have experimented with lateral arrangements similar to those at Playco. Strongly entrenched functional structures remain, and more dramatic and confrontational conflict management processes have emerged, centered around the arts of the meeting duels and the ritually aggressive social influence. Ironically, the opposite tendency has occurred at Playco, where the matrix structure has been partially dismantled through radical reorganizations and the selling of some of the corporation's holdings. Playco executives now experience two dominant patterns of conflict management: one that rests on ritualistic confrontation and a second which rests on the prerogatives of superiors. Independent Accounting's dominant minimalist conflict management has undergone further changes, moving toward greater confrontation and negotiation.

Beyond these particularistic developments lie theoretical implications that extend beyond the contexts in the study and even beyond organizational contexts. In the sections below, I first discuss the implications of the study for organizational analysis and organizational change. I then discuss implications that focus more broadly on the relationship between conflict management, identity, and conflict intervention. I close with more speculative implications for conflict management and the wider society.

Orthodoxy in Organizational Analysis

The arguments of this work call attention to the fact that the proximate factors which influence conflict management choices and pro-

cesses identified in cross-cultural anthropological studies influence the
ways of handling conflict at the tops of large, modern corporations.
The habitualized, scripted forms of decision making about conflict ascribed to North American working-class disputants (Merry and Silbey
1984) appear to fit appropriately with the experience of organizational
elites as well. Studying up, then, reveals more similarities than differences between the powerful and the less powerful in terms of how
they manage conflict among themselves. In an ironic way, this argument would seem to partly contradict the new orthodoxy in organizational analysis that has developed over the past fifteen years.

Whereas the old orthodoxy focused on "intendedly rational" (Simon
1976) action inside organizations and how such action emanated from
organizations to their environments (Powell 1985), the new orthodoxy
views organizations as functions of environments, whether environments are conceived as organizational populations (e.g., Hannan and
Freeman 1989), sets of institutional arrangements (Meyer and Rowan
1977; Powell and Dimaggio 1991), functional fields as used in the present work (see generally Scott 1991), or some combination of structural
and institutional arrangements (Fligstein 1990). If one peruses any of
the mainstream organizational journals (*Administrative Science Quarterly, Academy of Management Journal,* and *Organizational Science,* for example), the new orthodoxy does indeed seem to have conquered the
myopia of the old orthodoxy. In so doing, however, it may be substitut-
ing a new shortcoming, which, for want of a better term could be
called "organizational presbyopia": a tendency to dismiss proximate
social relations inside organizations as so much local noise that plays
little role in the long run and is unimportant for the big picture of how
organizations behave.[1]

Organizational analysis has increasingly become data analysis from
afar born of surveys and large data archives, and massaged by statistical tools that remove scholars from the stuff of organizations themselves. There is no question that macrosociological analysis utilizing
large data sets and sophisticated quantitative techniques is important
for understanding organizational action. But such analysis also misses
the role of local social and interpretive structures among actual actors
in and between organizations. As Granovetter has argued, "No adequate link between macro- and micro-level theories can be established
without a much fuller understanding of these relations" (1985:507).

This argument is particularly true for the tops of organizations. The
well-demarcated exclusivity of the executive levels means that executives are embedded in a highly insular world that powerfully mediates
their perceptual and behavioral exposure to organizational environments. An executive's vision of the world is constructed and sustained

within their local contexts. Whether they enact weak or strong formal chains of command, create and sustain loose-knit or dense-knit communication networks, experience and carry perceptions of contextual stability or instability, the longer executives work inside the executive ranks, the more tenuous their ties to parties outside that world become and the more likely they are to develop schemas for understanding drawn exclusively from their insular local contexts (Starbuck and Milliken 1988). These schemas, therefore, will include large portions of what is appropriate for those local contexts, rather than what may be appropriate for organizational efficiency or the elusive big picture about which executives are so fond of talking. More to the point: many students of the modern corporation assume that organizational adaptation occurs as if the organization is collectively rational in part because they assume that top managers act in ways that contribute to collectively rational problem solving. The findings in this book suggest that executive decision making is quite often decoupled from substantive rationality, focused instead on the customs of local interpersonal relations. Despite this decoupling and the feelings of powerlessness executives can feel (see chapter 2), their decisions still carry great weight in the sense that elite intervention can play critical roles in the creation and maintenance of organizational structures and institutional arrangements (Powell 1991). If this is so, understanding organizational action requires that serious attention be paid to the microdynamics of action within organizations, particularly among top managers and others who have access to the means of organizational power. Such an argument also implies, then, that we need theoretical constructs that are neither purely "macro" or "micro," but theoretical efforts which have as their foci the relationships between proximate and broader social contexts. Until then, organizational analysts will be able to tell only part of the story of how organizations function.

Indigenous Conflict Management and Organizational Change

The theoretical arguments as well as the descriptive materials in this book also point to the tenuous relationship between conflict management and fundamental (second-order) organizational change. As argued in chapter 1, a dual normative boundary exists in most established social contexts; the first bounds nongrievance-related social relations, while the second bounds routine conflict management. If fundamental change is to occur as an outcome of conflict management, the second normative boundary governing indigenous conflict management must be crossed. This means that a transformation of the contextual schemas through which people interpret nonconflict *and* conflict relations must occur. In effect, fundamental change requires that organizational members develop qualitatively different understandings of their proximate contexts (Kanter 1983). Yet a fundamental tenet of the new orthodoxy in organizational analysis is that organizations exhibit strong tendencies toward structural inertia; social structures within and surrounding organizations are not plastic and do not easily change (Hannan and Freeman 1989). To the social-structural inhibitors of organizational change, we can add interpretive inertia and the discourse processes that help to perpetuate the meanings held for familiar events (e.g., Bartunek 1988). In other words, the common meanings that people impute to their surroundings do not easily change either. Any fundamental change, therefore, must occur through behavioral, interpretive, and discourse transformations.

It is typically so difficult for transformations of these kinds to occur within formal organizations that Bartunek and Reid, for example, argue that fundamental change is likely only where "situations or events (especially crises) [arise] that are so drastically different from the usual situation that they short-circuit the application of typically applied scripts because no one knows how to deal with them" (1992:141). Even crisis situations, Bartunek and Reid further argue, require explicit models that people can refer to during the implementation of completely new schemas, scripts, and social structures or recombinations of existing ones; otherwise people are likely to revert back to their older, more familiar habits. In business organizations, such crises might arise during restructurings, mergers, hostile takeovers, or radical divestitures, or by radically changing functional fields (as experienced by Old Financial, for example). Barring such crises, most routine conflict management in organizations ultimately results in the perpetuation of the status quo, at least in the short term.

However, this is not to imply that change in some ways is not "routine" itself in most organizational contexts. Routine change does occur, but of the first-order variety that only slightly alters the schemas, scripts, and social relations in a given context. First-order change occurs within existing normative boundaries via social processes that, like routine conflict management, perpetuate the fundamental parameters of its social context. Without exogenous shocks, second-order change may occur only as a slow accretion process through minute recombinations and slight alterations in existing schemas. Although the data in this study do not allow for a complete examination of how organizational orders relate to processes of change, they do allow for some speculations about routine first-order change.

Consistent with the prerogatives of superiors, first-order change in authoritative orders (as seen in mechanistic organizations) would likely occur via direct imposition from above, as when a superior issues a direct order about how a subordinate should behave, or via indirect imposition through the establishment of rules that specify modified routines to be followed (while still articulating with existing rules and patterns of relations). There would also likely be negative sanctions attached to noncompliance with new rules or directives. At Old Financial dozens of such directives and rules flow down the corporate hierarchy every week. Because of the prevalence of mechanistic bureaucracies and their attendant authoritative orders, imposed change processes are well documented throughout the organizational literature (e.g., Edwards 1979; Gouldner 1954).

Less documented are processes of first-order change that occur within the minimalist orders that are typical of atomistic bureaucracies. Minimalist orders would appear inimical to widespread change because of the lack of ties between incumbents that enable the diffusion of innovations. Yet incremental change, like conflict management, may occur in highly fragmented fashions. Such a process resembles innovation via "structural equivalence" as individuals independently adapt to similar structural conditions. As Burt (1987) argues, structural equivalence processes of change occur via social comparisons. Individuals attempting to live up to the images and generalized standards of their roles (for example, a partner's role as a professional at Independent Accounting), compare their abilities, procedures, and adequacies with like comparators and, on the fly, adopt innovations that they believe will make them more competitive or that will live up to their idealized role images of their structural positions (1987:1291). This may explain why incremental collaborative change (called *cohesion* by Burt 1987), such as that illustrated by the increasing interdependence of the traditional practices and management consulting at Independent Accounting, has been so difficult for partners in the traditional practices to accept. Partners in the traditional practices are accustomed to the fragmented change processes of structural equivalence. Change via direct contact is incomprehensible to partners in the traditional practices.

Reciprocal orders should exhibit very different patterns of change. First-order change where there is positive reciprocity (negotiation) should occur through direct, constant communication between innovators about changes under way or proposed as they socialize with one another and come to a normative understanding of the costs and benefits of adoption (Burt 1987; Coleman et al. 1966; Rogers 1983). In this sense, diffusion of first-order change in negotiated orders should occur through a process of what could be called *continuous cohesion,* reflecting the cooperation between actors. First-order change where there is negative reciprocity (vengeance) should occur through processes by which parties adopt innovations to go one up on the other party. Again, there will be little fundamental change in the context as parties simply recapitulate the fundamental elements of their routine behaviors and negative reciprocity in their change processes.

These speculations focus on indigenous change processes within social contexts. But what implications does the present study carry for conflict management intervention and change? To answer this question, I turn to the relationship between conflict management and identity.

Identity and Conflict Management Intervention

A diverse literature has developed on the relationship between identities and social contexts. At least three levels of identity exist: the personal, social, and collective.[2] Personal identities are imputed to the self by actors themselves, while social identities are imputed to individuals by others (Snow and Anderson 1987:1347). Collective identity focuses on projections of identity to and from groups. Rosenberg writes that a contextual perspective on identity means "to investigate the bearing of some general property of the *group* on the thoughts, acts, or norms of its constituent members" (1992:608). In this sense, constituent members could be individual persons or collectivities. For most sociologists, social identity contexts (salient contexts in which people are most often labeled with particular identities and come to identify themselves in particular ways) consist of racial, religious, ethnic, and economic foci.

In this book, I focus on social contexts that are embedded in rationalized work organizations and that specifically consist of intersections of social and interpretive structures. This view of context thus suggests locus for identity other than the broad sociological categories above: the customs and pragmatics of routine social interaction. That is: *Personal, social and group identities may have as much to do with how people accomplish and frame basic activities within organizations (such as communication, evaluation, innovation, change, and, routine indigenous conflict management) as with the substantive goals of action.* Because conflict management often ritualizes and brings into relief basic assumptions and actions about how people go about their daily lives, it in turn may be a key factor in establishing, maintaining, and dissolving personal and social identities. Moreover, the relationship between customs of conflict management and identity may be particularly important in contexts in which there exist tight embracement and congruence between structurally based roles and personal identities. In such contexts, as Snow and Anderson argue, structurally based roles and relationships do indeed function as an important "springboard for personal identities" (1987:1366). In executive contexts top managers typically embrace their roles despite the inherent difficulties of being an executive. Moreover, executives derive much if not all of their social and personal identities from what Jackall terms an "unrelenting attentiveness to the social intricacies" of their roles in their organizations (1988:202). A large portion of those social intricacies involve the management of conflict between themselves and their colleagues.

Evidence for the relationship between identity and conflict management can be found in executive accounts about what it means to be an effective executive in their local contexts and what is distinctive about their contexts relative to other executive contexts. In these accounts one often finds references to the "way an effective executive handles people problems here." Recall the accounts at the outset of the organizational case-study chapters. At the outset of chapter 4, for example, the Old Financial executive focused on the machinelike qualities of Old Financial, but also how one should control subordinates. At Independent Accounting, the beehives contain silent bees who don't sting one another, unlike in other firms. And Playco, of course, is a brave new world in which executives are continually looking for a fight or for "fresh meat."

The relationship between conflict management and identity appears outside of modern American business corporations as well. In Japanese organizations, managerial roles involve a high investment in conflict-dampening activities so that conformity and ostensible harmony are maintained (Rohlen 1974). Moreover, there is "little capacity to separate the people from their roles" (Rohlen 1974:119). A Japanese manager's personal identity, then, is intimately bound up with their ability to manage conflict nonconfrontationally. Cross-cultural research far removed from business corporations indicates that in many contexts, social, personal, and collective identities are fused with role relations in cultures of conflict management. The traditional societies that surround the Mediterranean, for example, offer a wealth of illustrations of the relationship between vengeance and male social identity. Males who do not participate with skill and panache in games of vengeance suffer the ignominious fate of being known as less than a full man (Rieder 1984:138). Vengeance games also relate to collective identity among traditional Balkan herders: "Each man is obligated to defend his group against both physical and symbolic attack. The latter category includes a wide range of acts that diminish a group's reputation for honor. Response in kind is required for the sullied group to retain its honor" (Denich 1974:248–49). It is not only violent conflict management that fuses with identity. Laura Nader (1990) describes how traditional peoples in southern Mexico preserve social and collective identities through conflict management framed around conciliation and compensation. To handle conflict management by "making the balance" is to be identified as a local and to retain autonomy at the group level apart from the state or, historically, from colonial regimes. In social contexts with even less violent and more restrained indigenous conflict management, such as among traditional hunter-gatherers or modern suburbanites, to name two seemingly disparate contexts, all levels of identity—personal, social, and collective—are bound up with conflict management (Balicki 1970; Baumgartner 1988; Furer-Haimendorff 1967; Turnbull 1961).

The relationship between conflict management and identity raises further questions concerning the transplantation of conflict management forms into contexts and groups other than those in which they naturally arise. It is currently fashionable in some circles of scholars and practitioners of conflict management to assume that most if not all conflicts are amenable to negotiation or mediation. The panacea, we are told, for contemporary organizations, international conflicts, intergroup ("gang") conflict in American cities, or environmental disputes, is to have the parties sit down and immerse themselves in the cool medium of rational dialogue oriented toward reaching a mutually agreeable resolution. Such a prescriptive program ignores the fact that to ask disputants who are not already in contexts in which conflict management of this sort is customary is to ask them not only to engage in activities in which they have little pragmatic experience but to ask them to give up a part of their identities. To ask gang members to negotiate conflicts, for example, is to ask them to give up part of what makes them who they are: collective liability, codes of honor, and vengeance (e.g., Jankowski 1991; Rieder 1984). To ask suburbanites to go to mediation is to ask them to forfeit their identities as reasonable people who do not engage in confrontation to pursue their grievances: "Common sense in the suburbs dictates that normal people will see the advantages of avoidance for the prevention and containment of conflict" (Baumgartner 1988:131). Thus, intervention in ongoing disputes is not only about creating discourses of conflict management that disputants can understand (or can perhaps piggyback onto their indigenous schemas and scripts for conflict management), it is also about facing the reality that how people handle conflict may have as much to do with how they see their local worlds, experience and enact their daily routines, and see themselves as it does with the contents of their conflicts. This is not to argue that practitioners should abandon attempts to transplant nonviolent conflict management into violent contexts. Rather, conflict management intervention requires attention to the personal, social, and collective identities of the disputants it is intended to serve, particularly as those identities relate to customs of indigenous conflict management.

*   *   *

It seems unlikely that a single normative order will dominate executive contexts in the future. In this work I have attempted to identify and describe three elementary forms of normative order that currently exist among American corporate executives. Indeed, one challenge for contemporary and future managers lies in recognizing the multiple organizational contexts in which they work and being able to quickly adjust to the conflict management repertoires called for in such contexts. Such adjustments require the ability to master a number of conflict management skills and leave far behind the idea that there is one best conflict management process to which all people should aspire.

The idea of multiple organizational orders also means that the future of conflict management in wider society will not be dominated by a single vision of conflict management. The growth of a mass society of atomistic and fluid individuals has been a part of sociological analysis since the nineteenth century. Recently, scholars have turned this argument specifically on the question of conflict management to argue that as transiency and fragmentation of social relations increase, moral minimalism will become more pervasive among disputants of all kinds (Baumgartner 1988). Such an analysis neglects the importance of organizations in contemporary society and, moreover, that people increasingly spend much of their waking (and perhaps sleeping) lives in complex organizations. As a result, the corporate normative orders of the future will not reflect an inexorable, linear path born of atomization, but will reflect the diversity of organizational forms in society. The question of the future trajectory of conflict management in contemporary society therefore lies in the contraction and expansion of the diversity of organizational forms themselves.

ANATOMY OF AN
ETHNOGRAPHY
OF BUSINESS
ELITES

The style, voice, and attempt at dispassionate description in this book belong to the "realist" genre of ethnographic literature (Van Maanen 1988). This writing style developed during the later decades of the nineteenth century and matured into the dominant literary genre in American and English ethnography during the first two-thirds of the twentieth century. Despite its success at capturing the minds, if not the scientific longings, of most of those who practice qualitative fieldwork, ethnographers and humanities scholars have recently indicted realist ethnography on several counts. A large part of this critical attack centers on the issue of "representation" (Snow and Morrill 1993:8), questioning whether ethnographic text in general is ever anything other than a projected fantasy of the ethnographer via their own authorial voice.[1] Certainly one cannot expect any science, broadly understood, to represent a phenomenon under study exactly "right" without any personal or contextual biases. The most one can hope for is a "close approximation of the empirical world" (Snow and Morrill 1993:10). Crucial to this effort are systematic methods and a delineation about how the authorial self forms a part of those approximations.

My intent in the next few pages, therefore, is not simply to recount the frontstage methods used in creating my realist tale of executive conflict management, but to take readers backstage to the method behind the method, to the tacit knowledge I gained about how to effectively execute fieldwork in executive settings as well as my own critical reflection of my methods. As such, this appendix continues the realist slant of the book, but also injects some "confessional tales" (Van Maanen 1988) into the account. My confessional methodological tales convey a sense of my personal experiences and feelings in the field (see also the preface and acknowledgments) and will hopefully give readers some sense of the problems I encountered while I worked among the "other." My realist methodological tales adhere more closely to the traditional methodological concerns of social "science."

Going to the Field

Imagine yourself standing alone on a sidewalk one early morning in a large city looking up at a sixty-story tower of glass and steel.[2] You are dressed in a gray suit carrying nothing but a leather notebook and a small tape recorder. Noise fills the air around you. Car engines roar and horns blare. The doors to a city bus shush open and then close. Exhaust fumes itch your nose and eyes, and the aroma of a nearby food cart penetrates directly into your half-empty stomach. Men and women dressed in dark-colored suits rush in and out of the tower's entrance. A doorman eyes you suspiciously as you continue to stare up and into the building. Finally, and deliberately, you stride into the building and find a gold colored sign that reads Executive Elevator by the side of an elevator at the far end of the main lobby.

You walk toward the sign and encounter two attendants sitting at a desk with television monitors facing them. One of them asks with whom you have an appointment and what your name is. As confidently as possible, you state: "Calvin Morrill to see Mr. Brown." "Hmmm," the attendant says, "Mr. Brown. And you [he says with disbelief], *you* have an appointment with Mr. Brown?" "Yes, at 7:30," you reply with as much certainty as you can muster. The attendant then asks if you would wait a moment while he calls ahead. As he calls, you begin to wonder if in fact you have the right day. You open a small date book to find that you have the correct date. Still, you calm an anxious urge to stop the attendant in midcall, to tell him that you were mistaken about the appointment, and that you will come back another day. You begin thinking about sports, about music, about the ocean, about just what Marx *did* mean by "species being"—about anything that will remove you from the present. Just as you are drifting off into one of those other worlds, the attendant smiles broadly at you and says: "Mr. Brown will see you, sir. I'll accompany you to the executive level." The attendant leads you on to the elevator and pushes A3, which is above the last numbered floor, which is 59. Ah, you think, the executive floors at last!

The elevator ascends quickly, reminding you of your empty stomach and the food cart that you left far below on the street. The elevator slows and levels. The doors open and the attendant waves you forward into an entryway with a woman sitting behind a huge dark desk. "Mr. Morrill [he even pronounces your name correctly] to see Mr. Brown," the attendant says. "Thank you, Bill," the woman replies. Bill nods and exits toward the elevator. "Mr. Morrill [*she* pronounces your name correctly as well], Mr. Brown is just finishing up some other business. Can I get you some coffee or tea? We have some delightful pastries this morning. Perhaps some coffee and a pastry?" You think: What if I spill coffee or drop pastry filling on my suit? I'll blow every ounce of credibility I've got! You politely decline the offer and walk over to an overstuffed leather couch.

Sitting down, you admire the view of the city through a twenty-foot-tall-by-forty-foot-wide window facing the couch. You begin to feel self-conscious without something in hand to read. You decide not to read over the questions you want to ask Mr. Brown. You committed them to memory anyway and reviewing them one more time might simply muddle your delivery during the interview. *What do I want to read?* you ask yourself. You see several magazines on the marble coffee table in front of the couch. *Harvard Business Review, Sloan Management Review, New Management Magazine, Fortune,* and *Forbes* seem a little too "businessy." *Sailing* and *Golf Digest* seem a bit too light. Perhaps a newspaper would be more interesting, but you already read some of the *Times* before leaving for the appointment. The *Wall Street Journal* is too businessy as well. . . . Your selection process is abruptly interrupted by a distinguished-looking, gray-suited Anglo man in his late fifties who, extending his hand, introduces himself in a baritone voice: "Calvin Morrill, Stu Brown. I'm very glad we could arrange this. Did Patty get your pastry order? We've got a dynamite chef now for the stuff. Come on back and let's talk a bit."

You follow Mr. Brown [he insists that you call him Stu, and he calls you Cal] through a maze of corridors until you reach a long hallway with another woman sitting at a large desk who smiles at you as you walk through a double door into another room with a woman and a man sitting at two desks placed on either side of another set of large double doors. Finally, you enter what you believe to be Mr. Brown's (uh, Stu's) office. He asks again about your pastry order, says he thinks he is going to "indulge himself," and you feel you should follow his lead. He makes the orders via an intercom on his desk. At one end of his office is a large mahogany desk. At the other end is a marble, oval table with chairs around it. His view of the city is as majestic as Patty's, only he has two views because his office is on a corner. You notice that the ceiling is probably over twenty feet above you because it looks to be over two basketball stanchions high. He invites you over to an enclave of slightly overstuffed chairs between the oval table and his desk and asks you to take a seat. "Now," he says, "what can I do for you, Cal?"

This scene occurred dozens of times over the two-year period (1984–1986) during which the fieldwork for this book was conducted. But this scene really describes the "kill," so to speak—what happens in the minutes before a typical initial interview with a corporate executive and during initial interaction with that informant. It does not describe how one "gets in" to study executives or the factors that transform fearful first encounters into sustained ties with informants.

Initial Access

While I was planning the present investigation, it was apparent that close empirical study of top business managers would be difficult unless I devised a strategy to ensure adequate access to executive settings. I found few helpful clues for gaining access to corporate executives per se in the sociology or anthropology literatures, although ethnographic studies of organizations at the middle and lower levels, particularly essays on organizational field methods by W. Richard Scott (1965) and Dalton (1964), as well as an article on interviewing "ultra-elites" by Zuckerman (1972), proved helpful for understanding how to go about collecting data once I gained access to the tops of organizations. I began my preparation for the study by talking with a number of business scholars who described to me the arduous task of contacting business executives, waiting for months to receive word back from them, and then being turned down for access to their corporations. When asked if I could contact some of their contacts, most scholars proved quite protective of their resources and declined. One scholar even suggested that I embark on a nonethnographic research plan because, in his words, "No one [no executives] will talk with you."

Ethnographic research in settings far removed from corporate elites proved more helpful in developing strategies for access. My eclectic taste led me to fine models of fieldwork contained in William Foote Whyte's *Street Corner Society*, Klaus-Friedrich Koch's *War and Peace in Jalemo* (on the management of conflict in highland New Guinea), and Bruno Latour and Steve Woolgar's *Laboratory Life* (an influential ethnography of the production of scientific knowledge at the Salk Institute). The authors of these disparate studies all shared the same problem: how to gain access to a socially insulated setting in order to study delicate issues therein. Access in each of these studies developed through a close, personal tie of the authors constituted before going to the field or upon their arrival. For Whyte that tie proved to be with Doc, an influential corner boy. For Koch, Wasa, the ablest medicine man in the village he studied, provided that tie. For Latour and Woolgar, the key tie emerged through the latter author's "girlfriend."[3] All of these works also underscored the need for one's in-group tie to be well respected and knowledgeable about the context. A close friend served that role for my initial "pilot" forays into the field. A close relative, call him Tag, who was (and, at this writing, is) a longtime management consultant and respected member of the local business community chosen for the study, consented to be my focal contact in executive contexts for the full study. Even with such ties, it took eighteen months to gain access to my first set of executive contexts from the time I began planning the project (in the winter of 1983) to the time I actually entered the field.

In the summer of 1984, Tag and I developed a list containing twenty-four executives chosen to represent a mixture of kinds of businesses, from whom five executives were chosen as initial prospective informants because of their likelihood of being receptive to being interviewed. Tag then suggested that he "prime the pump" by mentioning the project on "people problems among managers" to each of the five informants during routine meetings with them on other matters. It seemed prudent during the priming that Tag mention only the topic of the project to prospective informants, ask whether it would be appropriate if they were contacted for an initial interview, and that he establish the independence of the study from any of his business endeavors. Tag would also mention to the five initial informants that the study would become the basis for my sociology doctoral dissertation at Harvard University.

Each of the five prospective informants then received cover letters asking them for an initial, informational interview during which the project, identified as a "study of how corporate executives influence each other about work-related people problems," would be discussed and they would be asked whether they would want to participate. I then called the five executives using the direct-line phone numbers which Tag supplied. Secretaries initially responded to my name, the contact letter, and requests for interviews with disinterest and, in one case, hostility, until I mentioned that "Tag suggested that Mr. X might be interested in talking with me." At that point, secretaries raised questions such as, "How is Tag?" or "We haven't seen Tag in a long time, tell him to come around." These statements were typically followed by, "You're related to Tag, eh? Well, Mr. X will certainly want to see you. Just a minute." The secretary typically left the phone for a minute, presumably for quick consultation with Mr. X or a scheduling secretary. A short negotiation for an appointment date concluded the call. Four of the five executives consented to an initial interview.[4] Three of the four granted partial access to their organizations,[5] and one of them worked in a corporation that became one of the corporations selected for in-depth study.

At various times during initial interviews or informal chats with executives, I asked whether any other executives they knew might be interested in participating. This snowball strategy was necessitated by the fact that only in the organizations I later classified as mechanistic bureaucracies did the CEO issue a blanket order to cooperate with me. This strategy also enabled me to gain access to other corporations and far-flung departments within the same organization. During many conversations, informants would think partially out loud about whether a colleague or competitor might be suitable to participate in the study, and whether I might have any further luck with access in the informant's organization or department. Contact letters sent to these executives generated by referral from other executives differed from the initial contact letter in that it referenced the source of the referral.[6]

Site Selection

The lack of studies of elite conflict management and comparative executive ethnographies, the sensitive nature of the data collection, and the limited funds available for this study dictated three overriding concerns in the selection of study sites. First, the initial contacts at each firm needed to be willing to personally support the study in order to facilitate access to all parts of their firm's executive levels. I discuss how I further facilitated access through initial contacts in subsequent sections of this appendix.

Second, research sites of the firms needed to be located in roughly the same region of the country to facilitate easy and inexpensive travel to and from them and the researcher's home base. This criterion produced few organizations (save Bailey Construction, General Utility, Playco, Commco) that engage significantly in international activities. The study therefore does not include a multinational firm in the truest sense of the term, although two of the four firms engaged in international business (Playco and Commco) have, at this writing, entered major product bids into several international markets. This criterion, then, inevitably introduced a regional bias into the study, which from another perspective was a blessing for a lone fieldworker trying to cover the organizational countryside in as thorough a manner as possible. I excluded subsidiary corporations from the study because of my desire to study the relatively independent action of executives, because of the difficulty in traveling to and from multiple sites within the same organization, and because I alone collected all data and could be in only so many locales. Only one regional headquarters (Independent Accounting) was included in the study because of its unique characteristics and weak ties to its headquarters.

Third, I needed to maximize within the field constraints described above the types of firms included in the study. The selection of firms was executed with what in retrospect could loosely be described as a "maximum variation" sampling logic (Lincoln and Guba 1985). An initial foray into the field attempted to secure access to firms that exhibited variation in products, revenues, financial health, and numbers of employees and executives. A second stage focused more closely on the internal and external contexts of each firm, attempting to maximize variation within the sample, both in internal structural and cultural properties at the executive level and in the organizational environments. The goal of the second stage, therefore, was to extend and begin to cross-check information already obtained in initial data collection efforts and collect information from contexts that could possibly contrast with those already obtained (Lincoln and Guba 1985:199–201; Patton 1980).

The group of organizations included in this study, then, represents the culmination of good fortune, but also somewhat more systematic selection processes than in previous studies of executives. At the same time, the firms in the study do not make up a random or perfectly representative sample of all business types and corporations. Nor does the sample contain matched pairs of businesses on particular variables that would allow a great deal more control than the current study possesses. The sample is thus purposive, but within the constraints of the resources available for the study and of access imposed by the social insularity of executive contexts.

Excluded Organizations

Even though I found many executives willing to participate in the study once I had established my snowball technique, my "hit" rate for suitable organizational access was sixty-two percent, with thirteen of the twenty-one firms I contacted being included in the sample. Table A.1 presents the summary characteristics of the eight excluded firms. Like the firms included in the study, those excluded vary considerably in products and services, sizes (in terms both of numbers of employees

Table A.1   Summary Characteristics of the Eight Corporations Excluded
from the Study

Corporation (Industry)	Number of Employees	Number of Executives	Total Revenues ($\times$ $1,000)[a]	Financial Health[a]	Exclusion Rationale
Worldtech (Electronics)	130,000	33	44,000,000	profit	sparse data
Megabank (Finance)	150,000	57	11,000,000	loss	sparse data
U.S. Law (Law)	20,000	150	2,000,000	profit	sparse data
Agricorp (Agriculture)	1,400	18	1,100,000	profit	sparse data
St. Olaf's (Health)	1,300	13	25,000	loss	ethical dilemma
Industrial Supply (Maintenance)	500	7	10,000	loss	ethical dilemma
Windfall Indemnity (Insurance)	200	4	5,000	profit	size
Gresham Design (Architecture)	75	2	3,000	profit	size

Note: All corporate names are pseudonyms. Firms are listed in order of gross revenues in 1986.
[a] Data for this variable were gathered from year-end reports for 1986 provided by each corporation.

and executives and of revenues), and financial health. Every type of
business represented by the organizations included in the study (electronics, financial services, professional, health, insurance, agriculture)
is also represented by the excluded firms. Those excluded also exhibit
a higher rate of financial health than those in the included group. The
most striking limitation in the study revealed by the comparison of
tables 2.1 and A.1 may be the inability to compare executive action in
two of the very largest multinational corporations in the world:
Worldtech and Megabank. Neither Commco or General Utility approaches the size of Worldtech or Megabank.

The reasons for excluding these eight firms fell into three categories:
sparse data, ethical dilemmas, and the size of the executive ranks in
particular companies. Access difficulties at Worldtech, Megabank, U.S.
Law, and Agricorp resulted in sparse data and their subsequent exclusion from the study. At both Worldtech and Megabank, exogenous factors (governmental investigations of the former and stockholder and
governmental calls for reorganizing the latter in the aftermath of heavy
financial losses) prevented the completion of more than a few preliminary interviews. This meant that the opportunity to watch executive
behavior in the face of external threats was lost as was the opportunity
to observe an externally forced reorganization. Interviews at U.S. Law
were discontinued because the firm's headquarters was located several

thousand miles away from the researcher's primary field locale. After initially agreeing to participate in the study, the Agricorp CEO decided that his executives "had better things to do than speak with [the researcher]," and without further explanation terminated interviews.

Ethical dilemmas prevented the inclusion of data collected at St. Olaf's and Industrial Supply. In the first corporation, an initial contact became implicated in a legal investigation of the firm's tax reporting practices and requested that I use my cover as a fieldworker to spy on those specifically targeted by federal authorities. I declined to perform this role, terminated data collection in the firm, and also decided that the data collected was too sensitive for public presentation. At Industrial Supply, I was also asked to report on the activities of a competing group of executives attempting to buy out another group led by an initial informant. I declined again to act as a spy, terminated data collection in the firm, and also decided against using the data lest it be read by those involved and used in their (now legal) struggle against one another.

More mundane reasons led to the exclusion of data collected at Windfall Indemnity and Gresham Design. Both companies are quite small and have extremely small numbers of executives (four and two, respectively) that strained the credibility of contextual comparisons between the two firms and other firms in the sample.

Sustained Access and Leave Taking

One of the most striking features of doing ethnography among corporate executives, beyond the material wealth, are their educational attainments, life experiences, and worldly sophistication. Nearly all executive informants had BAs and over half held some kind of graduate degree (as indicated in chapter 2). More than a few were familiar with the latest academic literature on organizations, and a few, who had academic backgrounds in the social sciences, were familiar with research on conflict management. More important, each of my informants was a veteran of the "wars" of corporate upward mobility. Most had done more than survive; they had thrived to get to their executive positions. All of this meant that the "cover story" for the project had to tread a fine line between complete disclosure (with the consequence of irreparably biasing the data) and gloss (with the consequence of having the study perceived as dull or even deceptive).

In effect, the cover story had to do more than inform; it had to function rhetorically to convince highly able informants of my abilities and the general interest of the project. The cover story also had to demonstrate what informants might gain out of the study. The cover story still contained the phrase "people problems" to describe its object of study, but evolved into a five-minute presentation on different approaches to people problems, how "objective" observation of conflict management by a disinterested third party might enhance informants' and their organizations' reflections about how they manage trouble with colleagues, and how their "wisdom" and experiences might educate me as well. Informants had their own conditions for participating in the study: (1) that I not disseminate any of the information I collected from their organizations with the original names of the actors or corporations attached; (2) that I not disrupt ongoing routines in the corporation; and (3) that they not have to fill out any questionnaires or forms related to the study. This last condition eliminated the possibility of self-report checklists or written self-administered questionnaires.

In exchange for executive cooperation I offered them two "services": 1) public presentations consisting of general observations of their organization and 2) private exit interviews with any informant covering observations of their personal "strengths and weaknesses." Few organizations took me up on these offers, although every organization assigned a trusted manager to interview me about what I found out about it prior to my leaving the site. I also warned every informant about the delicate nature of much of the information that I might learn and that fieldwork in their organization would be disengaged if access became contingent upon disclosure of informant confidences. Nearly every informant in the thirteen organizations ostensibly agreed to these terms. Those that did not I did not contact about participating in the study.

Nevertheless, what Bonacich calls "communication dilemmas"—in which individual and collective interests diverge regarding the disclosure of information—still arose during fieldwork (1990:449). These dilemmas sometimes occurred in routine interviews or at social gatherings when informants would attempt to extract information about specific colleagues or groups "for the good of the company" which would break an informant's confidence.[7] Especially difficult were situations in which such information could, in the right hands and in a timely fashion, be used to forestall potentially harmful situations to an organization or its publics. I would politely ignore inquiries of this nature when I could. To more pointed inquiries, a humorous retort of some kind would suffice as a rebuff. In a few situations, I restated the original conditions of the fieldwork to which the informants had already agreed during initial interviews. I also avoided situations in which executives created conversational structures in which silence could be construed as an affirmation of particular actions learned of in confidence. My first allegiance in all of these situations was to informant confidentiality.

Another problem I faced in the fieldwork concerned the age difference between the informants and me (I was in my mid- and late twenties at the time of the study, nearly thirty years younger than the average executive). "Why would an experienced executive want to divulge the secrets of corporate goings on to young Mr. Morrill?" wrote a reviewer of a grant proposal I submitted to the Law and Social Sciences Program of the National Science Foundation, which eventually supported the field portion of the study. This was an important concern and one that I managed ironically by adopting the role of the naive young man eager to be educated in the ways of the business world. In part, the initial credibility granted by my association with Tag and further facilitated by successive credible references to almost every executive informant in the study facilitated this social identity. At the same time, my social characteristics (being white and from Harvard University) also lent credence to my image.

This identity proved sufficient for securing solitary interviews and observations with executives, but insufficient for other opportunities for observation, such as at meetings or social gatherings. The same social identity that motivated executives to speak candidly in private militated against completely throwing open their operations for study. The layers of secretaries, assistants, and junior executives surrounding each executive further exacerbated this problem. During the first few months of fieldwork I found it infeasible to hang around and watch what executives do on a daily basis. The question became how to project a secondary social identity that would create a reason for executives to allow, even encourage, casual conversations and observations.

The answer to this question occurred one afternoon just before going to lunch with an executive named Greeley. Greeley had begun running to get himself into shape and kept his running gear in his private commode adjacent to his office. One day, the gear was visible for only a moment when he went to wash his hands prior to going to lunch. To a casual question about whether he ran often, he enthusiastically responded that he "loved" running every afternoon and that there were quite a few "serious" runners at the executive levels in the firm. This started a long conversation during which I disclosed that I had run competitively in high school and college. Thereafter, he and other executives at his corporation occasionally asked me advice about running and even ran with me on occasion. These interactions became the occasions for informal observations and conversational interviewing and, more important, invitations to other formal and informal gatherings, including executive committee meetings, parties, new product presentations, and strategy sessions. In effect, informants could now receive something in exchange for information on their corporation: affiliation with a person who was a competent actor in another social world they admired and of which some even wanted to be a part. The most successful medium of informal rapport building during the study was sports (particularly running), but in some settings other topics, such as mutual interests in jazz, popular music, art, films, or experiences at Harvard (more than a few executives hoped that their children might be admitted as undergraduates) served nearly as well.

As useful as such superficial identities were, my identity as a nonthreatening, nonjudgmental, and intently interested listener provided the final piece to sustained access and created the conditions for increasingly personal self-disclosures as the fieldwork progressed, sometimes to the point of embarrassment. After particularly disclosive conversations (mainly with men and always one-sided), executives would sometimes end the interview by asking me, "When can you come back?" or saying, "This was really great, see my secretary about scheduling another visit." Salutations signaling the beginnings of disclosive informal conversations were often begun with "Hey, it's good to see you. I really need to talk with you." At first, such salutations and leave-takings merely seemed to indicate the depth of the rapport that had been established with informants. Some executives displayed little personal intimacy in their verbal or nonverbal communication, but still freely offered the most intimate details of their work and personal lives. (For nearly a year, for example, the same hour and day of every month was reserved for a painfully self-disclosive one-hour interview with an executive named Banks. After almost every meeting, Banks would say some variation on "That was a good session. I'll see you next month.")

The longer I was in the field, the more apparent it became that these disclosive, private interviews with executives played important therapeutic functions in their lives and combated their sense of loneliness. At no time in any interview did I make any pretense at therapy, aside from the offering of a nonjudgmental, sympathetic ear. Towards the end of my fieldwork, Greeley eloquently commented on the cathartic aspects of interviews with executives in the study:

> Look, it *is* lonely at the top. A guy in an organization with a lot of politics can't confide in his colleagues because whatever he says will come back and bite him in the ass. A guy in an organization without a lot of politics is going to be thought of as weird if he starts telling other guys stuff. Your wife is bored with it. Your kids don't

care. Some guys spend lots of money on shrinks. More than a few
guys find their therapy in alcohol and drugs. But to have someone
really listen, care about what you're saying, who only costs you
time, doesn't come around very often.

Consequently, disengagement from informants as I left the field sometimes became difficult, requiring several lengthy and emotionally
draining "exit" conversations (other than those the corporation required me to have prior to disengagement) with many of those whom
Greeley called my "patients."

I terminated my fieldwork using three traditional criteria: I had
spent over a full "season," as field anthropologists are fond of saying,
with my "people." I had metaphorically seen the crops harvested, re-
planted, and harvested again. Second, my money ran out after over a
year in the field. Third, I began, as Donald Black, the chair of my dissertation noted, to be overly "saturated" with the contexts I was studying. In other words, I had absorbed as much information as I could
handle and needed to get beyond the collection and initial coding
phases of the study to the write-up.

Research Procedures and Data Base

Table A.2 summarizes the research procedures used in the field once
I established sustained access to executive contexts. The hours devoted
to the project presented in table A.2 can be multiplied many times to
cover the time spent arranging meetings and interviews over the phone
and via mail with executives, traveling to and from research sites, and
writing up articles and this book.

Interviewing

The most fruitful yield of data, particularly related to conflict, derived from formal interviews with executives. I conducted the majority
of formal interviews in executives' private offices, favorite eating and
drinking establishments, and homes. Formal interviews varied in
length from nearly six hours to thirty minutes. The median formal
interview was just under ninety minutes. Nearly all formal interviews
occurred with single informants. Three hundred five executives
worked for the thirteen firms in the study during field work. Of these,
I interviewed 228 (75%). In the three executive contexts chosen for case
study presentation, my response rates were higher—nearly 100% at
Playco and Independent Accounting and in the western and central
divisions of Old Financial. I conducted informal interviews where and

Table A.2   Summary of Research Procedures and Data Base

Data Sources and Procedures	Research Activity	Data Produced
(1) Field observation and informal interviews of executives and their staffs during their daily routines over 18 months: 1 March 1984 to 31 May 1984, 15 August 1984 to 15 September 1985, and 1 December 1985 to 31 January 1986	(a) 631 hours in the field (b) 702 hours typing field notes (c) 156 hours coding 87 sets of field notes from OF, IA, and P[a] 1489 hours	(a) Descriptions of physical layouts and work rhythms @ OF, IA, and P (see chapters 4–6) (b) "Day-in-the-life" descriptions (see chapters 5–6) (c) 39 episodes from extended trouble cases at OF, IA and P
(2) Formal executive interviews	(a) 401 hours of taped and untaped interviews of 227 executives (b)—taking notes from taped interviews and field notes of untaped interviews (hours included in 1b) (c)—coding (hours included in 1c) 401 hours	(a) Organizational characteristics, executive demographics, common themes across executive life (see chapter 2 and tables B1–B9 in appendix B) (b) 303 extended trouble cases decomposed into 822 conflict management actions (see chapters 3–6 and appendix B, esp. tables B.10–B.15)
(3) Formal and informal staff interviews	(a) 138 hours of untaped interviews with 91 staff members (b)—taking notes from field notes (hours included in 1b) (c)—coding (hours included in 1c) 138 hours	(Data yield included in 2a and 2b)
(4) Additional coding during 1988 and 1990–93[b]	(a) 30 hours typing 31 sets of untyped field notes (b) 546 hours coding 257 sets of field notes 576 hours	(Data yield included in 2a and 2b)

Table A.2 (continued)

Data Sources and Procedures	Research Activity	Data Produced
(5) Follow-up formal interviews with key informants during 1990	(a) 8 hours of untaped interviews with 7 executives (b) 8 hours typing field notes (c) 6 hours coding 7 sets of field notes 22 hours	(a) Changes in corporations during 1986–90 (b) 9 extended trouble cases decomposed into 22 grievance expressions
(6) Collection during 1990 of historical data on matrix diffusion in American business corporations	(a) 15 hours collecting articles on matrix management in business and popular journals (1945–90) (b) 8 hours coding journals for adoption, effects, and persistence of matrix in American corporations 23 hours	(a) Historiography of matrix diffusion in American corporations (see chapter 2)
(7) Collection of corporate documents	(a)—collecting in-house documents from corporations (hours included in 1a) (b)—coding in-house documents (hours included in 1b and 4b)	(a) Organizational characteristics (see chapter 2) (b) Exec. communication (see chapter 3 and appendix B, tables B.1 and B.2)

[a] A portion of the observational and interview notes for Old Financial, Independent Accounting, and Playco were originally coded for my dissertation (Morrill 1986) and subsequent articles (Morrill 1989, 1991a, 1991b, 1992a, 1992b) related to these corporations.
[b] Additional coding of field notes includes notes uncoded from Old Financial, Independent Accounting, Playco, and all of the remaining ten corporations in the study.

when I could. Sometimes these interviews consisted of nothing more than a few conversational turns, while sometimes a hallway conversation might stretch for an hour as an informant and I "shot the breeze."

To direct my questions I used a loosely structured format contained within an interview "guide." The guide contained a repertoire of question clusters on topics I tried to ask about in every formal interview and, when I could, in informal interviews. Because of time constraints, not every question was asked across all informants, although I attempted to maintain as much consistency as possible in terms of topics and key questions within each cluster. The interview guide used for executive interviews evolved through the first thirty executive interviews and remained relatively stable thereafter. I also found that it was particularly important during the developmental phase to ask questions in the vernacular of executives. This did not mean adopting local slangs (such as those that appear in the glossary of Playco native terms in appendix C), for I found early on that my using these terms as an outsider took on a disingenuous ring to insider ears. More appropriate for my questions, except in special situations, was what I call "businessspeak"—a vaguely decision making–oriented vernacular with which I had grown up in my family.

I designed the first part of the guide to obtain information on an informant's workaday context (in his or her corporation) and to draw responses which could contain trouble cases. When I detected such information, I would then ask several questions in detective-like fashion regarding the basis of the conflict, its management, and its participants and their relationships and backgrounds. As a result, the interview guide only portrays a skeletal menu of the questions asked and not their exact wording. Nor does it portray how the conversational rhythms developed during an interview. Sometimes I delivered the questioning about trouble cases in the innocent and slightly bumbly style of actor Peter Falk's television detective, Columbo, in order to put informants at ease. Always, I attempted to maintain an even emotional balance—not too excited, but interested. As my time in the field progressed, I became particularly adept, for example, at reading verbal and nonverbal cues that communicated reluctance or immediate rapport. Some informants began interviews with an impatient "How long did you say this will take?" or seemed uneasy at answering even the most innocuous opening questions; others rarely gave me a chance to ask questions and instead plied me with a flurry of detailed statements about their corporations, in effect answering all or many of the questions in my interview guide. I also became conscious of not wasting informants' time by asking questions about topics available from company documents. At the same time, I also wanted to hear every informant's perspective on general issues of relevance to the study whether I had asked every one of their colleagues the same question or not. It became crucial, therefore, to learn when and how to ask certain questions. I also used, although I did not have a label for it at the time, a form of what Snow et al. (1982) call "interviewing by comment." Instead of only using direct questions to elicit information from informants, I would sometimes repeat back an informant's statements or try out an informal hypothesis about a particular situation (particularly when in the Columbo mode). These techniques would often yield information which direct questions about the same topics did not. Interviewing by comment proved particularly useful during informal interviews.

The following clusters of questions were asked during an initial interview if the informant had already granted me more than one interview or during the initial part of a single interview if subsequent interviews would not occur with the informant:

1. How long has _____ been in operation? How many employees does _____ have? What would you consider the main lines of business here at _____? What were _____ total sales in 1984/ 85/86?

2. How many executives are at the executive levels? How are the senior executive levels organized (i.e., divisions, titles, departments)?

3. What are your responsibilities here at _____?

4. Who do you report to? (Questions sometimes followed about who reports to whom formally, what it means to "report" to someone in the firm, how one informally "gets things done" outside of formal reporting lines, etc.)

5. If you wanted to talk with your superior about a not-so-serious issue, how would go about doing it? If you wanted to talk with your superior about a serious issue, how would you go about doing it? Would you need an appointment? Is there an open-door policy among executives?

6. What is your day-to-day routine like around here? Where do you spend most of your time during the day? What do you do when you come into the office in the morning? What does your schedule usually look like? (About one-third of the informants shoved an appointment book toward me to demonstrate their "typical" schedule. Others invited me to chat with their secretaries about their typical schedules.)

7. Would you say there's a shared philosophy at the executive level about how work is to be approached by an executive? Do different groups of executives or divisions/departments/practices have different shared philosophies? How are they different? How are they similar? How do these differences or similarities manifest themselves in behavior? in decision making? in ways of thinking about problems and solutions in the firm?

8. On a weekly basis, how many face-to-face contacts would you have with your peers in the same division/department/practice? with peers outside the division/department/practice? with your superior(s)? with your subordinates?

9. On a weekly basis, how many written or oral messages/communications would you estimate you send to your direct superior? to your direct subordinates? to your peers? Among your executive colleagues, are there any that you regularly need to receive information from in order to make timely and effective decisions? (This last question was clarified to mean two or three times per week.)

10. What do you and your colleagues generally talk about when you communicate face-to-face at work? work-related issues? personal topics? What percentage of each would you say fills out your conversations with your colleagues during a routine week? Among your colleagues, who do you regularly talk with about work-related issues only? (This cluster was also asked as: Do you ever talk about interpersonal problems or conflicts with other executives? If so, who in the organization? In whom do you confide on a weekly basis?)

11. Do executives at the senior level get together much informally, say for lunch or after work for a drink? What do you guys talk about then? Who do you usually go with? Is it always the same bunch? If not, why not?

At this point in interviews, I asked a few questions that executives would expect someone studying managers to want to know and in which they might be particularly interested:

12. A lot of people talk about how business has changed over the past few years. Have you noticed any changes at _____? If so, what brought about these changes? If not, why not? How would you say _____ is positioned relative to its competitors?

13. What characteristics do you believe make an executive effective? Are there any older or younger executives in the company now who you think fit those characteristics?

14. How is performance measured at the executive levels? How is it related to compensation? Are there personal meetings used in evaluation? statistics? Do executives actually use quantitative measures in assessing individual and group performance?

Near the end of an initial interview, I would always begin asking questions about the informants themselves. After several of the initial informants indicated how "therapeutic" their interviews had been, I determined that asking personal but not "soul-searching" questions about an informant might leave the executive with a stake in continuing the interviews. I always asked informants final self-appraisal questions which they would most likely answer in a positive fashion. These final "stake" questions appear below in clusters 15 and 16:

15. What is your background? Where did you go to school? Did you start out with _____? What positions did you hold prior to your present position?

16. What strengths do you think you bring to your present position? How do you see yourself improving in the future? What are your personal work goals? What do you enjoy about your job?

I reserved the questions below for later in single interviews or for follow-up interviews. These questions more naturally led into information on trouble cases:

17. How do you survive long enough in this company to get to the top?

18. What kind of executive do you respect?

19. How do you enforce a decision down the line (i.e., to a subordinate)? across divisions/departments/practices?

20. How much latitude do you feel you have in the decisions you make? Are there a lot of procedures you have to follow or other people in the organization you have to notify before making an important decision?

21. Have you ever had what you might call a "personality clash" with a colleague? How did you handle it? Can you give me an example?

22. Have you ever experienced a situation in which a top executive subordinate wasn't performing up to your expectations? How did you handle that situation? What would you consider the proper way to handle such a situation? Do you have any formal procedures or guidelines for these kinds of situations?

23. Have you ever known of a dispute between two execs to spill over into other parts of the company? If so, did people choose sides? Which side were you on? Why?

24. What do executives complain about around here? Do they ever complain about their colleagues? What kinds of things annoy execs here about their colleagues? Why? Can you give me an example?

25. Do you think the gender composition of the top ranks of your firm is going to change over the next few years? How do you think your colleagues will react to these changes? How will you react? Is the hiring of more women and minorities for executive jobs a top priority at the company?

26. What kinds problems arise between people you supervise? between yourself and people you supervise? between people to whom you report and yourself? between people to whom you report? How are these usually handled? Can you give me some examples?

27. What kinds of pressures do you face in your job? What happens if you don't meet your goals or the expectations of your superiors?

28. Have you ever had to terminate another executive? How was that done? Why? Have you ever felt as though you might be fired? If so, what were the circumstances?

29. If you need to find out about a delicate situation, say one involving a serious disagreement between senior executives or unethical behavior by one of your colleagues which could affect you or harm the company, and you've already spoken to the people involved, how would you learn more about the situation?

30. Have you ever been asked to intervene or intervened on your own account in an executive dispute? What were the circumstances?

31. Do you remember the foreign payment scandals in the '70s? There was a lot of talk then that if a company had honest people at the top the whole company was honest; if not, the whole company was crooked. Do you buy into that argument? If not, why not? If so, why?

32. Does _____ have a code of ethics, written or otherwise? How would you describe the personal ethics held by execs here? What happens if an executive doesn't comply with ethical standards (written or unwritten)? How are these things usually discovered?

If executive informants appeared a bit anxious towards the end of a multiple-session set of interviews in which they had disclosed quite a lot of trouble cases, I would ask wrap-up questions that would end the last session on a "businessy" or relatively noncontroversial note. When successful, these questions functioned as part of a process reminiscent of Goffman's (1952) notion of the "cooling out process" wherein individuals attempt to lessen the potential loss of face to others in the aftermath of uncomfortable or failed interactions.

33. What are the company's goals at present? What strengths would you say _____ has at the moment? What do you look forward to in your job in the near and long term?

Recording Field Data

I initially taped all formal interviews and continued to do so throughout the fieldwork in two (Commco and General Utility) of the thirteen corporations. In the other eleven corporations, I found that a tape recorder, no matter how small or unobtrusive, made many informants anxious. I found that oftentimes when I turned off the tape recorder and an informant was still speaking "on the record" (but off the tape), they opened up considerably. I also found early on that I could not keep up with the transcription of tape-recorded interviews (which contained a fair amount of dross as well). I therefore relied exclusively on note taking, except at Commco and General Utility, where I recorded most of my formal interviews.[8] I never taped conversational interviewing because of logistical constraints.

My information gathering in the field and the transformations of such "field jottings" into field notes and finally into analytic categories were activities well described in a number of guides to qualitative fieldwork (Bernard 1988; Lincoln and Guba 1985; Lofland and Lofland 1984; Miles and Huberman 1984; Spradley 1979). My field jottings contained scribblings about the actors, situations, problems in the field, physical layouts of offices, and anything else that seemed important from my observations and in response to my questions during interviews. At all times when I visited an executive context (except at a few social gatherings), I kept a leather notebook with me and jotted down my observations wherever I could without seeming obtrusive to the actors with whom I was interacting. When I was unable to write down observations, conversational shards, or descriptions on site, I kept my notebook in my car or another secure place and wrote down as much as I could remember immediately after leaving.

At the end of data collection each day, I converted my field jottings into full-fledged field notes by entering them into a personal computer in three phases. First, I simply expanded on the jottings as they appeared in my notebook, trying to remember as many things that I didn't write down as possible. I used a standard journalistic template for recording my jottings during this first phase: who, what, when, where, why, and how. My second pass over the jottings took a more structured process described in most qualitative field methods textbooks: I categorized field notes into descriptive, methodological, and analytic notes. Descriptive notes contained raw observations very close to the core of the original field jottings (except far more elaborated for intelligibility during coding). Methodological notes focused on my techniques of data collection, particularly when I tried a new technique or ran into problems using a technique with which I previously enjoyed success. Analytic notes contained my initial thoughts about how executive contexts were organized and theoretical leads. In this way, I immediately began coding and organizing my data as I harvested it every day.

Problems in the Field

Despite the overall success of my field methods, I should also note some of their shortcomings. First, any fieldworker faces the risk that what they see or hear in the field is what they "want" to see or hear—

the nightmare extreme of the "projected fantasy" critique of ethnography. Some ethnographers (Snow et al. 1986) argue that "team" fieldwork can partially combat self-fulfilling prophecies by multiplying informant and research perspectives during data collection and coding. As a lone fieldworker I did not have the option of team fieldwork. I did address this problem through (1) periodic conversations ("member checks") with "deep informants" at each firm (executives who were especially receptive to my study and me, were "veterans" of the executive ranks, and had high knowledge of their contexts or, as one informant commented, "know where all the bodies are buried"); (2) meetings during and after fieldwork with my dissertation committee, Donald Black, Harrison White, and Alessandro Pizzorno, as well as periodic conversations with Donald Cressey; and (3) presentations of work-in-progress to various faculties at the University of California at Berkeley, the University of Virginia, and Harvard University. All of these public exposures of my data forced me to continually rethink and refine my interpretations in the field, each time trying to better approximate the empirical realities of the contexts I was studying.

Second, other investigators have found that field methods tend to overestimate dramatic trouble cases and to overlook those handled via subtle strategies that may remain hidden to outsiders' eyes (Koch 1974:23–24). This problem can be particularly troublesome if the fieldworker bases the majority of their information about a social context on informant accounts because informants tend to remember more dramatic cases of conflict and forget those that occur without much fanfare. This field problem taps into broader issues of informant accuracy that arise due to faulty recall or selective memory (e.g., Killworth and Bernard 1976). Recently, Freeman et al. (1987) argued that collecting accurate data is less a question of which type of data is best for all research purposes—observational or informant recall data—than a question of the purposes for which the data will be used. Informants tend to be an inaccurate data source for synchronic social interaction but do seem to accurately capture behavioral norms in a particular context over time. Data on communication networks and formal structure were intended to approximate routine behaviors over time, thus suggesting the appropriateness of recall data. Trouble cases tend to be even more focused, however, on particular episodes of action, suggesting that such data may be even more prone to distortion than other aspects of the data collected in the study. Freeman et al. (1987) also argue that such distortions will tend to be biased toward what *usually* happens in a particular context or situation. Trouble cases gleaned from informants' memory should therefore tend to be biased in the direction of the customs of conflict management in particular contexts.

A related aspect of informant accuracy concerns whether or how much informants lie or "put on the researcher" when giving accounts about their social contexts (e.g., Douglas 1976). From one perspective, the themes I pursued (what some informants called "dirty laundry" or "skeletons in closets") and my age could easily lend themselves to fictitious accounts or at the very least embellishments by informants. The rapport that I established with most informants leads me to believe that most executives were relatively "straight" with me, although the level of disclosure obviously varied among informants. Moreover, I tried to maintain a dispassionate, but interested, stance toward executive tales of conflict management. This stance meant that it was difficult for informants to get "a rise" out of me with stories of trouble cases and thus know that they could draw me into a ruse. Nonetheless, I uncovered some embellished and fabricated stories by cross-checking my data with my deep informants.

As in all fieldwork, however, the ethnographer must not, as anthropologist Laura Nader once told me, fall into the trap of "explaining the world like your informants explain it." I believe her advice focused on the idea that indigenous interpretations and accounts of behavior must be regarded as data. To be sure, gross errors of misrepresentation must and can be avoided through member checks, but they must be regarded as but one arbiter of ethnographic validity if the fieldworker takes the notion of a multiperspectival reality seriously.

Coding Procedures for Field Data

I initially open-coded descriptive notes broadly for manifestations of (1) formal and informal hierarchies; (2) gender relations; (3) informal relations; (4) decision-making processes; (5) firm history; (6) biographies of executives; (7) motivations for being an executive; and (8) what I called, for want of a better label, life styles of executives. Subcategories emerged through intensive taxonomic analysis as I sifted and resifted through my field notes on a daily basis.[9]

I coded descriptive notes for trouble cases taking cues from procedures used by fieldworkers in the anthropology of law (Epstein 1967; Gluckman 1973; Koch 1974; Nader 1964; Van Velsen 1967; see also Burawoy 1991) and the sociology of conflict management and social control (Baumgartner 1984a, 1988; Black 1980). I constructed the narrative architecture of each trouble case from the following information: (1) focal grievance issues; (2) the principals' relationship, including past trouble; (3) the principals' interpretation of grievance issues using one of the five grievance schemas (penal, compensatory, conciliatory, therapeutic, or indifferent); (4) the threat to organizational health that each participant believed the case to pose; (5) the behaviors used to handle grievances; and (6) the case outcomes. I did not include any trouble cases for which I did not have information on these categories from at least two sources, one of whom had to be a principal. The only exception to this rule occurred in the atomistic organizations where aggrieved parties often unilaterally pursue grievances against an offending party without the knowledge of their target or other colleagues. I wrote narrative cases using this information, thirty-five of which appear in whole in the text of chapters 1 and 4 through 6. I decomposed the rest of the cases for the aggregate analysis in chapter 3. Trouble cases sometimes spanned months or even years, bounded only by the continuing participation of the principals and the issues involved. As such, trouble cases could contain numerous types of actions pursued by the principals (and other principals) to pursue their grievances. Moreover, trouble cases could also overlap with one another, and at times I represented such overlaps in my field notes using Venn diagrams of intersecting circles.

I also collected forty-one trouble cases which could not be analyzed due to incomplete information and difficulties in coding. Many of these cases were collected from the atomistic organizations where sparse communication among executives constrained my ability to develop multiple sources for extended trouble cases. To the degree that was possible, I compared the patterns in these cases to the ones included in the present study. The unincluded cases contain a number of highly covert, unilateral conflict management actions that is disproportionate to those included in the study. In other respects, they do not appear to be any different from those in the study.

Indigenous meanings given to grievance issues and conflict management actions (grievance expressions), including the language executives use to label such actions, proved critical to the writing of trouble case narratives, particularly during the second aspect of the coding process, in which I decomposed trouble cases into conflict management actions using a combination of emic and etic categories. In all of my coding efforts for trouble cases, I drew heavily from the cross-cultural literature on disputing, primarily the works of Baumgartner (1984a, 1984b, 1988) on nonconfrontational grievance pursuit and upward social control, Black (1976, 1980, 1983, 1989, 1990) on law and other forms of social control, Black and Baumgartner (1983) on third-party intervention, Horwitz (1982) on therapeutic social control, Nader and Todd (1978) on law and other forms of social control, Koch (1974) on self-help, and Gulliver (1979) on negotiation. I used emic categories when an appropriate equivalent did not exist in the conflict and disputing literature. The contemporary setting in which this research occurred, as well as the advanced educations of most informants, led to indigenous understandings of and labels for conflict management that in some instances were identical to those found in the scholarly literature (particularly the uses of the terms *negotiation, bargaining, avoidance,* and *therapy*). At other times, informant framing and scripts for action required quite a bit of decoding to understand the nature of the action in question. In some cases, I categorized similar indigenous grievance expressions into more inclusive categories drawn from the literature. In all of these coding efforts, every attempt was made to carry forth the indigenous meaning of the conflict management into the final analysis. I also checked for consistency in my codings by calculating some inter-rater reliabilities. Inter-rater reliabilities during the additional coding for the aggregate analyses that appear in chapter 3 yielded acceptable levels, averaging .71 across the outcome measures. The individual reliabilities for these categories appear in note 5 of chapter 3.

Collecting and Coding Historical Data for Playco

Historical information on executive conflict management before Playco's restructuring, the restructuring itself, and its executives' reaction to the hostile takeover movement derive from three sources: (1) a systematic review of the popular business press (the *Wall Street Journal, Fortune,* and *Business Week*) for reports of Playco's activities from 1965 to 1987; (2) a review of Playco internal publications and memoranda from 1965 to 1987; and (3) interviews with Playco personnel (described below) about Playco's history.

Writing Up the Study

Like every ethnographer before me, my systematic data collection and coding efforts yielded a Mount Everest of information which even before I left the field I anxiously began to scale. Gideon Kunda (1991:238), in his recent ethnography of organizational culture control, wrote of his own difficulties writing up his fieldwork; he accurately captured many of my feelings at the time I faced my field data:

> Having returned to safer shores, I discovered that, chained to a desk like the mythical hero, I was forced to relive the essence of the dangers and pain of the field adventure over and over again: facing the unknown, the incomprehensible. Masses of facts, stories, vignettes, numbers, rumors, and endless pages of field notes documenting the observed trivia of everyday life—their sheer volume offered daily testimony to the seeming impossibility of making any valid statement at all.

My first stab at writing up my coded field notes and trouble cases took the form of a dissertation in which I concentrated on the behavioral aspects of conflict management at Old Financial, Independent Accounting, and Playco. During this initial write-up, I also continued to manically write up trouble case narratives from the other ten corporations in the study. Throughout this phase of the write-up, I faced what all ethnographers face: the tension between writing too analytically (i.e., not providing rich enough ethnographic description) and writing too descriptively (i.e., not providing enough analysis or theoretical payoff).

Transforming the dissertation into published form first occurred via refereed articles and chapters in edited collections. I again focused on the three organizations used in the dissertation, using various parts of the data sets for each organization. Because I had already completed the analysis of a portion of the data and write-ups for the three case study organizations, I believed that I could write this book in about a year. That year stretched into two years as I continued to code and analyze the data from the other ten organizations in the study. I also discovered that as the time since completing the fieldwork grew longer and I grew more mature as a scholar, my depth of understanding about my field data increased. This proved both a blessing and a curse because I constantly had to be on guard against reading too much into my data.

Readers of my earlier works will also recognize theoretical continuities as well as discontinuities in my treatment of conflict management. My earliest work on conflict management adhered very closely to the behavioral-structuralist position invented by Donald Black and used by his students and intellectual fellow travelers. In recent years, my work on conflict management has been moving toward the contextual or, more specifically, structural-interpretivist position espoused in chapter 1 of this book. My reasons for moving in this theoretical direction relate to my longstanding interest in the investigation of interpretive processes associated with social control, social order, and social change, which began under the tutelage of Donald Cressey at the University of California at Santa Barbara and has continued at the University of Arizona with the collaboration of my colleagues in the department of communication and the department of sociology, particularly David Snow. I view my turn toward the relationships between the structural and the cultural aspects of social life not as a regression to an earlier stage of my intellectual development, but as an attempt to take what I have learned from the behavioral-structuralist school and relate that to recent advances in cognitive and interpretive analysis.

This change does not mean that I repudiate the behavioral-structuralist position, for one could hardly repudiate a theoretical stance with which one is sympathetic. My theoretical stance in this book simply means that I have taken a slightly different path toward the same general goal as proponents of the behavioral-structuralist approach: a general theory of social control. As such, the theoretical approach herein is complementary, rather than antithetical, to the behavioral-structuralist project. It is but a beginning to what I hope will be an intellectual journey of theoretical discovery, refinement, and extension.[10]

AGGREGATE
COMPARATIVE
DATA

Note: In all the tables in appendix B, the numbered columns represent the sample corporations as follows: 1 = Bailey Construction; 2 = Commco; 3 = Container Corporation; 4 = Continental Design; 5 = General Utility; 6 = Hightower Construction; 7 = Independent Accounting; 8 = Infotain; 9 = New Financial; 10 = Old Financial; 11 = Playco; 12 = Smith Brothers; 13 = Sunset Group.

Table B.1 Average Information Flows between Executives per Week per Executive

	Corporation													
	1	2	3	4	5	6	7	8	9	10	11	12	13	Mean
Written	4.4	6.7	3.3	3.1	5.9	3.4	2.4	10.4	6.2	6.2	4.7	8.3	1.1	5.77
Face-to-face	6.1	2.4	4.1	1.1	8.6	1.8	0.7	14.0	20.8	3.8	11.9	1.7	15.5	7.73
Indirect	5.6	0.6	1.1	0.5	4.8	0.8	1.4	11.1	7.4	1.3	7.8	0.8	8.9	3.55
Total	16.1	9.7	8.5	4.7	19.3	6.0	4.5	35.5	34.4	11.3	24.4	10.8	25.5	17.05
Informant n	7	16	10	9	15	13	19	11	13	53	39	14	9	228

Note: Flows consist of messages sent, regardless of initiator. Data for this table derive from estimates by informants in interviews. The total number of flows for each channel was divided by the number of respondents to this question in each firm. Secretaries and other staff members working with each informant, as well as in-house documents, were also consulted to obtain estimates and checks of informant self-reports. Corporate ns do not include CEOs because they report to boards of directors. Some corporation totals are lower than the actual number of executives below the CEO level because information could not be verified for all executives. Only executives working at or near corporate headquarters are included in these figures. Total informant $N = 228$. See appendix A for a general discussion of problems encountered in the field.

Table B.2 Average Face-to-Face Information Flows between Superiors and Subordinates and between Formal Peers per Week per Executive

	Corporation													
	1	2	3	4	5	6	7	8	9	10	11	12	13	Mean
Hierarchical	1.4	1.1	3.0	0.3	4.5	0.7	0.2	3.7	5.7	3.1	3.1	1.1	4.1	2.5
Peer	4.7	1.3	1.1	0.8	4.1	1.1	0.5	10.3	15.1	0.7	8.8	0.6	11.4	4.7
Ratio of H:P	0.30	0.85	2.72	0.38	1.10	0.64	0.40	0.36	0.38	4.43	3.52	1.83	0.36	1.33
Informant n	7	16	10	9	15	13	19	11	13	53	39	14	9	228

Note: Flows consist of messages sent, regardless of initiator. Data for this table derive from estimates by informants in interviews. The total number of flows for each channel was divided by the number of respondents to this question in each firm. Secretaries and other staff members working with each informant, as well as in-house documents, were also consulted to obtain estimates and checks of informant self-reports. Corporate *n*s do not include CEOs because they report to boards of directors. Some corporation totals are lower than the actual number of executives below the CEO level because information could not be verified for all executives. Only executives working at or near corporate headquarters are included in these figures. Total informant $N = 228$. See appendix A for a general discussion of problems encountered in the field.

Table B.3 Access Process to Executive Superiors for a Quick Matter

	Corporation													
	1	2	3	4	5	6	7	8	9	10	11	12	13	Total
Formal appointment	4	3	2	5	0	4	7	8	8	17	26	3	6	44.7 (93)
Informal appointment	2	12	4	3	4	7	9	2	3	31	6	7	1	43.8 (91)
Open door	0	0	3	0	8	0	2	0	0	2	5	3	1	11.5 (24)
Total	6	15	9	8	12	11	18	10	11	50	37	13	8	100.0 208

Note: See chapter 2 for definitions of "quick" and "complex" matters. Frequencies refer to the number of subordinates indicating their "typical" access routine for discussing matters—quick in table B.3, complex in B.4—with superiors. Percentages appear for row totals only. Marginal frequencies for rows appear in parentheses. Numbers do not include CEOs because they report to boards of directors. Some corporation totals are lower than the actual number of executives below the CEO level because information could not be verified for all executives. See appendix A for a general discussion of problems encountered in the field.

Table B.4   Access Process to Executive Superiors for a Complex Matter

	\multicolumn{13}{c}{Corporation}												
	1	2	3	4	5	6	7	8	9	10	11	12	13	Total
Formal														96.6
appointment	6	15	9	8	10	11	18	8	9	50	36	13	8	(201)
Informal														2.4
appointment	0	0	0	0	2	0	0	1	2	0	0	0	0	(5)
														1.0
Open door	0	0	0	0	0	0	0	1	0	0	1	0	0	(2)
														100.0
Total	6	15	9	8	12	11	18	10	11	50	37	13	8	208

Note: See chapter 2 for definitions of "quick" and "complex" matters. Frequencies refer to the number of subordinates indicating their "typical" access routine for discussing matters—quick in table B.3, complex in B.4—with superiors. Percentages appear for row totals only. Marginal frequencies for rows appear in parentheses. Numbers do not include CEOs because they report to boards of directors. Some corporation totals are lower than the actual number of executives below the CEO level because information could not be verified for all executives. See appendix A for a general discussion of problems encountered in the field.

Table B.5   Access Process to Executive Superiors for a Quick Matter

	\multicolumn{13}{c}{Corporation}												
	1	2	3	4	5	6	7	8	9	10[a]	11	12	13	Total
Formal														41.1
appointment	1	3	0	2	0	3	4	4	4	4	11	1	2	(39)
Informal														37.9
appointment	1	2	0	2	0	1	0	1	2	21	2	2	2	(36)
														21.1
Open door	0	0	2	0	2	0	0	0	1	9	3	3	0	(20)
														100.1
Total	2	5	2	4	2	4	4	5	7	34	16	6	4	(95)

Note: See chapter 3 for definitions of "quick" and "complex" matters. Frequencies refer to the number of superiors indicating their "typical" access routine for discussing matters—quick in table B.5, complex in B.6—with subordinates. Percentages appear for row totals only. Marginal frequencies appear in parentheses. The numbers represent executives above the vice-presidential level. See appendix A for a general discussion of problems encountered in the field.

[a] At Old Financial, information on this variable could not be verified for four executives.

Table B.6   Access Process to Executive Subordinates by Superiors for a Complex Matter

	\[Corporation\]													Total
	1	2	3	4	5	6	7	8	9	10[a]	11	12	13	
Formal														78.9
appointment	2	5	1	4	2	4	4	5	5	23	11	5	4	(75)
Informal														20.0
appointment	0	0	1	0	0	0	0	0	2	11	5	0	0	(19)
														1.1
Open door	0	0	0	0	0	0	0	0	0	0	0	1	0	(1)
														100.0
Total	2	5	2	4	2	4	4	5	7	34	16	6	4	(95)

Note: See notes to table B.5.

Table B.7   Face-to-Face Communication with Colleagues by Work Unit Membership by Percentage

	\[Corporation\]													Mean
	1	2	3[a]	4	5	6	7	8	9	10	11	12	13	
With work-unit colleagues	57	74	0	90	40	74	77	21	61	80	63	74	55	52
With interunit-team colleagues	33	22	0	10	30	12	15	56	30	12	26	21	26	28
With other colleagues	10	4	100	0	30	14	8	23	9	8	11	5	19	20
Total	100	100	100	100	100	100	100	100	100	100	100	100	100	100
Informant *n*	7	16	10	9	15	13	19	11	13	53	39	14	9	228

Note: Work units were defined as functions, practice specialties, and departments at the vice-presidential and senior-vice-presidential level and as divisions or practices (whatever higher unit organized functions, specialty practices, or departments) at the executive-vice-presidential level. CEOs were asked these questions in relation to corporate-level officers and aides appointed as special staff who are not members of any particular function or practice. Each informant was asked to make their personal communication distribution add up to 100%. The percentages for each category were then divided by the number of executives interviewed in each firm (see table 2.2 for numbers of informants per firm).

[a] Container Corporation had only one executive per work unit and did not have any sort of standing interunit teams, task forces, or committees. All executive communication is therefore with colleagues of neither the same team nor unit.

Table B.8   Communication Content among Executives by Percentage

	Corporation													
	1	2	3	4	5	6	7	8	9	10	11	12	13	Mean
Work	11	59	66	78	35	67	74	26	12	68	27	55	16	46
Social	37	18	13	12	23	22	6	33	46	10	9	23	27	21
Work and social	53	23	22	10	42	11	21	41	42	23	64	22	57	34
Totals	101	100	101	100	102	100	101	100	100	101	100	100	100	101
Informant *n*	7	16	10	9	15	13	19	11	13	53	39	14	9	

Note: Executives were asked to estimate what percentage of their communications with their executive colleagues fall into each category. The percentages for each category were then divided by the number of executives interviewed in each firm (the number of informants per firm table 2.2). See chapter 3 for descriptions of work and social activities.

Table B.9   Characterizations of Personal Relations among Executives by Percentage*

	Corporation													
	1	2	3	4	5	6	7	8	9	10	11	12	13	Mean
Acquaintances	65	68	78	86	24	61	72	52	49	63	42	61	44	59
Friends	27	22	14	11	45	29	23	34	30	27	32	27	41	28
Close friends	9	10	8	3	31	10	5	14	21	10	25	13	15	14
Totals	101	100	100	100	100	100	100	100	100	100	99	100	100	101
Informant *n*	7	16	10	9	15	13	19	11	13	53	39	14	9	

Note: Executives were asked to estimate what percentage of their executive colleagues fall into each category. The percentages for each category were then divided by the number of executives interviewed in each firm (the number of informants per firm appears in table 2.2).

Table B.10   Conflict Management Schemas by Percentage

	Corporation													
	1	2	3	4	5	6	7	8	9	10	11	12	13	Total
Accusatory	62	23	61	7	59	14	19	58	57	69	59	65	60	46
	(13)	(41)	(11)	(2)	(78)	(5)	(15)	(19)	(35)	(61)	(61)	(32)	(12)	(385)
Remedial	38	34	39	43	33	30	32	42	39	25	32	29	40	33
	(8)	(60)	(7)	(12)	(44)	(11)	(25)	(14)	(24)	(22)	(33)	(14)	(8)	(282)
Indifferent	0	42	0	50	8	57	48	0	3	7	9	6	0	21
	(0)	(74)	(0)	(14)	(11)	(21)	(37)	(0)	(2)	(6)	(9)	(3)	(0)	(177)
Total	2	21	2	3	16	4	9	4	7	11	12	6	2	100
	(21)	(175)	(18)	(28)	(133)	(37)	(77)	(33)	(61)	(89)	(103)	(49)	(20)	(844)

Note: Based on conflict management actions uncovered in fieldwork. Figures are column percentages; parenthetical figures are the numbers of actions of each type at the given corporation.

Table B.11   Conflict Management Forms by Percentage

							Corporation							
	1	2	3	4	5	6	7	8	9	10	11	12	13	Total
Unilateral	33	54	67	54	54	70	73	24	31	66	34	63	35	52
	(7)	(95)	(12)	(15)	(72)	(26)	(56)	(8)	(19)	(59)	(35)	(31)	(7)	(422)
Bilateral	29	35	22	32	26	24	23	27	34	21	24	22	25	28
	(6)	(62)	(4)	(9)	(35)	(9)	(18)	(9)	(21)	(19)	(25)	(11)	(5)	(233)
Trilateral	38	10	11	14	20	5	4	48	34	12	42	14	40	20
	(8)	(18)	(2)	(4)	(26)	(2)	(3)	(16)	(21)	(11)	(43)	(7)	(8)	(169)
Total	2	21	2	3	16	4	9	4	7	11	12	6	2	100
	(21)	(175)	(18)	(28)	(133)	(37)	(77)	(33)	(61)	(89)	(103)	(49)	(20)	(844)

Note: Based on conflict management actions uncovered in fieldwork. Figures are column percentages; parenthetical figures are the numbers of actions of each type at the given corporation.

Table B.12   Conflict Management Directness by Percentage

							Corporation							
	1	2	3	4	5	6	7	8	9	10	11	12	13	Total
Confrontation	76	37	44	29	62	24	23	70	57	56	78	55	50	51
	(16)	(65)	(8)	(8)	(82)	(9)	(18)	(23)	(35)	(50)	(80)	(27)	(10)	(431)
Non-confron-tation	24	63	56	71	38	76	77	30	43	44	22	45	50	49
	(5)	(110)	(10)	(20)	(51)	(28)	(59)	(10)	(26)	(39)	(23)	(22)	(10)	(413
Total	2	21	2	3	16	4	9	4	7	11	12	6	2	100
	(21)	(175)	(18)	(28)	(133)	(37)	(77)	(33)	(61)	(89)	(103)	(49)	(20)	(844

Note: Based on conflict management actions uncovered in fieldwork. Figures are column percentage parenthetical figures are the numbers of actions of each type at the given corporation.

Glossary of
Native Terms
at Playco

AMBUSH   Covert action to inconvenience an adversary (synonyms: *bushwhack* and *cheap shot;* in takeover imagery, *ambush* refers to a swift and premeditated takeover attempt).

AMNESIA   Feigned ignorance of a colleague's grievances.

ART   The aesthetics of executive comportment.

BLACK HAT   An executive who often engages in covert action to manage conflict with opponents (synonym: *pirate;* compare *black knight*).

BLACK KNIGHT   An executive who often engages in covert action against opponents, does not support his intradepartmental colleagues in disputes (compare *black hat;* in takeover imagery, *black knight* refers to an unfriendly acquirer from the perspective of an acquired firm).

BLINDSIDING   An intentional and surprising public embarrassment by one executive at another's expense.

BOZO   An executive who ineptly attempts to follow the code of honor to press his grievances against opponents (compare *dick*).

BULLETS   Criticisms of an executive's plan by an opponent delivered in the midst of a meeting *duel* or *shoot-out.*

BURNING
  FIGHTER   A particularly aggressive executive dispute.

BUSHWHACK	Covert action to inconvenience an adversary (synonyms: *ambush* and *cheap shot*).
CALL OUT	Public challenge to a colleague for a *shoot-out* or *duel*.
CATFIGHT	An argument between less honorable executives.
CAVALRY	Departmental executives who come to a colleague's aid in an interdepartmental dispute.
CHEAP SHOT	Covert action to inconvenience an adversary (synonyms: *ambush* and *bushwhack*).
CRYING	Secretly complaining to a colleague about another's behavior without the offender's knowing.
DECLARING WAR	Collectivization to aggressively and overtly pursue grievances against a collective opponent (also expressed as *"to go to war"*).
DICK	A belligerent executive who ineptly attempts to follow the code of honor to press his grievances against opponents (compare *bozo*).
DOG	An inept and low-status (less honorable) executive (compare *bozo* and *dick*).
DOGS ON A LEASH	Mental health (not having one's *dogs on a leash* indicates mental instability).
DUEL	Ritualized contest of elaborate formal presentations used to settle an interdepartmental executive dispute (synonym: *shoot-out*).
EXEC IN DISTRESS	Executive who ineptly follows the code of honor, but who colleagues feel can be saved; also an honorable executive caught in a *burning fighter* (see also *white knight*).
FAILED GAMBIT	Loss of a *duel* or *shoot-out*.
FIGHTING FIRE WITH FIRE	Matching the aggressiveness of an executive adversary's grievance pursuit in kind.
FLAK VEST	Suit vest worn by honorable executives during a *shoot-out* or *duel* to ward off *bullets* from the opposition (in takeover imagery, *flak* refers to impediments to a takeover raised by a target).

FLIGHT DECK	The executive suites in the multistory main tower at headquarters from which most "big ideas are launched."
FLYING LOW	Not confronting an offender with longstanding grievances against their behavior.
GAS ATTACK	Nonverbal expression of scorn against an offending colleague.
HAND GRENADE	Particularly aggressive insults expressed directly between disputants.
HIDING	Avoiding an opponent.
HONORABLE	Held in high esteem by one's colleagues.
HUNTING BIG GAME	Looking for honorable executives with whom to dispute in order to establish a reputation (in takeover imagery, *hunting big game* refers to looking for large corporate takeover candidates).
IRON MAN	The senior vice president of operations known for his "stiffness" in interpersonal affairs, his background in the steel industry, and reputation as one of the most honorable executives at Playco.
ITALIAN LIRA MONEY ORDER	Worthless promise of an executive (related to the takeover imagery of *Russian rubles,* used to describe early noncash takeover offers).
JUMPING SHIP	Resigning from the corporation.
KILLING AN IDEA	Refuting (by another principal) and wholly rejecting as viable (by a wider audience) of a principal's idea or proposal in a meeting duel (compare *withdrawal*).
LIFE VEST	Suit vest worn by less honorable executives when engaged in a *shoot-out* or *duel* to keep their "heads above water."
MELTDOWN	Physical fight between executives.
OUTLAW	An executive who handles conflict in unpredictable ways but who is regarded as especially task competent.
PATCHING UP	An agreement to cease hostilities between disputants.

PEACE TALKS   Collective negotiations to cease interdepartmental hostilities.

PIGEON   An executive who avoids all conflict and has a reputation as particularly *weak* (in takeover imagery, a "pigeon" refers to a highly vulnerable takeover target).

PIRATE   An executive who often engages in covert action to manage conflict with opponents but who is regarded as especially task competent (compare *black knight* and *black hat*).

PLAYING BY THE RULES; PLAYING THE GAME   Engaging in honorable vengeance.

PRINCESS OF POWER   The senior vice president of marketing; known to have the ear of the chairman of the board, she sometimes "succumbs" to emotional outbursts and is believed to be the next president of domestic affairs.

RAID   Covert action taken to inconvenience an opposition department (compare *ambush, bushwhack,* and *cheap shot;* in takeover imagery, a "raid" refers to a hostile takeover).

RAPE   An executive's allowing him- or herself to be publicly criticized by another colleague without *calling out* the challenger.

REDLINE   An argument which unpredictably escalates to physical violence.

RESCUING   Helping an executive colleague disengage from a dispute with another executive or group of executives.

ROADBLOCK   Impediment raised by an executive to block another's decisions (similar to the hostile takeover imagery of *barricade,* meaning impediments to a takeover attempt).

SECOND   An aid to a principal in a meeting *duel.*

SERIOUS PLAYER   An executive who adeptly engages in honorable conflict management (compare *strong executive* or a *white hat*).

SHOOT-OUT	Ritualized contest of elaborate formal presentations used to settle an interdepartmental executive dispute (synonym: *duel*).
SIT DOWN	Negotiations between two principals to suspend a dispute.
SKIRMISH	Intradepartmental argument.
SLEEPING BEAUTIES	Executives enamored with their own abilities but ignorant of their negative perception by other top managers (in takeover imagery, "sleeping beauties" refers to vulnerable takeover targets).
SMALL BURSTS OF FIRE	Short public criticisms of a colleague delivered in rapid succession.
STRONG EXECUTIVE	Adhering to the code of honor in handling trouble with colleagues.
SUCKED IN	Having become an ally in an interdepartmental feud through no purposive action of one's own.
TARGET	An opponent in a conflict; typically used by less honorable executives to refer to adversaries.
TEMPORARY AMNESIA	Temporary feigned ignorance of a colleague's grievances.
TERMINATOR	Sales executive who adopted the nickname from Arnold Schwarzenegger's movie of the same name because he closes big deals for Playco and "hunts big game any way he can."
TEXAS BOYS	Texas takeover men (refers to *big-hat boys* who are Texas moneymen interested in hostile takeovers in takeover imagery).
VALIANT EFFORT	Performing in a particularly honorable way during an executive conflict or other activities; often used to describe executive conflict management actions in a particular dispute that are admired because of their honorable style, but which did not lead to winning the dispute.
VAPORIZING	Terminating an executive from the company or creating the conditions under which an executive resigns from the corporation.

WALTZ
  AROUND
Polite argument between less honorable executives (related to *dancing*, which refers to preliminary negotiations during a takeover in takeover imagery).

WAR
Aggressive and overt collective pursuit of grievances against a collective opponent (*war* refers to an extremely hostile takeover attempt in takeover imagery, such as the American Express attempt to take over McGraw-Hill in 1979).

WEAK
Not adhering to the code of honor in managing trouble with colleagues.

WHITE HAT
An honorable executive (compare *black hat, outlaw, pirate, white knight*).

WHITE
  KNIGHT
An honorable executive who supports his colleagues in interdepartmental disputes and "rescues execs in distress" (compare *white hat* and *black knight;* in takeover imagery, white knight refers to an acceptable acquirer sought after by a potential acquirer to forestall a hostile takeover).

WILD BUNCH
A successful product team known for its *outlaw* behavior.

WITHDRAWAL
Unilateral concession of defeat in a *duel* or *shoot-out.*

WIZARD
Senior vice president of research and development who has numerous inventions and patents, has long hair, and wears loose hopsack clothing.

WOUNDED
  LIST
Executives who have lost individual conflicts in a larger *war* with another department (in takeover imagery, *wounded list* refers to executives of an acquired firm who develop health or career problems from the deal).

NOTES

Chapter One

1. I borrow the framing of these conflict "myths" from Kolb and Putnam (1992:1).

2. Definitional issues related to conflict management versus conflict resolution versus social control, etc., are discussed in note 16 of this chapter.

3. For analysis of this case in context, see chapter 4. The year or years in parentheses refer to the approximate time span over which the cases unfolded.

4. For analysis of this case in context, see chapter 5.

5. For analysis of this case in context, see chapter 6.

6. This section draws on Black's (1984) observations on the history of social control, Baumgartner's (1988: 4–5) discussion of the theoretical context of contemporary conflict management studies, Kochan and Verma's (1983) review of the organizational conflict and negotiation literatures, Kolb and Putnam's (1992) review of trends in organizational conflict studies, and my own reading of the primary literature.

7. The study of conflict management, of course, has a much longer history than Weber's analysis of bureaucracy. Questions of how social groups handle conflict have their origins in writings on the maintenance of societal order by seventeenth- and eighteenth-century political philosophers such as Hobbes, Locke, and Rousseau. Hobbes (1962 [1651]), of course, argued that nation-states emerged out of a state of nature characterized by a "war of all against all." In essence, he proposed that social order could be maintained only through conflict management (social control) by the state. Locke (1952 [1690]) also assigned a central place to the state for securing social order—not a state borne of narrow self-interest, but one borne of enlightened human reason. Locke also argued that natural law secures social order without states. In such orders, every person has an obligation to punish transgressions and refrain from committing offenses against others. Conflict management by the state, then, is one formal manifestation of normative relations that already exist in the state of nature. Nearly a century after Locke, Rousseau (1968 [1762])

further argued for the importance of the state in securing social order. He believed that under the most favorable conditions, states reinforce indigenous social orders. To the extent that states do not do so (are in opposition to indigenous mores), they would eventually weaken and cease to exist, thereby creating the opportunity for social chaos.

Nineteenth-century social thinkers, such as Marx, Weber, and Durkheim, originally tied the problem of order and disorder to nation-state formation and politics. Durkheim (1933 [1893]) advanced the notion that legal forms reflect and reproduce social order. He argued that all conflict management feeds into the social order of a social system, either by reproducing it or by ushering in change. Marx and Engels argued that the *way* societal conflicts are managed— for example, via overt violence between groups (e.g., open class warfare) or via mechanisms introduced by the state (e.g., repression)—provide insight as to the alignment of power and the likelihood and processes of fundamental social change (see the edited collection in Tucker [1978]). Weber (1968 [1922]) traced the historical rise of different forms of social order, which he argued resulted from the coupling of particular social structures, value orientations, and forms of legal decision making. Contemporary sociologists continue this state-centered approach in much of their work on conflict management in modern society, exhibiting a decided orientation toward studies of the legal system and related social-control institutions.

Anthropologists, in contrast, have for decades investigated how tribal groups without formal governments maintain order and handle disputes (Roberts 1979). Anthropologists have also studied how people in traditional societies resist the replacement of indigenous disputing mechanisms with the legal apparatuses of colonial powers or combinations of colonial and newly organized local regimes (e.g., Burman and Harrell-Bond 1981; Moore 1986; Nader 1990). Many of these investigations use trouble case methods together with other ethnographic and historical techniques. As a result, a diverse body of cross-cultural materials richly documents the vast array of informal and formal (e.g., state-centered) conflict management processes across several traditional societies (e.g., Avruch et al. 1991; Bohannan 1967; Nader and Todd 1978). Baumgartner (1988), Black (1984, 1990, 1993), and Horwitz (1982, 1990) use these central tendencies in sociology and anthropology as a point of departure for their examinations of extralegal social control. For other interfaces between the sociological and anthropological literatures on extralegal and legal conflict management, see the representative collections in Abel (1982), Black and Mileski (1974), Evan (1980), Starr and Collier (1989), and Tomasic and Feeley (1982), and contributions in the journals *Law and Society Review, Law and Social Inquiry,* and *Virginia Review of Sociology.*

8. As many managerial scholars and sociologists in the 1960s focused on the design implications of the previous decade's studies, another group of scholars spurred by social-psychological research on personality and group dynamics addressed what they called conflict management "styles." These investigators generally argued that negotiation and compromise (code words in these studies for preventing or suppressing conflict, and again, echoing the human-relations preference for cooperation) more likely resulted in organizational

productivity than other styles of conflict management (Blake and Mouton 1964; Lawrence and Lorsch 1967a; Walton and Dutton 1969). In turn, these arguments led to the development of psychometric scales intended to measure interpersonal conflict management styles and to diagnose the repertoire of managerial conflict management styles used by individual managers (Hall 1969; Thomas and Kilmann 1978). The 1980s and early 1990s also ushered in a reawakening of interest in social-psychological research using more advanced and wide-ranging instruments (Putnam and Wilson 1982; Rahim 1983; Morrill and King Thomas 1992); prescriptive and descriptive research on the social psychology of negotiation (Bazerman and Lewicki 1983; Bazerman and Neale 1992; Fisher and Ury 1981; Neale and Bazerman 1991; Raiffa 1982) are two areas generally regarded as "growth industries" in organizational-conflict studies. Social psychologists also returned to organizational contexts to focus on personality factors in conflict management (Greenhalgh 1987; Jones and Melcher 1982). Management scholars began investigating the organizational control implications of interdepartmental conflict management as well (Eccles 1985; Eccles and White 1984).

9. The distinction between *productive* and *destructive* organizational conflict also harkens back to more general ideas about functional and dysfunctional conflict in the writings of Coser (1956) and Deutsch (1973). In radical strands of this approach, the question became and continues to be how to widen the scope of conflict by negotiatory or other means so that fundamental issues such as gender and minority discrimination or alternative nonhierarchical organizational structures could be considered (e.g., Burawoy 1979; Hearn et al. 1986; Martin 1992a).

10. The use of the terms *contemporary* and *traditional* throughout the text are not intended to imply normative evaluations of the settings characterized. Traditional settings generally refer to aggregates of people who are socially homogeneous and utilize relatively simple technology, while contemporary settings refer to aggregates of people who are socially heterogeneous and utilize relatively complex technology (e.g., Felstiner 1974). These distinctions do not begin to capture the subtleties contained within societal typologies used in cross-cultural and evolutionary research (e.g., Netting 1986; Johnson and Earle 1987). However, these distinctions *are* widely used in empirical studies of conflict management and so appear to be a reasonable classification for present purposes (e.g., Baumgartner 1988; Black 1976, 1984, 1990). The distinction between formal and informal conflict management evokes Weber's characterization (1968: 226) of *formal* and *substantive* justice, the former referring to justice which conforms to legal precepts and procedures and the latter to justice which occurs outside the official legal system. On the use of these concepts in empirical studies of contemporary conflict management, see generally Abel (1982) and Black (1976). Empirical studies across a wide range of disciplines corroborate the argument that people use law to handle interpersonal conflict less frequently than other means. Social psychologists, communication researchers, legal scholars, and family-studies scholars have found that conflicts among family members, friends, neighbors, and romantic partners in American society are handled by a range of informal mechanisms, ranging from

violence to subtle nonverbal shunning (Bochner and Eisenberg 1987; Braiker and Kelley 1979; Cahn 1990; Cupach and Metts 1986; Ellickson 1991; Fitzpatrick 1988; Sternberg and Dobson 1987; Sternberg and Soriano 1984). Galanter (1983) also raises doubts about the empirical grounds for claiming that modern society is especially litigious (cf. Lieberman 1983), particularly when compared to other periods in American history, such as the immediate postrevolutionary decades when legal suits per capita were far higher than in the contemporary United States.

11. On the paucity of ethnographic studies of elites in general, see Marcus (1983). Ironically, some organizational scholars would argue that the dominant paradigm guiding research on organizations emanates from the concerns of top managers (Alvesson and Wilmot 1992), particularly male managers (Martin 1992a). As noted earlier, this study departs from the mainstream concerns of managers or managerial scholars because its intellectual origins lie in the study of disputing and conflict management, rather than the study of management structures, or more broadly, the study of organizational efficiency and effectiveness. At the same time, I attempt to avoid the preoccupation with conflict as a negative force in organizations. Scholars within this perspective argue that managers do not indigenously manage conflict effectively because they often use nonconfrontational or aggressive confrontational strategies that result in destructive rather than constructive organizational and interpersonal outcomes (e.g., Walton 1969). At the other end of the spectrum, more radical scholars argue for techniques that will politicize conflict, resulting in productive (i.e., change-oriented) outcomes. Because of these value orientations, there has been far more attention paid to how organizational members *should* handle conflict than how they *do* handle it (Lewicki and Sheppard 1985).

12. To this list, one can add Whyte's *The Organization Man* (1967) and Mills's *White Collar*. Both of these works primarily focus on the whole of middle-class life, but also present occasional and insightful sketches of the conditions of executive life. At the same time, there is an extensive array of observational works on middle and lower managers, some of which touch on corporate executives (e.g., Dalton 1959; Kanter 1977; Kunda 1992; O'Barr and Conley 1992; Powell 1985; see the review in Martynko and Gardner 1985).

13. In this literature, "complete" or "successful" executives are typically described in terms of their central "functions" in organizations. Chester Barnard's *The Functions of the Executive* provides one classic and abstract exemplar of this genre by arguing that executives function "first, to provide the system of communication, second, to promote the securing of essential efforts, and third, to formulate and define purpose" (1968: 217). Along the same lines Luther Gulick, a contemporary of Barnard, coined the awkward acronym "POSDCORB" to characterize the functions of corporate executives as planning, organizing, staffing, directing, coordinating, reporting, and budgeting (1937). According to some business writers (e.g., Drucker 1954), the actions associated with these functions describe what executives actually do. The orientation of this typology continues to thrive explicitly and implicitly in contemporary popular treatises on management written for executives and people aspiring to the executive levels (Levinson 1981; Lundsborg 1981; Stern 1990; Wareham 1991).

Although functional managerial typologies enjoy widespread appeal, they enjoy little empirical support. Empirical investigations of their validity consistently demonstrate the difficulty that executives and observers have in classifying executive activities into discrete functions. Executive ethnographies, in particular, demonstrate the shortcomings of such schemes and suggest that executive work is more differentiated from, but at the same time more similar to, work at other managerial levels of organizations than functional executive typologies would suggest (Mintzberg 1973:10–11).

At its best, the prescriptive literature on executives contains images of executive decision making and action that may prove useful as ideals for which executives can strive (e.g., Srivastva 1983). At its worst, the prescriptive literature may lead down a path that is at variance with the realities of executive life altogether.

14. Needless to say, this approach does not begin to capture the plethora of theoretical lenses through which conflict is studied. Two frameworks that have enjoyed particular currency in studies of conflict management focus on *interests* and *culture*. Authors typically pose these frameworks as antipodes, although some approaches explicitly draw from both (e.g., Ross 1993).

Scholars who explain conflict management in organizations as a function of interests assume disputing is a consciously instrumental decision-making process. March (1988) argues that such assumptions underlie much of the descriptive and prescriptive wisdom about all decision making in organizations. As outlined by March (1988:2), decision making from an interest ("choice") perspective is "intentional, consequential, and optimizing." In organizations, managers, particularly *top managers*, are "cast in the role of rational men" who must optimize profit for their organizations (Collins and Moore 1970:7; McDonald 1985). These assumptions also undergird some human-relations approaches to organizational conflict (e.g., Likert and Likert 1976; Walton 1969) and social-psychological studies of managerial conflict (Lewicki and Sheppard 1985; Neale and Bazerman 1991). For scholars operating out of this perspective, managers make rational choices about how to handle interpersonal and group conflict. In the structural version of this approach, conflict management results from rational decision-making processes about how best to assure the smooth functioning of organizational parts (Lawrence and Lorsch 1967a; Pondy 1967). In the political vision of organizations, such interests concern the struggle over power and control among managers (e.g., Bacharach and Lawler 1980; Fligstein 1990; Pettigrew 1973). Regardless of the theoretical strain, a prominent consideration in managerial decision-making processes focused on rationally handling conflict is the "seriousness" of conflict issues (McDonald 1985). In general, serious conflict issues are regarded from a choice perspective as those that "seriously and rapidly impede the progress of the organization" (Frost 1987:510).

Walton (1969), for example, argues that managers lower the personal and organizational costs of organizational conflict by confronting colleagues, particularly with the use of third parties acting as settlement agents of some type. This is especially true when conflicts are deeply felt and longstanding among the principals. In a similar vein, Bergman and Volkema (1989) suggest that the greater the number of people affected by a conflict, the more likely managers are to confront the principals head-on. Lewicki and Sheppard (1985) provide one of the clearest examples of choice theory applied to managerial conflict. They argue that the amount of control exercised by managerial third-party settlement agents over outcomes will vary with the seriousness of issues.

Cultural approaches to conflict management depart from the methodologically individualist orientations of interest perspectives, working down from collectively shared sentiments to individual actions. In traditional cultural approaches conflict was defined as a breakdown in pervasively held values and expectations within organizations. Conflict management from this perspective functioned to reintegrate adversaries into or "flush" them from the organization. Contemporary cultural theories of conflict management, in contrast, focus on how collectively held values define what is worth pursuing grievances over and how such grievances are to be pursued (Merry and Silbey 1984). A central concern in such theories is how aggrieved individuals define their grievances (e.g., as injustices, nuisances, etc.) within their local contexts (Van Maanen 1992). Other scholars have emphasized the existence of subcultures within organizations that may or may not contain similar values (Martin 1992b). From a subcultural perspective, there may exist many culturally defined customs of conflict management within a single organization.

Gender explanations of conflict management appear to straddle both interest and cultural approaches. Over the past two decades feminist and other scholars investigating gender differences in behavior have argued that systematic differences exist between the ways men and women approach issues of normative import, including conflict management. Much of these investigations have taken a discourse slant, focusing on "conflict talk" and other communication processes (Tannen 1993a). Some scholars claim that such differences reside in the domination of women by men. From this perspective, gendered conflict management processes are one way by which the privileged interests of men are institutionalized (e.g., Thorne and Henley 1975; Thorne, Kramarae, and Henley 1983). The cultural study of gendered conflict management emanates from the claim that men and women are socialized into cultures with different moral ethoses: women into cultures of connection and care and men into cultures of justice, status hierarchies, and rule orientations (Gilligan 1982). Consider Deborah Tannen's argument from her well-known book, *You Just Don't Understand* (1990:150): "To most women, conflict is a threat to connection, to be avoided at all costs. Disputes are preferably settled without direct confrontation. But to many men, conflict is the necessary means by which status is negotiated, so it is to be accepted and may be sought, embraced, and enjoyed." It should be noted that the interest and cultural approaches to gendered conflict management are not purely antithetical. When women attempt to enact their moral ethos in social institutions dominated by the male moral ethos, for example, their discourse does not articulate well with those institutions and they can be disadvantaged relative to actors using justice- or rule-oriented discourses (Conley and O'Barr 1990).

A review of the empirical support of these approaches is beyond the purview of the present work. Suffice it to say that a multidisciplinary literature has grown up around the study of gender and conflict management during the last two decades. Gender differences in conflict management have been investigated ethnographically (Conley and O'Barr 1990; Kolb 1992), via discourse analysis (see the review in Tannen 1993a and the collections in Tannen 1993b; Gilligan et al. 1988; Grimshaw 1990), and experimentally (see the results and review in Gayle 1991; Morrill, Johnson, and Harrison 1994). The findings of these diverse studies indicate a potentially more complex picture than the above quote would indicate, although it is unclear just how gendered cultures systematically affect conflict management. The ultimate promise of organizational cultural approaches to conflict management also remains unclear because there have been relatively few studies to take such a perspective and because the emphasis of normative consensus in traditional studies of organizational culture naturally leads researchers away from conflict to concentrate on what is agreed upon by organizational members (e.g., Martin 1992b; Sackman 1991).

Empirical support for interest approaches in the experimental literature is far more substantial. Conflict management tactics, for example, can be accurately predicted under artificially induced payoff structures (Lewicki and Sheppard 1985; Neale and Bazerman 1991). Using completely different methods, scholars studying broad historical trends have demonstrated that interest-driven organizational conflicts over control of large corporations do result in dramatic changes in the strategy and structure of firms unexplained by efficiency arguments alone (Fligstein 1987, 1990). Yet, the data used to support these arguments largely derive from mobility trends over time which are far removed from the day-to-day interactions of executives themselves. Indeed, there have been virtually no studies to date which have investigated the claims made by these approaches with qualitative and quantitative data systematically drawn from a variety of organizational contexts.

Other scholars favor the so-called conflict-styles approach to conflict management and have been searching for transcontextually consistent styles of conflict management for decades (Sternberg and Dobson 1987; Sternberg and Soriano 1984). Robert Blake and Jane Mouton's (1964) *Managerial Grid* represents one of the most durable and influential attempts to argue that personality traits form the basis for transcontextually consistent conflict styles within organizations. They argue that managers possess different levels of two enduring traits: concerns for people and concern for production. Their "managerial grid" measures managers' individual-level traits along these dimensions and results in five conflict-handling modes consistently used by individuals depending upon the levels of each trait they possess. In the thirty years since Blake and Mouton proposed this approach, countless studies have taken it as a point of departure for studies of conflict within organizations, typically relying on checklists of statements concerning how managers usually or generally would handle conflict in their organizations (see the reviews in Putnam 1988; Morrill and King Thomas 1992).

More recently psychologists have argued that personality has little predictive value in the study of conflict management, but that in controlled laboratory studies, student subjects do exhibit some transcontextual consistencies in conflict styles (Sternberg and Dobson 1987). One wonders about the generalizability of these results to actual social contexts in which people face conflicts embedded in the routines of day-to-day living.

Another theoretical approach, which has not to my knowledge been used in organizational contexts and which remains largely at the paradigmatic level, locates the seeds of conflict and its management in the biological makeup of humans. Much of this work concerns intraspecies human aggression, its role in social and biological selection, and its diffusion or redirection via peaceful means. Charles Darwin in his *The Descent of Man* (1871) provided one early and influential voice to this bio-evolutionary view of human aggression. More recently Konrad Lorenz (1963) and E. O. Wilson (1975) have argued that human aggression has biological bases which interact with environmental influences to ensure the survival of certain social groups and institutions.

15. "Interest" assumptions can also be found in some of these works, as well as a wide array of social exchange approaches to interpersonal and relational conflict (Peterson 1983; Roloff and Cloven 1990; Thibault and Kelley 1959). Students of international conflict also draw upon interest notions (e.g., Pruitt and Rubin 1986).

16. Black (1984:4–6) and Horwitz (1990:8–11) provide more complete discussions of the diversity of the ways the concepts of conflict management and social control have been used. Both of these authors use *social control* as a synonym for *conflict management* in the sense that the concept is used in the present work: the purposive pursuit of grievances against people defined as deviant (from the perspective of aggrieved parties). The term *conflict management* is used in lieu of *social control* throughout the present work to avoid confusion with a usage of *social control* common in some sociological traditions and a usage of *control* (without *social* preceding it) in contemporary organizational studies. I should also note that *conflict management* does not necessarily imply *conflict resolution* in that the latter term conventionally refers to the suspension of hostilities or settlement of some kind. Conflict management may or may not lead to conflict resolution. Traditionally, *social control* has referred to the ways that society regulates its members (e.g., Janowitz 1975). This meaning of social control closely resembles that used in early twentieth-century works by sociologists Ross (1901) and Thomas and Znaniecki (1927). These authors argued that social control efforts via education, public opinion, and socialization channeled individuals toward legitimate pursuits in the face of social change brought about by rapid industrialization and large-scale immigration. *Organizational control* refers to the process of channeling individual interests toward collective interests in organizational life defined either by management or workers or some combination of both. Beginning with Weber (1968), scholars have devoted a great deal of attention to how formal organizational structures imposed from above by management or from below by workers achieve control through incentives and rules (e.g., Edwards 1979; Etzioni 1961; Tannenbaum 1968). More recently, White (1986, 1992) and Eccles and White (1984) have explored how social networks within formal organizational structures induce control through the creation of self-reproducing goal structures. In some sense, the concept of control as used in relation to organizational life simply recycles the earlier meanings of societal social control; individuals and groups are still being regulated (e.g., influenced) not by society, but by components of the organizational systems in which they work and that in some instances they themselves have created.

17. In extensions of this approach outside of legal processes, conflict management/social control is also treated as a dependent variable (Black 1984). For analyses and descriptions of a variety of conflict management processes, see the works of sociologists M. P. Baumgartner (1984a, 1984b, 1985, 1988, 1992), Marian Borg (1992), Mark Cooney (1986, 1992), John Griffiths (1984), John Herrmann (1992), Allan Horwitz (1982, 1990), Candace Kruttschnitt (1982), and James Tucker (1989, 1993), as well as that by social historian Roberta Senechal (1992). Viewing conflict management as a dependent variable thus differs from traditional organizational approaches which are concerned with the etiology of conflict (Walton et al. 1969) and functionalist concerns about the integrative or nonintegrative consequences of organizational conflict (Pondy 1967; Corwin 1969).

18. Some of the headwaters of this stream can be found in works by Herbert Blumer (1969), George Herbert Mead (1934), and Alfred Schutz (1962). More contemporary treatments of these fields can be found in works in interpretive anthropology by Geertz (1973, 1983) and Turner (1967); in dramaturgical sociology by Goffman (1959, 1961); in cultural organizational studies by Frost et al. (1991), Kunda (1992), Sackman (1991), Schein (1984), Thompson (1976), and Trice (1985); and in social cognition by Fiske and Taylor (1991) and Schank and Abelson (1977). For a broad review of studies in organizational culture, see Martin (1992b) and Dobbin (1994).

19. Donald Black's emphasis lies in the behavioral manifestations of social structures that pattern reactions to deviance. Because of the behavioral emphasis in his work, he is unconcerned with the mechanisms by which structure, culture, and cognition intertwine with conflict management. See Cooney (1986), Greenberg (1983), and Horwitz (1983) on the radical "behavioralism" contained within Black's approach to the study of law and conflict management. Mayhew (1982) further suggests that Black's theoretical framework may actually represent a "pure" structuralist approach.

20. Several social theorists have tackled the problems of agency, structure, and culture via different "balancing acts" which emphasize various levels of voluntarism and determinism. Giddens (1979, 1984) addresses this problem by arguing that individual agents both create and reproduce social structures over time in a never-ending process. Bourdieu's (1977) treatment of action and "habitus" also concentrates on structured pragmatic action within highly confined cultural contexts. See Granovetter (1985), Hays (1994), Sewell (1992) for excellent reviews and attempts to sort out aspects of these thorny theoretical problems with specific relevance to economic contexts and historical change, respectively.

21. A number of scholars in the last three decades have attempted to corral the somewhat messy concept of local context. Geertz provides a discussion of local context that focuses on proximate meanings and symbols (1973, 1983). Hymes (1974), Applegate and Delia (1980), Giles and Coupland (1991), and Goodwin and Duranti (1992) discuss how communication and linguistic forms constitute local contexts. Garfinkel (1967) focuses on local contexts as emerging from pragmatic action. Goffman (1967) focuses on normative interaction rituals as constitutive of local context. Black (1979a, 1990) provides a multidimensional notion of context that could be couched at the local level or more

distant ones. Black uses the term *social field*, instead of social context, to denote particular constellations of what he calls dimensions of "social space" (1979a). Social space, from Black's perspective, consists of five dimensions: vertical (the distribution of resources), horizontal (distribution of social intimacy), symbolic (distribution of symbols), corporate (distribution of the capacity for collective action), and evaluative (the distribution valorization). Another notable allusion to social context in law and society studies originates in Moore's (1978:55) "semi-autonomous social field"—a context that contains and reproduces internal rules and customs that are distinctive but also somewhat vulnerable to influences from the larger society of which it is a part. Each author stresses what the other limits in their usage of social field: Black stresses structures of observable behavior, while Moore stresses the cultural, particularly norms and values. I use social context as a concept in an attempt to recognize the interweaving of structural, cultural, and cognitive elements in particular settings.

22. Formal hierarchy can also legitimate social hierarchies grounded in social class, gender, or ethnicity, thus ensuring that such hierarchies are perpetuated without resort to overt coercion (e.g., Ferguson 1984).

23. The number of labels for interpretive structures appear as numerous as the number of authors who write about them. At the most general level, schemas provide individuals with preconscious bases for interpreting phenomena. Scripts provide preconscious bases for action. I chose to settle on one term, *schemas*, to label interpretive structures. For a more complete review of the usages of *frames* and *schemas*, see Fiske and Taylor (1991) and Tannen (1979, 1990). See also Bateson's original usage of the concept of frame (1972:184–8, 190–2). Schemas and scripts are not purely localized phenomena, certainly having interconnections with the wider societal context within which people live. Schemas and scripts are often overlaid, one flowing out of and into the other. However, this correspondence is not perfect because of pragmatic concerns in particular situations.

24. My usage of *culture* in this book thus departs from the conceptual usage by Black (1976:61–83), who defines culture by example as language, beliefs, values, and systems of thought (e.g., scientific, artistic). He primarily uses culture as a quantitative variable, arguing that the quantity (e.g., complexity) of culture can be used to predict conflict management processes and outcomes. The usage here differs from this approach in that culture exists as a meaning system composed of schemas and scripts through which people make sense of and act in and on their surroundings.

25. Burt (1992), in contrast, characterizes gaps in actors' social networks as "structural holes." Contextual holes, as conceived here, focus attention on the social structural gaps between interactants and on interpretive gaps caused by a lack of overlapping schemas and scripts. A contextual hole could thus be characterized by communication or other action that is mutually unintelligible to interactants, particularly when such interactants have never previously interacted with one another and when they originate from very different cultures.

26. Conflict scholars generally refer to the interpretive structures that enable people to define dimensions of their conflicts in a number of ways. Klar et al. (1987) and Kruglanski et al. (1993), for example, argue that "conflict schemas"

have at their core the notion that the principals to an interaction have incompatible goals. Comaroff and Roberts (1977, 1981) argue that "paradigms of argument" invoke normatively based interpretations of conflict talk, processes, and strategies. Pinkley (1990) provides a useful review of some of this literature.

27. The use of conflict management *styles* in this book differs from that found in the social psychological and communication literatures (see the review in Putnam and Poole 1987). In those literatures, conflict styles refers to behavioral functions of personality traits used to manage conflict.

28. Social escalation is akin to what Horwitz (1990:97) calls *social expansion,* which is "the extent that grievances radiate outward beyond the disputants themselves into informal and formal networks for resolution." Social escalation differs from social expansion, however, in that it leaves open the question of whether greater involvement of the social system in which grievances arise leads to resolution or to the continuation of grievance pursuits. Third parties, for example, can both exacerbate and reduce hostilities.

29. Black and Baumgartner (1983) define authoritativeness in a purely behavioral sense, eschewing the legitimacy with which the concept is traditionally linked. From the present perspective, authoritativeness refers to the degree to which a third-party settlement agent uses their recognized, legitimated position(s) in some institutionalized hierarchy to impose outcomes on disputes between other parties.

30. Baumgartner (1992) provides empirical illustration and an extended discussion on the effects of hierarchical dependence on conflict management.

Chapter Two

1. All figures for firm characteristics are for fiscal year 1986.

2. The actual product mixes, revenues, and financial status and business strategies of each firm have been slightly modified in order to protect the confidentiality of all sources and the identities of the firms in the study.

3. Drawing on Moore's (1962) notion of "homosexual reproduction," Rosabeth Kanter (1977:48) wrote in *Men and Women of the Corporation* that the *white men* who manage large corporations "reproduce themselves in kind" by largely excluding women and minorities from top executive ranks. Executives, she claimed, were overwhelmingly educated white men in their forties to seventies. More recently, Ferguson (1984:106) has argued that "the more similarity there is in outwardly identifiable characteristics, such as race, sex, dress, language, and style, the more likely is an aspirant to be seen as the 'right kind of person' and given access to positions of discretion and power. Thus, the patterns of racial, sexual, and class stratification of the larger society are reproduced in the organization." These claims are supported by several sources over a two-decade period. Kanter noted that women held *none* of the top management positions in three-fourths of 163 corporations participating in a 1971 national survey conducted by the editors of the magazine *Personnel Policies Forum.* Moreover, she argued, a U.S. Bureau of the Census report in 1973

indicated that nonwhite men made up less than 5% of all managers earning more than $30,000 per year in 1973—a sum that even in the early 1970s would be far below that earned by most top managers, particularly in large corporations. Thus, these figures seem to indicate that fewer executives are nonwhite men than even the percentage above suggests. Evidence on demographic changes in the ranks of American executives since the 1970s is difficult to come by and even more difficult to interpret because of the inclusiveness of occupational classifications used in many of the available statistics. For example, the U.S. House of Representatives Report (United States House of Representatives 1991:553) accompanying the Glass Ceiling Act of 1991 (a civil rights act passed to strengthen the access of qualified women and minorities to educational and occupational opportunities) contains statistics culled from U.S. Department of Labor statistics over the last three decades. The House Report contains two tables that are interpreted in the accompanying text as providing "evidence" of the changes in minority and female composition in the managerial workforce. The first table shows the percentage of women holding the occupation of "executive" for the years 1972, 1978, 1983, and 1988. These statistics indicate that the percentage of women holding executive positions increased from 19.7% of the women in the American labor force in 1972 to 39.3% in 1988. A second table in the report presents the ratio of minority worker employment to white worker employment by occupational category, 1960–1988. This table indicates a doubling of the minority-to-white "office and managerial" worker ratio. The text accompanying these tables gushes that "the charts . . . dramatically illustrate the significant improvement in opportunities for women and minorities during the last two decades" (United States House of Representatives 1991:553). Inspection of the actual *Handbook of Labor Statistics* on which the House Report rests reveals that the range of occupations included in the "executive" category ranges from middle-level supervisors to CEOs. The number of women at the corporate vice president or higher levels (the working definition of *executive* in the present work) included in this wide occupational category is unclear. The second table on minority and white workers is even more problematic because the category "office and managerial" occupations includes positions from administrative assistants to CEOs. Again, the percentage of top managers represented in this category remains unknown. Other available surveys significantly contrast these statistics. A recent U.S. Bureau of Labor Statistics report (1992; cited in Segal and Zellner 1992) reports that women hold 3% of the senior executive posts (defined as those who report to the CEO of a firm) in American corporations. The results of three national surveys—two published in *Fortune Magazine* (Fierman 1990) and one in *Business Week* (Segal and Zellner 1992)—also present less than optimistic pictures of executive demographics. The first *Fortune* survey of the 1,000 largest American industrial and service companies revealed that of the 4,012 personnel listed as the highest paid officers and directors of these companies, only 19 (0.5%) were women. The second *Fortune* survey focused on the officers listed in the back of 255 annual reports of corporations who subscribe to *Fortune*. Of the 9,293 officers listed in these reports, roughly 5% were women. In the *Business Week* survey of 400 women executives during 1992 (performed by Louis Harris & Associates), a majority of women (64%) felt that the hiring policies by large corporations of women executives had improved since 1986. Yet 52% of those surveyed also believed that the rate of progress in hiring women to top managerial posts had slowed in more recent years and only 13% of those surveyed believed that their own companies would be more likely to promote a woman over a man if both were equally qualified for the job. It is against this backdrop, then, that one should consider the social characteristics of executives in the present study.

4. Only Old Financial and New Financial contain the title "senior executive vice president." This title was coded as executive vice president because of the similarity of duties between Old and New Financial SEVPs and the EVPs in other firms. Classifying CEOs, chief operating officers (COOs), and presidents raised further difficulties. In firms with both CEOs and COOs, the latter were treated as EVPs because their duties appeared to be similar to those of EVPs in firms with only CEOs and EVPs. In firms with both CEOs and presidents (particularly divisional presidents), presidents were classified as EVPs, again because their duties seemed equivalent to those of EVP's in firms without both presidents and CEOs. In either of these instances, if the firm also contained EVPs, they were classified as SVPs; SVPs and VPs in these instances were then classified together.

5. Two more aspects of these categories bear mention before reviewing the social characteristics of executives in various positions. Some organizations subsume certain functions under one another. For example, Infotain and Sunset Group subsume sales under marketing, each having a single executive overseeing the combined department. In these instances, executives were placed in the category that best described their de facto activities (e.g., marketing or sales). Some executives also hold more than one position in an organization (such as executive vice president of both engineering and research and development). The same decisional rule was applied in these instances: executives were classified in the category closest to their actual activities. Finally, CEOs, presidents, and chief operating officers were classified according to their last executive function prior to their current position.

6. All executive informants were asked how much cash salary they earned. Only 151 of 227 executives replied with meaningful, nonevasive responses. Asking executives about their salaries, in fact, proved to be the most delicate subject broached during the study. Average middle manager salaries derive from several sources: (1) interviews with middle managers themselves; (2) estimates by executives; and (3) estimates by clerical personnel.

7. Personal computers during the mid-1980s were not yet the office fixtures that they are in the 1990s.

8. When one departs from the "objective" data produced in year-end organizational performance reports, official organization charts, and counts of demographic characteristics of individuals, one necessarily confronts the particularly thorny issue of equivalency of meaning for phenomena studied across different contexts (Abrams 1982:154–62; Nadel 1951). This problem was handled by balancing between etic and emic categories for classifying executives' "dictionary knowledge" (Sackmann 1991) of their local contexts and the fields within which their organizations operate. See appendix A for further discussion of coding issues and methodological caveats.

9. See Morgan (1986) for an updated discussion of the "machine" metaphor used to describe organizations.

10. The physical location of executives vis-à-vis one another could certainly affect all of the indices described in this section for each organization. The data for executive communication networks include only those executives who have offices at their corporate headquarters. Another factor that could confound both information-flow data and personal-tie data is the number of executives at each firm. Obviously, a small executive corps could facilitate communication whereas a large one could inhibit the development of communication contacts or personal relationships. The average number of executives in mechanistic firms is 33 (skewed because of the 76 executives at Old Financial), at atomistic firms 19, and at matrix firms 20. As will be discussed below, the sparsest and densest communication networks occur among atomistic and matrix executives, respectively, with the mechanistic top managers falling somewhere between these two extremes. Thus, size appears to be less of a factor than other features of context in determining information flow and personal ties. Another factor that could affect information flow would be electronic communication networks (e.g., electronic mail; see generally Sproull and Kiesler 1992 on the communication functions of such systems). At the time of the fieldwork, none of the organizations studied had implemented such systems across the executive levels.

11. For the purposes of this index, *work units* are defined as divisions or practices at the executive vice presidential level. CEOs were asked these questions in relation to corporate level officers and aides appointed as special staff who are members of any particular function or practice. Each informant was asked to make their personal communication distribution add up to 100%.

12. The atomistic organizations described here should not be confused with "atomized organizations" described by Deal and Kennedy (1982) that combine decentralization and computer-mediated communication to tie work units together (see also Drucker 1988; Sproull and Kiesler 1992). Nor should atomistic organizations be confused with the processes by which some large corporations externalize the costs of particularly mutable production processes to smaller, more flexible organizations embedded in resource and relational networks (e.g., Powell 1990; Sabel 1982). Atomistic bureaucracies do not enjoy the interdependence or the mutability of any of these organizational forms.

Chapter Three

1. Critics of the trouble case method (e.g., Cain and Kulcsar 1982; cf. Gluckman 1973; Greenhouse 1986:24–27) claim that it distorts the relationship between conflict and its social-contextual surroundings, reifying the structural boundedness of ongoing disputes. But, as Nader (1990:135) argues, cases are used to "examine particulars prior to, or as part of, forming generalized conclusions" about social contexts, thus leading to an articulation of cases with their contexts.

2. The total amount of grievance expressions collected number fewer than the total number of grievance issues because multiple issues could be associated with single expressions.

3. The labels for these actions again combine etic categories drawn from the cross-cultural and organizational literature on conflict management and emic categories that emerged from the data. See appendix A for details.

4. This argument would seem to contradict self-report studies indicating that violence occurs in fifty to sixty percent of all intimate dyads (Straus 1978). However, these figures may reflect not only the popular visibility of domestic violence as a legitimate object of public inquiry, but also the changing nature of intimate interpersonal relationships and family structures as indicated in divorce and separation rates and other measures of relational dissolution (Bumpass 1990; Kitson 1992:11; Norton and Moorman 1987). Indeed, one could speculate that an increase in social support institutions acting intendedly (e.g., lawyers) or unintendedly (e.g., counselors and social workers) as allies of divorcing individuals may actually increase the likelihood of violence because the *increase* in the relational distance between parties by introducing an additional communication step between them. I discuss the association between coalitions and confrontational conflict management later in this chapter. I do not mean to imply that social policy should be directed away from supportive institutions for individuals involved in relational dissolution; only that such individuals in such institutions should be aware of how they can exacerbate rather than heal confrontations between former intimates.

5. Two independent coders coded a random sample of 10% of the grievance expressions for each of the outcome variables in order to assess inter-rater reliabilities. These analyses yield reliabilities for issue (.66), schema (.71), form (.81), and directness (.68).

6. One of the failings of the fieldwork was the gathering of few grievance expressions among executives of ethnic minorities. Only 4 of the 15 African-American, Hispanic, and Asian-American executives granted me interviews, which in turn generated 3 extended cases and 6 grievance expressions. Therefore, it is difficult to analyze with any sense of rigor the relationship between conflict management and ethnicity. In chapter 4, I analyze one highly confrontational dispute involving a minority executive at Old Financial. In general, minority executives did not talk openly about grievances they had. Nor did European-American executives speak freely about conflict among or with minority executives. As a result, I did not undertake a quantitative analysis of ethnicity and conflict management.

7. Indifferent schemas were not included in the individual level analyses.

8. On the linguistic effects of social subordination on women, see generally Lakoff (1978).

9. The measure of association used is the Cramer C coefficient. $C = \sqrt{x^2/[N(L-1)]}$, where N is the total number of observations and L is the lesser of the number of rows and the number of columns in the contingency table from which the observations are drawn. Like the Pearson product-moment correlation, the Cramer C has a maximum value of 1 and will be equal to 0 when the variables of interest are independent of one another. Unlike the Pear-

son product-moment correlation, C cannot be negative because the statistic only measures relationships between unordered (nominal) variables (Siegel and Castellan 1988:225–27).

10. Baumgartner (1984b:334–36) describes procedures that occur in downward and upward directions in social hierarchies as *authoritarian*. This style of procedure differs from the *authoritative* orders in mechanistic bureaucracies in that authoritative conflict management is grounded in and limited to some degree by the formal authority of role positions in formal organization. Baumgartner (1984b:335), in contrast, argues that authoritarian procedures are "grounded in available resources and opportunities. . . . Where the authoritarian mode prevails, then, which people are processed for what conduct depends heavily on the inclinations of those who are offended, even as those vary with the same person or group over time." Although some overlaps exist between the two types of orders, authoritarian procedures appear more personalistic in nature than the authoritative order described herein.

Chapter Four

1. Fligstein (1985:378) defines the "multidivision form" as a "decentralized management structure [with] product divisions and [a] unitary structure." A unitary structure in his sense (compare the use of the term in Davis and Lawrence 1977, which is used through out the present work) "implies an organization divided into manufacturing, sales, and marketing" (Fligstein 1985:378). The corporation under study, strictly speaking, is a hybrid of multidivision and what Fligstein terms "geographical" forms (1985:378). Perhaps the corporation should properly be labeled a "geographical-multidivision form."

2. Because of space limitations, only those extended cases presented in text are numbered and given formal titles.

3. Not every executive sent to a management-training program (particularly those organized as retreats or designed exclusively for top managers) or to college (whether at the undergraduate or graduate levels) is the target of grievances. At times, such practices are often seen by Old Financial executives as investments in promising junior executives. Such was the case, from all accounts, with the female executive who had her entire way through college paid by Old Financial and who is now a vice president in the firm. However, nongrievance-related practices of this sort enable conflict management practices of similar forms to occur without much notice.

4. The subtlety of this process created certain problems for data collection. Many executives were ignorant of its existence, while others regarded its use with cynicism and smiled or laughed about its occurrence without relating any details. Much of the information on it derives from the president, two executive vice presidents, and a senior vice president who claim to engage in it regularly, and who argued that other executives did so as well. None of these informants, of course, believed they had ever been the targets of grievance-based reassignment.

Chapter Five

1. The Big Six were the Big Eight until 1989, when two mergers occurred. See Stevens (1991) for an account of these mergers and their consequences for big-league accounting.

2. See appendix A for a discussion of the decision to conduct field research at Independent's main regional office, rather than its world headquarters. Such a choice, of course, raises questions about the comparability of observations at Independent and the other twelve headquarters studied. Informants who had worked in Independent's world headquarters as top managers argued that the social relations among partners at the large regional office were substantially the same as at world headquarters. Moreover, many of the top partners in the main regional office kept offices at the world headquarters as well and regularly participated in top management decisions at headquarters.

3. Further evidence for the sparse communication network density among Independent partners can be found in Morrill (1991a).

Chapter Six

1. In 1991, two female executives were promoted beyond the vice presidential level.

2. Quantitative evidence for the network density among Playco executives can also be found in Morrill (1991b).

3. When weak executives wore suit vests for "duels" or "shoot outs," their vests were sometimes referred to as "life" vests, indicating their need for "help [keeping] their heads above water" (winning a conflict in a proper manner).

Chapter Seven

1. However, the view of managerial action as more habituated and scripted than most theories of organizational decision making would recognize ironically converges with the observations by Hannan and Freeman (1989:40), the most ardent proponents of the new orthodoxy, about the "antiheroic" implications of organizational population ecology for conventional notions of managerial action and decision making.

2. Social identity as used here is closer to the traditional notions of the concept, although it would be included in the broader versions such as that found in White, who defines identity as "any source of action not explicable from biophysical regularities, and to which observers can attribute meaning" (1992:6).

Appendix A

1. Representative critical reflections of ethnography by both anthropologists and sociologists appear in works by Clough (1992), Denzin (1989, 1994), Geertz (1988), Krieger (1991), Lofland (1994), Marcus and Fisher (1986), Rosaldo (1989), Stocking (1989, 1991, 1992), and Van Maanen (1988). Literary scholars and historical scholars also offer their own critique of ethnography in works by Herbert (1991) and Kuklick (1991). See the review essay by Snow and Morrill (1993) and the collection in Denzin and Lincoln (1994) on the general arguments and dilemmas raised by these works.

2. Of course, this scene is far from a typically imagined setting in which the ethnographer is "suddenly set down surrounded by all your gear, alone on a tropical beach close to a native village, while the launch or dinghy which has brought you sails away out of sight," as Malinowski (1922:4) so ably captured. Even though I had grown up in the business "culture" and was in familiar North American settings, I still experienced an initial fear, desperately wanting to turn back yet not able to turn back, as well the excitement of going on an adventure in a land rarely seen by anyone except "natives."

3. After leaving the field, I encountered an article by Hoffman (1980) on his experiences while gaining access to hospital boards of directors in Quebec. He specifically argues for the approach I stumbled onto and empirically demonstrates the increased informational yield from elite informants with personal contacts to the interviewer. Hoffman also argues that personal contacts enhance the validity of information in interviews because informants feel freer to express themselves and focus more on their *own* accuracy, rather than focusing on not divulging too much insider information.

4. The nonrespondent on the initial list had apparently had a falling out with Tag. The nonrespondent's secretary, upon hearing Tag's name as a reference, said, "I think such an appointment would be quite impossible at present or at any time in the near future." She added curtly, "I'm sorry this has been such a waste of time for you," and hung up. Access via personal ties, then, can cut both ways.

5. The only lack of access after an initial interview resulted from government security clearance investigations the informant claimed would be needed before conducting fieldwork. The informant also claimed that such investigations could take up to a year. Part of this "brush-off" could certainly be ascribed to the scrutiny of the defense industry by federal authorities and other watchdog organizations at the time of fieldwork. This informant also barely knew Tag and so had little obligation to help in the access process.

6. It should be noted that only a small percentage of the group of executives I studied actually knew these four executives. After the first round of referrals, the connectedness of informants to these initial informants was nearly nonexistent. However, snowball techniques still leave one with something of a convenience sample and all of its potential for sample selection bias, depending on where the snowball began.

7. Of course, I recognize that executives could have been masking their own personal interests or desire for gossip behind a rhetoric of public good.

8. Commco and General Utility executives may not have minded being tape-recorded because of their relationships to regulatory agencies and regular exposure to the representatives of the print and electronic media.

9. Although I did not explicitly use what Snow and Morrill (forthcoming) refer to as an "integrated approach" to ethnographic data analysis, I did attend to coding data in each of the broad analytic categories we refer to as (1) actors (e.g., individuals and/or collectivities), (2) time (e.g., sequences, careers, rhythms, tempos), (3) sociocultural domains (behaviors, artifacts, resources, meanings), and (4) place (e.g., scenes, settings, arenas, and stages).

10. I borrow the notion of theoretical discovery, refinement, and extension from Snow and Morrill (forthcoming).

REFERENCES

Abbot, Andrew
    1988   *The Systems of the Professions.* Chicago: University of Chicago Press.

Abel, Richard L. (ed.)
    1982   *The Politics of Informal Justice: The American Experience.* New York: Academic Press.

Abrams, Philip
    1982   *Historical Sociology.* Ithaca, NY: Cornell University Press.

Alvesson, Mats, and Hugh Wilmot (eds.)
    1992   *Critical Management Studies.* Newbury Park, CA: Sage Publications.

Ansoff, H. I., and R. G. Brandenburg
    1971   "A Language for Organizational Design: Part I and II." *Management Science* 17:705–31.

Applegate, James L., and Jesse G. Delia
    1980   "Person-Centered Speech, Psychological Development, and the Contexts of Language Usage." Pp. 245–82 in *The Social and Psychological Contexts of Language,* edited by Robert St. Claire and Howard Giles. Hillsdale, NJ: Erlbaum.

Argyris, Chris
    1967   "Today's Problems with Tomorrow's Organizations." *Journal of Management Studies* (February):31–55.

Aubert, Vilhelm (ed.)
    1969   *Sociology of Law.* New York: Penguin Books.

Avruch, Kevin, Peter W. Black, and Joseph Scimecca (eds.)
    1991   *Conflict Resolution: Cross-Cultural Perspectives.* New York: Greenwood Press.

Bacharach, Samuel B., and Edwin J. Lawler
    1980   *Power and Politics in Organization.* San Francisco: Jossey-Bass.

Balicki, Asen
1970   *The Netsilik Eskimo.* Garden City, NJ: Natural History Press.

Barker, Jeffrey, Dean Tjosvold, and I. Robert Andrews
1988   "Conflict Approaches of Effective and Ineffective Project
            Managers: A Field Study in a Matrix Organization." *Journal
            of Management Studies* 25:167–78.

Barley, Stephen R.
1991   "Contextualizing Conflict: Notes on the Anthropology of
            Disputes and Negotiations." Pp. 165–203 in *Research on Nego-
            tiation in Organizations,* vol. 3, edited by Max H. Bazerman,
            Roy J. Lewicki, and Blair H. Sheppard. Greenwich, CT: JAI
            Press.

Barnard, Chester I.
1968   *The Functions of the Executive.* Cambridge, MA: Harvard Uni-
            versity Press (originally published 1938).

Barnes, J. A.
1969   "Networks and Political Process." Pp. 51–76 in *Social Net-
            works in Urban Situations,* edited by J. Clyde Mitchell. Man-
            chester: Manchester University Press.

Bartunek, Jean M.
1984   "Changing Interpretive Schemes and Organizational Re-
            structuring: The Example of a Religious Order." *Administra-
            tive Science Quarterly* 29:355–72.

1988   "The Dynamics of Personal and Organizational Reframing."
            Pp. 137–62 in *Paradox and Transformation: Toward a Theory of
            Change in Organization and Management,* edited by Robert E.
            Quinn and Kim S. Cameron. Cambridge, MA: Ballinger Pub-
            lishing Company.

Bartunek, Jean M., and Robin D. Reid
1992   "The Role of Conflict in a Second-Order Change Attempt."
            Pp. 116–42 in *Hidden Conflict in Organizations: Uncovering
            Behind-the-Scenes Disputes,* edited by Deborah M. Kolb and
            Jean M. Bartunek. Newbury Park, CA: Sage Publications.

Bateson, Gregory
1972   *Steps to an Ecology of Mind.* New York: Random House.

Baumgartner, M. P.
1984a   "Social Control in Suburbia. Pp. 79–103 in *Toward a General
            Theory of Social Control,* vol. 2: *Selected Problems,* edited by
            Donald Black. Orlando, FL: Academic Press.

1984b   "Social Control from Below." Pp. 303–45 in *Toward a General
            Theory of Social Control,* vol. 1: *Fundamentals,* edited by Don-
            ald Black. Orlando, FL: Academic Press.

1985   "Law and the Middle Class: Evidence from a Suburban
            Town." *Law and Human Behavior* 9:3–24.

1988   *The Moral Order of a Suburb.* New York: Oxford University Press.

1992   "War and Peace in Early Childhood." Pp. 1–38 in *Virginia Review of Sociology,* vol. 1: *Law and Conflict Management,* edited by James Tucker. Greenwich, CT: JAI Press.

Baumhart, Raymond C.
1961   "How Ethical Are Businessmen?" *Harvard Business Review* 39:6–19.

Bazerman, Max H., and Roy J. Lewicki (eds.)
1983   *Negotiating in Organizations.* Beverly Hills, CA: Sage Publications.

Bazerman, Max H., and Margaret A. Neale
1992   *Negotiating Rationally.* New York: Macmillan.

Bennis, Warren
1965   "Beyond Bureaucracy." *Trans-Action* 2:31–35.

1980   "Why Leaders Can't Lead." Pp. 36–48 in *Life in Organizations: Workplaces as People Experience Them,* edited by Rosabeth Moss Kanter and Barry A. Stein. New York: Basic Books.

Berger, Peter L., Brigitte Berger, and Hansfried Kellner
1973   *The Homeless Mind: Modernization and Consciousness.* New York: Vintage.

Berger, Peter L., and Thomas Luckmann
1966   *The Social Construction of Reality.* New York: Doubleday.

Bergman, T. J., and R. J. Volkema
1989   "Understanding and Managing Interpersonal Conflict at Work: Its Issues, Interactive Processes, and Consequences." Pp. 7–19 in *Managing Conflict: An Interdisplinary Approach,* edited by M. Rahim. New York: Praeger.

Bernard, H. Russell
1988   *Research Methods in Cultural Anthropology.* Newbury Park, CA: Sage Publications.

Bersheid, Ellen, David Boye, and Elaine Walster
1968   "Retaliation as a Means of Restoring Equity." *Journal of Personality and Social Psychology* 10:370–76.

Black, Donald
1976   *The Behavior of Law.* New York: Academic Press.

1979a   "A Strategy of Pure Sociology." Pp. 149–68 in *Theoretical Perspectives in Sociology,* edited by Scott G. McNall. New York: St. Martin's Press.

1979b   "Comment: Common Sense in the Sociology of Law." *American Journal of Sociology* 44:18–23.

1980   *The Manners and Customs of the Police.* New York: Academic Press.

1983   "Crime as Social Control." *American Sociological Review* 48:34–45.

1984   "Social Control as a Dependent Variable." Pp. 1–36 in *Toward a General Theory of Social Control*, vol. 1: *Fundamentals*, edited by Donald Black. Orlando, FL: Academic Press.

1989   *Sociological Justice*. New York: Oxford University Press.

1990   "The Elementary Forms of Conflict Management." Pp. 43–69 in *New Directions in the Study of Justice, Law, and Social Control*, prepared by the School of Justice Studies, Arizona State University. New York: Plenum.

1993   *The Sociology of Right and Wrong*. San Diego, CA: Academic Press.

Black, Donald, and M. P. Baumgartner
1983   "Toward a Theory of the Third Party." Pp. 84–114 in *Empirical Theories about Courts*, edited by Keith O. Boyum and Lynn Mather. New York: Longman.

Black, Donald, and Maureen Mileski (eds.)
1974   *The Social Organization of Law*. New York: Seminar Press.

Blake, Robert R., and Jane S. Mouton
1964   *The Managerial Grid*. Houston: Gulf.

Blau, Peter M.
1955   *The Dynamics of Bureaucracy*. Chicago: University of Chicago Press.

1968   "The Hierarchy of Authority in Organizations." *American Journal of Sociology* 73: 453–67.

1970   "A Formal Theory of Differentiation in Organizations." *American Sociological Review* 35:201–18.

Bloch, Marc
1961   *Feudal Society*. vol. 2: *Social Classes and Political Organization*. Chicago: University of Chicago Press.

Blumer, Herbert
1969   *Symbolic Interactionism*. Englewood Cliffs, NJ: Prentice-Hall.

Bochner, Arthur P., and Eric M. Eisenberg
1987   "Family Process: Systems Perspectives." Pp. 540–63 in *Handbook of Communication Science*, edited by C. R. Berger and S. H. Chaffee. Newbury Park, CA: Sage Publications.

Bohannan, Paul (ed.)
1967   *Law and Warfare: Studies in the Anthropology of Conflict*. Austin: University of Texas Press.

Bonacich, Phillip
1990   "Communication Dilemmas in Social Networks: An Experimental Study." *American Sociological Review* 55:448–59.

Borg, Marian J.
1992   "Conflict Management in the World System." *Sociological Forum* 7:261–82.

Boulding, Kenneth
1962   *Conflict and Defense: A General Theory.* New York: Harper and Row.

1964   "A Pure Theory of Conflict Applied to Organizations." Pp. 41–49 in *The Frontiers of Management*, edited by George Fisk. New York: Harper and Row.

Bourdieu, Pierre
1965   "The Sentiment of Honour in Kabyle Society." Pp. 191–244 in *Honour and Shame: The Values of Mediterranean Society*, edited by J. G. Peristiany. Chicago: University of Chicago Press.

1977   *Outline of a Theory of Practice.* Cambridge: Cambridge University Press.

Braiker, Harriet B., and Harold H. Kelley
1979   "Conflict in the Development of Close Relationships." In *Social Exchange in Developing Relationships*, edited by R. L. Burgess and T. L. Huston. New York: Academic Press.

Buckle, Leonard G., and Suzann R. Thomas-Buckle
1982   "Doing unto Others: Dispute and Dispute Processing in an Urban American Neighborhood." Pp. 78–90 in *Neighborhood Justice: Assessment of an Emerging Idea*, edited by Roman Tomasic and Malcolm M. Feeley. New York: Longman.

Bumpass, L. L.
1990   "What's Happening to the Family? Interactions Between Demographic and Institutional Change." *Demography* 27: 483–98.

Burawoy, Michael
1979   *Manufacturing Consent: Changes in the Labor Process under Monopoly Capitalism.* Chicago: University of Chicago Press.

1991   "The Extended Case Method." Pp. 271–87 in *Ethnography Unbound: Power and Resistance in the Modern Metropolis*, edited, by Michael Burawoy, Alice Burton, Ann Arnett Ferguson, Kathryn J. Fox, Joshua Gamson, Leslie Hurst, Nadine G. Julius, Charles Kurzman, Leslie Salzinger, Joseph Schiffman, and Shiori Ui. Berkeley: University of California Press.

Burman, Sandra B. and Barbara E. Harrell-Bond (eds.)
1981   *The Imposition of Law.* New York: Academic Press.

Burns, Lawton R.
1989   "Matrix Management in Hospitals: Testing Theores of Matrix Structure and Development." *Administrative Science Quarterly* 34:349–68.

Burns, Tom, and G. M. Stalker
1961   *The Management of Innovation.* London: Tavistock.

Burt, Ronald S.
1987   "Social Contagion and Innovation: Cohesion versus Struc-

tural Equivalence." *American Journal of Sociology* 92:1287–1335.

1992   *Structural Holes: The Social Structure of Competition.* Cambridge, MA: Harvard University Press.

Butler, Arthur
1973   "Project Management: A Study in Organizational Conflict." *Academy of Management Review* 16:84–101.

Cahn, Dudley D. (ed.)
1990   *Intimates in Conflict: A Communication Perspective.* Hillsdale, NJ: Earlbaum.

Cain, Maureen, and Kalman Kulcsar
1982   "Thinking Disputes: An Essay on the Origins of the Dispute Industry." *Law and Society Review* 16:375–402.

Carlson, Sune
1951   *Executive Behavior: A Study of the Work Load and the Working Methods of Managing Directors.* Stockholm: Strombergs.

Chandler, Alfred D.
1962   *Strategy and Structure: Chapters in the History of the American Industrial Enterprise.* Cambridge, MA: MIT Press.

1977   *The Visible Hand: The Managerial Revolution in American Business.* Cambridge, MA: Harvard University Press.

Chandler, Alfred D., and Herman Daems (eds.)
1980   *Managerial Hierarchies: Comparative Perspectives on the Rise of the Modern Industrial Enterprise.* Cambridge, MA: Harvard University Press.

Chandler, Alfred D., and Takasi Hikino
1990   *Scale and Scope: The Dynamics of Industrial Capitalism.* Cambridge, MA: Belknap Press.

Christie, Nils
1977   "Conflicts as Property." *British Journal of Criminology* 17:1–15.

Cicourel, Aaron V.
1974   *Cognitive Sociology.* New York: Free Press.

Cohn, Bernard
1967   "Some Notes on Law and Change in North India." Pp. 139–59 in *Law and Warfare,* edited by Paul Bohannan. Austin: University of Texas Press.

Coleman, James S.
1982   *The Asymmetric Society.* Syracuse, NY: Syracuse University Press.

Coleman, James S., Elihu Katz, and Herbert Menzel
1966   *Medical Innovation.* New York: Bobbs-Merrill.

Collins, O. F., and D. G. Moore
1970   *The Organization Makers.* New York: Appleton.

Colson, Elizabeth
    1953   "Social Control and Vengeance in a Plateau Tonga Society."
                  Africa 23:199–212.

Comroff, John L., and Simon Roberts
    1977   "The Invocation of Norms in Dispute Settlement." Pp. 77–112
                  in *Social Anthropology and Law*, edited by Ian Hammet. New
                  York: Academic Press.

    1981   *Rules and Processes: The Cultural Logic of Dispute in an African
                  Context*. Chicago: University of Chicago Press.

Conley, John M., and William M. O'Barr
    1990   *Rules versus Relationships: The Ethnography of Legal Discourse*.
                  Chicago: University of Chicago Press.

Cooney, Mark
    1986   "Behavioural Sociology of Law: A Defence." *Modern Law Re-
                  view* (March):262–71.

    1992   "Racial Discrimination in Arrest." Pp. 99–120 in *Virginia Re-
                  view of Sociology*, vol. 1: *Law and Conflict Management*, edited
                  by James Tucker. Greenwich, CT: JAI Press.

Corwin, Ronald G.
    1969   "Patterns of Organizational Conflict." *Administrative Science
                  Quarterly* 14:507–21.

Coser, Lewis
    1956   *The Functions of Social Conflict: An Examination of the Concept of
                  Social Conflict and Its Use in Empirical Sociolegal Research*. New
                  York: Free Press.

Cough, Patricia Ticineto
    1992   *The End(s) of Ethnography: From Realism to Social Criticism*.
                  Newbury Park, CA: Sage Publications.

Cressey, Donald R.
    1953   *Other People's Money: A Study in the Social Psychology of Embez-
                  zlement*. Belmont, CA: Wadsworth.

Cressey, Donald R., and Charles A. Moore
    1983   "Managerial Values and Corporate Codes of Ethics." *Califor-
                  nia Management Review* 25:53–77.

Cupach, William, and Sandra Metts
    1986   "Accounts of Relational Dissolution: A Comparison of Mari-
                  tal and Non-marital Relationships." *Communication Mono-
                  graphs* 53:311–33.

Cyert, Richard M., and James G. March
    1963   *A Behavioral Theory of the Firm*. Englewood Cliffs, NJ:
                  Prentice-Hall.

Dalton, Melville
    1959   *Men Who Manage: Fusions of Feeling and Theory in Administra-
                  tion*. New York: Wiley.

    1964   "Preconceptions and Methods in *Men Who Manage*." Pp. 50–

95 in *Sociologists at Work,* edited by Phillip E. Hammond. New York: Basic Books.

Darwin, Charles
1898   *The Descent of Man.* New York: Appleton (originally published 1871).

Davis, Stanley M.
1974   "Two Models of Organization: Unity of Command versus Balance of Power." *Sloan Management Review* (Fall):29–40.

Davis, Stanley M., and Paul R. Lawrence
1977   *Matrix.* Reading, MA: Addison-Wesley.

Deal, Terrence E., and Allan A. Kennedy
1983   *Corporate Cultures: The Rites and Rituals of Corporate Life.* Reading, MA: Addison-Wesley.

Denich, Bette S.
1974   "Sex and Power in the Balkans." Pp. 243–63 in *Woman, Culture, and Society,* edited by Michelle Zimbalist Rosaldo and Louise Lamphere. Stanford, CA: Stanford University Press.

Denzin, Norman K.
1989   *Interpretive Interactionism.* Newbury Park, CA: Sage Publications.

1994   "The Art and Politics of Interpretation." Pp. 500–15 in *Handbook of Qualitative Research,* edited by Norman K. Denzin and Yvonna S. Lincoln. Newbury Park, CA: Sage Publications.

Denzin, Norman K., and Yvonna S. Lincoln (eds.)
1994   *Handbook of Qualitative Research.* Newbury Park, CA: Sage Publications.

Deutsch, Morton
1973   *The Resolution of Conflict.* New Haven, CT: Yale University Press.

DiMaggio, Paul J., and Walter W. Powell
1991   "Introduction." Pp. 1–38 in *The New Institutionalism in Organizational Analysis,* edited by Walter W. Powell and Paul J. DiMaggio. Chicago: University of Chicago Press.

Dobbin, Frank
1994   "Organizational Models of Culture: The Construction of Rational Organizing Principles." Pp. 117–41 in *Sociology of Culture: Emerging Theoretical Perspectives,* edited by Diana Crane. Oxford: Basil Blackwell.

Domhoff, William J.
1967   *Who Rules America?* Englewood Cliffs, NJ: Prentice-Hall.

1970   *The Higher Circles: The Governing Class in America.* New York: Random House.

Douglas, Jack D.
1976   *Investigative Social Research: Individual and Team Field Research.* Beverly Hills, CA: Sage Publications.

Drucker, Peter
 1954   *The Practice of Management.* New York: Harper and Row.
 1988   "The Coming of the New Organization." *Harvard Business Review* (January–February):45–53.

Duck, Steve
 1991   *Understanding Relationships.* New York: Guilford Press.

Durkheim, Emile
 1933   *The Division of Labor in Society.* New York: Free Press (originally published 1893).

Eccles, Robert G.
 1985   *The Transfer Pricing Problem: A Theory for Practice.* Lexington, MA: Lexington.

Eccles, Robert G., and Harrison C. White
 1984   "Firm and Market Interfaces of Profit Center Control." Working Paper, Harvard Business School.

Edgerton, Robert B.
 1977   *Alone Together: Social Order on an Urban Beach.* Berkeley: University of California Press.

Edwards, Richard C.
 1979   *Contested Terrain: The Transformation of the Workplace in the Twentieth Century.* New York: Basic Books.

Ellickson, Robert C.
 1991   *Order without Law: How Neighbors Settle Disputes.* Cambridge, MA: Harvard University Press.

Engel, David M.
 1984   "The Oven Bird's Song: Insiders, Outsiders, and Personal Injuries in an American Community." *Law and Society Review* 18:551–82.

Epstein, A. L.
 1967   "The Case Method in the Field of Law." Pp. 205–30 in *The Craft of Social Anthropology,* edited by A. L. Epstein. London: Tavistock.

Etzioni, Amitai
 1961   *A Comparative Analysis of Complex Organizations.* New York: Free Press.

Evan, William M. (ed.)
 1980   *The Sociology of Law: A Social-Structural Perspective.* New York: Free Press.

Evans-Pritchard, E. E.
 1940   *The Nuer: A Description of the Modes of Livelihood and Political Institutions of a Nilotic People.* New York: Oxford University Press.

Ewing, David W.
 1983   *Do It My Way or You're Fired: Employee Rights and the Changing*

Role of Management Prerogatives. New York: John Wiley and Sons.

Fausch, Richard
　1971　　　　"Teamwork through Conflict." *Business Week* (20 March): 44–50.

Feld, Scott L.
　1981　　　　"The Focused Organization of Social Ties." *American Journal of Sociology* 86:1015–35.

Felstiner, William L. F.
　1974　　　　"Influences of Social Organization on Dispute Processing." *Law and Society Review* 9: 63–94.

Ferguson, Katherine
　1984　　　　*The Feminist Case against Bureaucracy.* Philadelphia: Temple University Press.

Fierman, Jaclyn
　1990　　　　"Why Women Still Don't Hit the Top." *Fortune Magazine* (30 July): 40–62.

Fisher, Roger, and William Ury
　1981　　　　*Getting to Yes.* Boston: Houghton Mifflin.

Fiske, Susan T., and Shelley E. Taylor
　1991　　　　*Social Cognition.* New York: McGraw-Hill (first edition, 1984).

Fitzpatrick, Mary Ann
　1988　　　　*Between Husbands and Wives: Communication in Marriage.* Beverly Hills, CA: Sage Publications.

Fligstein, Neil
　1985　　　　"The Spread of the Multidivisional Form." *American Sociological Review* 50:377–91.

　1987　　　　"The Intraorganizational Power Struggle: Rise of Finance Personnel to Top Leadership in Large Corporations, 1919–1979." *American Sociological Review* 52:44–58.

　1990　　　　*The Transformation of Corporate Control.* Cambridge, MA: Harvard University Press.

Foster, S. L.
　1987　　　　"Issues in Behavioral Assessment of Parent-Adolescent Conflict." *Behavioral Assessment* 9:253–69.

Freeman, Linton C., A. Kimbal Romney, and S. C. Freeman
　1987　　　　"Cognitive Structure and Informant Accuracy." *American Anthropologist* 89:310–25.

Freidson, Eliot
　1970　　　　*Professional Dominance.* New York: Atherton.

　1973　　　　*The Professions and Their Prospects.* Beverly Hills, CA: Sage Publications.

Friedel, Morris F.
　1967　　　　"Organizations as Semilattices." *American Sociological Review* 32:46–54.

Frost, P., L. Moore, M. Louis, C. Lundborg, and J. Martin (eds.)
1991   *Reframing Organizational Culture.* Newbury Park, CA: Sage
            Publications.

Frost, Peter J.
1987   "Power, Politics, and Influence." Pp. 503–48 in *Handbook of
            Organizational Communication: An Interdisciplinary Perspective,*
            edited by Frederick J. Jablin, Linda L. Putnam, Karlene H.
            Roberts, and Lyman W. Porter. Newbury Park, CA: Sage
            Publications.

Fulmer, R. M.
1971   "Business Ethics: Present and Future." *Personnel Administra-
            tion* 34:46–52.

Furer-Haimendorff, Christoph von
1967   *Morals and Merits: A Study of Values and Social Controls in
            Southeast Asian Societies.* Chicago: University of Chicago
            Press.

Galanter, Marc
1983   "Reading the Landscapes of Disputes: What We Know and
            Don't Know (And Think We Know) about Our Allegedly
            Contentious and Litigious Society." *UCLA Law Review*
            31:4–71.

Garfinkel, Harold
1967   *Studies in Ethnomethodology.* Englewood Cliffs, NJ: Prentice-
            Hall.

Gayle, Barbara Mae
1991   "Sex Equity in Workplace Conflict Management." *Journal of
            Applied Communication Research* 19:152–69.

Geertz, Clifford
1973   *The Interpretation of Cultures.* New York: Basic Books.

1983   *Local Knowledge: Further Essays on Interpretive Anthropology.*
            New York: Basic Books.

1988   *Works and Lives: The Anthropologist as Author.* Stanford, CA:
            Stanford University Press.

Geneen, Harold (with Alvin Moscow)
1984   *Managing.* New York: Doubleday.

Giddens, Anthony
1979   *Central Problems in Social Theory: Action, Structure, and Contra-
            diction in Social Analysis.* Berkeley: University of California
            Press.

1984   *The Constitution of Society: Outline of a Theory of Structuration.*
            Berkeley: University of California Press.

Giles, Howard, and Nikolas Coupland
1991   *Language: Contexts and Consequences.* Pacific Grove, CA:
            Brooks/Cole Publishing.

Gilligan, Carol
1982   *In a Different Voice: Psychological Theory and Women's Develop-
            ment.* Cambridge, MA: Harvard University Press.

Gilligan, Carol, Janie Victoria Ward, and Jill McLean Taylor, with Betty Bar-
dige (eds.)
1988   *Mapping the Moral Domain.* Cambridge, MA: Harvard Uni-
            versity Press.

Gluckman, Max
1955a   *The Judicial Process among the Barotse of Northern Rhodesia.*
            Manchester: Manchester University Press.

1955b   *Custom and Conflict in Africa.* Glencoe, IL: Free Press.

1967   *Custom and Conflict in Africa.* New York: Barnes & Noble
            (originally published 1956).

1973   "Limitations of the Case-Method in the Study of Tribal Law."
            Law and Society Review 8:611–41.

Goffman, Erving
1952   "On Cooling the Mark Out: Some Aspects of Adaptation to
            Failure." *Psychiatry* 15:451–63.

1959   *The Presentation of Self in Everyday Life.* New York: Anchor
            Books.

1961   *Asylums: Essays on the Social Situation of Mental Patients and
            Other Inmates.* New York: Anchor Books.

1967   *Interaction Ritual.* Garden City, NY: Doubleday.

1974   *Frame Analysis.* Cambridge, MA: Harvard University Press.

1983   "The Interaction Order." *American Sociological Review* 48:1–17.

Goggin, William C.
1974   "How the Multidimensional Structure Works at Dow Corn-
            ing." *Harvard Business Review* (January–February):54–65.

Goldstein, S. G.
1985   "Organizational Dualism and Quality Circles." *Academy of
            Management Review* 10:504–17.

Goode, William J.
1960   "Norm Commitment and Conformity to Role-Status Obliga-
            tions." *American Journal of Sociology* 66: 246–58.

1978   *The Celebration of Heroes.* Berkeley: University of California
            Press.

Goodwin, Charles, and Alessandro Duranti
1992   "Rethinking Context: An Introduction." Pp. 1–43 in *Rethink-
            ing Context: Language as an Interactive Phenomenon,* edited by
            Alessandro Duranti and Charles Goodwin. Cambridge:
            Cambridge University Press.

Goodwin, Marjorie Harness
1993   "Tactical Uses of Stories: Participation Frameworks within

Boys' and Girls' Disputes." Pp. 110–42 in *Gender and Conversational Interaction*, edited by Deborah Tannen. New York: Oxford University Press.

Gouldner, Alvin W.
1954   *Patterns of Industrial Bureaucracy: A Case Study of Modern Factory Administration*. New York: Free Press.

Granovetter, Mark S.
1973   "The Strength of Weak Ties." *American Journal of Sociology* 78:1360–80.

1985   "Economic Action and Social Structure: The Problem of Embeddedness." *American Journal of Sociology* 91:481–510.

Greenberg, David F.
1983   "Donald Black's Sociology of Law: A Critique." *Law and Society Review* 17:337–68.

Greenhalgh, Leonard
1987   "Interpersonal Conflicts in Organizations." Pp. 229–71 in *International Review of Organizational Psychology*, edited by C. L. Cooper and I. T. Robertson. New York: John Wiley and Sons.

Greenhouse, Carol J.
1986   *Praying for Justice: Faith, Order, and Community in an American Town*. Ithaca, NY: Cornell University Press.

Griffiths, John
1984   "The Division of Labor in Social Control." Pp. 37–70 in *Toward a General Theory of Social Control*, vol. 1: *Fundamentals*, edited by Donald Black. Orlando, FL: Academic Press.

Grimshaw, Allen D. (ed.)
1990   *Conflict Talk: Sociolinguistic Investigations of Arguments in Conversations*. Cambridge: Cambridge University Press.

Gulick, Luther
1937   "Notes on the Theory of Organization." Pp. 7–21 in *Papers on the Science of Administration*, edited by Luther Gulick and L. F. Urick. New York: Columbia University Press.

Gulliver, P. H.
1979   *Disputes and Negotiations: A Cross-Cultural Perspective*. New York: Academic Press.

Haber, Samuel
1991   *The Quest for Authority and Honor in the American Professions 1750–1900*. Chicago: University of Chicago Press.

Hall, Jay
1969   *Conflict Management Survey*. Conroe, TX: Teleometrics.

Hambrick, Donald C. (ed.)
1988   *The Executive Effect: Concepts and Methods for Studying Top Managers*. Greenwich, CT: JAI Press.

Hannan, Michael T., and John Freeman
1989   *Organizational Ecology.* Cambridge, MA: Harvard University Press.

Hawes, Leonard C.
1974   "Social Collectivities as Communication." *Quarterly Journal of Speech* 60:497–502.

Hays, Sharon
1994   "Structure and Agency and the Sticky Problem of Culture." *Sociological Theory* 12:57–72.

Hearn, Jeff, D. L. Sheppard, P. Tancred-Sheppard, and G. Burrell (eds.)
1986   *The Sexuality of Organization.* Newbury Park, CA: Sage Publications.

Herbert, Christopher
1991   *Culture and Anomie: Ethnographic Imagination in the Nineteenth Century.* Chicago: University of Chicago Press.

Herrmann, John
1992   "Gossip in Science: A Study of Reputation and Social Control." Paper presented at the Annual Meeting of the American Sociological Association, Pittsburgh, Pennsylvania.

Hirsch, Paul M.
1986   "From Ambushes to Golden Parachutes: Corporate Takeovers as an Instance of Cultural Framing and Institutional Integration." *American Journal of Sociology* 91:800–37.

1987   *Pack Your Own Parachute: How to Survive Mergers, Takeovers, and Other Corporate Disasters.* Reading, MA: Addison-Wesley.

Hirsch, Paul M., and John A. Y. Andrews
1983   "Ambushes, Shootouts, and Knights of the Roundtable: The Language of Corporate Takeovers." Pp. 145–55 in *Organizational Symbolism,* edited by Louis R. Pondy, Peter J. Frost, Gareth Morgan, and Thomas C. Dandridge. Greenwich, CT: JAI Press.

Hirschman, Albert O.
1970   *Exit, Voice, and Loyalty: Responses to Declines in Firms, Organizations, and States.* Cambridge, MA: Harvard University Press.

Hobbes, Thomas
1962   *Leviathan: Or the Matter, Forme and Power of a Commonwealth, Ecclesiasticall and Civil.* New York: Collier Books (originally published 1651).

Hoebel, E. Adamson
1967   "Law-Ways of the Comanche Indians." Pp. 183–203 in *Law and Warfare: Studies in the Anthropology of Conflict,* edited by Paul Bohannan. Austin: University of Texas Press (originally published 1940).

Hoffman, Joan Eakin
1980   "Problems of Access in the Study of Social Elites and Boards of Directors." Pp. 45–56 in *Fieldwork Experience: Qualitative Approaches to Social Research,* edited by William B. Shaffir, Robert A. Stebbins, and Alan Turowetz. New York: St. Martin's Press.

Horwitz, Allan V.
1982   *The Social Control of Mental Illness.* New York: Academic Press.

1983   "Resistance to Innovation in the Sociology of Law: A Response to Greenberg." *Law and Society Review* 17:369–84.

1990   *The Logic of Social Control.* New York: Plenum Press.

Hymes, Dell
1974   *Foundations in Sociolinguistics: An Ethnographic Approach.* Philadelphia: University of Pennsylvania Press.

Iacocca, Lee (with William Novak)
1984   *Iacocca: An Autobiography.* New York: Bantam Books.

Ibarra, Hermina
1992   "Structural Alignments, Individual Strategies, and Managerial Action: Elements Toward a Network Theory of Getting Things Done." Pp. 165–88 in *Networks and Organizations: Structure, Form, and Action,* edited by Nitin Nohria and Robert G. Eccles. Boston: Harvard Business School Press.

Jackall, Robert
1988   *Moral Mazes: The World of Corporate Managers.* New York: Oxford University Press.

Janis, Irving L.
1989   *Crucial Decisions: Leadership in Policymaking and Crisis Management.* New York: Free Press.

Jankowski, Martin Sanchez
1991   *Islands in the Street: Gangs in American Urban Society.* Berkeley, CA: University of California Press.

Janowitz, Morris
1975   "Sociological Theory and Social Control." *American Journal of Sociology* 81:82–108.

1960   *The Professional Soldier.* New York: Free Press.

Jennings, Eugene Emerson
1962   *The Executive: Autocrat, Bureaucrat, Democrat.* New York: Harper and Row.

Johnson, Allen W., and Timothy Earle
1987   *The Evolution of Human Societies: From Foraging Group to Agrarian State.* Stanford, CA: Stanford University Press.

Jones, Robert E., and Bonita H. Melcher
1982   "Personality and the Preference for Modes of Conflict Resolution." *Human Relations* 35:649–58.

Jones, Schuyler
    1974   *Men of Influence in Nuristam: A Study of Social Control and Dispute Settlement in the Waigal Valley, Afghanistan.* New York: Seminar Press.

Kahn, Robert L., and Elise Boulding
    1964   *Power and Conflict in Organizations.* New York: Free Press.

Kanter, Rosabeth Moss
    1977   *Men and Women of the Corporation.* New York: Basic Books.

    1983   *The Change Masters: Innovation for Productivity in the American Corporation.* New York: Simon and Schuster.

Kanter, Rosabeth Moss, and Barry Stein
    1980   "Life at the Top: The Struggle for Power." Pp. 3–20 in *Life in Organizations: Workplaces as People Experience Them,* edited by Rosabeth Moss Kanter and Barry A. Stein. New York: Basic Books.

Karikas, Angela
    1980   "Solving Problems in Philadelphia: An Ethnography of a Congressional District Office." Pp. 345–77 in *No Access to Law: Alternatives to the American Judicial System,* edited by Laura Nader. New York: Academic Press.

Katz, Jack
    1977   "Cover-Up and Collective Identity: On the Natural Antagonisms of Authority Internal and External to Organizations." *Social Problems* 25:3–17.

Kaufer, David S., and Kathleen M. Carley
    1993   *Communication at a Distance: The Influence of Print on Sociocultural Organization and Change.* Hillsdale, NJ: Earlbaum.

Kellerman, Kathy
    1992   "The Conversational MOP II. Progression Through Scenes in Discourse." *Human Communication Research* 17:385–414.

Kelman, Herbert C., and V. Lee Hamilton
    1989   *Crimes of Obedience.* New Haven, CT: Yale University Press.

Killworth, Peter D., and H. Russell Bernard
    1976   "Informant Accuracy in Social Network Data." *Human Organization* 3:269–86.

Kipnis, David, Stuart M. Schmidt, and Ian Wilkinson
    1980   "Intraorganizational Influence Tactics: Explorations in Getting One's Way." *Journal of Applied Psychology* 65:440–52.

Kitson, Gay C. (with William M. Holmes)
    1992   *Portrait of Divorce: Adjustment to Marital Breakdown.* New York: Guilford Press.

Klar, Y., Daniel Bar-Tal, and Arie W. Kruglanski
    1987   "On the Epistemology of Conflicts: Toward a Social Cognitive Analysis of Conflict Resolution." Pp. 112–37 in *Social Psychology and Intergroup and International Conflict,* edited by

W. Stroebe, Arie W. Kruglanski, Daniel Bar-Tal, and Michael Hewstone. New York: Springer-Verlag.

Knapp, Mark L., Linda L. Putnam, and Laura J. Davis
1988   "Measuring Interpersonal Conflict in Organizations: Where Do We Go from Here?" *Management Communication Quarterly* 1:414–29.

Knorr-Cetina, Karin D.
1981   "Introduction: The Micro-Sociological Challenge to Macro-Sociology: Towards a Reconstruction of Social Theory and Methodology." Pp. 1–47 in *Advances in Social Theory and Methodologies: Toward an Integration of Micro- and Macro-Sociologies,* edited by Karin D. Knorr-Cetina and Aaron V. Cicourel. Boston: Routledge and Kegan Paul.

Koch, Klaus-Friedrich
1974   *War and Peace in Jalemo: The Management of Conflict in Highland New Guinea.* Cambridge, MA: Harvard University Press.

1984   "Liability and Social Structure." Pp. 95–129 in *Toward a General Theory of Social Control,* vol. 1: *Fundamentals,* edited by Donald Black. Orlando, FL: Academic Press.

Koch, Klaus-Friedrich, Soraya Altorki, Andrew Arno, and Letita Hickson
1977   "Ritual Reconciliation and the Obviation of Grievances: A Comparative Study in the Ethnology of Law." *Ethnology* 16:269–84.

Kochan, Thomas A., and Anil Verma
1983   "Negotiations in Organizations: Blending Industrial Relations and Organizational Behavior Approaches." Pp. 13–32 in *Negotiating in Organizations,* edited by Max H. Bazerman and Roy J. Lewicki. Beverly Hills, CA: Sage Publications.

Kolb, Deborah M.
1992   "Women's Work: Peacemaking in Organizations." Pp. 63–91 in *Hidden Conflict in Organizations: Uncovering Behind-the-Scenes Disputes,* edited by Deborah M. Kolb and Jean M. Bartunek. Newbury Park: Sage Publications.

Kolb, Deborah M., and Jean M. Bartunek (eds.)
1992   *Hidden Conflict in Negotiations: Uncovering Behind-the-Scenes Disputes.* Newbury Park, CA: Sage Publications.

Kolb, Deborah M., and Linda L. Putnam
1992   "Introduction: The Dialectics of Disputing." Pp. 1–31 in *Hidden Conflict in Organizations: Uncovering Behind-the-Scenes Disputes,* edited by Deborah M. Kolb and Jean M. Bartunek. Newbury Park, CA: Sage Publications.

Kolb, Deborah M., and Blair H. Sheppard
1985   "Do Managers Mediate, or Even Arbitrate?" *Negotiation Journal* (October):379–88.

Kotter, John
1983   *The General Managers.* New York: Free Press.

Krieger, Susan
   1991   *Social Science and the Self: Personal Essays on an Art Form.* New
                 Brunswick, NJ: Rutgers University Press.

Kruglanski, Arie W., Daniel Bar-Tal, and Yechiel Klar
   1993   "A Social Cognitive Theory of Conflict." Pp. 45–56 in *Conflict
                 and Social Psychology,* edited by Knud S. Larsen. Oslo: Inter-
                 national Peace Research Institute; London: Sage Publica-
                 tions.

Kruttschnitt, Candace
   1982   "Women, Crime, and Dependency: An Application of the
                 Theory of Law." *Criminology* 19:495–513.

Kuklick, Henrika
   1991   *The Savage Within: The Social History of British Anthropology,
                 1885–1945.* Cambridge, England: Cambridge University
                 Press.

Kunda, Gideon
   1991   *Engineering Culture: Control and Commitment in a High-Tech
                 Corporation.* Philadelphia: Temple University Press.

Lakoff, Robin
   1978   *Language and a Woman's Place.* New York: Harper and Row.

Lamont, Michele
   1992   *Money, Morals, and Manners: The Culture of the French and the*
                 American Upper-Middle Class. Chicago: University of Chi-
                 cago Press.

Larson, Erik W., and David H. Gobeli
   1987   "Matrix Management: Contradictions and Insights." *Califor-
                 nia Management Review* 29:126–38.

Latour, Bruno, and Steve Woolgar
   1979   *Laboratory Life.* Beverly Hills, CA: Sage Publications.

Lawrence, Jay W., and Paul R. Lorsch
   1967a   *Organization and Environment.* Boston: Harvard Business
                 School Press.

   1967b   "Differentiation and Integration in Complex Organizations."
                 Administrative Science Quarterly 12:1–47.

Lempert, Richard, and Joseph Sanders
   1986   *An Invitation to Law and Social Science.* Philadelphia: Univer-
                 sity of Pennsylvania Press.

Levinson, Harry (with the assistance of Cynthia Lang)
   1981   *Executive.* Cambridge, MA: Harvard University Press.

Levitt, Barbara, and James March
   1988   "Organizational Learning." *Annual Review of Sociology*
                 14:319–40.

Lewicki, Roy J., and Blair H. Sheppard
   1985   "Choosing How to Intervene: Factors Affecting the Use of

Process and Outcome Control in Third-Party Dispute Resolution." *Journal of Occupational Behaviour* 6:49–64.

Lieberman, Jethro K.
1983   *The Litigious Society.* New York: Basic Books.

Lincoln, James R.
1982   "Intra- (and Inter-) Organizational Networks. *Research in the Sociology of Organizations* 1:1–38.

Lincoln, Yvonna S., and Egon G. Guba
1985   *Naturalistic Inquiry.* Beverly Hills: Sage Publications.

Llewellyn, Karl, and E. Adamson Hoebel
1983   *The Cheyenne Way: Conflict and Case Law in Primitive Jurisprudence.* Norman: Oklahoma University Press (originally published 1941).

Locke, John
1952   *The Second Treatise of Government.* New York: Bobbs-Merrill (originally published 1690).

Lofland, John
1994   "Analytic Ethnography: Features, Failings, Futures." *Journal of Contemporary Ethnography:* (forthcoming).

Lofland, John, and Lynn Lofland
1984   *Analyzing Social Settings: A Guide to Qualitative Observation and Analysis:MDIÑ* Belmont, CA: Wadsworth Publishing Company.

Lorenz, Konrad
1963   *On Aggression.* New York: Harcourt, Brace, and World.

Lundsborg, Louis B.
1981   *The Art of Being an Executive.* New York: Free Press.

Lundsgaarde, Henry P.
1977   *Murder in Space City: A Cultural Analysis of Houston Homicide Patterns.* New York: Oxford University Press.

Luthans, Fred, and Janet Larsen
1986   "How Managers Really Communicate." *Human Relations* 39:161–78.

Macaulay, Stewart
1963   "Non-contractual Relations in Business: A Preliminary Study." *American Sociological Review* 28:55–67.

Macy, Michael W.
1991   "Chains of Cooperation: Threshold Effects in Collective Action." *American Sociological Review* 56:730–47.

1993   "Social Learning and the Structure of Collective Action." Pp. 1–35 in *Advances in Group Processes,* vol. 10, edited by Edward J. Lawler, Barry Markovsky, Karen Heimer, and Jodi Obrien. Greenwich, CT: JAI Press.

Malinowksi, Bronislaw
   1926   *Crime and Custom in Savage Society.* London: Kegan Paul,
                 Trench, Truber.

March, James G.
   1988   "Introduction: A Chronicle of Speculations About Organiza-
                 tional Decision-Making." Pp. 1–21 in *Decisions and Organiza-
                 tions,* edited by James G. March. Oxford: Basil Blackwell.

March, James G., and Herbert A. Simon
   1958   *Organizations.* New York: John Wiley and Sons.

Marcus, George E. (ed.)
   1983   *Elites: Ethnographic Issues.* Albuquerque: University of New
                 Mexico Press.

Marcus, George E., and Michael M. J. Fisher
   1986   *Anthropology as Cultural Critique: An Experimental Moment in
                 the Human Sciences.* Chicago: University of Chicago Press.

Marquis, Donald G.
   1969   "A Project Team + PERT = Success. Or Does It?" *Innova-
                 tion* 5:26–33.

Martin, Joanne
   1992a   "The Suppression of Gender Conflict in Organizations." Pp.
                 165–86 in *Hidden Conflict in Organizations: Uncovering Behind-
                 the-Scenes Disputes,* edited by Deborah M. Kolb and Jean M.
                 Bartunek. Newbury Park, CA: Sage Publications.

   1992b   *Cultures in Organizations: Three Perspectives.* Oxford: Oxford
                 University Press.

Martynko, Mark J., and William L. Gardner
   1985   "Beyond Structured Observation: Methodological Issues
                 and New Directions." *Academy of Management Review*
                 10:676–95.

Mayhew, Bruce H.
   1980   "Structuralism Versus Individualism: Part 1, Shadowboxing
                 in the Dark." *Social Forces* 59:335–75.

McDonald, Alonzo
   1985   "Conflict at the Summit: A Deadly Game." Pp. 15–29 in *The
                 Executive Dilemma: Handling People Problems at Work,* edited
                 by Eliza G. C. Collins. New York: John Wiley and Sons (origi-
                 nally published 1980).

Mead, George Herbert
   1934   *Mind, Self, and Society,* vol. 1. Chicago: University of Chi-
                 cago Press.

Mee, John
   1964   "Ideational Items." *Business Horizons* (summer):70–72.

Mentschikoff, Soia
   1961   "Commercial Arbitration." *Columbia Law Review* 61:846–69.

Merry, Sally Engle
1979   "Going to Court: Strategies of Dispute Management in an
            Urban Neighborhood." *Law and Society Review* 13:891–926.

1984   "Rethinking Gossip and Scandal." Pp. 271–302 in *Toward a
            General Theory of Social Control*, vol. 1: *Fundamentals*, edited
            by Donald Black. Orlando, FL: Academic Press.

Merry, Sally Engle, and Susan Silbey
1984   "What Do Plaintiffs Want? Reexamining the Concept of Dis-
            pute." *Justice System Journal* 9:151–78.

Meyer, John W., and Brian Rowan
1977   "Institutionalized Organizations: Formal Structure as Myth
            and Ceremony." *American Journal of Sociology* 83:340–63.

Miles, Matthew B., and A. Michael Huberman
1984   *Qualitative Data Analysis: A Sourcebook of New Methods*. Bev-
            erly Hills, CA: Sage Publications.

Miller, Delbert C., and William H. Form
1980   *Industrial Sociology: Work in Organizational Life*. New York:
            Harper and Row (third edition; first edition, 1951).

Mills, C. Wright
1940   "Situated Actions and Vocabularies of Motive." *American So-
            ciological Review* 34:904–13.

1956   *White Collar: The American Middle Classes*. New York: Oxford
            University Press (originally published 1951).

Mills, Peter K., James L. Hall, Joel Leidecker, and Newton Margulies
1983   "Flexiform: A Model for Professional Service Organiza-
            tions." *Academy of Management Review* 8:118–31.

Mintzberg, Henry
1973   *The Nature of Managerial Work*. New York: Harper and Row.

1979   *The Structuring of Organizations*. Englewood Cliffs, NJ:
            Prentice-Hall.

Mnoonkin, Robert H., and Lewis Kornhauser
1979   "Bargaining in the Shadow of the Law: The Case of Divorce."
            Yale Law Journal 88:950–97.

Monge, Peter R., and Eric M. Eisenberg
1987   "Emergent Communication Networks." Pp. 304–42 in *Hand-
            book of Organizational Communication: An Interdisciplinary Per-
            spective*, edited by Fredrick M. Jablin, Linda L. Putnam, Kar-
            lene H. Roberts, and Lyman W. Porter. Newbury Park, CA:
            Sage Publications.

Moore, Sally Falk
1978   *Law as Process: An Anthropological Approach*. London:
            Routledge and Kegan Paul.

1986   *Social Facts and Fabrications: Customary Law on Kilimanjaro,
            1880–1980*. New York: Columbia University Press.

Moore, Wilbert
    1962   *The Conduct of the Corporation*. New York: Random House.

Morgan, Gareth
    1986   *Images of Organization*. Newbury Park, CA: Sage Publications.

Morrill, Calvin
    1986   "Conflict Management Among Corporate Executives: A Comparative Study." Ph.D. diss., Department of Sociology, Harvard University.

    1989   "The Management of Managers: Disputing in an Executive Hierarchy." *Sociological Forum* 4:387–407.

    1991a   "Conflict Management, Honor, and Organizational Change." *American Journal of Sociology* 97:585–621.

    1991b   "The Customs of Conflict Management among Corporate Executives." *American Anthropologist* 93:871–93.

    1992a   "The Private Ordering of Professional Relations." Pp. 93–116 in *Hidden Conflict in Organizations: Uncovering Behind-the-Scenes Disputes*, edited by Deborah M. Kolb and Jean M. Bartunek. Newbury Park, CA: Sage Publications.

    1992b   "Vengeance among Executives." Pp. 51–72 in *Virginia Review of Sociology*, vol. 1: *Law and Conflict Management*, edited by James Tucker. Greenwich, CT: JAI Press.

Morrill, Calvin, Michelle Johnson, and Tyler Harrison
    1994   "In a Different Voice or in a Different Context? Gender, Social Ties, and Legal Discourse in Small Claims Disputes." Paper presented at the Law and Society Meetings, Phoenix, Arizona.

Morrill, Calvin, and Cheryl King Thomas
    1992   "Organizational Conflict Management as Disputing Process: The Problem of Social Escalation." *Human Communication Research* 18:400–28.

Morrill, Calvin, Ellen Snyderman, and Edwin J. Dawson
    1994   "Social Context and the Labelling of Unethical Acts in Organizational Life: A Test of Black's Theory of Social Control." Paper presented at the annual meetings of the American Sociological Association, Los Angeles.

Nadel, S. F.
    1951   *The Foundations of Social Anthropology*. New York: Free Press.

Nader, Laura
    1964   "An Analysis of Zapotec Law Cases." *Ethnology* 3:404–19.

    1965a   "Choices in Legal Procedure: Shia Moslem and Mexican Zapotec." *American Anthropologist* 67:394–99.

    1965b   "The Anthropology of Law." *American Anthropologist* (special issue: *The Ethnology of Law*, edited by Laura Nader) 67:3–32.

1969   "Up the Anthropologist: Perspectives Gained from Studying
            Up." Pp. 284–311 in *Reinventing Anthropology,* edited by Del-
            bert Hymes. New York: Random House.

1990   *Harmony Ideology: Justice and Control in a Zapotec Mountain
            Village.* Stanford, CA: Stanford University Press.

Nader, Laura, and Harry F. Todd
1978   *The Disputing Process—Law in Ten Societies.* New York: Co-
            lumbia University Press.

Neale, Margaret A., and Max H. Bazerman
1991   *Cognition and Rationality in Negotiation.* New York: Free Press.

Netting, Robert M.
1986   *Cultural Ecology.* Prospect Heights, IL: Waveland Press (first
            edition, 1977).

Norton, A. J., and J. E. Moorman
1987   "Current Trends in Marriage and Divorce among American
            Women." *Journal of Marriage and the Family* 45:3–14.

O'Barr, William M., and John M. Conley
1992   *Fortune and Folly: The Wealth and Power of Institutional In-
            vesting.* Homewood, IL: Business One Irwin.

Patton, Michael Quinn
1980   *Qualitative Evaluation Methods.* Beverly Hills: Sage Publica-
            tions.

Perham, John
1970   "Matrix Management: A Tough Game to Play." *Dun's*
            (August):31–34.

Peristiany, J. G.
1965   "Introduction." Pp. 9–18 in *Honour and Shame: The Values of
            Mediterranean Society,* edited by J. G. Peristiany. Chicago:
            University of Chicago Press.

Perrow, Charles R.
1967   "A Framework for Comparative Organizational Analysis."
            American Sociological Review 32:194–208.

1986   *Complex Organizations: A Critical Essay.* New York: Random
            House (third edition; first edition, 1972).

Peters, Thomas J., and Robert H. Waterman, Jr.
1982   *In Search of Excellence: Lessons from America's Best-Run Compa-
            nies.* New York: Warner.

Peterson, Donald R.
1983   "Conflict." Pp. 360–96 in *Close Relationships,* edited by Har-
            old H. Kelley, Ellen Berscheid, Andrew Christensen, John H.
            Harvey, Ted L. Huston, George Levinger, Evie McClintock,
            Letitia Anne Peplau, and Donald R. Peterson. New York:
            W. H. Freeman.

Pettigrew, Andrew
 1973   *The Politics of Organizational Decision-Making.* London: Tavistock.

Pfeffer, Jeffrey, and Gerald R. Salancik
 1978   *The External Control of Organizations: A Resource Dependence Perspective.* New York: Harper and Row.

Pinkley, Robin L.
 1990   "Dimensions of Conflict Frame: Disputant Interpretations of Conflict." *Journal of Applied Psychology* 75:117–26.

Pitt-Rivers, Julian
 1965   "Honour and Social Status." Pp. 19–77 in *Honour and Shame: The Values of Mediterranean Society,* edited by J. G. Peristiany. Chicago: University of Chicago Press.

Pondy, Louis R.
 1967   "Organizational Conflict: Concepts and Models." *Administrative Science Quarterly* 17:296–320.

Posner, Barry Z., and Warren H. Schmidt
 1987   "Ethics in American Companies: A Managerial Perspective." *Journal of Business Ethics* 6:23–36.

Powell, Walter W.
 1985   *Getting into Print.* Chicago: University of Chicago Press.
 1990   Neither Market nor Hierarchy: Network Forms of Organization." Pp. 295–336 in *Research in Organizational Behavior,* vol. 12, edited by Barry M. Staw and L. L. Cummings. Greenwich, CT: JAI Press.
 1991   "Expanding the Scope of Institutional Analysis." Pp. 183–203 in *The New Institutionalism in Organizational Analysis,* edited by Walter W. Powell and Paul J. DiMaggio. Chicago: University of Chicago Press.

Powell, Walter W., and Paul J. DiMaggio (eds.)
 1991   *The New Institutionalism in Organizational Analysis.* Chicago: University of Chicago Press.

Pruitt, Dean G., and Jeffrey Z. Rubin
 1986   *Social Conflict: Escalation, Stalemate, and Settlement.* New York: Random House.

Putnam, Linda L.
 1983   "The Interpretive Paradigm: An Alternative to Functionalism." Pp. 31–54 in *Communication and Organizations: An Interpretive Approach,* edited by Linda L. Putnam and Michael E. Packanowsky. Newbury Park, CA: Sage Publications.
 1988   "Communication and Interpersonal Conflict in Organizations." *Management Communication Quarterly* 1:293–301.

Putnam, Linda L., and M. Scott Poole
 1987   "Conflict and Negotiation." Pp. 549–99 in *Handbook of Organizational Communication: An Interdisciplinary Perspective,* ed-

ited by Frederick J. Jablin, Linda L. Putnam, Karlene H. Roberts, and Lyman W. Porter. Newbury Park, CA: Sage Publications.

Putnam, Linda L., and Charmain E. Wilson
1982   "Communicative Strategies in Organizational Conflicts: Reliability and Validity of a Measurement Scale." Pp. 629–52 in *Communication Yearbook* 6, edited by Michael Burgoon. Beverly Hills, CA: Sage Publications.

Rahim, M. Afalzur
1983   "A Measure of Styles of Handling Interpersonal Conflict." *Academy of Management Journal* 26:368–76.

Raiffa, Howard
1982   *The Art and Science of Negotiation.* Cambridge, MA: Harvard University Press.

Reich, Robert
1985   "The Executive's New Clothes." *New Republic* (13 May): 23–28.

Rieder, Jonathan
1984   "The Social Organization of Vengeance." Pp. 131–62 in *Toward a General Theory of Social Control*, vol. 1: *Fundamentals*, edited by Donald Black. Orlando, FL: Academic Press.

Rieff, Philip
1959   *Freud: The Mind of the Moralist.* Chicago: University of Chicago Press.

Roberts, Simon
1979   *Order and Dispute.* London: Penguin Books.

Rogers, Everett M.
1983   *Diffusion of Innovations.* New York: Free Press.

Rohlen, Thomas P.
1974   *For Harmony and Strength: Japanese White-Collar Organization in Anthropological Perspective.* Berkeley: University of California Press.

Roloff, Michael E., and Denise H. Cloven
1990   "The Chilling Effect in Interpersonal Relationships: The Reluctance to Speak One's Mind." Pp. 49–76 in *Intimates in Conflict: A Communication Perspective*, edited by Dudley D. Cahn. Hillsdale, NJ: Erlbaum.

Rosaldo, Renato
1989   *Culture and Truth: The Remaking of Social Analysis.* Boston: Beacon Press.

Rosenberg, Morris
1992   "The Self-Concept: Social Product and Social Force" Pp. 593–624 in *Social Psychology: Sociological Perspectives*, edited by Morris Rosenberg and Ralph H. Turner. New Brunswick, NJ: Transaction Publishers.

Ross, Edward A.
1901   *Social Control: A Survey of the Foundations of Order.* New
            York: Macmillan.

Ross, Mark Howard
1993   *The Culture of Conflict: Interpretations and Interests in Compara-*
            tive Perspective. New Haven: Yale University Press.

Rothenberger, John E.
1978   "The Social Dynamics of Dispute Settlement in a Sunni Mus-
            lim Village in Lebanon. Pp. 152–180 in *The Disputing Pro-*
            cess—Law in Ten Societies, edited by Laura Nader and Harry
            F. Todd. New York: Columbia University Press.

Rousseau, Jean-Jacques
1968   *The Social Contract.* New York: Penguin Books. (originally
            published 1762)

Sabel, Charles F.
1982   *Work and Politics: The Division of Labor in Industry.* Cambridge:
            Cambridge University Press.

Sackmann, Sonja A.
1991   *Cultural Knowledge in Organizations: Exploring the Collective*
            Mind. Newbury Park, CA: Sage Publications.

Sahlins, Marshall D.
1961   "The Segmentary Lineage: An Organization of Predatory
            Expansion." *American Anthropologist* 63:322–45.

1974   *Stone Age Economics.* London: Tavistock.

Schank, Roger C., and Robert C. Abelson
1977   *Scripts, Plans, Goals, and Understanding: An Inquiry into Hu-*
            man Knowledge. Hillsdale, NJ: Earlbaum.

Scheff, Thomas J.
1990   *Microsociology: Discourse, Emotion, and Social Structure.* Chi-
            cago: University of Chicago Press.

Schein, Edgar H.
1984   "Coming to a New Awareness of Organizational Culture."
            Sloan Management Review, 25:3–16.

Schutz, Alfred
1962   *Collected Papers,* vol. 1, *The Problem of Social Reality.* The
            Hague: Martinus Nijhoff.

Scott, W. Richard
1965   "Field Methods in the Study of Organizations." Pp. 261–304
            in *The Handbook of Organizations,* edited by James G. March.
            New York: Random House.

1991   "Unpacking Institutional Arguments." Pp. 164–82 in *The*
            New Institutionalism in Organizational Analysis, edited by
            Walter W. Powell and Paul J. Dimaggio. Chicago: University
            of Chicago Press.

Scott, William G.
1965   *The Management of Conflict: Appeal Systems in Organizations.* Homewood, IL: Irwin-Dorsey.

Segal, Amanda Troy, and Wendy Zellner
1992   "Corporate Women." *Business Week* (8 June): 74–76.

Selznick, Philip
1947   *Leadership in Administration.* New York: Harper and Row.
1949   *TVA and the Grass Roots.* Berkeley: University of California Press.
1969   *Law, Society, and Industrial Justice.* New York: Russell Sage Foundation.

Senechal, Roberta
1992   "Collective Violence as Social Control." Paper presented at the annual meetings of the American Sociological Association, Pittsburgh.

Sewell, William H., Jr.
1992   "A Theory of Structure: Duality, Agency, and Transformation." *American Journal of Sociology* 98:1–29.

Siegel, Sidney, and N. John Castellan, Jr.
1988   *Nonparametric Statistics for the Social Sciences.* New York: McGraw-Hill (second edition; first edition, 1956).

Siegel, Sidney, and Louis Fouraker
1960   *Bargaining and Group Decision Making: Experiments in Bilateral Monopoly.* New York: McGraw-Hill.

Simon, Herbert A.
1976   *Administrative Behavior: A Study of Decision-Making Processes in Administrative Organization.* New York: Free Press (third edition; first edition, 1945).

Sloan, Alfred P. (edited by John McDonald with Catharine Stevens)
1963   *My Years with General Motors.* New York: Doubleday.

Smoke, Richard
1977   *War: Controlling Escalation.* Cambridge, MA: Harvard University Press.

Snow, David A., and Leon Anderson
1987   "Identity Work among the Homeless: The Verbal Construction and Avowal of Personal Identities." *American Journal of Sociology* 92:1336–1371.
1992   *Down on Their Luck: A Study of Homeless Street People.* Berkeley: University of California Press.

Snow, David A., Robert Benford, and Leon Anderson
1986   "Fieldwork Roles and Informational Yield: A Comparison of Alternative Settings and Roles." *Urban Life* 15:377–408.

Snow, David A., and Calvin Morrill
1993   "Reflections on Anthropology's Crisis of Faith." *Contemporary Sociology* 22:8–11.

forthcoming   "Linking Ethnography and Theoretical Development: Sys-
               tematizing the Analytic Process." *Sociological Quarterly*.

Snow, David A., E. Burke Rochford, Jr., Steven K. Worden, and Robert Benford
    1986   "Frame Alignment Processes, Microbilization, and Move-
               ment Participation." *American Sociological Review* 51:464–81.

Snow, David A., Louis Zurcher, and Gideon Sjoberg
    1982   "Interviewing by Comment: An Adjunct to the Direct Ques-
               tion." *Qualitative Sociology* 5:285–311.

Spradley, James
    1970   *You Owe Yourself a Drunk: An Ethnography of Urban Nomads.*
               Boston: Little Brown.

    1979   *The Ethnographic Interview.* New York: Holt, Rinehart and
               Winston.

Sproull, Lee, and Sara Kiesler
    1992   *Connections: New Ways of Working in the Networked Organiza-
               tion.* Cambridge, MA: MIT Press.

Srivastva, Suresh (ed.)
    1983   *The Executive Mind.* San Francisco: Jossey-Bass Publishers.

Starbuck, William H., and Frames J. Milliken
    1988   "Executives' Perceptual Filters: What They Notice and How
               They Make Sense." Pages 35–65 in *The Executive Effect: Con-
               cepts and Methods for Studying Top Managers,* edited by Don-
               ald C. Hambrick. Greenwich, CT: JAI Press.

Starr, June, and Jane F. Collier (eds.)
    1989   *History and Power in the Study of Law: New Directions in Legal
               Anthropology.* Ithaca, NY: Cornell University Press.

Stephenson, Karen
    1990   "The Emergence of Virtual Groups." *Ethnology* 29:279–97.

Stern, Paul G.
    1990   *Straight to the Top: Beyond Loyalty, Gamesmanship, Mentors, and
               Other Corporate Myths.* New York: Warner Books.

Sternberg, Robert J., and Diane M. Dobson
    1987   "Resolving Interpersonal Conflicts: An Analysis of Stylistic
               Consistency." *Journal of Personality and Social Psychology*
               52:794–812.

Sternberg, Robert J., and L. J. Soriano
    1984   "Styles of Conflict Resolution." *Journal of Personality and Con-
               flict Resolution* 47:115–26.

Stevens, Mark
    1991   *The Big Six: The Selling Out of America's Top Accounting Firms.*
               New York: Touchstone Books.

Stinchcombe, Arthur L.
    1959   "Bureaucratic and Craft Administration of Production." *Ad-
               ministrative Science Quarterly* 4:168–87.

1985   "Authority and the Management of Engineering on Large Projects." Pp. 225–56 in *Organizational Theory and Project Management: Administering Uncertainty in Norwegian Offshore Oil*, edited by Arthur L. Stinchcombe and Carol A. Heimer. Bergen: Norwegian University Press.

Stocking, George W.
1989   *Romantic Motives: Essays on Anthropological Sensibilities.* Madison: University of Wisconsin Press.

1991   *Colonial Situations: Essays on the Contextualization of Ethnographic Knowledge.* Madison: University of Wisconsin Press.

1992   *The Ethnographer's Magic and Other Essays in the History of Anthropology.* Madison: University of Wisconsin Press.

Stone, Christopher
1975   *Where the Law Ends: The Social Control of Corporate Behavior.* New York: Harper and Row.

Straus, Murray A.
1978   "Wife Beating. How Common and Why?" *Victimology* 23:443–58.

Strauss, Anselm
1978   *Negotiations: Varieties, Contexts, Processes, and Social Order.* San Francisco: Jossey-Bass Publishers.

Suchman, Lucy A.
1987   *Plans and Situated Actions: The Problem of Human-Machine Communication.* Cambridge: Cambridge University Press.

Swanson, Guy
1971   "An Organizational Analysis of Collectivities." *American Sociological Review* 36:607–24.

Swidler, Ann
1986   "Culture in Action: Symbols and Strategies." *American Sociological Review* 51:273–86.

Tannen, Deborah
1979   "What's a Frame? Surface Understanding for Underlying Expectations." Pp. 137–81 in *New Directions in Discourse Processing*, edited by R. Freedle. Norwood, NJ: Ablex.

1990   *You Just Don't Understand: Women and Men in Conversation.* New York: Ballantine Books.

1993a   "Editor's Introduction." Pp. 3–13 in *Gender and Conversational Interaction*, edited by Deborah Tannen. New York: Oxford University Press.

Tannen, Deborah (ed.)
1993b   *Gender and Conversational Interaction.* New York: Oxford University Press.

Tannen, Deborah, and Cynthia Wallat
1987   "Interactive Frames and Knowledge Schemas in Interaction:

Examples from a Medical Examination/Interview." *Social Psychology Quarterly* 50:205–16.

Tannenbaum, Arnold S.
1968   *Control in Organizations.* New York: McGraw-Hill.

Taylor, Michael
1982   *Community, Anarchy, and Liberty.* Cambridge: Cambridge University Press.

Thibault, John W., and Harold H. Kelley
1959   *The Social Psychology of Groups.* New York: John Wiley and Sons.

Thoden van Velzen, H. U. E., and W. van Wetering
1960   "Residence, Power Groups and Intra-societal Aggression: An Enquiry into the Conditions Leading to Peacefulness within Non-stratified Societies." *International Archives of Ethnography* 49:169–200.

Thomas, Kenneth W., and Ralph H. Kilmann
1978   "A Comparison of Four Instruments Measuring Conflict Behavior." *Psychological Reports* 42:1139–45.

Thomas, W. I., and F. Znaniecki
1927   *The Polish Peasant in Europe and America.* Chicago: University of Chicago Press.

Thompson, James D.
1967   *Organizations in Action: Social Science Bases of Administrative Theory.* New York: McGraw-Hill.

Thompson, Victor
1976   "Dramaturgy." Pp. 329–37 in *Drama in Life: The Uses of Communication in Society,* edited by James E. Combs and Michael W. Mansfield. New York: Hastings House Publishers (originally published 1963).

Thorne, Barrie, and Nancy Henley (eds.)
1975   *Language and Sex: Difference and Dominance.* Rowley, MA: Newbury House.

Thorne, Barrie, Cheris Kramarae, and Nancy Henley (eds.)
1983   *Language, Gender, and Society.* Rowley, MA: Newbury House.

Tomasic, Roman, and Malcolm L. Feeley (eds.)
1982   *Neighborhood Justice: Assessment of an Emerging Idea.* New York: Longman.

Trice, Harrison M.
1985   "Rites and Ceremonials in Organizational Cultures." Pp. 221–70 in *Research in the Sociology of Organizations,* vol. 4. Greenwich, CT: JAI Press.

Trice, Harrison M., James Belasco, and Joseph A. Alutto
1969   "The Role of Ceremonials in Organizational Behavior." *Industrial and Labor Relations Review* 23:40–51.

Tucker, James C.
  1989   "Employee Theft as Social Control." *Deviant Behavior* 10:319–34.
  1993   "Everyday Forms of Employee Resistance: How Temporary Workers Handle Conflict with Their Employers." *Sociological Forum* 8:25–45.

Tucker, Robert C.
  1978   *The Marx-Engels Reader.* New York: Norton.

Turnbull, Colin M.
  1961   *The Forest People.* New York: Simon and Schuster.

Turner, Victor
  1967   *The Forest of Symbols.* Ithaca, NY: Cornell University Press.

United States House of Representatives
  1991   *U.S. House Report 102-40, part I,* 102d Cong., 1st sess. (attached to the "Glass Ceiling Act").

Useem, Michael
  1984   *The Inner Circle: Large Corporations and the Rise of Business Political Activity in the U.S. and U.K.* New York: Oxford University Press.

Van Maanen, John
  1973   "Observations on the Making of Policemen." *Human Organization* 32:407–18.
  1988   *Tales of the Field: On Writing Ethnography.* Chicago: University of Chicago Press.
  1992   "Drinking Our Troubles Away: Managing Conflict in a British Police Agency." Pp. 32–62 in *Hidden Conflict in Organizations: Uncovering Behind-the-Scenes Disputes,* edited by Deborah M. Kolb and Jean M. Bartunek. Newbury Park, CA: Sage Publications.

Van Maanen, John, and Stephen R. Barley
  1985   "Cultural Organization: Fragments of a Theory." Pp. 31–53 in *Organizational Symbolism,* edited Louis R. Pondy, Peter J. Frost, Gareth Morgan, and Thomas C. Dandridge. Newbury Park, CA: Sage Publications.

Van Velsen, J.
  1967   "The Extended-Case Method and Situational Analysis." Pp. 129–49 in *The Craft of Social Anthropology,* edited by A. L. Epstein. London: Tavistock.

Veyne, Paul
  1987   "The Roman Empire." Pp. 5–233 in *A History of Private Life,* vol. 1: *From Pagan Rome to Byzantium.* Cambridge, MA: Harvard University Press.

Walton, Richard E.
  1969   *Interpersonal Peacemaking: Confrontations and Third-Party Consultation.* Reading, MA: Addison-Wesley Publishing.

Walton, Richard E., and John M. Dutton
  1969   "The Management of Interdepartmental Conflict: A Model
              and Review." *Administrative Science Quarterly* 14:73–84.

Walton, Richard E., John M. Dutton, and Thomas P. Cafferty
  1969   "Organizational Context and Interdepartmental Conflict."
              Administrative Science Quarterly 14:522–42.

Wareham, John
  1991   *The Anatomy of a Great Executive.* New York: Harper Busi-
              ness Books.

Weber, Max
  1946   *From Max Weber: Essays in Sociology,* translated and edited by
              H. H. Gerth and C. Wright Mills. New York: Oxford Univer-
              sity Press.

  1968   *Economy and Society: An Outline of Interpretive Sociology,* ed-
              ited by Guenther Roth and Claus Wittich. Berkeley: Univer-
              sity of California Press.

Weick, Karl E.
  1976   "Educational Systems as Loosely Coupled Systems." *Admin-
              istrative Science Quarterly* 21:1–19.

  1979   *The Social Psychology of Organizing.* Reading, MA: Addison-
              Wesley.

  1984   "Small Wins: Redefining the Scale of Social Problems."
              American Psychologist 39:40–49.

Whistler, Thomas L.
  1984   *Rules of the Game: Inside the Corporate Boardroom.* Homewood,
              IL: Dow Jones–Irwin.

White, Harrison C.
  1961   "Management of Conflict and Sociometric Structure." *Ameri-
              can Journal of Sociology* 67:185–99.

  1986   "Agency as Control." Pp. 187–212 in *Principals and Agents: The
              Structure of Business,* edited by John W. Pratt and Richard J.
              Zeckhauser. Boston: Harvard Business School Press.

  1992   *Identity and Control: A Structural Theory of Social Action.*
              Princeton, NJ: Princeton University Press.

White, Ralph K.
  1965   "Images in the Context of International Conflict: Soviet Per-
              ceptions of the U.S. and the U.S.S.R." Pp. 236–76 in *Interna-
              tional Behavior: A Social-Psychological Analysis,* edited by Her-
              bert C. Kelman. New York: Holt, Rinehart and Winston.

Whyte, William Foote
  1973   *Street Corner Society.* Chicago: University of Chicago Press
              (originally published 1943).

Whyte, William H., Jr.
  1957   *The Organization Man.* New York: Anchor Books. (originally
              published 1956)

Williamson, Oliver E.
1975   *Markets and Hierarchies: Analysis and Antitrust Implications.*
            New York: Free Press.

1985   *The Economic Institutions of Capitalism.* New York: Free Press.

Wilson, Edward O.
1975   *Sociobiology: The New Synthesis.* Cambridge, MA: Harvard
            University Press.

Wilson, William Julius
1987   *The Truly Disadvantaged: The Inner City, The Underclass, and
            Public Policy.* Chicago: University of Chicago Press.

Witty, Cathy J.
1981   *Mediation and Society: Conflict Management in Lebanon.* New
            York: Academic Press.

Wolf, F. M.
1981   "The Nature of Managerial Work: An Investigation of the
            work of the Audit Manager." *Accounting Review* 16:861–81.

Wyatt-Brown, Bertram
1984   *Southern Honor: Ethics and Behavior in the Old South.* New
            York: Oxford University Press.

Yngvesson, Barbara, and Lynn Mather
1983   "Courts, Moots, and the Disputing Process." Pp. 51–83 in
            Empirical Theories about Courts, edited by Keith O. Boyum
            and Lynn Mather. New York: Longman.

Zillman, Dolf
1990   "The Interplay of Cognition and Excitation in Aggravated
            Conflict Among Intimates." Pp. 187–208 in *Intimates in Con-
            flict: A Communication Perspective,* edited by Dudley D. Cahn.
            Hillsdale, NJ: Earlbaum.

Zuckerman, Harriet
1972   "Interviewing an Ultra-elite." *Public Opinion Quarterly*
            36:159–75.

INDEX

grievances *(cont.)*
  work performance in, 68–69, 78, 105, 155, 167–68
Gulliver, P. H., 165

hierarchy, formal
  in atomistic organizations, 53–55, 141, 144–47
  in matrix system, 61–63, 183–85, 210
  in mechanistic bureaucracy, 46–48, 94–99, 135–37, 180–81
honor
  importance in matrix system, 185, 190, 192–97, 199, 203–7, 209–12, 214–15
  nature of, 193

identity
  in conflict management, 225–28
  and social context, 225–26
"Independent Accounting." *See* atomistic organization
information-gathering
  as function of lead personal assistants, 100–101
  in matrix system, 213–14
In Search of Excellence (Peters and Waterman), 60
interpretive structures in organizational culture. *See* sense-making

Japanese organizations, conflict management in, 226
jurisdictional authority
  in authoritative normative order, 136–37
  history and universality of, 135–37

Kanter, Rosabeth, *Men and Women of the Corporation*, 279n3
Koch, Klaus-Friedrich, *War and Peace in Jalemo*, 232–33
Kunda, Gideon, 253

Laboratory Life (Latour and Woolgar), 232–33
Latour, Bruno, and Steve Woolgar, *Laboratory Life*, 232–33
lead personal assistants
  information-gathering and gatekeeping functions, 100–101, 114, 119–20, 123–26, 131–32
  personal loyalty among, 100–101, 126

liquidation of resources as disciplinary action, 114–16

management by objectives, 97
Managerial Grid, The (Blake and Mouton), 273n14
matrix system
  accusatory schema in, 87–89, 209–11
  ambiguous lines of authority in, 182, 184–85, 210, 212
  budget control, 62–63
  collective action in, 186–90, 209–10
  communications networks in, 63–65, 186–90
  compromise in, 195, 198
  confrontational competition in, 184–85, 189–90, 212–13
  corporate uncertainty in, 211, 213
  dense social interaction in, 186–87
  development of, 59–60
  discussion of proposals, 63
  formal hierarchy in, 61–63, 183–85, 210
  formal meetings in, 191, 210
  function of gossip in, 186
  gender and ethnic hierarchies in, 185–86, 211–12
  importance of honor in, 185, 190, 192–97, 199, 203–7, 209–12, 214–15
  information-gathering in, 213–14
  lack of loyalty in, 211
  mechanistic bureaucracy restructured as, 182–83, 209
  nature of, 59, 62, 67, 183, 214–16
  promotion process, 62–63
  reciprocal normative order in, 91, 191–92, 195–98, 219
  remedial schema in, 88–90
  reorganization and change, 220, 224–25
  respectability in, 185
  stability in, 65–67, 190
  stress in, 190
  and takeovers, 182–83, 192–93, 209, 211, 215–16
  third-party mediation in, 201–2, 210
  use of slang and imagery in, 180, 183, 185, 188, 190, 192–94, 196–200, 203–9, 244
Mayo, Elton, 7
mechanistic bureaucracy
  accusatory schema in, 87–89, 91, 106, 134
  authoritative normative order in, 91,